Jane's
WAR AT SEA
1897–1997

Jane's
WAR AT SEA
1897–1997

BERNARD IRELAND & ERIC GROVE

HarperCollins*Publishers*

In the USA for information address:
HarperCollins*Publishers* Inc.
10 East 53rd Street
New York
NY 10022

In the UK for information address:
HarperCollins*Publishers*
77–85 Fulham Palace Road
Hammersmith
London W6 8JB

First Published in Great Britain by HarperCollins*Publishers* 1997

3 5 7 9 10 8 6 4 2

Colour illustrations (except p182–3) © Aerospace Publishing

Illustrations p182–3 Tony Bryan (aircraft) and Tony Gibbons (USS *Yorktown*)
ISBN 0 00 472065 2

Editor: Ian Drury
Design: Amzie Viladot Lorente
Page Layout: Amzie Viladot Lorente and Rod Teasdale
Production Manager: David Lennox

Colour reproduction by Colourscan
Printed in Italy

The publishers would like to thank the following organisations and individuals for providing photographs:

3: IWM. 4: IWM. 7: Jane's Information Group. 8: Naval Historical Center. 9: IWM. 10: Jane's Information Group/IWM. 11: IWM/IWM. 12: Jane's Information Group/IWM. 14: Jane's Information Group/IWM/IWM. 15: IWM/Jane's Information Group/IWM. 18: Jane's Information Group/IWM. 19: Jane's Information Group/IWM/IWM. 20: IWM. 22: IWM/Naval Historical Center. 24: IWM/IWM. 25: IWM. 26: Jane's Information Group/IWM. 27: Jane's Information Group/US Navy. 28: Jane's Information Group. 29: Jane's Information Group. 30: IWM/ Jane's Information Group. 34: IWM. 36: IWM/Jane's Information Group. 38: IWM. 39: IWM. 40: Jane's Information Group (two). 41: IWM. 44: IWM. 45: Naval Historical Center. 46: IWM/IWM. 47: IWM. 48: IWM. 49: IWM. 50: IWM. 51: IWM. 54: IWM. 55: IWM. 60: IWM. 63: Jane's Information Group. 65: IWM. 66: Jane's Information Group. 68: IWM. 70: Jane's Information Group. 71: Jane's Information Group (two). 72: IWM. 73: Jane's Information Group (two). 74: Jane's Information Group/IWM. 75: IWM. 76: IWM. 77: IWM. 78: IWM. 79: IWM (two). 80: IWM (two). 82: Jane's Information Group. 83: IWM (two). 84: IWM. 85: Jane's Information Group. 86: IWM. 87: IWM. 88: IWM. 89: Jane's Information Group/IWM. 90: IWM/ Jane's Information Group. 91: IWM. 92: IWM (two). 93: IWM. 94: IWM (two). 95: IWM. 96: IWM (two). 97: IWM (two). 100: IWM. 101: IWM. 104: IWM. 105: IWM. 106: IWM. 107: IWM. 108: IWM. 109: IWM. 110: IWM. 111: IWM. 112: IWM. 113: IWM. 114: IWM. 115: IWM (two). 116: IWM. 117: IWM (two). 118: IWM. 119: IWM. 120: IWM. 122: Vickers/IWM. 123: IWM. 124: Jane's Information Group/IWM. 125: Jane's Information Group/IWM. 126: Jane's Information Group/Naval Historical Center. 127: Jane's Information Group/IWM. 128: IWM. 129: Naval Historical Center. 130: Naval Historical Center. 131: Naval Historical Center. 132: Naval Historical Center. 133: IWM. 134: IWM. 135: IWM. 136: IWM (two). 137: Jane's Information Group. 138: IWM (two). 139: Jane's Information Group. 140: Jane's Information Group. 141: Jane's Information Group. 142: Jane's Information Group. 143: Naval Historical Center. 146: US Navy. 147: IWM. 148: IWM/Naval Historical Center. 149: IWM. 151: Naval Historical Center. 153: IWM. 154: IWM. 155: IWM. 156: IWM. 157: IWM. 158: Naval Historical Center (two). 159: US Navy. 160: US Navy. 161: US Navy. 162: Naval Historical Center. 164: Naval Historical Center/IWM. 165: Naval Historical Center (two). 166: Naval Historical Center (two). 167: Naval Historical Center. 168: Naval Historical Center. 169: US Navy (two). 170: Naval Historical Center (two). 171: US Navy (two). 172: Naval Historical Center (two). 173: Naval Historical Center (two). 174: US Navy. 175: US Navy (two). 176: Naval Historical Center. 177: US Navy (two). 180: US Navy (two). 184: US Navy (two). 185: US National Archives. 186: US National Archives. 187: US Navy (two). 188: US National Archives. 189: Jane's Information Group. 190: US Navy. 191: Jane's Information Group/US Navy. 192: US Navy/ Jane's Information Group. 193: Jane's Information Group. 194: Jane's Information Group/Giogio Arra/US Air Force. 195: McDonnell Douglas. 196: Jane's Information Group /Giorgio Arra. 197: General Dynamics Electric Boat Division. 198: Royal Australian Navy/US Navy. 199: Giorgio Arra. 200: Martin Marietta. 201: US Department of Defense (two). 202: Jane's Information Group. 203: US Navy. 204: Dassault. 205: H.M. Steele-Jane's Information Group (two). 206: H.M. Steele-Jane's Information Group. 207: H.M. Steele-Jane's Information Group. 208: H.M. Steele-Jane's Information Group/Jane's Information Group. 209: H.M. Steele-Jane's Information Group. 210: US Navy/Dassault/ H.M. Steele-Jane's Information Group. 210: H.M. Steele-Jane's Information Group. 212: McDonnell Douglas/ H.M. Steele-Jane's Information Group. 213: H.M. Steele-Jane's Information Group. 214: Van Ginderen Collection. 214: Jane's Information Group. 215: H.M. Steele-Jane's Information Group. 216: H.M. Steele-Jane's Information Group. 217: H.M. Steele-Jane's Information Group. 218: H.M. Steele-Jane's Information Group (two). 219: H.M. Steele-Jane's Information Group. 220: H.M. Steele-Jane's Information Group (two). 221: Ingalls Shipbuilding/ H.M. Steele-Jane's Information Group. 222: H.M. Steele-Jane's Information Group/Van Ginderen Collection/Ingalls Shipbuilding. 223: Ingalls Shipbuilding. 224: H.M. Steele-Jane's Information Group. 225: H.M. Steele-Jane's Information Group/DCN Cherbourg. 226: H.M. Steele-Jane's Information Group (two). 227: Van Ginderen Collection. 228: US Navy/Van Ginderen Collection. 229: H.M. Steele-Jane's Information Group. 230: H.M. Steele-Jane's Information Group/US Navy. 231: US Navy. 232: US Navy. 233: US Navy. 234: US Navy. 235: US Navy. 236: US Department of Defense. 237: North China Industries. 238: US Navy. 240: Central Office of Information/US Navy241: US Navy. 242: Van Ginderen Collection. 243: US Navy. 244: Central Office of Information/Van Ginderen Collection. 245: H.M. Steele-Jane's Information Group/Central Office of Information. 246: Dr Robert L Scheiner/Dassault. 247: H.M. Steele-Jane's Information Group (two). 248: H.M. Steele-Jane's Information Group/US Navy. 249: Giorgio Arra. 250: H.M. Steele-Jane's Information Group. 252: US Navy.

Contents

Fred T Jane and *Fighting Ships*

*J*ane's *Fighting Ships* is one of the world's most
famous titles, yet many must have wondered just who
was this androgynous naval expert. He himself joked
about his own name, once signing a sketch 'Fred
Mary-Ann'. Fred T Jane, as he was really known,
was born on 6 August 1865, the son of a Church
of England clergyman. He grew up during a
period of rapid technological change that
profoundly affected the two worlds he
inhabited: journalism, and the Royal
Navy. New printing processes, and more
general literacy created a wider reading
public, taking a more active interest in
defence matters, partly inspired by the
spectacular pace of naval and military
change, and partly by the
international instability this brought
with it.

Fred T Jane, however, grew up in
the peace of Cornwall, and Devon,
where his father held various
benefices. He attended Exeter School
as a day boy, where it cannot be said he
shone academically, describing himself
later as an awful thickhead. He did better
on the football pitch, being recognised as a
plucky and straight running half-back, apt to
get too near the scrimmage through over-
eagerness: an observation often borne out in later
life. Significantly Jane was also responsible for the
Toby, an alternative school magazine which enjoyed
much success for its illustrations, and total disregard for
veracity, or the law of libel.

Unable to enter the Royal Navy for health reasons,
Jane went to London, where he occupied an attic above
41 Gray's Inn Road, scraping a living by pictorial
journalism. This was poorly paid work, and recognition
came slowly. Jane's chance came in July 1890 with a
cruise on board HMS *Northampton*, an elderly ironclad,
to cover that summer's naval manoeuvres for the
Pictorial World. Over the next two months a flood of
sketches appeared over his name. These were something
quite out of the ordinary. Not only did Jane's ships lie in
the water as ships really do, but he drew everything that
happened, by day or night, starting in Tor Bay with what
became Jane's trademark: a display of electric
searchlights.

Jane's participation in these annual events allowed him
to extend a portfolio of warship sketches dating back to
an album he started at school. Inspired by the Royal
Navy's bombardment of Alexandria in 1882, 'Ironclads
of the World' gradually began to merit its ambitious title.
Fred T Jane became an accepted authority on foreign
warships as well as British. When the Russian fleet
visited Toulon to seal the Franco-Russian Entente, or a
Spanish cruiser was wrecked off Gibraltar it was Jane
who sketched the occasion for the *Illustrated London
News*. So remarkable was his ability to conjure up

Left: Pioneer defence analyst Fred T Jane
developed *All The World's Fighting Ships* in
1897. He provided a uniquely impartial and
comprehensive record of the world's navies just
as naval construction became a source of
international tension.

warships he had never seen, that for years Jane was
believed to have taken part in the Chilean Civil War of
1891, on the strength of his illustration of the torpedo
attack on the *Blanco Encalada*, a Chilean cruiser. Only
after Fred's death did his brother reveal that the sketch
was made in Devon. In 1897 Fred T Jane used the
expertise he had developed to produce a revolutionary
new warship directory, to be known as *All The World's
Fighting Ships*, the engraved blocks for which, laid end
to end, stretched some 400 feet.

The frequent naval scares that followed the
development of steam warships fed upon ignorance of
the true state of the strategic balance between the leading
naval powers, particularly Great Britain and France.
Journalists, novelists, and politicians exploited public
fears, deliberately exaggerating the strengths, and
weaknesses of both sides for their own commercial or
political advantage. In the 1880s Lord Brassey, still a
significant name in defence publishing, began to publish
the *Naval Annual*, tabulating many of the world's
warships. However, as a directory of warships it was not
entirely successful. Illustrations appeared separately from
ships' specifications, and gave little idea of their true

appearance. The format of the data tables varied, making
it impossible to compare British and foreign warships, or
armoured ships with unarmoured. Some information was
misleading. Original trial speeds appeared for ships
which were notoriously immobile, for example the
Turkish fleet which never left the Bosphorus. Ordnance
was described in terms of calibre, or weight of shot,
which was unhelpful when modern 6-inch quick-firers
rivalled older 10-inch guns with a slow rate of fire, and
low muzzle energy.

Fighting Ships addressed all these shortcomings. Jane's
contacts among the Royal Navy's engineering branch
ensured he quoted only the latest speeds. Illustrations
appeared next to the standard set of data provided for all
ships. Jane insisted on documenting the most obscure
auxiliary warships, 'on the same principle that a
dictionary includes words on account of the mere fact of
their existence'. He classified guns alphabetically,
according to their muzzle energy, so their performance
could easily be compared. Conversely he classified
armour by its ability to keep shells out. Thus "A" class
guns, such as the 12-inch guns of the Royal Sovereign
class battleships of 1891-92, could penetrate "a" class

Above: Fred T Jane developed a highly detailed naval wargame which enabled military and civilian players to evaluate the comparative strengths and weaknesses of the world's warships.

armour out to 4000 yards, then the tactical range for heavy naval guns. "A" class guns also included older 16-inch and 13.5-inch weapons, whose heavier rounds made up for their lower velocity.

Although the level of detail varied over the years, Jane never forgot the needs of the man on the bridge, in a hurry to identify another ship on the horizon. It was for him that Jane provided his most striking innovation. The first issue of *Fighting Ships* included a visual index of ship silhouettes to assist recognition. *The Naval Warrant Officer's Journal*, the mouthpiece of the professional 'bone and muscle of the service', recognised the value of this, recommending that the new directory should be in every chart-house, within reach of the signal-man and officer on watch.

The same journal in 1902 described *Fighting Ships* as, 'more indispensable than ever', and made a plea for the Admiralty to place a copy within reach of all naval personnel. Although ships did acquire copies, officialdom never took Jane seriously. To some extent this was due to his irreverent sense of humour, that found an outlet in outrageous practical jokes, most notoriously the kidnapping of a Labour MP in 1909. Jane infuriated

the Navy League by suggesting that if they really wanted to help modernise the Navy, they would do well to throw Nelson overboard. When the 1903 *Fighting Ships* carried an article describing a revolutionary fast battleship, armed exclusively with 12-inch guns, the proposal was derided as more suitable for the pages of HG Wells than a serious naval publication. The Admiralty, however, was already considering such a ship, the *Dreadnought*, justifying the claim of a later editor of *Fighting Ships* that, 'Never before had Jane so clearly attained his ambition of making *Fighting Ships* the mirror of naval progress'.

Jane's lack of official favour was clearly demonstrated by the failure to use his talents during the First World War. Unlike modern defence experts, he profited little from the opportunity to play the pundit. Perhaps his views were not to the taste of a jingoistic public who regarded the war as a football match, with ships sunk instead of goals scored. Jutland and its aftermath vindicated Jane's unfashionable prediction that the war would end without a decisive Trafalgar-style victory over the German battle fleet, but he did not live to comment on the battle. He had undertaken an exhausting lecture

tour, from Plymouth to Dundee, to defend the conduct of the naval war, and in October 1915 was soaked to the skin driving from Portsmouth to Cheltenham in his open topped racing car. He caught a chill. The following March Fred T Jane died alone in his apartment in Southsea, apparently of heart failure brought on by influenza. Fortunately he had made careful arrangements for the continued publication of *Fighting Ships* which, alone among its rivals, continued to appear throughout the war.

Richard Brooks

Introduction

The purpose of this book is to chart the development and functions of the warship through the 20th century, a century of accelerating progress which produced greater change than resulted from the whole of the previous two millennia. Commencing in 1897, and with Fred T. Jane's *All the World's Fighting Ships*, the first comprehensive review of the world's navies, we inevitably set out in a maritime world still dominated by Great Britain and by British practice.

The year in question marked Queen Victoria's Diamond Jubilee, the celebrations for which, feeding on their own success, resulted in (by British standards at least) quite uncharacteristic and spontaneous demonstrations of enthusiasm. The British felt that they had something to be pleased about. Life was not easy, but they were buoyed by the notion of being at the heart of things, of being at the head of an Empire that generated interests world-wide. Little of the resulting wealth filtered down to the man in the street, yet the trappings of wealth were all about him. For a while, he could take vicarious pleasure from them and, for a while, life seemed good.

The Empire was a very real concept, even to ordinary people, and the period was one of intense public debate as to where it was going. People were also well aware that this tapestry of possessions, protectorates and mandates was connected by the threads of a multitude of trade routes, served largely by British shipping. Red ensigns were worn by the majority of the world's ships. These myriad hulls imported raw materials from around the globe, returning with the manufactured goods that had provided employment. Except on the cosseted Atlantic route, the great passenger liners were filled not with tourists but with the administrators and functionaries who operated the apparatus of Empire, and officers of the military that supported them. Service tours being of long duration, these personnel were usually accompanied by families and servants.

Underpinning this vast structure was the very visible power of the Royal Navy. The service had never been more popular, its activities a matter of close interest to the population at large in a way that is quite difficult to imagine in present times now that patriotism has become so unfashionable.

Below: US naval construction proceeded at a leisurely pace until the 1898 Spanish-American war. The cruisers *Chicago* and *Newark* seen here were ordered as barque-rigged vessels in the 1880s.

US NEWARK CHICAGO

The celebrations peaked with the Jubilee Fleet review, held at Spithead on 27 June. Comprising, as it did, only the more modern of Her Majesty's ships, the 167 that were mustered still occupied six columns, each five miles in length. Such assembled might was awe-inspiring to the onlookers but, quite deliberately, carried a clear signal for those who needed to read it.

For, far removed from the bunting, the bands and the patriotic songs, grave doubts and misgivings were surfacing. The Empire was not the tranquil and smoothly functioning conglomeration that was portrayed for public consumption. Nations, after all, are not willingly subjugated by foreign states, however powerful. Although the British perceived themselves as benign rulers, bringers of law and order, those ruled more often viewed them as oppressors and plunderers. Other European settlers had sometimes staked prior claims. Thus, for instance, the British, fired by the promise of land rich in gold and diamonds, were on a collision course with the Dutch settlers, the Boers, in South Africa. The King of Burma had recently been deposed and humiliated by the British, apparently for his close links with the French. Egypt was being taken over by an inexorable process of British infiltration of its administration.

There was risk of more direct confrontation with powerful European states. In Africa, where Great Britain was accustomed to virtually a free hand, both France and a recently unified Germany were energetically extending their territories, moving steadily inland from coastal enclaves. Even Russia, with its royal kinship with the Queen, was relentlessly expanding, so that Afghanistan (itself a hot-bed of insurrection) stood as the only buffer short of India. Even India itself, through the medium of the recently formed National Congress, was beginning to challenge British rule.

One aspect, particularly of the colonies of White settlement, was the large-scale production of food staples. These so undercut the price of home production that Great Britain was already reliant on its merchant marine to import about half its foodstuffs.

The Royal Navy, in protecting the long trade routes, was on hand to deal with what might be termed "imperial brush fires". Typical recent events had been operations along the Red Sea coast following the rising in the Sudan, suppression of the thriving slave trade along the east coast of Africa, policing action in Somaliland, Sierra Leone, the Virgin Islands and on Lake Nyassa, interventions in Chile and the Gambia, and the quashing of a rebellion in Zanzibar

Above: Completed in 1897, the French battleship *Jauréguiberry* displaced 11,000 tons and was armed with single 12-in guns fore and aft, with single 10.8-in guns on either beam.

These, however, were the affair of the Navy's smaller warships; it was the function of the Battle Fleet to act as a deterrent. It achieved this not only by its sheer size but also by maintaining what today would be termed a "high profile". Its smartness and efficiency were the stuff of legend yet it, too, faced a major problem. In short, this age of invention and innovation was proceeding at such a pace that the service was faced with virtual block obsolescence. Despite the huge inertia of a mass of senior ranks trained, and still thinking, in sail, the fleet was not short of forward thinkers; but the impending crisis had more to do with the depth of the public purse, the immense cost of maintaining the world's largest fleet and its considerable infrastructure. If the fleet was satisfactorily discharging its duties, there was little point in adopting new technologies that would hasten obsolescence and the need for replacement. Because of this, the Board of Admiralty was often portrayed as a group of diehards who opposed progress. Progress, however, was now being thrust upon them.

France, still obsessed with the view of Great Britain as the traditional enemy, was developing her fleet in a manner that, at once, threatened British trade and aimed to offset the size of the Royal Navy by innovative technology. The United States, having just defeated the Spanish, found themselves with overseas possessions, a mini-empire, by default. The American fleet had acquired enormous prestige through the Spanish war and, on the back of this and its new-found colonial duties, was keen to expand.

The major catalyst was the Queen's grandson who, as Kaiser Wilhelm II, had come to power in 1888. Vain, ambitious and strongly attracted to the concept of sea power, he was influenced powerfully by the recent writings of the American Captain Alfred Thayer Mahan. Taking Great Britain as an example, Mahan had developed the argument that the existence of a battle fleet led naturally to the acquisition of the overseas possessions which were the key to national wealth and international influence. Wilhelm's enormous energy and intensely focused vision were already transforming Germany into a first-class industrial power. Unfortunately, he was pursuing a naval construction programme that directly challenged the maritime dominance regarded by the British as a God-given right. Their response was rapid and, by 1897, a new generation of warships was entering service.

The Royal Navy, which, like its peers, had recently undergone the painful transition from sail to steam, was in the process of further rapid development. This inevitably triggered responses elsewhere. The process was accelerating and was to end in tears.

Above: In the first issue of what became the celebrated annual yearbook, Fred Jane provided a sketch of each major warship, emphasising how each vessel appeared at sea – something not always apparent from photographs. This is the French battleship *Amiral Duperré.* note the side-by-side funnels and massive ram.

Below: The Infanta Maria Theresa class cruiser *Almirante Oquendo* was part of the ill-fated Spanish squadron destroyed by the US fleet at Santiago in 1898. Armed with two 11-in and ten 5.5-in guns, these cruisers had excellent firepower but were poorly protected and caught fire easily.

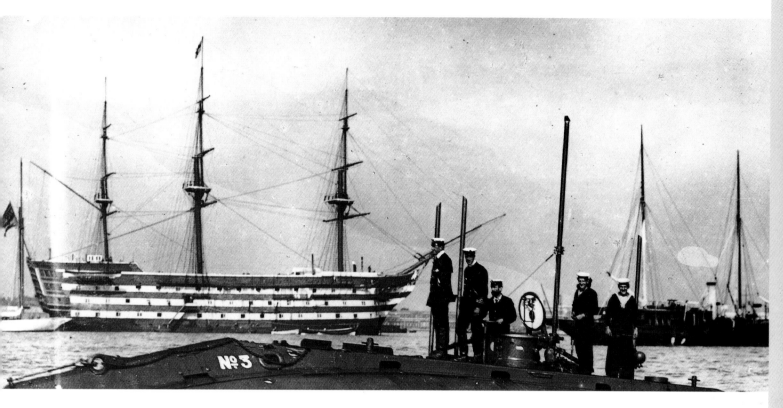

Above: The old and the new: one of the first Holland submarines built by Vickers for the Royal Navy. With a crew of eight, the Holland types carried a single 18-in torpedo. Trials began in 1902 and they served for ten years without mishap.

Below: The launch of the British battleship *Canopus* in 1897: note the prominent ram bow that had become a feature of major warships since the American civil war. The battle of Lissa in 1866 also seemed to suggest that ramming was a valid tactic.

Chapter One – The Navy & Fred T. Jane

'This is far less a review than a great Naval manifestation, or ... a solemn affirmation of the sea power of England. ...Their supremacy at sea has long since been established on the ruin of nations who once had a sea power that balanced theirs. But never has their sea power been greater than at the present moment.' Thus wrote one M. Maurice Loir, a French press correspondent attending the Jubilee Review.

This year of 1897 was appropriate for such a show, not only because of its royal connotations but also because events abroad demanded a show of strength. For this, the mass of new tonnage funded under the 1889 Naval Defence Act was very appropriate. Decades without a major war had left the Royal Navy with a rag-bag of ships, many of them so out-dated that, in the contemporary phrase, 'they could neither fight nor run away'. Growing concern at foreign aspirations demanded that the situation be rectified. For the first time, therefore, the peacetime strength of the Fleet was quantified. Known as the 'Two-Power Standard', this was not an absolute figure but that one which would give equality with an alliance between the next two largest maritime powers, at that time France and Russia.

Fleet strength was gauged primarily by the crude yardstick of numbers of capital ships. Figures for fully battleworthy units differ according to the method of reckoning but the Royal Navy's twenty-two battleships already out-numbered France's fourteen and Russia's seven. However, their quality as fighting ships varied too much to ever allow them to form a coherent battle line. The Naval Defence Act sought to remedy this with a series of eight first-class and a pair of second-class battleships.

The concept of second-class units was still strong. Essentially diminutive versions of the first-class battleships, they were intended to act as flagships on foreign stations, where they would provide the necessary 'presence' but not be required to match first-line ships of other major fleets.

H. M. S. Prince of Wales 1st Class Battle Ship.

There was intense debate at this time regarding the relative merits of mounting large-calibre guns in turrets (well-protected but heavy) or barbettes (less well-protected but lighter). The Act thus provided for the seven Royal Sovereigns, whose barbette arrangement permitted a high freeboard and, for direct comparison, the one-off *Hood*, very similar but necessarily reduced in freeboard in order to offset the weight of her turrets. The Royal Sovereigns, which were also significantly larger than preceding classes, proved to be infinitely better sea-boats and their design formed the basis of those that followed. The second-class pair (*Barfleur* and *Centurion*) also had paired heavy guns revolving on a barbette turntable, but their arrangement was better in that the gun crews were protected by a six-inch-thick shield.

Four of the Royal Sovereigns appeared at the review, together with six of the nine Majestics built after them. Improvements in the latter took the protected barbette

Above: HMS *Prince of Wales* was a typical British battleship of the turn of the century. Laid down at Chatham in 1901, she was part of the Channel fleet in 1914 and served at the Dardanelles in the second squadron under Rear-Admiral Thursby.

forward to the point where it was virtually a turret in the modern sense. They were also protected by the new Harvey cemented armour, which gave the same resistance to penetration for only half the weight of the earlier compound armour.

British cruisers were also grouped into first-, second- and third-class units. Sixteen of the Navy's 34 first-class cruisers were present. Half of them, including the two impressive (but ultimately ineffective) Powerfuls, had been built since 1889. All were 'protected cruisers', which relied on a protective deck, sited just above the waterline, to prevent major damage. Selected areas of the superstructure were also lightly armoured but the upper

The Edgar class protected cruiser *St. George* was completed at Hull in 1894. Displacing 7,700 tons she was armed with two 9.2-in and ten 6-in guns. The colour scheme of black hulls, white upperworks and buff funnels was widely imitated. Note the torpedo nets deployed to protect the ships at anchor.

hull depended mainly on the stopping power of full coal bunkers. Improved armour plate would soon see the return of the 'belted cruiser', which, for no penalty in weight, could now add vertical side protection to the protected deck. Evolution would then naturally increase size to incorporate larger calibre armament, enabling transverse protective bulkheads to be added to belts and decks, and a new generation of 'armoured cruiser' would be born.

First-class cruisers were intended to work either with the battle fleet, in force in the role of reconnaissance, or individually on assignments requiring extended endurance. Second-class units were built for the primary purpose of commerce protection (in an age when the threat was only from surface raiders). Such duty was one of the Navy's major functions, reflected in the 29 second-class cruisers ordered under the Naval Defence Act. At this time the fleet had 47 in commission and 6 under construction. Earlier units, such as the Apollo and Hermione classes, shipped only two 6-inch guns and a secondary battery of 4.7-inch quick-firers. The developing threat, however, saw the later Eclipses take eleven 6-inch backed by nine 3-inch guns, then usually termed 'twelve-pounders'

For the multitude of duties on distant imperial stations, small third-class cruisers were displacing a heterogeneous collection of masted cruising ships. Initially intended for scouting, they were unsuccessful as the machinery of the day usually left them slower than the forces that they were to reconnoitre. Of the 34 in service, the 2130-ton *Pelorus* was the first of eleven of a new 20.5 knot class.

With an undoubted requirement for large numbers of cruisers worldwide, and some influential voices in Parliament, the Royal Navy was well ahead of minimum requirements dictated by the Two-Power Standard. Despite the Naval Defence Act resulting in a continuous stream of new warships, creative forecasting demonstrated (quite erroneously) that French and Russian construction programmes would again result in equality by the end of the century. The resultant supplementary Spencer Programme of 1893 was already bearing fruit, of which the Majestics, Powerfuls and *Pelorus* were examples.

Right: Line drawings of HMS *Pelorus* from the 1906 edition of *Jane's Fighting Ships*. The hashed lines indicate the armoured deck while the compartments are notional, relating to the damage system in Jane's naval wargame.

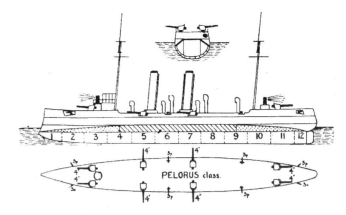

The other important group represented in strength at the review were torpedo-armed craft. These were early days in torpedo development, the weapon's still limited endurance requiring it to be taken to within almost suicidal range of its target before being launched. Torpedo boats were small and narrow-gutted to squeeze the maximum speed from their reciprocating machinery. However, any sort of sea slowed them drastically, and never was the 'hard-lying' money (bonus payments for particularly arduous service) better-earned. Larger ships were obviously required. These, termed 'torpedo gunboats', were introduced in 1886 and, in the space of the next eight years, ran to five separate classes. Where

the latest 440-ton torpedo boats could make 30 knots in fine conditions, the more weatherly torpedo gunboats, displacing between 735 and 1070 tons, were unable to better twenty, some barely seventeen. They could carry 4- or even 4.7-inch guns against a torpedo boat's 12-pounders, and up to five torpedo tubes with the torpedo boat's two. Nonetheless, their lack of speed meant they were able neither to destroy a torpedo boat by gunfire nor to attack an enemy line with torpedoes. They were soon found alternative employment as minesweepers, as fishery protection ships or even as a support ships for early submarine flotillas.

It was the torpedo boat that spawned its own antidote, the torpedo-boat destroyer, which even by 1897 was becoming known simply as a 'destroyer'. Essentially overgrown torpedo boats, destroyers remained shorter and narrower than the gunboats but boasted up to twice the installed power. Very wet, highly exhilarating, they made splendid first commands. As their superior size permitted the shipping of torpedo tubes in addition to guns, the future line of development was plain.

The rapid evolution of torpedo craft is evident from a comparison between those mustered for the 1887 and 1897 reviews. At the former were 38 torpedo boats and just one torpedo gunboat. Ten years later there were twenty torpedo boats and twenty gunboats but, already, thirty destroyers.

Left: The second class cruiser *Highflyer* was laid down in 1897. Armed with 11 6-in guns, she was still in service in 1914 and took part in the search for German commerce raiders. On 26 August, she discovered the 24,000 ton armed liner *Kaiser Wilhelm der Grosse* in a remote anchorage in Spanish Saharan waters and sank her.

Right: Displacing 14,000 tons and over 500 feet long, the two enormous cruisers *Powerful* and *Terrible* were built by the British in response to rumours of giant Russian commerce-raiding cruisers. Longer than contemporary battleships and requiring even more crew (nearly 900) they were soon recognised as white elephants. Both landed naval brigades for service during the Boer war, aiding the relief of Ladysmith with some of the ships' guns on improvised field carriages.

Left: White hulls and buff upperworks was the almost universal scheme for service in hot climates. Several of the Pelorus class were still active at the outbreak of war. *Pegasus* was sunk by the German cruiser *Konigsberg* off South Africa in 1914.

Right: Line drawings of the Powerful class as shown by the 1905 edition of *Jane's Fighting Ships*. The fore and aft turrets mounted single 9.2-in guns, with armoured tubes extending down to the protective deck, protecting the shell hoists. The secondary 6-in guns were mounted in casemates: a layout that often left the lower weapons unworkable in a sea way, but the sheer size of the Powerfuls ensured that this was rarely a problem.

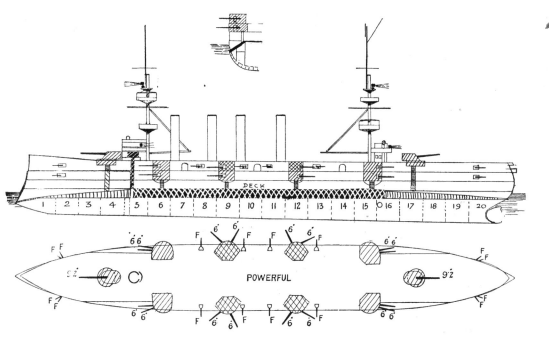

Right: Hermes served on the East Indies station and at the Cape before returning to England to pay off in 1913. She was converted at Chatham to a seaplane carrier and re-commissioned that year with a launching platform forward and stowage for three seaplanes aft. Returning after ferrying seaplanes from Portsmouth to Dunkirk in October 1914, she was sunk by *U-27* off Calais.

Royal Sovereign class

data:

Displacement standard	14,150 tons
Displacement full load	15,580 tons
Length	380 ft
Beam	75 ft
Design draught	27.5 ft
Complement	712

Class: *Royal Sovereign, Empress of India, Ramillies, Repulse, Resolution, Revenge, Royal Oak.*

Armament:
4 x 13.5-in guns
10 x 6-in guns
16 x 6-pdr guns
7 x 18-in torpedo tubes

Machinery:
2 triple expansion steam engines, 11,000 ihp
2 shafts
16.5 kts

Armour:
Belt	18 in
Belt ends	14 in
Decks	3 in
Barbette	17 in
Casemates	6 in

Below: Built under the 1889 Naval Defence Act which decreed that the Royal Navy must be able to match the world's second and third largest navies, the Royal Sovereign class were a deck higher than the low freeboard battleships then in vogue. As a result, they were much better sea boats, all except for the one-off low freeboard eighth unit *Hood* which had its main armament in turrets.

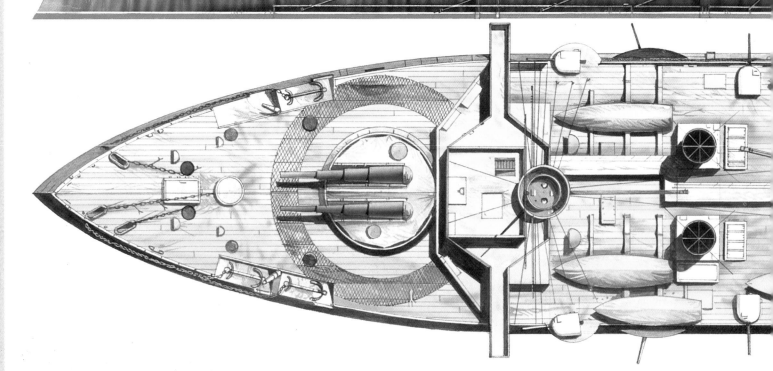

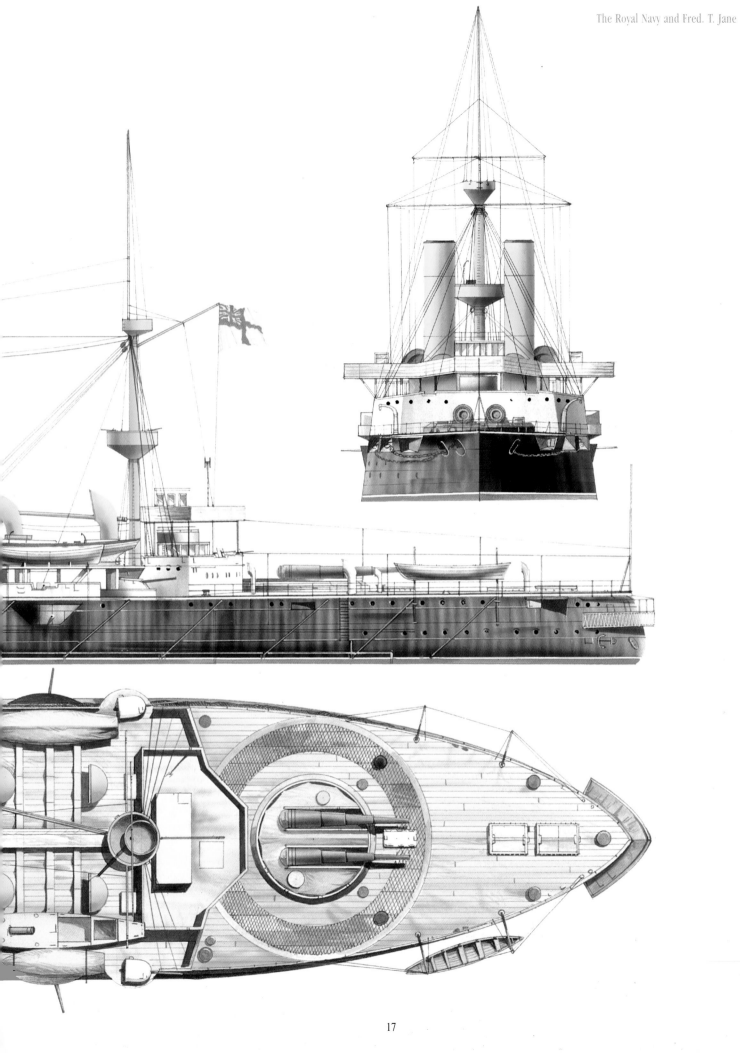

Chatham Dockyard.　　　　　　　H.M.S. Albemarle.

Left: The Duncan class battleship *Albemarle* was built at Chatham 1900-03 and served in the Mediterranean from 1904-5. She had an active war after 1914: serving with the 6th battle squadron and losing her bridge to heavy seas off the Pentland Firth in 1915. She was used as an ice-breaker at Archangel as Allied supplies were shipped to Russia in 1916.

Anybody interested in the new concept of the submersible would have been disappointed at the 1897 review, for it would be a further three years or so before the Royal Navy would commit itself, although developments abroad were not wanting.

Further advanced were the French, who saw in it a useful means of defending their coasts and ports from assault or close blockade. Their first really practical design was produced by the renowned Dupuy de Lôme, but his untimely death saw the craft completed by Gustave Zédé. An improved and enlarged version was then overtaken by that of another pioneer, soon to become famous, Maxime Laubeuf. Resulting from this activity the French had by 1897 introduced the double hull, separate propulsion systems for surfaced and submerged navigation, and the periscope. Zédé and Laubeuf both thought in terms of a torpedo-armed craft, an objective also being pursued abroad, notably by John Holland in the United States, Isaac Peral in Spain and Thorsten Nordenfelt in Sweden.

In Britain, the Admiralty Board was having to commit large funds also to a rapidly changing and enlarging infrastructure. Pure sailing ships were able to spend considerable periods at sea with minimal or no support. Machinery, even with an auxiliary sailing rig, required reliable repair yards and frequent access to considerable quantities of good steam coal. Scattered outposts of Empire thus provided not only one of the Navy's primary reasons for being but also necessary locations for its support. The increasing size of major ships was reducing the choice of dry docks worldwide for maintenance or the repair of battle damage. Once recognised, the problem was tackled with considerable energy. In 1895, Parliament approved the Naval Works Bill, voting £8.8 million for improvements. It says much for the status of the Royal Navy that, over the next two years, this sum was increased, first to £14 million then to £17 million. The scale of this expenditure is evident when compared with the £21.5 million voted for the 1889 Naval Defence Act, which sum paid for a five-year, seventy-ship programme.

Works were commenced on a huge and varied scale. Naval barracks ashore replaced the unwholesome accommodation hulks, hitherto used by crews standing by ships under refit. Dartmouth Naval College moved from the Britannia hulks to splendid new buildings ashore. The growing fear of torpedo attack saw huge moles added or extended at Portland, Dover, Malta, Gibraltar, Simonstown (South Africa) and Bermuda. Dry docks, dredged channels and machine shops were added in varying degrees to the three main home dockyards (Portsmouth, Devonport/Keyham and Chatham/Sheerness) and foreign yards at Bermuda, Colombo, Gibraltar, Haulbowline (Ireland), Hong Kong, Malta and Simonstown. It was policy also to quietly subsidise colonial port authorities to provide facilities well in excess of any required by the merchant marine. The Navy could thus count on support in ports from Halifax to Sydney and from Vancouver to Durban.

A Royal Commission was appointed to consider the provision of coaling stations. A network of facilities already paralleled the major trade routes, but the Navy required reliable stocks to be maintained in remote areas also. These were established in places such as Mauritius, Labuan (Borneo) and on the barren Cape York peninsula in Australia. Not an area of prime interest, the Pacific was poorly served, with nothing between Suva (Fiji) and the Falklands in the South Atlantic. Enormous numbers of colliers were on charter, either to coal ships directly or to replenish stocks.

At this point, the high tide of British imperial dominance, the Navy's commitments were so wide-ranging that there were fifteen independent commands, ten of them of a significance to warrant a Commander-in-Chief (C-in-C). Of these, three were Admirals Superintendent of the Home Stations – Portsmouth, Plymouth and the Nore. Abroad there were Australia, Cape of Good Hope/West Africa, China, the East Indies, the Mediterranean, North America/West Indies and the Pacific. A further, South Atlantic, command was about to be established.

In home waters, the active fleet was centred on the Channel Squadron, which included six of the latest battleships. The Reserve Squadron was built around five older capital ships and, though scattered around the kingdom, could be quickly concentrated. There was also the Training Squadron, whose ships, although older, were permanently active and, being fully worked-up, would contribute a rapid reinforcement in an emergency.

Below: Royal Navy warships assembled in the Solent for a fleet review in 1907. Entente with France enabled more British warships to be concentrated in home waters, facing the rapidly developing threat from Germany.

Of the foreign stations, the Mediterranean (which included the Red Sea) was the most important. Its strength in 1897 was 37 combatant ships and, with a major base at Malta, it was practice to retain ships on station, refitting them between commissions. Three-year commissions were the norm, crews being transferred and exchanged by troopship. Where the Royal Navy had run its own 'troopers', these were now being sold out of service or, like the *Malabar*, found alternative roles, in this case base ship at Bermuda. Mercantile tonnage was now being chartered for trooping voyages.

The Australian station differed in that the squadron's Royal Naval units were complementary to the seven third-class cruisers paid for and maintained by the various, and still separate, states. In time of war the ships would be retained exclusively for the defence of these states.

The Navy exercised intensively, culminating in the annual manoeuvres, of which those of 1897 were typical. Here were no gunnery duels, high-speed melees or massed night torpedo attacks. Manoeuvres developed along the stately lines of a court masque, products of an era that was still showing evidence of placing tradition above a ready acceptance of new technology and procedure.

Each reinforced by ships dispersed from the review, the Channel and Reserve Fleets were set different problems. For the purpose of the exercise, the Channel Fleet was divided into two divisions, the First based on Lough Swilly in the north of Ireland, the Second on Blacksod Bay, to the south-west. Anticipating a declaration of war, the Second was to proceed to sea, leaving behind one fast cruiser. On the outbreak of hostilities, a few hours later, this ship was to overhaul its division with the news, meeting it at a pre-arranged rendezvous. Two First Division cruisers were to be pre-positioned to the north and south of Blacksod Bay, with orders to sail at a specific time (actually four hours after the 'messenger'), and endeavour to intercept her. If successful, they would learn the rendezvous point of the Second Division. They would inform their own Admiral, who would try to prevent the Second from regaining its base at Blacksod.

The total forces involved, near equally divided, comprised eleven battleships, seventeen cruisers and two torpedo gunboats. The exercise occupied a circle of 700 miles diameter, and a period of ninety hours. The First Division admiral failed utterly. Rather than approaching his task rationally, he used tortuous reasoning to establish the likely position of the Second. He thus intercepted neither it nor its messenger. Something, nonetheless, was learned about Victorian admirals.

British maritime supremacy extended also to the merchant marine, and enormous numbers of men served at sea. Crews were large by modern standards, ships were many, and round trips slow. Nearly a quarter million men crewed British-flagged merchantmen, of whom about one third were fishermen, Lascars or 'foreigners'. This provided a vast pool of trained personnel for an emergency, for which 25,000 reserves were also available.

The 1896-7 Naval Estimates provided for a Royal Navy strength of nearly 94,000. Already an increase of 5,000 over the previous year, the figure was forecast to rise to 105,000 by the turn of the century.

Right: Built by British yards for Chile, but purchased by the British government in response to a possible Russian purchase in 1903, *Swiftsure* and her sister *Triumph* were too small and too lightly armed to match the latest battleship designs. Nevertheless, *Swiftsure* served in the Dardanelles; *Triumph* assisted in the capture of the German navy's Chinese base at Tsingtao before her loss at the Dardanelles, torpedoed by *U-21*.

Above: Spartiate was one of the eight Diadem class cruisers laid down 1895-7. Smaller versions of the Powerful class, they were still longer than most battleships and displaced 11,000 tons. The fore and aft 9.2-in guns were replaced by shielded 6-in guns to give an armament of 16 6-in guns.

Right: The 12-in guns of HMS *Russell*, a Duncan class battleship built at Jarrow 1899-1901. She covered the evacuation of the Gallipoli peninsula in January 1916 but was mined off Malta in April.

Seamen in the Royal Navy were recruited as 'boys' or 'youths'. Initial training was either in the *Impregnable* hulk at Plymouth or in one of those at Harwich, Portland, Portsmouth or Queensferry, all four of which would shortly be replaced by the Ganges establishment, ashore at Shotley, Suffolk.

The eight months of training accorded to boys before their being drafted included, at this time, twelve weeks of military training. Insurrections and emergencies within the Empire often necessitated the landing of naval brigades or smaller parties of bluejackets for the restoration of order. Three months' sea time followed in a cruiser of the training squadron before the new recruit emerged as an ordinary or able seaman. He would then sign on for twelve years, extendible by a further ten to qualify for a pension. All had to complete a gunnery course, while selected volunteers also underwent the torpedo specialist's course. Training schools for both existed within each of the Home commands and there was real incentive to qualify. Seamen torpedomen or gunners earned an extra fourpence (4d.) per day. If this does not sound impressive, the resulting £6.1s.8d. per annum represented an increase of some 26 percent on the basic pay of an ordinary seaman!

Engine room personnel were divided into artificers and stokers. In 1897 the former were still recruited directly from the ranks of skilled shore-side tradesmen, and were selected by examination. Only in 1903 was naval machinery recognised as a subject sufficiently specialised to require in-house training, commencing with the recruitment of boy artificers

Prior to 1902, executive and engineering branch officers were also subject to completely separate conditions of entry. Cadets underwent four years of shore training, of which about half would be spent at Dartmouth, still aboard the two training hulks known collectively as HMS *Britannia*. Osborne House would shortly (1903) be acquired to give cadets preliminary training prior to their time at Dartmouth. A further six months' sea time aboard a training cruiser was required before a cadet could be drafted in the rank of midshipman. It then took three years to qualify as a sub-lieutenant, followed by more examinations and a year's seatime to gain the watchkeeper's certificate necessary to win promotion to lieutenant. This was the minimum rank for commencing specialisation in, for instance, navigation, gunnery, torpedoes or engineering.

The true 'University of the Navy' was in the old royal palace at Greenwich, which commenced as the Royal Naval College in 1873. Engineers, however, underwent specialist training at the college at Keyham, Devonport, which opened in 1880. Although established as a grade as early as 1837, engineers were still looked upon as a 'non-fighting' branch and, therefore, apart from executive grades. They had to be total specialists, which barred them from any chance of command. This division, a throwback to the Navy's transition from sail to steam, caused real friction in the Service; the Common Entry system was still in the future.

About 20 percent of personnel strength was accounted for by the Royal Marines, who formed part of the complement of every major ship. Marines were still trained separately as either artillerymen or infantry, the former being considerably better paid.

Much is made, particularly in foreign publications, of the manner in which both general and specialist training laid emphasis on the traditions and qualities of the Royal Navy.

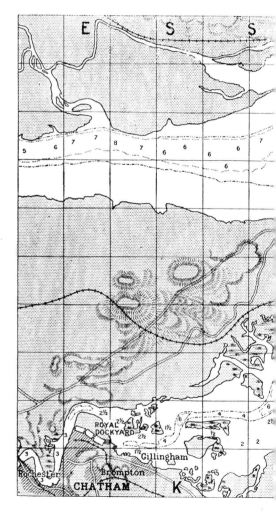

Right: Jane's Fighting Ships provided scale plans of the naval bases and facilities of the world's major navies as well as details of the warships themselves. At the turn of the century, Chatham was one of the main British construction yards.

Below: Canopus served in the Channel and Mediterranean fleets before going into reserve in 1912. Commissioned as part of the 8th battlesquadron in 1914 (Channel) she was soon sent to the south Atlantic where she fired the first shots in the battle of the Falklands.

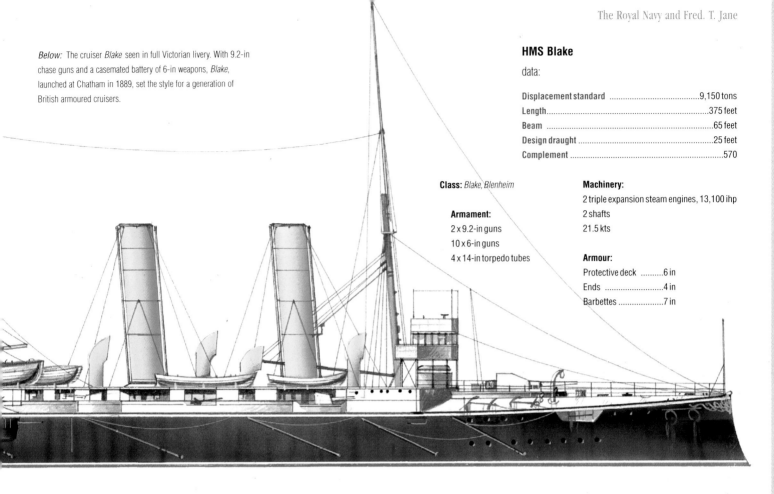

Below: The cruiser *Blake* seen in full Victorian livery. With 9.2-in chase guns and a casemated battery of 6-in weapons, *Blake*, launched at Chatham in 1889, set the style for a generation of British armoured cruisers.

HMS Blake

data:

Displacement standard	9,150 tons
Length	375 feet
Beam	65 feet
Design draught	25 feet
Complement	570

Class: *Blake, Blenheim*

Armament:
2 x 9.2-in guns
10 x 6-in guns
4 x 14-in torpedo tubes

Machinery:
2 triple expansion steam engines, 13,100 ihp
2 shafts
21.5 kts

Armour:
Protective deck ....6 in
Ends ....4 in
Barbettes ....7 in

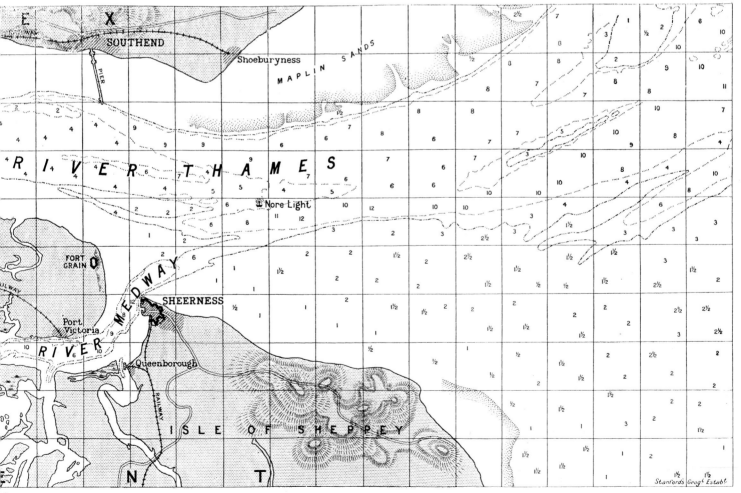

Chapter Two – **The Major Players in 1897**

Great Britain

It is easy to be beguiled into the traditional view that the British Empire was a sort of benevolent club, with contented peoples ruled by others better suited to organise them. Empire, in reality, was all about acquisition and exploitation, although the colonies did benefit in inheriting a proven system for law, order and administration, together with one of the world's largest markets for their raw materials. Great Britain, in turn, had a reciprocal outlet for her manufactured goods. The Empire, despite a genuine belief in the merits of free trade, was a tightly-knit trading bloc. Inevitably, in this loose and disparate community of peoples, challenges arose in the form of Popular Fronts. A Governor's first

line of defence was the local military garrison but, if the revolt against authority was serious or prolonged, the Navy almost invariably became involved in one way or another. The military skills of the bluejackets were frequently subjected to the most severe of tests, and many a naval gallantry award was earned at a considerable distance from salt water.

Commanding officers of those of Her Majesty's ships engaged on colonial commissions were still very much 'Captains under God'. Communications remained unreliable, so the senior officer was expected to exercise personal judgement and initiative. He could do little wrong in assisting a Governor to run a 'tight ship'.

While underpinning the structure of Empire, however, the Royal Navy had yet more important roles in the direct defence of the realm and its trade. Threats to either would necessarily be diverse, and totally removed from the requirements of imperial peacekeeping, necessitating a wide diversity of warship types.

As a quantitative yardstick, the Two-Power Standard applied, irrespective of the politics or the perceived threat from the two powers operating the fleets concerned. In terms of commissioned first- and second-class battleships, the relative strength of the world's leading maritime powers in the mid-1890s was Great Britain 31, France 16, Russia 9, Germany 6, the United States 5 and Japan 2. Italy's force, although considerable on paper, could not at that time be rated as being capable of engaging those of the above powers. While the fighting value of individual units varied enormously in this era of rapid development, there is no doubt that Great Britain was already well in advance of its own Two-Power Standard, and was pulling even further ahead. By the turn of the century, when the disparity was approaching 3:1, the pace of construction slackened.

Below: In 1897 the US Navy was little more than a coast defence force, with only five ocean-going battleships and a modest force of cruisers available. The *Miantonomoh* seen here was one of six obsolete monitors that were retained, although seldom in full commission until World War I. The US Navy's enthusiasm for the type was unabated: four new monitors were authorised in 1898 as part of the major building programme that followed the war with Spain.

Above: Laid down at Brest in 1887 but not completed until 1893, *Isly* was one of three Alger class protected cruisers. Capable of 19 kts, she was armed with four 6.4-in guns and six 5.5-in guns. Note the heavy masts with fighting tops: these mounted light calibre cannon.

Below: The French fleet arrives at Spithead in 1905 not, as had been feared for 50 years, as a hostile force, but as a potential ally. Since the late 1850s, the British and French navies had regarded each other as their likely opponent in a future war.

France

Britain's major maritime rival remained France, but the above figures disguise the fact that the French fleet was in a period of decline. This had begun in the early 1870s and was to continue until some years after the turn of the century, by which time the tricolour had dropped from second to fifth place in world naval ranking. Catastrophic defeat in the 1870–1 Franco-Prussian war had highlighted the fact that the major threat to France came from across its borders. As a result the navy was reduced in order to improve the capability of the army.

Political instability dogged the Third Republic, and an endless succession of Ministers of Marine changed naval policy as quickly as it was formulated. The French naval budget was not ungenerous, being a little less than half that of the British (in 1896 some £10.6 million compared with £21.8 million) for a fleet that was considerably smaller proportionally. Far too much was being swallowed up in an over-large inefficient shore-side organisation. Understandably, French naval thinking was in turmoil. Native originality abounded, manifested in such as the floating armoured batteries in the Crimea, the pioneering application of armour to battleships, and experiments with submersibles.

Many senior French naval officers still believed Great Britain to be the natural enemy, but realised that she could be defeated only at sea. They were thus trying to square the circle, for they knew full well that Britain would never allow herself to be out-built, and that she possessed the wealth, industrial capacity and political will to guarantee it. Admirals Aube and Bourgeois created a major stir by pointing out that history demonstrated Britain's weakness to be her inability to protect the seaborne trade upon which her very existence depended, and that this should be targeted rather than the battle fleet. Their supporters, the so-called *Jeune école*, were numerous and vociferous but their enthusiasms, breaking against the solidly entrenched ideas of the traditionalists, effectively split the Service. The school's tenet was that resources, instead of being invested in expensive battle fleets, should be used to build fast cruisers for waging a *guerre de course* and large numbers of torpedo-armed craft to defeat any attempt by the Royal Navy to impose close blockade.

Threats to trade always alarmed the British, but Aube's writings were couched in the sort of terminology that made his ideas uniquely unacceptable. For instance, torpedo craft should not only sink merchantmen but should '...send to the bottom cargo, crew and passengers, not only without remorse but proud of the achievement'. Aube's lofty intention was that the excesses of total war

Amiral Charner

data:

Displacement standard	4,700 tons
Length	360 feet
Beam	46 feet
Design draught	20 feet
Complement	393

Class: *Amiral Charner, Bruix, Chanzy, Latouche-Tréville.*

Armament:
2 x 194 mm (7.6-in) guns
6 x 138 mm (5.4-in) guns
4 x 450 mm (17.7-in) torpedo tubes

Machinery:
2 triple expansion steam engines, 8,300 ihp
2 shafts
18.5 kts

Armour:
Belt ....90 mm (3.5-in)
Ends ....70 mm (2.7 in)

Left: Amiral Charner was the lead ship of a class of armoured cruisers built with the express intention of attacking British merchant shipping if another Anglo-French war broke out. Three were still active in 1914, serving in the eastern Mediterranean, evacuating Armenians from Syria in 1915. *Amiral Charner* was sunk by *U-21* off Beirut in 1916, only one member of her crew surviving.

would persuade nations to abandon hostilities entirely, but much of the French naval establishment assumed that such atrocities would be viewed by the international community as no better than piracy.

British thoughts on combating such a form of warfare were interesting in that the arguments advanced against the ancient defence of convoy were identical to those repeated later during two world wars. In the event, the *Jeune école* was self-defeating for the reason that France, like its notional opponent, was becoming a major imperial power and, again like the British, required a largely similar type of fleet to support it. France had possessions in North Africa and great business interests in the Levant, to say nothing of latent rivalry with the Italians. These demanded a strong Mediterranean fleet, optimised for fighting power rather than endurance. Colonies, however, were scattered as far afield as West Africa, the West Indies, Madagascar, the central Indian Ocean, Indo-China and Polynesia, requiring ships of opposite qualities.

By the 1890s, perhaps even to the annoyance of Admiral Aube's diehards, France was undergoing something of a rapprochement with Great Britain. The *Entente Cordiale* was, admittedly, still some years distant, but the threat of hostilities had receded. France, politically isolated by the machinations of the wily Bismarck was, with his dismissal in 1890 by the new Kaiser, seeking to improve relationships abroad. These began with the conclusion of an alliance with Russia in 1893, an agreement that found little favour in Britain.

Right: Built at Lorient 1893-98, *Bouvet* was the last of the Charles Martel type battleships. She carried single 12-in guns fore and aft, with single 10.8-in weapons on either beam. With 32 Belleville boilers, *Bouvet* was capable of 18 knots when new.

The latter's suspicions were well justified. Plans for activities at sea, in the event of war with Britain, called for holding actions on the Baltic while French forces threatened an invasion of England. Such a threat would tie down the bulk of the Royal Navy's strength in home waters, leaving the way clear for a Russian fleet to issue from the Black Sea to land an expeditionary force in Egypt. A French fleet, based on Madagascar, would create a cordon sanitaire in the Indian Ocean to act as distant cover to a Russian army marching into India. Much of this was make-believe, not least because of the exceedingly low opinion by the French of the Russian Navy: 'They are so poorly handled that their cumbersome mass could do nothing but weigh down and paralyse our own [squadrons]'. British views were even less complimentary.

French capital ship design showed originality, but any advantage built into their conception was usually more than offset by extended construction time. The new one-off, *Brennus*, completed in 1896, was typical in being seven years in the building. Her 340-mm (13.4-in) main battery out-classed that of the 12-in (305-mm) gunned Royal Sovereigns, but was housed in heavy, full-scale turrets, whose revolving protective gunhouse projected beyond and below the upper level of the fixed barbette. The resultant weight limited the main battery to only three barrels, sited in a twin mounting forward and a single aft. Even this eccentricity saved too little weight to achieve the stipulated command and hull freeboard. The result was, by British standards, insufficient protection, exacerbated by the French refusal to accept the principle of 'soft-ends', so that the full-length belts were very shallow. The armour itself was of the obsolete compound type, and the belt was totally submerged at even moderate angles of heel.

The later trio of Martels, laid down in 1891, had an extraordinary arrangement of single 305-mm (12-in) guns at either end, and single 275-mm (10.8-in) guns on either beam. All were in full turrets, however, capable of being reloaded on any bearing. This increased the rate of fire typical of barbette ships, whose guns could be loaded only on the fore-and-aft axis, and at a specific elevation.

Having adopted the water-tube boiler earlier than the British, the French were well ahead. Such units were smaller and, containing less water, were considerably lighter than the cylindrical boilers with which the Royal

Right: A Fred Jane sketch from the first edition of *Jane's Fighting Ships* shows the distinctive lines of the French battleship *Brennus*. Built at Lorient 1889-1896, she had twin 13.4-in guns in the fore turret and a single one in the aft turret. The first major warship to have Belleville boilers, *Brennus* was unusual in not having a ram bow.

BRENNUS (FRENCH)

Navy was still largely equipped. The latter well recognised the potential advantages, not least in the greater efficiency of higher-pressure steam, and several ships including the Powerfuls were in the process of evaluating them.

Notable French armoured cruisers were the three Amiral Charner class and the improved *Pothuau*, completed in 1895–6. Their exaggerated 'ram' bows and extreme tumblehome were intended to improve

seakeeping, reduce topweight and to improve axial fire, but it is difficult to see how they could have survived for very long in their designed raiding role, as their 18–19 knot speed would have proved deficient. As with British practice, they were fitted with a single large-calibre (194-mm/7.6-in) gun at either end and an amidships battery of six to ten smaller (138-mm/5.5-in) weapons.

Torpedo craft, the other major plank of the *Jeune école*, existed in large numbers, but in sizes too small to be

Below: Amiral Baudin, displaced 11,700 tons and carried three 371 mm (14.6-in) guns in individual barbettes. Protected by 22 inches of compound armour and capable of 15 knots, she was completed in 1888 and served until 1909. The central barbette was removed in 1898 and the main armament changed to two 10.8-in guns. The 1905 edition of *Fighting Ships* noted that their boilers were worn out and no further reconstruction was planned.

seriously considered as seagoing. The 34 largest dated from between 1888 and 1896 and carried two or four tubes on displacements of between 100 and 150 tons. Capable of 27 knots in calm conditions, they were faster than their British contemporaries but their submarine-like hulls permitted no scuttles to be opened in any sea, suggesting noisome standards of habitability.

Russia

The Russian naval budget was only about two-thirds that of France but, in contrast, was rapidly increasing. Its value was distorted by the high cost of indigenous construction and by geography, which caused a self-sufficient land power to require an over-sized fleet. Then, as now, it was divided, with the most important segment based on the Baltic, and a lesser component in the Black Sea. A division of the latter was usually detached to provide a presence in the Mediterranean, a procedure facilitated by the French permitting anchoring rights at Villefranche. The Pacific coast did not merit a dedicated fleet at this time, but was covered by the combination of a 'Siberian squadron' and a detached force from the Baltic fleet. There was no White Sea fleet.

Progress was inconsistent, as the Tsar was supreme commander of the armed forces, while the General-Admiral, who headed the Navy, was either a relation of the Tsar or at the mercy of his whim. Nicholas II combined autocracy with weakness. He was enthusiastic

about his fleet, but had a lack of understanding of its purpose. His system saw wide abuse from an army of officials. Funds purchased generally capable ships but did not permit their sufficient exercise. The lack of sea-time fostered inefficiency and discontent.

Above: The Russian cruiser *Rurik*, rumours of which triggered the British Powerful class cruisers. Completed with a barque rig in 1895, she was sunk by Japanese cruisers in the Russo-Japanese war.

Below: French and Russian warships at Saigon, French Indochina, in the 1890s. The old battleship on the left is the station ship, *Loire*, originally the *Prince Jerome*, a 90-gun screw-powered two-decker launched in 1853. To her right, behind the gunboat in the foreground, is the Russian cruiser *Pamiat Azova*, completed in 1890 and sunk (when in Bolshevik hands) by British torpedo boats in 1919. The cruiser in the centre is probably *Vladimir Monomakh*, later sunk at the battle of Tsushima.

Despite its already huge area, Russia was eager to expand strategically. Her aim of controlling the Black Sea exit, following the successful outcome of the 1877–8 war with Turkey, had been frustrated by British diplomacy. Shifting attention to the Far East, by 1896 Russia had won the concession to drive the new Trans-Siberian railroad across Manchuria. Its eastern terminus, the naval port of Vladivostok was, however, ice-bound for several months each year. Japan had recently defeated China, but Russia used her considerable muscle not only to prevent Japan's use of the Liaotung peninsula but also, in 1897, to obtain a lease on the 'warmwater' harbour of Port Arthur.

The Russian fleet's fourteen coast defence ships reflected a defensive mentality resulting from the seaborne threats of the Crimean War. A seven-year construction programme, commencing in 1898, is not easy to justify even in the context of Russian territorial ambitions. Far-Eastern expansion, and a growing antagonism with Japan, explains the building-up of the Pacific Squadron but, for the rest, it can best be attributed to the personal gift of the Tsar, who was greatly influenced by Mahan's writings. With his own yards unable to meet his demands, Nicholas II placed orders widely abroad, but noticeably not in Britain. This building spree raised Russia's naval ranking to third in the world by the beginning of the twentieth century.

Like its ally, France, Russia built large cruisers for raiding. These, the *Rurik*, *Rossia* and *Gromoboi*, dwarfed the *Dupuy de Lôme*. Between them, they stimulated construction of the British 22-knot white elephants, *Powerful* and *Terrible*.

An interesting component of the Russian Navy was the so-called Volunteer Fleet. Foreshadowing the Fleet Auxiliary, it comprised commercial tonnage built to an enhanced standard through Government subsidy. Its vessels were available for use as armed transports or auxiliary warships in time of war.

Tsarevitch

data:

Displacement standard	12,915 tons
Length overall	388 ft
Beam	76 ft
Design draught	26 ft
Complement	782

Armament:
4 x 12-in guns
12 x 6-in guns
20 x 11-pdr guns
20 x 3-pdr guns
4 x 15-in torpedo tubes

Machinery:
2 triple expansion steam engines,
16,500 ihp
2 shafts
18.5 knots

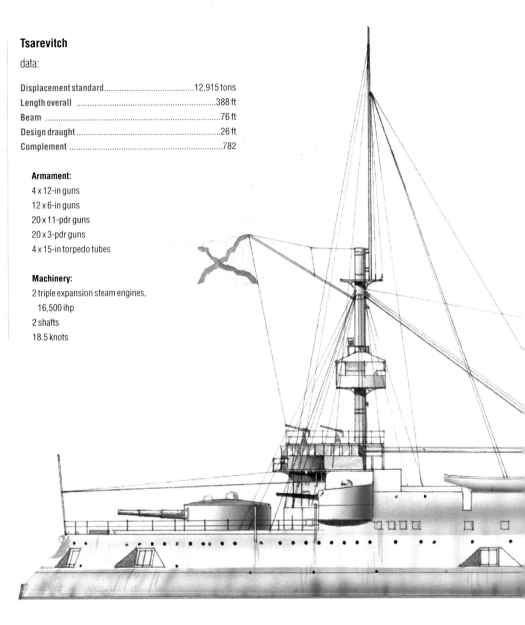

"POBIEDA."

Below: Completed in 1902, the *Pobieda* was the third unit of the Peresviet class battleships. Armed with four 10-in guns when 12-in weapons were becoming the norm, and with only modest protection, two were sunk in Port Arthur in 1904 and later raised by the Japanese.

Armour:
Belt ....up to 10 in
Ends ....6 in
Main deck ....2.5 in
Turrets ....10 in
Secondary turrets ......6 in
Conning tower ....10 in

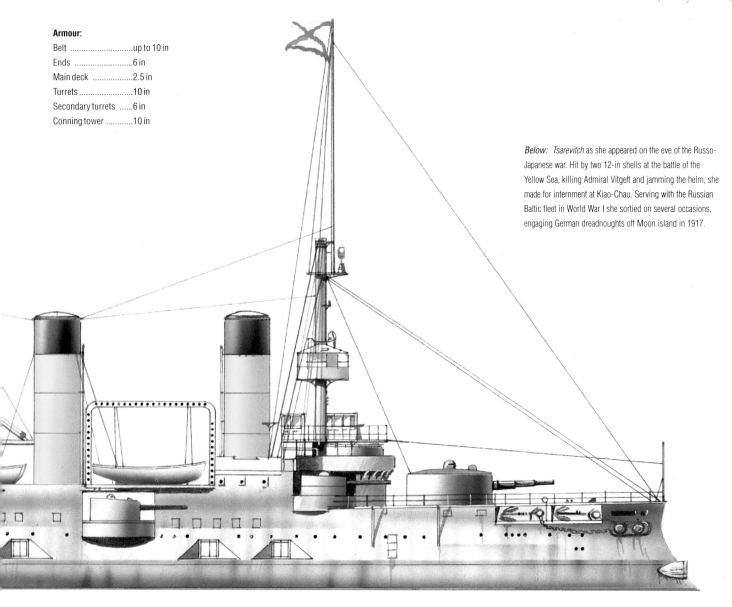

Below: Tsarevitch as she appeared on the eve of the Russo-Japanese war. Hit by two 12-in shells at the battle of the Yellow Sea, killing Admiral Vitgeft and jamming the helm, she made for internment at Kiao-Chau. Serving with the Russian Baltic fleet in World War I she sortied on several occasions, engaging German dreadnoughts off Moon island in 1917.

The United States

American attitudes toward Great Britain, the old colonial power, were at best ambivalent, but the comforting expanse of the North Atlantic dulled the fear of any naval threat. A nationwide revulsion at the excesses of the Civil War saw funds channelled decisively away from armaments, and led to a radical shift in American naval policy. Secure in its isolation, the United States feared no intrusion. The US Navy was allowed to stagnate with a dozen or so mixed, composite-built, steam and sail cruisers, and a handful of shallow-draught monitors for use on the extensive river systems.

By the 1880s the scars were healing. The West was being opened up and industry was booming. Growing production levels demanded export markets, which were sought aggressively. It was soon apparent that the American merchant marine was inadequate to capitalise on success, while the Navy could protect neither it nor the nation's extensive coastline. Even the minor states then involved in the war on the Pacific Coast of South America could dispose of naval forces superior to those of the United States. An Advisory Board was, therefore,

USS *Iowa* (BB4) took part in the battle of Santiago on 3 July 1898. Against her four 12-in and eight 8-in guns, the Spanish cruisers stood little chance.

appointed in 1881 to report on the needs of the Navy,. Not surprisingly, it recommended expansion but, due to American industry's limited experience in warship construction, this resulted by 1887 in only a modest increase of three protected cruisers and a despatch vessel. With the prospect of further orders, however, industry

Above: USS *Brooklyn* was Commodore Winfield Scott Schley's flagship at the battle of Santiago, engaging the Spanish flagship *Infanta Maria Theresa* which led the Spanish breakout.

Mississippi class

data:

Displacement standard	13,000 tons
Length	382 ft
Beam	77 ft
Design draught	25 ft
Complement	800

Class: *Mississippi, Idaho*

Armament:
4 x 12-in guns
8 x 8-in guns
8 x 7-in guns
12 x 3-in guns
2 x 21-in torpedo tubes

Machinery:
2 triple expansion steam
engines, 10,000 ihp
2 shafts
17 knots

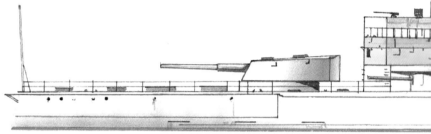

MAINE (U.S.A)

Above: The battleship *Maine*, sent to Cuba in February 1898 blew up in Havana: an accident attributed to Spanish sabotage by the American press.

quickly invested. By 1890 they were in better condition to take advantage of the recommendations of the new Naval Policy Board, which added up to a ten-year programme for a 100-ship expansion. For a fleet whose current largest commissioned warship was an armoured coast defence vessel, the prospect of an armada to include twenty first-class battleships, ten armoured, twenty protected and thirty lesser cruisers was ambitious to the point of absurdity. One can again see the influence of Mahan, whose theories had persuaded the Board that infinite, if indefinite, results would flow from the possession of significant naval power. Although the full recommendations had little prospect of realisation, they

resulted in a major step forward by the turn of the century, and a virtual transformation in the decade following.

American designs were already showing independent thought. Building at the time were the two Kentuckys, which incorporated what were to be the almost standard features of battle-worthiness and endurance enhanced

through the adoption of a moderate speed. While considerably smaller than the British Majestics, they mounted a larger, 13-in (330.2-mm) main battery. These guns could throw an 1100-pound (500-kg) projectile, compared with the 12-in (304.8-mm) guns' 850 pounds (386 kg). Although there were also fourteen 5-in (127-mm) guns, sited in a casemated centre battery, there

Armour:

Belt ....9 in
Ends ....4 in
Deck: ....2.5 in
Barbettes ....12 in
Casemates: ....6 in

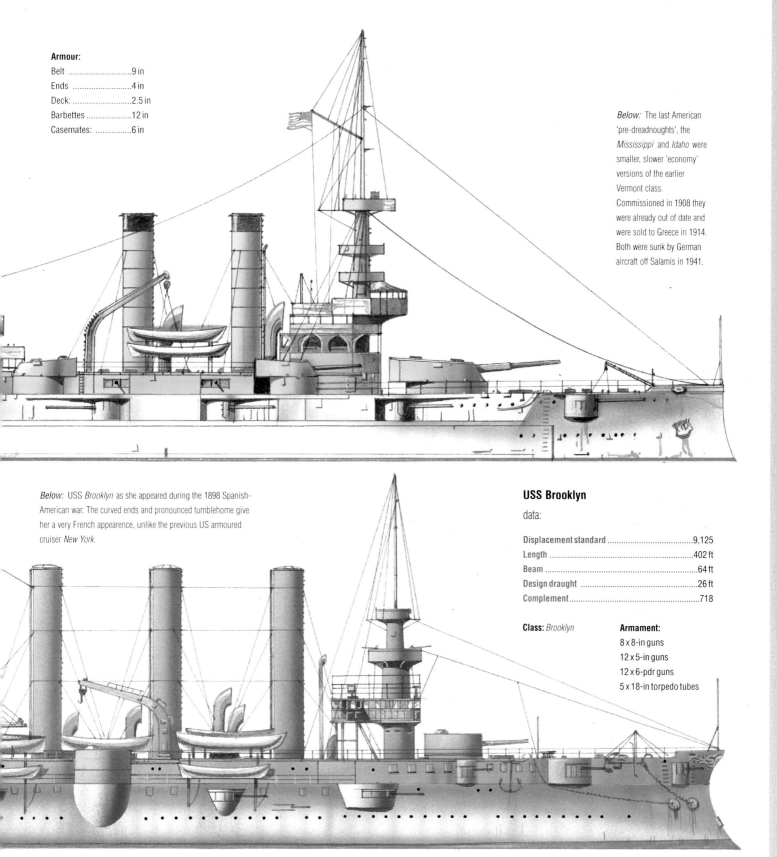

Below: The last American 'pre-dreadnoughts', the *Mississippi* and *Idaho* were smaller, slower 'economy' versions of the earlier Vermont class. Commissioned in 1908 they were already out of date and were sold to Greece in 1914. Both were sunk by German aircraft off Salamis in 1941.

Below: USS *Brooklyn* as she appeared during the 1898 Spanish-American war. The curved ends and pronounced tumblehome give her a very French appearence, unlike the previous US armoured cruiser *New York*.

USS Brooklyn

data:

Displacement standard	9,125
Length	402 ft
Beam	64 ft
Design draught	26 ft
Complement	718

Class: *Brooklyn*

Armament:
8 x 8-in guns
12 x 5-in guns
12 x 6-pdr guns
5 x 18-in torpedo tubes

were also four 8-in (203-mm) weapons. To save both weight and space, these were mounted in smaller gunhouses, built onto the roof of the main battery turrets. Thus, the one needed to train with the other, although they could elevate independently. The ammunition handling arrangements for the 8-in complicated the main turret, while a single fault could immobilise four major

weapons. The arrangement was not repeated.

Anglo-American relations had been jarred in 1895 by a border dispute between Venezuela and British Guiana. American attempts to demand British concessions failed absolutely, and forced home the lesson that foreign policy would need to be backed by a credible fleet if resolutions were not to become mere rhetoric.

Machinery:

4 triple expansion steam engines, 18,500 ihp
2 shafts
22 knots

Armour:

Belt ....8 in

Ends	3 in
Deck	3-6 in
Barbettes	8 in
Casemates	4 in

Germany

Where popular British concern, if that existed, might have been focused on the 'old' enemy, France, official attention was increasingly being directed toward Germany. This disparate collection of states had agreed unification into nationhood only as recently as 1871, and was dominated by Prussia. Within the space of the seven previous years, this martial state had concluded successful wars against Austria, Denmark and France. These were essentially military victories yet, while they firmly established the army as the senior service, they highlighted the need for a credible fleet, both for what may be termed 'total' defence and for the projection of a proud new sense of national identity.

Although the service acquired in 1871 the status of Imperial German Navy, it so lacked identity that its early administrators were army officers. These, notably General Stosch, diligently set about establishing the necessary infrastructure, in addition to building on what had been the Royal Prussian Navy. War at sea, understandably, was viewed as an extension to that ashore, and major energy was directed toward defending Germany's shores, particularly those of the Baltic, against (interestingly, in view of British preoccupations) an alliance of France and Russia.

Development proceeded at a modest rate and when, in 1887, the then Kaiser initiated the execution of the strategically important Kiel Canal, the fleet stood at eighteen each of ironclads and cruising ships, the former category embracing a varied collection of small seagoing turret, barbette and broadside ships.

Politically, Chancellor Bismarck, the architect of the German state, remained a moderating influence. In 1888, however, a new Kaiser, Wilhelm II, succeeded to the leadership. Very much in tune with his burgeoning nation, Wilhelm was a dangerous mix of character; at once bold and dynamic, impetuous and weak-willed. Greatly influenced by those around him, he was soon attended by those who could manipulate him, pandering to his vanity whilst exploiting his weaknesses. It was a tragedy for the world that he had a consuming passion for warships and naval affairs. In contrast his Chancellor believed that Germany should be content with being a naval power of the second rank. He also retained a mind of his own, so his dismissal in 1890, though a profound shock at the time should, in retrospect, be seen as inevitable.

Wilhelm II was another avid disciple of Mahan. The latter's writings convinced the Kaiser that Germany needed a blue-water navy. Overseas possessions, national prestige and trade would naturally follow. In a world already divided up by the major imperial powers, Wilhelm felt it quite in order to consider acquiring or, if necessary, appropriating, territory from 'declining' colonial powers. His grandmother, Queen Victoria, ruled the Empire that had inspired Mahan to put pen to paper: it served only to fuel in Wilhelm a mix of admiration, envy and resentment.

The German constitution defined the Kaiser as Supreme Commander of the state's military forces. Having finally divorced the functions of the Navy from those of the Army, however, he commenced a long series of changes to its organisation and command structure.

Endlessly exercising his right to meddle in the affairs of the Navy, he invariably ran out of interest and left others to sort out the problems that he had created.

In 1888 Wilhelm appointed the first naval officer to head the German Admiralty. Graf von Monts quickly moved construction on from a handful of armoured frigates to the quartet of Brandenburg-class battleships. Naval development, obviously in safe hands, was then disrupted by von Monts' early death in 1889, followed by the Kaiser dissolving the Admiralty hierarchy and, with it, unity of planning.

All four Brandenburg class battleships were completed in time to form the centrepiece of an impressive international naval gathering to celebrate the opening of the Kiel (or, more correctly 'Kaiser Wilhelm', or 'Nordsee-Ostsee') Canal in June 1895. Only in the following year did work commence on a second class of battleship, the quintet of Kaiser Friedrich III class battleships. These were of interest in having a main battery of 240-mm (9.4-in) guns in place of their predecessors' heavier 280-mm (11-in) weapons, in the belief that rate of fire was of greater significance than weight of projectile.

A continuing interest was taken in the armoured cruiser, whose fighting power was not matched by its speed, condemning it as a class to early obsolescence, being good for neither fleet work nor raiding.

In June 1897, the same month as Victoria's Diamond Jubilee Review, the Kaiser appointed Rear Admiral Alfred Tirpitz to head the Reichs Marineamt, or Imperial Navy Office. This department was responsible for the administration and the direction of development of the Navy. Ranked as State Secretary, and with parliamentary status, Tirpitz believed passionately in both the destiny of Germany and the power of a modern fleet to shape it. He was appointed largely on the strength of hypothetical plans, with which he had approached and enthused the Kaiser. Once in power, he proved adept at influencing those in parliament, and in industry, who could assist in realising his plans for the Navy. He was to transform the naval map of Europe, impressing his master to the extent that he was ennobled thereafter ('von' Tirpitz) within two years.

In April 1898, only ten months after his appointment, the Reichstag passed the First Navy Bill. 'To represent German interests everywhere energetically in peacetime and to be equal to warlike conflicts with countries across the sea not possessing any strong navy...', the Imperial German Navy was to be increased in strength by nineteen battleships (two squadrons of eight, plus a flagship, for the active fleet; two for reserve), eight 'large' (i.e. armoured) cruisers (seven for the active fleet, of which five would serve on foreign stations; one for reserve), and fifteen light cruisers. As ships of the existing fleet would require to be replaced over the same period of expansion, the whole programme was expected to run until 1916.

Not yet alarmed, but increasingly concerned, Britain listened carefully to the Kaiser's utterances. Those for public consumption ranged from the bellicose to the unrealistic but, when addressing his armed forces, his

words carried more meaning. Germany 'had regained her position in the council of nations' by virtue of his grandfather's rebuilding the army to the standards that it had enjoyed under Frederick the Great. 'As my grandfather did for the Army so will I for the Navy. Then I shall be enabled to procure for Germany the place among foreign nations which she has not yet obtained.' And, from the wording of the Navy Bill: '..Germany must have a fleet of such strength that, even for the mightiest Naval power, a war with her would involve such risks as to jeopardise its own supremacy. For this purpose it is not absolutely necessary that the German fleet should be as strong as that of the greatest Sea Power because, generally, a great Sea Power will not be in a position to concentrate all its forces against us'. The 'greatest Sea Power' was not mentioned by name, but its response was not long in coming.

Below: The final class of German pre-dreadnoughts were the five Deutschlands. Like their predecessors, they were optimised for short-range performance in the North Sea and Baltic.

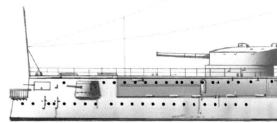

Below: The ten-strong Gazelle class built from 1897-1903 established the basic layout for German cruisers up to World War I. With exaggerated ram bows and reasonable freeboard, they had a severe roll but were very manoeuverable. *Frauenlob*, seen here, was sunk by HMS *Southampton* at the battle of Jutland.

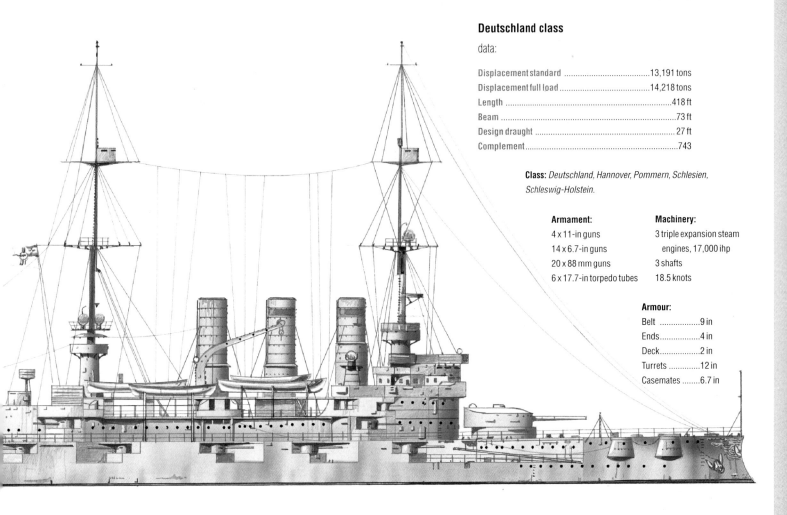

Deutschland class

data:

Displacement standard	13,191 tons
Displacement full load	14,218 tons
Length	418 ft
Beam	73 ft
Design draught	27 ft
Complement	743

Class: *Deutschland, Hannover, Pommern, Schlesien, Schleswig-Holstein.*

Armament:
4 x 11-in guns
14 x 6.7-in guns
20 x 88 mm guns
6 x 17.7-in torpedo tubes

Machinery:
3 triple expansion steam
  engines, 17,000 ihp
3 shafts
18.5 knots

Armour:
Belt	9 in
Ends	4 in
Deck	2 in
Turrets	12 in
Casemates	6.7 in

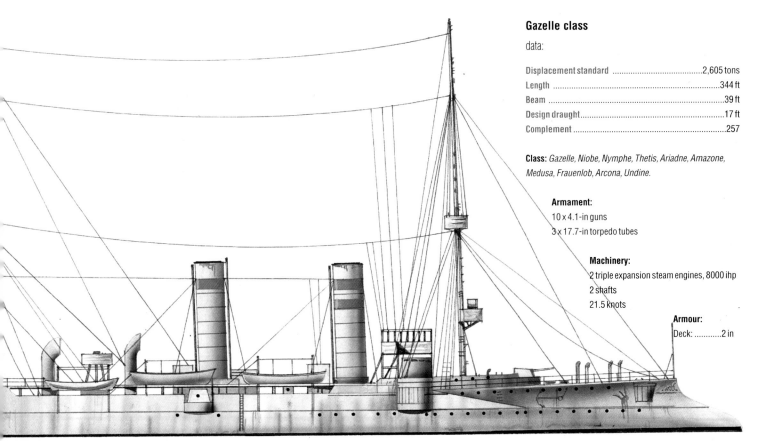

Gazelle class

data:

Displacement standard	2,605 tons
Length	344 ft
Beam	39 ft
Design draught	17 ft
Complement	257

Class: *Gazelle, Niobe, Nymphe, Thetis, Ariadne, Amazone, Medusa, Frauenlob, Arcona, Undine.*

Armament:
10 x 4.1-in guns
3 x 17.7-in torpedo tubes

Machinery:
2 triple expansion steam engines, 8000 ihp
2 shafts
21.5 knots

Armour:
Deck: 2 in

Chapter Three – Warship Design
1850–1914

A period of great advances and innovation in science and technology, the latter half of the nineteenth century saw the warship transformed. Major areas, such as machinery, armament and protection improved steadily, while around them raged controversy regarding the best hull to put them in. By the final decade of the century, some consensus was being reached, and a common international standard could be seen emerging. It may be of interest to review the primary stages whereby the sailing three-decker of the mid-century became what could be termed a 'modern warship'.

It is something of a cliché to state that the great ship of early Victorian days had changed little from that of two hundred years before. Hull construction had been improved but armament and rig could have been operated instantly by a Royal Navy crew from the mid-eighteenth century.

Just two years after Trafalgar, the *Clermont* demonstrated the application of a steam engine to a commercial hull but it was to be 1814 before Fulton built the *Demologos*, a 'kippered' wooden frigate, devoid of rigging but equipped with a steam-driven paddlewheel between the demi-hulls. For the next decade the British Admiralty monitored developments, recognising the value of steam propulsion but unwilling to introduce a revolution that would render the huge fleet of the Royal Navy obsolescent. Small paddle sloops were acquired during the 1820s, but served only as auxiliaries. Nonetheless, their performance worried the French into acquisition of the new technology.

Paddle frigates were introduced during the 1830s in France and the United States as well as in Great Britain. In this age of broadside armaments, however, their boilers, machinery and paddle boxes reduced fighting power. The paddles were vulnerable to damage while, when the ships were being sailed, they greatly increased resistance.

A practical marine propeller was demonstrated in 1838 to Admiralty representatives. It powered the commercial ship *Archimedes* and created an impression in allowing a hull to be better laid out for broadside armament. The first such warship, the sloop *Rattler* of 1843, was followed rapidly by the American *Princeton* and, two years later, by the French frigate *Isly*.

Improvements in hull construction allowed otherwise conventional two- and three-deckers to be built longer to accommodate machinery with minimum loss of fighting power. Full rig was retained, the two-bladed propeller being sited in the deadwood forward of the rudder post. When the ship was under sail, the screw was either feathered in a locked, vertical position, or decoupled and withdrawn upward into the hull above. Funnels were telescopic and, when retracted, they left the ship looking like a pure sailer.

Below: The distinctive profile of the Russian cruiser *Askold*, known to the Royal Navy as the 'packet of Woodbines'. Built for the Russians in Germany, 1898-1901, she was designed as a commerce raider: two-thirds of her hull devoted to machinery for a speed of 23.5 knots. Escaping the Port Arthur debacle, *Askold* got away to China and survived to fight in World War I, taking part in the hunt for the *Emden* before joining Allied forces off the Dardanelles.

Despite their poor industrial base, the French quickly grasped the potential of steam, producing the *Charlemagne* and *Napoléon* two-deckers in the early 1850s. The British responded with the *Agamemnon* in 1853. The impact of steam was such that both navies made the decision to convert entirely to steam-powered battle fleets, to be effected by a combination of new construction and by major surgery to existing hulls. Smaller fleets had to confine themselves to single-deckers, i.e. frigates, but with the extra length demanded by machinery, their shallow wooden hulls lacked longitudinal strength. With the extra weight of larger guns, however, the single-decker also became the established norm in larger fleets. Firepower was increasing at a rate that made the term 'frigate' increasingly meaningless. For instance, the two-decked *Agamemnon* was a nominal 90-gun, 70-metre ship of some 5,100 tons displacement. Just six years after her commissioning the frigate *Orlando* displaced some 5,700 tons on a length of 102 m. Their broadside armaments were of a hybrid nature, both including 68- and 32-pounders (30.9 and 14.5 kg) firing solid shot, together with 10- and 8-in (254- and 203.2-mm) shell guns, firing 84- and 56-lb (38.2- and 25.5-kg) spherical explosive projectiles.

Explosive shells owed much to the pioneering work of the French General Paixhans. Their slow development was validated suddenly during the 1850s, when the Russians annihilated a Turkish squadron at Sinope and an Anglo-French squadron was caused problems by the Sebastopol defences. Spherical shot was inaccurate, its wayward ballistics caused by castings of variable thickness and contents that settled after filling. The improved aerodynamics of a cylindrical projectile were appreciated, but, to prevent it tumbling in flight, the bore of the gun required to be rifled in order to impart spin stabilisation. With muzzle-loaded rifled (MLR) guns, reloading involved literally screwing the projectile home, engaging studs on its case with the rifling grooves in the barrel. This encouraged the re-introduction of an old concept, the breech. In breech-loaded rifles (BLR) loading was simplified, although the design of the breech itself caused considerable problems in the containment of the enormous pressures generated on firing.

Guns were growing both in size and weight. One-piece castings, in metals of varying quality, were superseded by a comparatively thin-walled tube strengthened by shrunk-on outer tubes until the diameter at the chamber end was about four time that of the bore. Great strength was required as the firing charge of black powder burned almost explosively. Slower-burning powders, and the introduction of steel of more consistent quality, would eventually reduce the weight of guns and encourage the lengthening of barrels in order to transfer the maximum proportion of the energy of the charge to the projectile.

Although decreasing in numbers, guns were still sited on open gundecks but on carriages that permitted both elevation and training. The latter was effected either by a heavy rack and pinion, or by castered wheels running on radial metal tracks, known as 'racers'. Nomenclature became increasingly bewildering. Early cannon were rated by the weight of their solid shot, e.g. 18-, 24- or 32 pounders (pdrs). It then became common to include the weight of the gun itself, e.g. a 68-pounder/95 hundredweight (cwt), or a 24-pdr/50cwt. As elongated shells became the norm, the gun calibre became the primary yardstick, e.g. 10-in/18-ton MLR.

The growing power of such artillery naturally had a profound influence on ship design. Two schools of thought predominated, that supporting the smashing effect of the largest projectiles and that concentrating on penetrations. The battle of Sinope, while over-dramatising the effect of shellfire on wooden hulls, effectively highlighted the danger which had already been foreseen by the British and French in firing trials against the *Prince George* and the range at Gavre. Only months later the forces of both nations were involved in the Crimea, with ships being required to engage fortifications. Over ten years previously, Dupuy de Lôme had advocated iron armouring for ships, the extra weight margin being found by incorporating iron members into the structure. For the Crimean application the French designed armoured box batteries, built by both fleets. Bluff and nearly flat-bottomed, they were steam-driven but carried a full rig. Their hulls were of wood, but clad with 4-in (101-mm) wrought iron plates, bolted to the hull and jointed to each other.

In their first action (1855) three French box batteries engaged the Russian fort at Kinburn. They absorbed many hits from 24-pounder solid shot without being pierced but, although this was generally hailed as a vindication of armour, the range was long enough for even wood to have resisted.

Below: Launched in 1883, HMS *Calypso* (right) was a 2,770 ton steam and sail-powered corvette, capable of 15 knots under steam. Armed with four 6-in and 12 5-in guns, she had a 1.5-in steel protective deck.

Right: In 1860 the Royal Navy had some 55 screw-powered ships of the line, carrying 90-130 guns. *Victoria*, launched in 1859 was typical: displacing 6,930 tons, she was 289 ft long and capable of 12 knots under sail or 13 knots under steam. Her armament consisted of 62 x 8-in smoothbore muzzle loaders, 58 x 32-pdr smoothbores and a single 68-pdr smoothbore chaser. Seen here at Malta in 1865, *Victoria* was sold in 1893.

New construction in wood, even for steam propulsion, was halted. In France, de Lôme designed a group of four protected ships, ordered in 1858. The first, *Gloire*, created a stir but, with the two following units, was literally an 'ironclad' with plates bolted to a wooden hull. Only the fourth, *Couronne*, was metal-hulled on metal frames. The great weight of the protection restricted them to being single-deckers, their hulls being greatly stressed and without watertight sub-division.

Rather leisurely evaluating the merits of armour protection following the end of the war, the British were jolted into activity by the ordering of the *Gloire* and her sisters. In terms of new and converted steam battleships, the Royal Navy had already lost the commanding numerical superiority that it had enjoyed in the days of sail. While not entirely abandoning wooden construction, the British used their greater industrial base to go straight for an all-metal pair of prototypes. The *Warrior* and *Black Prince* featured 4.5 in (114 mm) of wrought iron laid over a total of 18 in (457 mm) of timber backing, the latter required to assist the plate to absorb the shock of a large projectile which, otherwise, would have shattered it or sheared the bolts securing it.

Completed in 1861, HMS *Warrior* trumped the *Gloire* totally. Being metal-built, she could be longer (380 ft/115.8 m against 256 ft/78 m) and faster (14.3 against 12.8 knots). Her speed and heavier armament (ten 100-pounders and twenty-six 68-pounders against thirty 50-pounders) enabled her to choose her range. *Warrior*'s guns were spaced more generously but her armour was limited to the length of the main gundeck, its end being linked by transverse armoured bulkheads to defeat raking fire. Metal construction allowed also the provision of

watertight bulkheads. *Warrior* was still 'traditional' in having an armament that was overwhelmingly broadside, with minimal axial fire.

Over the next few years the British experimented with an extraordinary series of 'large frigates', leaving the French completely out-built. Armour necessarily grew thicker as guns grew larger, the extra weight resulting in increased ship dimensions and displacement. The centre battery, or casemate, ship was the first result, typified by the HMS *Bellerophon*, completed in 1866. This type incorporated a small number (in this case, ten) of the heaviest guns, mounted in a heavily protected box amidships. Through concentration of the armament, the protection around it was minimised in area and thus both casemate and belt could be thickened to 6-in (150-mm) plate. As ships now lacked the earlier extensive gundecks, they could be built shorter and handier. To permit a degree of axial fire, variations on the central box theme included overhangs, faceted hulls, pronounced tumblehome or angled box corners.

Training a gun took a long time compared with that taken by the ship to manoeuvre. The idea of mounting it on a revolving platform is usually credited to Captain Cowper Coles, who during the Crimean War explored its possibilities using a cannon on a floating raft, extending the concept to include a protective cover, or 'cupola'. Turrets became relatively common during the 1860s, featuring in the celebrated Civil War duel between the *Monitor* and *Virginia* (ex-*Merrimack*). Specimen turrets were constructed by the British Admiralty and tested by heavy bombardment, to which they proved resistant. They were applied quite extensively to low-freeboard coast defence ships, whose rapid roll was felt most in

deeper water and whose lack of sailing rig and endurance was not a vital factor.

The unreliability, low power and limited endurance of early steam machinery demanded that the Royal Navy retain auxiliary sailing rig. The all-round fire of turrets offered savings in weight and cost without loss of firepower. Masts and standing rigging unfortunately caused unacceptable obstruction. Coles designed a ship, the *Captain*, in which two turrets were set very low, with an overhead spar deck and self-braced tripod masts to avoid interference with firing arcs. Laws of stability were not fully developed in 1870 and the very low freeboard, whose lee side was quickly submerged by the force of a full rig, proved disastrous, leading to the ship's well-publicised capsize with severe loss of life, including Coles himself.

Machinery took a step forward with compounding, where the steam exhausted, still at high pressure, from the primary cylinder was used to drive a larger-diameter secondary cylinder. Its greater efficiency encouraged the removal of sailing rigs to produce a seagoing turret ship.

John Ericsson's *Monitor*, mentioned above, provided a model. Its hull little more than an armoured raft, it offered a minimal target to gunfire, although its ultra-low freeboard possessed little reserve buoyancy and risked rapid flooding through any hull opening. In the late 1860s, therefore, British designers added a low, armoured 'breastwork' to raise all apertures and the command of the turrets. Although designed for coast defence, they still displaced nearly 5,000 tons and had excessive draught, being poorly suited to their task. They were, however, important in proving the concept, resulting in the building of the 930-ton *Devastation* and

Thunderer in the early 1870s. These ships accommodated a 12-in gunned turret fore and aft of a narrow house of a superstructure, through which all hatch trunks led. Protection varied from 10- to 12-in (254- to 305-mm) and the ships proved able to steam 5,000 miles without coaling. Together with the following *Dreadnought*, they were the first battleships of the steam age, but the basic design suffered from its inherently low freeboard.

The big turret guns were muzzle-loaded, entailing running them back into the turret and depressing them to align the muzzles with inclined tubes emerging from a protected deck in front. Reloading was thus carried out entirely under armour, but was time-consuming. Turrets had to be of large diameter to allow the guns to be run back, but the guns themselves had to be short-barrelled to keep the heavy turret to minimum dimensions. With respect to the latter point, it should be pointed out that turret construction typically involved 12- to 14-in (305- to 356-mm) plate backed by 15- to 17-in (381- to 432-mm) teak.

With breech mechanisms still far from perfect, the Royal Navy was reluctant to make a final changeover, but this was finally forced upon it by an explosion in one of the *Thunderer*'s MLRs. This was caused by double-shotting, and would not have occurred with a breech loader.

Adoption of the new gun, with its longer barrel, meant that reloading was carried out much in reverse to earlier practice, the gun being elevated to an appropriate angle to allow projectile and firing charge to be rammed home from an underdeck assembly abaft the turret. Four 12-in BLRs were disposed in two turrets on the *Colossus* and

Edinburgh, completed in 1886/7 after eight-year building times that rivalled those of the French. The ships were of the central-citadel type, a concept originating with the Italian *Duilio* of 1876 and adopted by the British in HMS *Inflexible*. Both turrets were mounted amidships, the breastwork supporting them being as small and as heavily armoured as possible. The weight so saved allowed for 24-in (610-mm) protection on the *Inflexible* and 100-ton, 17.7-in (450-mm) guns on the *Duilio*. Subordinated to the requirements of the armaments, the superstructure was reduced to small masses. Vertical protection was limited to the length of the central citadel. Beyond this, reliance was placed on an armoured deck just below the waterline with a closely sub-divided level above.

The *Inflexible*'s 16-in (406-mm) MLRs and the *Colossus*' 12-in (305-mm) BLRs typified the trend to the largest possible guns. Mounted in suitably heavy turrets, they had to be sited low for reasons of stability. Not happy with this the French sought to increase freeboard, thereby both improving the command of the guns and the seakeeping of the ship. Dupuy de Lôme adopted the fortification technique of the guns firing *'en barbette'* i.e. over a low, armoured parapet. In warship terms this translated into a short, vertical circular tube, within which rotated a turntable supporting the gun. A smaller diameter tube, containing the ammunition hoist, projected downward from the barbette and through the protective deck to the magazine. As introduced, the barbette mounting was devoid of overhead protection except in way of the loading gear.

First with the new arrangement was the *Amiral Duperré*, launched in 1879. Four 340-mm (13.4-in) guns were mounted singly, two on the centreline aft and the

others sponsored from the ship's sides abreast the bridge structure. Because the hull was given pronounced tumblehome, the sided guns could fire almost directly ahead and astern. Higher freeboard permitted the guns to work effectively in heavy weather, leading the British to copy the idea in the *Collingwood*, completed in 1887. Each mounting a pair of 12-in BLRs, her barbettes were of a distinctive pear shape in plan, the elongation at the breech end housing the loading gear. A shallow main belt was 18 in (457.2 mm) thick but was limited to the central third of the ship, with each end being closed off by 16-in transverse bulkheads. The whole was roofed by a protective deck, which was extended fore and aft to the unprotected, but heavily sub-divided extremities. Much weight could now be saved through construction of mild steel rather than wrought iron.

Although of compound armour, i.e. steel-faced wrought iron, the short belt of the *Collingwood* was much criticised, while the *Duperré*'s full length belt was thought too shallow, though composed of up to 22-in (559-mm) wrought iron. Benedetto Brin in Italy believed that guns were now large enough to defeat any protection scheme and designed the two Italia class with no belts whatsoever. The ships relied on a double longitudinal bulkhead over their main length, together with a 75-mm (3-in) protective deck some two metres below the

waterline, divided from a continuous deck above by minute sub-division. The resultant great saving in weight, combined with the then large displacement of 13,900 tons and length and length of 124.7 m (409.1 ft) allowed for a high designed speed of 16 knots, although the ships were capable of eighteen. A high freeboard was combined with an elongated barbette that stretched diagonally across the ship amidships. At either end of the barbette was a turntable supporting a pair of monstrous 17-in (432-mm) guns, each weighing over 100 tons. By the end of the 1880s, when both Italias and a trio of follow-ons had been completed, the concept was out-moded by medium-calibre, quick-firing guns capable of riddling such unprotected hulls.

Something of Brin's ideas crept into the British 'Admiral' class, laid down in 1882–3. Their belt was both short and shallow, the ships' extremities depending upon close sub-division for protection. Except for the *Benbow*, with 16.25-in (413-mm) guns, the class had a pair of 13.5-in (343-mm) guns mounted in barbettes at either end. Weight control during their construction was poor, so the class proved wet through inadequate freeboard.

Camperdown of this class was involved in the celebrated collision that resulted in the sinking of the *Victoria*. It was one of several incidents that appeared to vindicate the ram as a weapon. Its return had followed the development of axial fire and powered manoeuvrability, and the new-style end-on tactics that they promised. During the Austro-Italian war of 1866, the *Ferdinand Max* sank the *Re d'Italia* by ramming during a battle off Lissa. The fact that the latter ship was wooden-built, had no watertight bulkheads, and had her

steering disabled so that she could not evade her attacker seemed lost on those eager to see 'lessons' in even the most insignificant incident. Rams thus continued to be a feature of major warships up until World War I, though there was never to be an instance of two large, fully-manoeuvrable surface warships deliberately attempting a ramming contest.

Like the *Benbow*, the *Victoria* had carried 16.25-in guns but, at the insistence of the Service, which wanted improved standards of protection, these were turret mounted. The effect on the design was drastic, with only one pair being accommodated, firing on restricted forward arcs, and very limited freeboard. Such a layout would necessarily have influenced tactics in action, while the guns had a command of only 15 ft (4.6 m) compared with 22 ft (6.7 m) in the *Benbow*.

Victoria was the first to be equipped with triple-expansion machinery. Improved boilers now delivered steam at pressures that permitted the cascading of three cylinders before it was exhausted to the condensers. Although triple-expansion engines were able to develop greater power for the same bulk and weight, this was of little consequence in driving the bluff forms of current battleships, whose length-on-breadth ratio was less than 5:1. More useful to a naval architect was to develop the same power with more compact engines, and then to increase the bonus with fewer boilers of improved design.

The Royal Sovereign class, funded by the Naval Defence Act, had two pairs of 13.5-in guns, mounted in barbettes. However, with the introduction of quick-firing guns, barbettes unprotected from above were no longer acceptable. In order to maintain a viable freeboard, therefore, the trend began towards smaller, i.e. 12-in,

Above: The Admiral class battleship *Camperdown* became notorious in 1893, accidentally ramming and sinking the flagship *Victoria* with heavy loss of life. Despite her typical ram bow, *Camperdown* herself was nearly lost in the collision. Note the size of the 13.5-in guns in open barbette mountings.

calibre armament and increased displacement. During the1890s international designs began to develop more similar characteristics as naval architects wrestled with common problems.

Developments in armour

Reference to armour during this period should note not only its thickness but also its type and, increasingly, its arrangement. Early thick wrought-iron plates had a 'puff-pastry' type of construction, resulting from rolling together a number of thin plates at very high temperature. Plates of up to 22-in (about 560-mm) thickness were produced by this process but it was more common to use two thinner plates, separated and backed by timber in a sandwich combination.

Iron was metallurgically tough and increasingly resistant to shattering, but was becoming ever thicker and heavier, and still being defeated by major calibre projectiles. In 1876, Creusot steel plate was introduced, more consistent in quality and more resistant to penetration, yet prone to shattering through being more brittle.

A British process then combined the better qualities of each, by heat-welding a resistant steel plate to the face of a resilient iron substrate. For similar thickness, the

Left: The ram bow and forward turret with two 16.25-in guns gave HMS *Victoria* a distinctive profile. The first to carry triple expansion engines, *Victoria* and her sister *Sans Pareil* exceeded 17 knots on trials and were known as good steamers, if a little wet forward. Controversy over the loss of *Victoria* continued for years. One important survivor was the then-lieutenant Jellicoe, who went on to command the Grand Fleet in World War I.

Right: Completed at Portsmouth in 1890, *Trafalgar* was a heavily-protected (20-in compound belt) turret ship, armed with four 13.5-in guns. Her low freeboard made her wet and unable to maintain speed in a seaway. Together with sistership *Nile*, she served in the Mediterranean fleet until the late 1890s and both were still on the strength as guard ships in 1905, although with speeds reduced to 14 knots, they were of low fighting value.

resulting 'compound' armour was 20 percent more effective than wrought iron alone. Creusot responded by developing a technique for surface tempering, resulting in a comparatively shatter-resistant plate with a very hard face. Proving trials, however, showed that despite its superiority over compound plate, it was still vulnerable to penetration by modern chilled shot. In the Royal Navy, the Royal Sovereigns marked a transition, having heavy belt armour of compound plates and more thinly-protected zones, such as casemates, protected by steel plate.

Improvements to steel plate depended increasingly upon developing heat treatments that would more smoothly graduate the boundary between hard and resilient phases, and identifying additives (such as nickel or chromium) which improved the metallurgy of the material with heat treatment. The American Harvey process, introduced in 1891, combined face-hardening with annealing. It proved to be some 38 percent more effective than compound plate but tended to spall on the inner surface under the shock from a heavy projectile, against which it required to be timber-backed.

Ships could now be given the same degree of protection for less weight, a trend taken further by Krupp

during the 1890s through the refinement of the Harvey process. By 1900, the so-called Krupp Cemented (KC) steel was shown to be a 25 percent improvement on Harveyised steel, and rapidly became a virtual standard.

Lighter protection could also permit deeper belts. Shallow vertical protection on all too many battleships could be fully submerged or exposed by even moderate rolling. As an example, the beam of a British battleship of the pre-Dreadnought era was about 75 ft (22.9 m), so a ten-degree roll would expose alternately an extra 13 ft (about 4 m) of side, or projected deck area. Gunnery was still thought of in terms of close-range encounters where trajectories were fairly flat, but already, without the plunging fire of longer ranges, a protective deck was vulnerable to penetration. Such decks were almost invariably thinner than vertical belts, due to their much greater area.

The Torpedo

To sink a ship, by whatever means, water must ultimately flood the hull sufficiently to destroy her buoyancy. The concept of the torpedo neatly short-circuited the contest between larger guns and thicker armour. Its function was to breach the hull, literally 'below the belt', and to allow external water pressure to do the rest.

Early torpedoes were synonymous with mines, but came to mean spar torpedoes. These, as the name implies, were explosive charges attached to a long spar that projected forward from, usually, a small launch. Its objective was to approach silently, use the spar to place the charge against the hull of the target as far below the waterline as possible, detonate it and disappear in the resulting confusion. Needless to say, successes were inversely proportional to the casualty rate.

This concept was developed further in the 'Davids' of the American Civil War. Able to flood down until only a minimum amount of topside broke surface, these semi-submersible craft were difficult to control at the low speeds of which they were capable. Despite successes such as the attack on the *New Ironsides*, they were still too hazardous to last.

As early as 1848 one Franz Pfeifer was credited with the first concept of a 'locomotive', or self-propelled, torpedo. It was, however, ahead of its time and the idea remained dormant until resurrected by Johannes Luppis, a commander in the Austro-Hungarian Navy. In 1866 he discussed his basic design with Robert Whitehead, the British director of an engineering factory in Fiume. A prototype was constructed, marrying for the first time the essential components of tubular hull, self-contained propulsion and space for a warhead. Elevators, controlled by hydrostatic valves, were incorporated to maintain a pre-set depth. A pendulum was introduced soon afterward to add a damping function to the control equation, maintaining smoother trajectories and ultimately 'porpoising' through over correction.

Whitehead was invited to England in 1871 and, following a long series of demonstration runs, the British purchased manufacturing rights. Within its first ten years of existence the torpedo progressed from a range of about 300 metres at less than 6 knots to 500 metres at 18 knots. By the early 1880s the diameter had been increased to 15 in (381 mm) and weight of warhead to 7 lb (31.8 kg). Most fleets had acquired them and several more states, including Germany, had purchased a licence to build.

Specialist torpedo craft were hampered by the still short range of the weapon. To close to effective launching range meant almost certain destruction by the quick-firing guns now carried by their intended targets.

Above: Rapid developments in torpedo design enabled small torpedo boats like this Italian launch to pose a real threat to warships of any size.

Speed and control of the torpedo had to be improved, as greater range involved increased 'dead time' and diminished accuracy. Hulls ceased to be tapered and became parallel cylinders with a 'blunt' nose and a finer after run. An increase to 18 in (457 mm) diameter in 1888 allowed an increase in the supply of compressed air used to power the propulsion engine. Another Austrian, Ludwig Obry, contributed a further major advance by adding a gyroscope to keep the weapon running straight. Soon afterward, speed was increased by almost 50 percent through burning liquid fuel in the compressed air. This produced a mass of rapidly-expanding gas, boosted by water vapour, used to power a four-cylinder radial engine.

Parallel with this steady development, other variations came and went. Electrical energy powered the Ericsson, Nordenfelt and the Sims-Edison torpedoes. Ericsson also tried rocket propulsion and the Howell stored its energy in a heavy flywheel. Both the Maxim and the Brennan had their propellers rotated by the rapid unreeling of about 3,000 yards (2,743 metres) of piano wire, stored within the torpedo but taken off by a fast-spooling winch aboard the launching ship. This type out-performed the Whitehead when first introduced but, unlike their competitor, were incapable of much improvement. Most types by now had contra-rotating propellers to offset the otherwise powerful torque reaction.

The increasing threat from the torpedo was not underestimated, and warship designers moved quickly to develop improved means to both deploy it and to safeguard against it. A major innovation in capital ships was the addition of longitudinal 'torpedo bulkheads'.

Running from the after magazine spaces to the forward, and flanking boiler and machinery rooms, these were set far enough inboard to prevent being breached by a torpedo exploding against the shell plating. The outboard space could be coal-filled, but was more effective if left void, giving the explosion space to vent itself.

Steel 'bullivant' nets, deployed from numerous booms, could be spread to form a continuous 'crinoline' around a ship at anchor, snaring any incoming torpedo. The whole assembly could be furled and stowed against the hull in a surprisingly short time in a smart ship

Both torpedo craft and capital ship deployed the weapon either from tube or launch cradle. As ranges were still reckoned in only hundreds of yards, attackers could be kept at bay by a combination of searchlights and quickfirers. The former had come with the introduction of electricity at sea, being first fitted in HMS *Alexandra* in 1876.

The first specifically anti-torpedo boat gun was the one-inch calibre, four-barreled Nordenfelt, which 'could damage the boiler of a torpedo boat at 300 to 500 yards'. This was followed by the 57-mm (2.24-in) Nordenfelt and Hotchkiss guns, both firing 6-lb (2.7-kg) fixed ammunition. An experienced gunner could, with these, loose up to twelve aimed shots per minute out to 4000 yards.

For a time, capital ships could extend the flexibility of the torpedo by deploying it from 'second-class' torpedo boats, carried aboard and slung under cranes. Used by the French and Italians, as well as the British, such 70-foot (21.3-metre) craft were really too small to pose a practical threat, and were abandoned in favour of 125-footers (38.1-metre) that could also act in the defence of larger ships.

Contemporary exercises explored the extent of the threat posed by the torpedo, and how best to use it in both offence and defence. During the Royal Navy's 1885 Fleet Exercise, for instance, a night attack was made by torpedo boats in ships anchored with nets deployed and covered by other ships, equipped with searchlights and quick-firers. Although every attempt to cross the lighted zone resulted in the attackers being 'sunk', spent torpedoes were afterwards recovered from the nets of three of the targets. By 1891, manoeuvres showed convincingly that 'catchers' severely hampered attacks by torpedo craft and led to the proposal that larger, gun-armed catchers should accompany larger units for their defence. In 1892 the term 'catcher' was abandoned in favour of 'destroyer', of which the first six '27-knotters' were ordered under the 1892–3 Programme.

As is so often the case, a significant development was first used in an insignificant circumstance. In 1877 the Laird-built turret monitor *Huascar*, manned by Peruvian revolutionaries, was deemed to have committed 'outrages' against local British interests. Brought to action by the big British frigate *Shah* and the corvette *Amethyst*, the Peruvian ironclad withstood 'seventy or eighty' hits from 9-in, 7-in and 64-pounder muzzle-loaders. The *Shah* finally launched a torpedo from an 'above-water ejector', only to see it run out of compressed air as the target manoeuvred to avoid it.

It was another fourteen years before a torpedo sank a target in anger. This occurred during the Chilean civil war, when the secessionist central-battery ship *Blanco*

Encalada was sunk by two Government destroyers while at anchor. One of five 14-in torpedoes fired was sufficient to cause her to capsize within five minutes but, as she had taken no precautions to confine flooding, the incident proved very little.

Following the introduction of heating, torpedo propulsion went in two directions; the Americans favouring turbines, the British a robust four-cylinder radial unit, whose lower speed of rotation required less reduction gearing. The 18-in weapon that was capable of 1,000 yards at 36 knots in 1906 could achieve 2,000 yards at over 40 knots, or 6,000 yards at 31 knots, by 1911. In 1908 the 21-in (533-mm) torpedo had been introduced and, by the outbreak of World War I, packed a warhead of about 100 kg (220 lb).

Destroyers

Having realised that the 'destroyers' were, at once, threat and antidote, Great Britain developed and built them at great speed, many to satisfy a healthy overseas demand. Thirty-six of the '27-knotters' were launched in 1894–5. Flush-decked, with a turtle-back forecastle, they were very wet. They carried two, single 18-in tubes, mounted on the centreline, together with one 12-pounder and five 6-pounder guns. Until 1899, a total of sixty-eight improved '30-knotters', followed in uninterrupted sequence. Of much the same specification, their displacement increased from about 280 to 360 tons.

Displacement and detail could vary considerably, with more than a dozen firms building to a similar specification, which was permitted to be interpreted with considerable freedom. Britain by no means possessed a monopoly in innovative construction and, by the later 1890s, French and German boats were reported to be making well in excess of 30 knots. The reports were exaggerated by a knot or two, and the British, even with water-tube boilers, were unable to match such speeds. At the 1897 review, Charles Parsons had electrified proceedings by dashing through the lines with his steam turbine-propelled *Turbinia*. The Admiralty, anxious to improve performance, was very ready to accept Parsons' offer to build a prototype based on a '30-knotter', but propelled by steam turbine.

Two prototypes, *Viper* and *Cobra*, were built in 1899 and, while both came to untimely ends, they demonstrated that speeds as high as 37 knots were feasible. Efficiency was, however, very low. The high-revving turbines were connected directly to the shafts, necessitating three propellers on each of four shafts. Coal consumption, particularly at low speeds, was up to twice that of a craft with reciprocating machinery. In a third ship, *Velox*, therefore, a compromise was attempted in the incorporation of turbines for high-speed use and reciprocating machinery for cruising. On slightly improved figures she still attained 35 knots.

Contemporary German designs featured a raised forecastle and the bridge structure set further aft, greatly improving their ability to fight in heavy weather. The British response was the extended series of River class destroyers, launched between 1903 and 1905. At 225 ft (68 m) in length, these were a full five metres longer than their German peers, improving sea-kindliness

further. Their raised forecastle was extended back to the bridge, in contrast to the foreign craft which had a short well between the break of the forecastle and the bridge front. In the well was a third torpedo tube, the Rivers carrying only two. As the Germans also carried two reloads, they had at their disposal five rounds to the British boats' two. Except for the turbine-driven *Eden*, all Rivers reverted to reciprocating machinery, conferring superior endurance.

Different requirements meant that the US Navy adopted the destroyer concept directly, without a preliminary torpedo boat stage. Sixteen Bainbridge class, launched in 1900–2, formed the initial class but, like their British counterparts, differed considerably from ship to ship. All were four-stacked, but variation in funnel spacing betrayed wide variation in internal layout. Although about 10 percent longer than the Rivers, they were narrower, gutted and thus of lower displacement. On average about three knots faster than the Rivers they were, nonetheless, criticised for being too slow. Like the British ships, they mounted only two 18-in torpedo tubes, but their extra length permitted a second 3-in/12-pounder gun.

Seven Bainbridges were flush-decked, with a pronounced turtleback forward; the remainder had a raised forecastle. Scantlings were light, which promoted structural problems, yet most come out overweight. All were powered by reciprocating machinery. In their following classes, both Americans and British increased both size and strength to correct structural shortcomings.

The dozen British Tribal class, which went into the water in 1907–9, were built to the simple but direct specification that they steam at 33 knots in a moderate sea, burn oil fuel, and carry three 12-pounders.

Below: French and American interest in submarines spurred the Royal Navy into acquiring five Holland submarines, built by Vickers with (initially secret) funding from the Treasury.

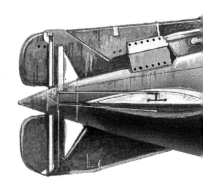

Interestingly, the size of individual boats grew with chronological order, ranging from the 855-ton *Afridi* (250ft/76.2 m) to the 1,090-ton *Viking* (280.3 ft/85.4 m). Steam turbines, now a more mature technology, were re-introduced and, with a triple shaft arrangement, all met their required maximum speed, some by a considerable margin.

Oil fuel was being adopted generally. Not only consistent in quality and being capable of simple pumping around the ship from remote tanks, it marked the end of the evolution of the 'coaling ship'. A drawback was that oil bunkers could not contribute to the protection of the ship. Despite the later Tribals shipping two 4-in guns in place of three 12-pounders, they were underarmed compared with the latest German 'torpedo boats', which carried three 105-mm (4.1-in) guns and no less than six torpedo tubes against two.

Lacking the urgency already evident in Europe, the US Navy waited almost nine years before building successors to the Bainbridges. Judged again to be lightly built, these 700/740 tonners were known popularly as the 'Flivvers', although their five 3-in (76-mm) guns and six tubes belied the flippancy of the nickname. All had raised forecastle. Despite adopting steam turbine propulsion, they returned disappointing speeds of below 30 knots maximum.

The French constructed torpedo boats (*Torpilleurs*) until 1902. As even the ultimate group averaged only 180 tons displacement, they were of little use beyond harbour defence. Even then, the 42-kg (92.4-lb) warhead and 600-metre range of their two 15-in (381-mm) torpedoes posed little threat to large ships. Only in 1900 did the French begin to build destroyers, although they were classified only as *Torpilleurs d'Escadre*. The term

Contre-torpilleur, i.e. torpedo-boat destroyer, was introduced only with the large 'super-destroyers' which began to enter service in the early 1920s. In common with the Germans and Italians, the French maintained a clear distinction between destroyers and torpedo boats through to World War II.

Once started, the French produced over fifty nominal 300-tonners between 1900 and 1908. Although built to a basic *Normand* design, they differed widely from yard to yard. They were characterised by a combination of low freeboard, marked tumblehome and turtleback sheerstrakes, some over their full length. In any sea they were awash, and all were therefore fitted with an elevated spar deck.

Thirteen nominal 450-tonners followed in 1906–10. They fell into three groups, which marked the progress of propulsion systems; viz. reciprocating, combined reciprocating and turbine, and turbine only. Six 65-mm (2.5-in) guns were carried and their three torpedo tubes were uprated to 450 mm (17.7 in). Their size was still too small to be effective beyond the Mediterranean, and the true destroyer type emerged only with the 800-tonner of 1911. With raised forecastle, two 100-mm (3.9-in) guns and four 450-mm (17.7-in) tubes, they were satisfactory, multi-purpose ships.

Submarines

Torpedo boats and destroyers were not to retain their pre-eminence as torpedo carriers. As noted above, the 1890s had seen a considerable experimentation in submersible craft, which proved an irresistible challenge to inventors. The torpedo was an ideal weapon, its then short range

being offset by a submersible's intended ability to creep up, unseen, on its target. Unfortunately, for a long time, ingenuity was insufficient to overcome the limitations of contemporary technology.

Submarines are complex beasts. Submerged, they are totally interactive; every movement or weapon discharge had to be instantly offset by shifting ballast to maintain trim. Depth control was feasible only under weigh, with sufficient flow over horizontal control surface, or 'hydroplanes' to provide lift. Equally important was the rate of application of hydroplane angle, which had to be a function of hull hydrodynamic response if potentially fatal 'porpoising' was to be avoided.

Holland class

data:

Displacement (surfaced)	113 tons
Displacement (submerged)	122 tons
Length	63 ft
Beam	12 ft
Design draught	10 ft
Complement	8

Class: *No.1, No.2, No.3, No.4, No.5*

Armament:
1 x 18-in torpedo tube (3 torpedoes carried)

Machinery:
4-cylinder petrol engine and electric motor, 160 hp/60 hp
7.5 knots surfaced, 6 knots dived

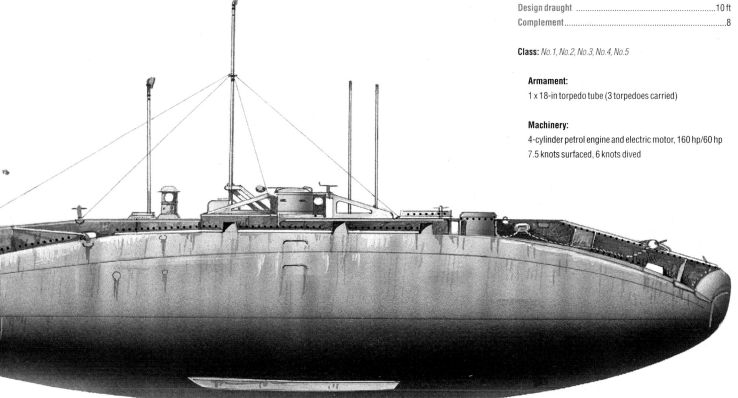

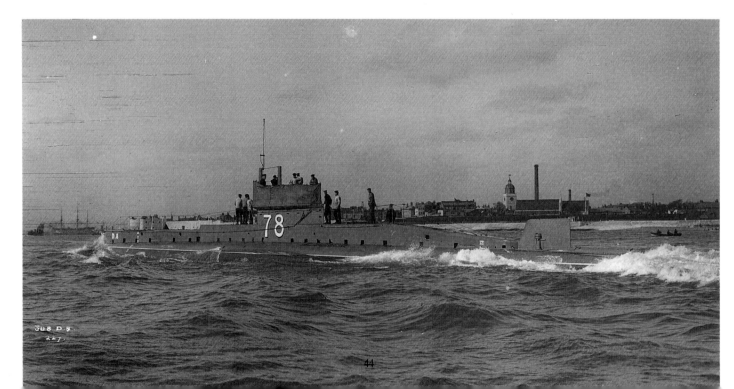

Below: The British 'E' class were the mainstay of the British submarine arm during World War I, with 55 constructed 1913–16. The *E-11* famously penetrated the Turkish defences, attacking shipping in Constantinople harbour and sank the battleship *Barbarossa.*

Any form of fuel-burning propulsion consumed oxygen and generated noxious gases – neither being compatible with crew survival. From the outset, electricity was the most attractive energy form, but then, as until very recently, it depended upon the simple cell for storage. Individually of low potential, cells needed to be connected in large numbers to yield a voltage sufficient to run a motor large enough for submarine propulsion. They also, of course, needed to be re-charged at frequent intervals, necessitating an air-breathing prime mover driving a suitable generator.

The French, never disciples of Mahan and active from the outset in submarine development, favoured steam propulsion, used in surface navigation for propulsion and battery charging. Submerging required shutting-down the boiler and securing all exhaust and ventilating arrangements before turning over to a battery-powered motor. Needless to say, the procedure was lengthy, laborious and vulnerable to human error, while the heat inside the hull was considerable. Following Gustave Zédé's death in 1890, the 48.5-metre boat that he was building was given his name. Problems in depth control

resulted in the staged development of the first practical hydroplanes. The boat also had a conning tower, introduced primarily to avoid the risk of flooding through open hatches when on the surface.

The *Zédé* was followed by the *Morse*, in which the extra height conferred by the tower was used to house the first effective periscope for submerged navigation. Both boats could accommodate three torpedoes, a feature that enthused the French Government to the extent that it staged an open design competition in 1896. The winner, Maxime Laubeuf, conceived what might be termed the sire of the modern submarine. Completed in 1899 as the *Narval*, the 200-ton boat incorporated a double hull to conveniently accommodate ballast and fuel tanks, an outer casing for surface navigation, and separate compartments for her steam and electric propulsion systems. Her batteries could be re-charged at sea, while oil fuel simplified stowage of bunkers. Four 450-mm (17.7-in) torpedoes were slung externally in deck-edge cradle/launchers.

Similarly interested in the submarine as a possible inexpensive deterrent to a fleet attempting close

blockade, the US Navy also promoted a competition during the 1890s. From this emerged the names of Simon Lake and John P. Holland. Holland, the winner, had been experimenting with submersible craft for nearly twenty years. His steam-propelled *Plunger* was completed in 1897, but her shortcomings meant that she was never accepted by the Navy. Holland's salvation was the new gasoline-fuelled internal combustion engine: smaller, producing less heat and, importantly, simple to stop and start, which greatly improved diving times. A speculative, alternative boat was quickly built, at 53.8 ft by 10.3 ft (16.4 x 3.1 m) less than half the size of the *Plunger*. With its obvious potential, the craft was purchased as the *Holland* in 1899.

Its inventor then stretched the basic design by about 17.5 percent to a displacement of 107/123 tons (surfaced/submerged). Between 1901 and 1903 seven were built to naval order. Known initially as the Adder

Below: The eight 'D' class were the first British submarines capable of more than coastal defence. Diesel engines were much safer than the petrol engines of the earlier boats.

'E' class

data:

Displacement submerged	667 tons
Displacement surfaced	807 tons
Length	181 ft
Beam	22 ft
Design draught	12 ft
Complement	30

Armament:
5 18-in torpedo tubes (two bow, two amidships and one stern)
10 torpedoes
1 x 12-pdr gun

Machinery:

2 diesel engines, 1,600 hp	2 electric motors, 840 hp
	14 knots surfaced, 9 knots dived

Left: USS *Narwhal* (SS17) was launched in 1909 and was designed to dive to a depth of 200 feet. Armed with four 18-in torpedo tubes, it had a crew of 15.

class, they later took the simple designations A1-7. The petrol engine, which could so reduce the size of a submarine, was also adopted by the French at this time.

Having closely monitored all this activity abroad, the British Admiralty finally decided to acquire submarines for evaluation. The 1901–2 Estimates thus officially funded five boats of the Holland improved type. In fact the craft had been ordered in 1900, to be built under licence by Vickers, Son and Maxim. Each carried one 18-in torpedo tube. Captain Reginald Bacon, one of the best brains in the Navy, who had been appointed Inspecting Captain of Submarines, devised a fold-down periscope, which greatly facilitated submerged navigation.

Officially, Vickers were building to the Holland design but, in practice, were well ahead of the Americans, having had to re-design it extensively and prepare many original drawings. As the company was thus having to develop its own solutions to Admiralty requirements, connections with the Holland Company were terminated as quickly as possible. From a standing start, the British

submarine service developed rapidly: thirteen A-class funded between 1902 and 1904, eleven B-class 1903–5, and no less than thirty-eight C-class 1905–9. All were single hulled, spindle-form boats, with no internal watertight bulkheads.

With negligible freeboard and no conning tower, the Hollands had been a nightmare in surface navigation, while their fighting value was very limited. Vickers' A-class development increased the length to 105 ft (32 m) and displacement to 190/206 tons. A tower was included and two, forward-firing tubes, for which there were four torpedoes. The B-class and very similar C-class took the process further, increasing length to 142.3 ft (43.4 m) and displacement to 287/316 tons. Rudimentary topside casings appeared with the Bs, facilitating crew movement on the surface and, by adding buoyancy forward, reducing any tendency to plunge. With the C-class, forward hydroplanes were introduced to assist control at slow submerged speeds.

This rapid expansion was not unconnected with the personal interest shown by Admiral Sir John ('Jackie')

Fisher, appointed First Sea Lord in 1904. A man with real vision when it came to naval matters, he stated in the same year that people had not even 'faintly realised … the immense impending revolution which submarines will effect as offensive weapons of war'. Even by 1907 it was widely believed that, in the event of a war with Germany, the North Sea would be too dangerous for the battle fleet, which would be split between the Channel and the Scottish west coast. Exercises had shown that submarines already had potential far beyond coastal defence.

With the D-class, constructed under the 1906–1910 Programmes, length moved up to 164.6 ft (50.2 m) and displacement to 495–620 tons, allowing a safer reserve buoyancy of about 20 percent. They were the first British twin-screw submarines and, for surface running, petrol engines were abandoned in favour of the heavy oil, or Diesel, engine. Although beset by teething problems, these were safer, having fuel of high flashpoint and not so prone to giving off dangerous fumes. During the 1910 manoeuvres the submarine D1 revised many an entrenched attitude when, despite trouble with one engine, she proceeded from Portsmouth to the west coast of Scotland, and remained off an 'enemy' anchorage for three days until being able to successfully 'torpedo' two cruisers.

Unlike Admiral Fisher and Kaiser Wilhelm II, Admiral von Tirpitz remained unconvinced of the submarine's potential, wanting proof of its capacity to operate far afield rather than simply in coastal waters before he would commit funds. In 1904 Russia (at war with Japan) ordered three 205/236-ton boats from Germaniawerft at Kiel, influencing Tirpitz to appoint a specialist officer to build Germany's first. This, the *U1*, was accepted by the German Navy in 1906 and was an improved derivative of the Russian design, but had only one 450-mm (17.7-in) torpedo tube. For surface navigation she had a paraffin-burning engine, petrol being held too dangerous. As the engine ran at constant speed and could not be reversed, controllable-pitch propellers were fitted.

Following in 1908, the *U2* was a considerable improvement. Four tubes were fitted, two forward and two aft. Saddle tanks gave her stockier proportions yet lines were still improved sufficiently for a 30 percent

Left: A1 was an improved Holland type, effectively the first all-British submarine class. Thirteen such boats were built, all by Vickers, with *A1* entering service in 1903. It unfortunately became the first British submarine loss, rammed and sunk by the liner *Berwick Castle* in 1904.

increase in speed for an increase of only 50 percent in installed power. Still viewing submarines as irrelevant to his task of creating a battle fleet, Tirpitz permitted their construction only at a very low rate. By 1911, therefore, only a dozen boats had been completed. With the U5-12, displacement increased to 505/636 tons. Submerged speed for short bursts was a creditable 10 knots, but the desired 15-knot surface speed could not be realised. A suitably-sized prototype diesel engine had been demonstrated as early as 1907, but production difficulties prevented its adoption until 1913, in the U19 class. These had tubes of an increased 500-mm (19.7-in) calibre, together with an 88-mm (3.5-in) deck gun. Their 7,600-mile surfaced endurance already theoretically allowed a return trip across the Atlantic, although habitability for the 35 crew was spartan. The design provided the basis for the first phase of expansion of the U-boat arm in war. As early as 1908 a senior German officer had called for a submarine capable of waging war on commerce, since the destruction of a large number of merchant men was 'more significant than defeating the opponent in a naval battle'. Tirpitz's opinions remained supreme, however and, even four years later, the modest official objective remained the creation of a 70-boat force, charged primarily with the control of German waters.

If the U19 type provided the base design for the first phase of expansion of the German submarine arm, the British equivalent was the E-class. Straightforward developments of the D's, the E-boats had sufficient beam to incorporate a pair of transversely mounted torpedo tubes. Torpedoes were still unguided and straight running, so that the submarine itself had to be aimed, with a deflection sufficient to allow for torpedo speed, and speed and range of target. As boats were getting larger and more configured for surface running, their submerged rates of turn were lower, so that opportunist shots could be missed. A stern tube in the D-class enabled a quicker response to be made, but the E's were able to fire ahead, astern or on the beam, so that the greatest angle through which they had to be turned was 45 degrees. Many of the Es were fitted as minelayers.

Below: The famous E11, still bearing traces of camouflage, seen at Lowestoft.

Below: The three Léon Gambetta class armoured cruisers completed 1905-7 bucked the trend towards heavier cruiser armament, retaining an enormous battery of 6.4-in guns. All served in World War I, *Gambetta* sunk by the Austrian *U-5* with heavy loss of life in 1915.

Léon Gambetta class

data:

Displacement standard	12,350 tons
Length	485 ft
Beam	70 ft
Design draught	27 ft
Complement	730

Class: *Léon Gambetta, Jules Ferry, Victor Hugo*

Armament:
4 x 7.6-in guns
16 x 6.4-in guns
2 x 65 mm guns
22 x 47 mm guns
4 x 17.7-in torpedo tubes

Machinery:
3 triple expansion engines, 27,500 ihp
3 shafts
22 knots

Armour:
Belt	6.7 in
Ends	3.5 in
Deck	2.5 in
Barbettes	7.8 in

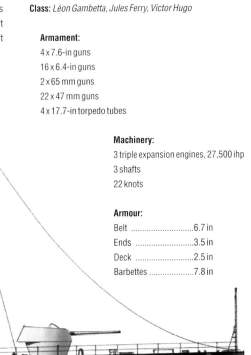

Cruisers

Cruiser development up to World War I followed several distinct paths. The armoured cruiser, with both belt and protective deck, was revived first by the Italians, finding favour also with the French and Americans. French ships required speed with protection, resulting in imposing hulls of considerable length. For survivability, their twenty or so boilers were sited in two groups, flanking the triple-expansion machinery. The resulting paired or tripled funnel groups were highly distinctive characteristics.

In the French manner, protection was spread thinly over large areas but, with improvements, inevitably led to increasing displacement. Between the first 'modern' cruisers, the trio of Kléber class, completed in 1903–4, and the last built, the two Waldeck Rousseau class of 1910, displacement climbed from 7,700 to nearly 14,000 tons full load. Belt thickness was up to about 140 mm (5.5 in), tapering to about 90 mm (3.5 in) at either end. Horizontal protection began with a single 65-mm (2.5-in) deck, developed to a 45-mm (1.8-in) deck in combination with a splinter deck, and finalised with a pair of decks, 34-mm (1.3-in) and 65-mm thick, which bridged the upper and lower edges of the main belt. Their armament moved from a logical layout of eight 164-mm (6.48-in) guns, paired in a lozenge arrangement, to various ineffectual schemes with single or twin 194-mm (7.64-in) turrets forward and aft, in combination with up to sixteen 164-mm pieces in turrets and/or

casemates, before finalising on a homogeneous battery of fourteen 164-mm in the *Waldeck Rousseau*. Although four of these guns were casemated, they were carried at a height sufficient to be worked in poor weather.

The US Navy discontinued building armoured cruisers after the four Tennessee class, launched 1904–6. At 14,500 tons standard displacement, they were even larger than their French contemporaries. With four 10-in (254-mm) and sixteen 6-in (152-mm) guns, they were scaled-down battleships. Belts of 5-in (127-mm) steel, tapering to 3 in (76 mm), first paralleled French practice,

but earlier protective decks, with 3-in horizontal plating and 6-in slopes, were thinned progressively to only 1 in and 3.5 in respectively. As some of the weight thus saved went into vertical protection, it illustrates a continuing concentration on tactics involving close-range gunfire.

Germany's first true armoured cruiser was the *Fürst Bismarck*, completed in 1900. She was a stretched, 10,690-ton version of the 5,650-ton Victoria Louise class

Below: HMS *Spartan*, one of the 21 Apollo class cruisers authorised by the 1889 Naval Defence Act.

protected cruisers which, once rebuilt, presented a very similar profile. Both types featured a high freeboard for good seakeeping, that of the *Bismarck* being sufficient to spread the secondary battery over three levels. The smaller ships also had armaments that were, effectively, diminutives of the larger i.e. two single 210-mm (8.2-in) mountings against two twin 240-mm (9.4-in), and eight 150-mm (5.9-in) guns against twelve. The *Bismarck*'s protective deck was only 30-mm thick, with 50-mm slopes (which were more likely to be struck by lower trajectory fire). Her 200-mm (7.9-in) belt tapered to 100 mm toward bow and stern, and also below the waterline. This balance of armour was not felt to be correct, subsequent first class cruisers having their belts substantially reduced to increase the much greater area of the protective deck. From the Prinz Adalberts of 1903–4, the main battery reverted to the faster-firing 210-mm gun, echoing a similar policy in battleships.

A basically sound cruiser design was refined through successive classes to the pairs of Roons (1905–6) and Scharnhorsts (1907–8). The latter were probably the finest of their type and, to achieve a maximum speed of 23.5 knots, their length was 144.6 m (474.4 ft) and standard displacement 11,620 tons. German armoured cruisers had thus evolved to a point where their size was considerably less than their foreign contemporaries but without yielding much in way of superiority owing to the penetrative power of their 210-mm and 150-mm guns.

Events then took a curious turn. It was the time when the British were building the *Dreadnought* and projected a new class of 'armoured cruisers'. The Germans supposed, correctly, that the latter would also be considerably upgraded on what had gone before but assumed, incorrectly, that they would retain the 9.2-in gun for their main battery. The one-off, 15,840-ton *Blücher* was produced as an answer. Her 25.4-knot speed was highly creditable, but the twelve 210-mm (8.3-in) guns, arranged in a diminutive of a battleship's hexagonal layout, were in no way a match for the 12-in that the British actually installed.

Below: The Amiral Charner class cruiser *Chanzy* seen in 1900. She was wrecked in Chinese waters in 1907.

Below: The six-strong Cressy class, completed 1901–2, continued the layout established with the Powerfuls. Single 9.2-in guns were mounted as chasers, with the 6-in battery sited in casemates that were too low to be worked in any seaway. Three of the Cressys were sunk by *U-9* in September 1914 with the loss of over 1,500 lives.

Cressy class

data:

Displacement standard	11,700 tons
Length	472 ft
Beam	69 ft
Design draught	26 ft
Complement	755

Class: *Aboukir, Bacchante, Cressy, Euryalus, Hogue, Sutlej*

Armament:
2 x 9.2-in guns
12 x 6-in guns
13 x 12-pdr guns
2 x 18-in torpedo tubes

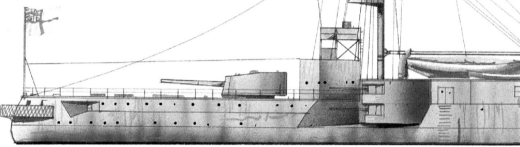

Until the turn of the century the British, too, had preferred the protected cruiser, mainly in the role of commerce protection. Cemented armour plate then offered equal protection for less weight; a given margin for protection could, therefore, be spread more widely.

As improved boilers were also permitting the generation of greater power per unit volume, it was possible to design 'armoured' cruisers, with belt, protective deck and the speed to pursue reconnaissance in force.

The first such class, the Cressys, used the 11,000-ton

protected cruiser *Diadem* as a starting point. Her 4-in (101-mm) armoured deck was changed to a 3-in (76-mm) deck and a vertical belt, 6-in (152-mm) thick amidships, tapering to 2 in (51 mm) at either end. Battleship-style, the central box was closed off with 5-in transverse bulkheads. Twelve of the Diadem's sixteen 6-in guns, half of them in very low casemates, were retained but the twin mountings forward and aft were exchanged for single 9.2-in (234-mm) weapons. The latter were excellent guns, but were too few and had too slow a rate of fire to be effective.

With the speed of a battle line slowly increasing with each new class introduced, so armoured cruisers had to become faster too. As the level of protection and firepower also had to be maintained, size inevitably increased. The four 23-knot Drakes, completed in 1902–3, had, otherwise, much the same specification as the Cressys, but displaced 14,100 tons. To put this in context, *Drake* was about the same displacement as the battleship *Duncan*, then completing. Each cost about £1 million. However, the cruiser's four-knot speed superiority demanded 30,000 ihp against 18,000, and a crew of 900 against 750, the extra number comprising the huge complement of stokers. The *Black Prince* that followed was shorter but beamier, with a greater stability range but also a livelier motion as a gun platform. Probably influenced by foreign armoured cruiser designs,

all of which took four guns of the primary calibre, the *Black Prince* mounted six 9.2s in single gunhouses. Despite the protective deck being slimmed to under an inch, draught was such as to put the secondary armament's barrels just eight feet above load waterline.

Above: The ultimate German armoured cruiser was the ill-fated *Blücher*, armed with 8.2-in guns after *Fighting Ships* had printed British 'disinformation' about the forthcoming Invincible class cruisers' armament.

As the above arrangement attracted justified criticism, the final four units of the class, known as the Warriors, exchanged all the 6-in weapons for four 7.5-in (190-mm) guns mounted in single turrets at upper-deck level. Because the casemate problem had thus been circumvented, a greater draught was permissible. Displacement was thus increased by some 700 tons in order to improve the horizontal protection, which ranged from three-quarters of an inch to two inches. This general arrangement was taken one stage further in the *Minotaur*. A twin 9.2-in turret was sited at either end but the reduction in number of main calibre barrels was more than offset by no less than five single 7.5s, sited along either side of the waist. This imposing array of firepower was complemented by further improved protection, reflecting the greater hazards now attending the armoured cruiser's tasks. However, the class was obsolete on completion, being overtaken by the Invincible class.

The size and value of armoured cruisers also made them quite unsuitable for many fleet functions, and there was a continuing need for smaller units whose protection lay primarily in their speed. In the Royal Navy, the 'Gem' type of Third-class Protected Cruiser was a bridge between old and new, the more so as the *Amethyst* was the first major British warship to evaluate steam turbine propulsion. The power/volume ratio was such that she could develop 30 percent more power than her reciprocating-engined sisters, although hydrodynamics translated this into only on extra 1.2 knots, i.e. 23.5 against 22.3.

Slightly smaller were the so-called 'Scouts', which sacrificed more armament and protection for speed. Capable of 25-26 knots, they found employment attached to Battle Squadrons or as leaders to the larger destroyer flotillas.

Both of these classes displaced 3000 tons or less, and were armed with 4-in guns. The scouts developed naturally through the *Arethusa*, which exchanged some of the smaller pieces for 6-inch, to the numerous groups of C- and D-class units, which were built throughout the

war. Their gradual evolution to an all 6-in gun armament was accompanied by a move from a 2-in protective deck to a 3-in vertical belt, recognising the smashing effect of larger guns at comparatively close ranges. The number of torpedo tubes increased by stages from just two to eight in the Cs and twelve in the Ds.

The Gems, on the other hand, begat the Bristols which, with a 6-in gun forward and aft, and an array of 4 in along the waist, had the appearance of diminutive armoured cruisers. As with the smaller units, these evolved through several groups, with successively more powerful armament. The fifteen 'Towns' would play classic cruiser roles in the forthcoming conflict.

Drake class

data

Displacement standard	14,150 tons
Length	533 ft
Beam	71 ft
Design draught	26 ft
Complement	900

Class: *Drake, Good Hope, King Alfred, Leviathan.*

Armament:
2 x 9.2-in guns
16 x 6-in guns
14 x 12-pdr
3 x 3-pdr
2 x 18-in torpedo tubes

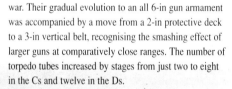

Left: The Devonshire class cruiser *Carnarvon*, armed with four 7.5-in and six 6-in guns. Admiral Stoddart's flagship, she took part in the battle of the Falklands in 1914, engaging the German flagship *Gneisnau* after the latter was slowed by the fire of the British battlecruisers. At the time of the action, *Carnarvon* was unable to make her designed speed of 22 knots.

Machinery:
2 triple expansion steam engines, 30,000 ihp
2 shafts
23 knots

Armour:
Belt ....6 in
Ends ....2 in
Decks.........................2.5 in
Turrets ....6 in
Barbettes ....6 in
Casemates ....5 in

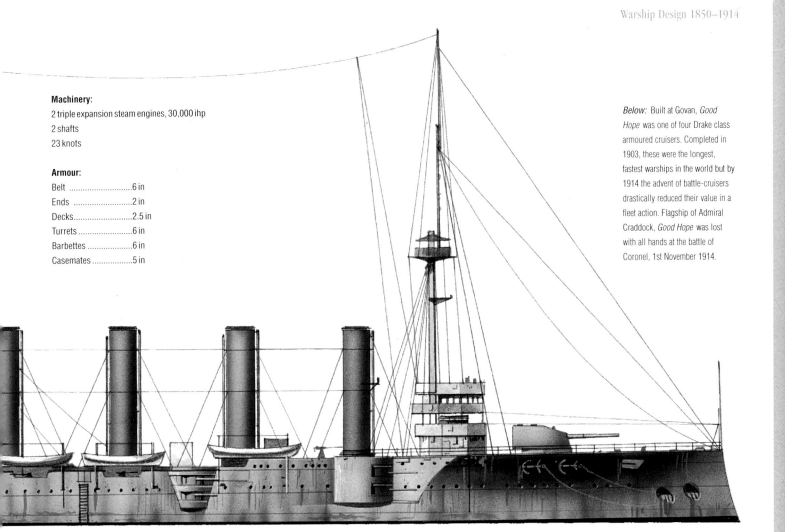

Below: Built at Govan, *Good Hope* was one of four Drake class armoured cruisers. Completed in 1903, these were the longest, fastest warships in the world but by 1914 the advent of battle-cruisers drastically reduced their value in a fleet action. Flagship of Admiral Craddock, *Good Hope* was lost with all hands at the battle of Coronel, 1st November 1914.

Below: The four Gem class, completed 1904-5 were the last 3rd class cruisers built for the Royal Navy. *Sapphire* seen here was attached to the 7th Battle Squadron, Channel Fleet in 1914 then served at Dover and with the Harwich flotilla before taking part in the Dardanelles operations.

German evolution was remarkably similar. The ten Gazelle class, completed 1899–1903, were very close to the Gems in concept, and developed between 1904 and 1918, through many small groups. These, too, were named after Towns and, totalling over thirty ships, were the backbone of the German fleet's cruiser force. Their displacement increased steadily from the 3,289 tons of the initial five Bremens to the 5,620 tons of the final pair of Dresdens.

Performance improved from 10,000 ihp for 22 knots to 31,000 shp to 27.5 knots, although German ships could usually manage an extra knot or two over published figures. In line with their British counterparts, their initial armament of ten 105-mm (4.1-in) guns altered by stages to eight 150-mm (5.9-in) weapons. They combined a light belt with a thin splinter deck for protection.

'Pre-Dreadnought' Battleships 1897–1905

Between 1897 and 1905 battleships were becoming better armed and better protected, with an improved balance between offence and defence. Unfortunately, the Royal Navy's much admired Royal Sovereigns were costing £940,000 apiece and there was much agitation in Parliament for smaller and cheaper designs. Studies, however, showed that economy would put future ships at a disadvantage compared with their foreign counterparts. The powerful naval lobby also 'proved' that, with current rates of building, the combined strength of France and Russia would leave the Royal Navy with unacceptably low margins of superiority. Faced with the threat of mass resignation by the whole Board of Admiralty, the Government agreed the so-called Spencer programme, resulting in the nine Majestic class battleships. Working out about 5 percent cheaper per unit than a Royal Sovereign, the class reverted to the handy-sized 12-in gun, paired at either end in what became an almost standard international arrangement. The guns were paired under 10-in armoured shields, which revolved with them on the turntables. With the final pair of the class, all-round loading was introduced, as was partial oil-firing.

A very satisfactory hull form, the *Majestic* formed the baseline for the Royal Navy's next three classes, the six Canopus class (completed 1899–1902), eight Formidable/Londons (1901–4) and six Duncans (1903–4). They shared similar primary and secondary armaments, with beam being limited to about 75 ft (22.9 m) by existing dry docks. Overall length, however, crept up from the Majestic's 420 ft (128.0 m) to the Duncans' 432 ft (131.7 m). This enabled the lines to be sweetened which, with improved machinery, resulted in a speed of 19 knots.

Similar external appearances disguised improvements based on battle experience of the Sino-Japanese War of 1894–5 and the Spanish-American War of 1898. Engagements during the latter were so unequal that little was learned beyond the danger of fire from unnecessary inflammable material, and the need for improved gunnery. (At the Battle of Santiago the victorious Americans registered 123 hits from 9,500 shells fired: a hit rate of 1.2 percent!)

Charlemagne class

data:

Displacement standard	11,100 tons
Length	387 ft
Beam	67 ft
Design draught	27 ft
Complement	725

Class: *Charlemagne, St. Louis, Gaulois*

Armament:	**Machinery:**
4 x 12-in guns	3 triple expansion steam engines, 14,500 ihp
10 x 5.4-in guns	3 shafts
8 x 3.9-in guns	18 knots
2 x 17.7-in torpedo tubes	

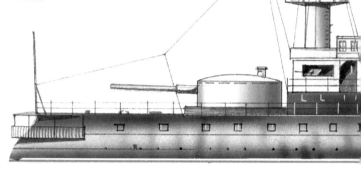

Below: The Minotaur class were the last British armoured cruisers and all were at Jutland. *Shannon*, seen here, and *Minotaur* in the 2nd cruiser squadron. *Defence*, flagship of the 1st cruiser squadron, was sunk: under fire from several Konig class dreadnoughts and the *Lutzow*, her aft 9.2-in magazine detonated and the flash shot along her 7.5-in ammunition passageways to detonate the forward magazine too. All 903 officers and men aboard were lost.

Minotaur class

data:

Displacement standard	14,600 tons
Length	519 ft
Beam	74 ft
Design draught	27 ft
Complement	755

Class: *Minotaur, Defence, Shannon.*

By contrast, Japanese experience in the Russo-Japanese war proved the value of saturation fire from secondary batteries, demonstrating the need for improved protection to the main armament. More-resistant armour was diminishing the effect from 6-in guns and a heavier secondary calibre was postulated to destroy an opponent's stability through flooding 'softer' regions of the hull. Secondary batteries also required guns to be

Armament:
4 x 9.2-in guns
10 x 7.5-in guns
14 x 12-pdr guns
5 x 18-in torpedo tubes

Machinery:
2 triple expansion steam engines, 27,000 ihp
2 shafts
23 knots

Armour:
Belt ....6 in
Ends ....3 in
Deck: ....1.5 in
Barbettes ....8 in

Above: The Charlemagne class were the first French battleships to adopt the 'two forward, two aft' layout for their main armament. Flying the flag of Admiral Guépratte during the attack on the Dardanelles on 18 March 1915, *Gaulois* was heavily damaged and forced aground. Repaired, she was sunk in 1916 by *UB-47*. Her sisterships survived the war.

separated by at least splinter-proof bulkheads to prevent progressive deflagration of ready-use charges in the event of a hit.

Speed was shown to be decisive in dictating the course of an action. Torpedo attack by small craft was successful only against stationary targets, but served to increase the overall anxiety felt by designers about torpedoes in general.

British battleships were designed with moderate metacentric heights, the resulting reduced stability being accepted for the slower roll which made for a superior gun platform. Torpedo bulkheads, the standard protection against torpedo attack, ran parallel to the shell plating and were set about three metres inboard. The space so formed was sub-divided to limit flooding but, in practice, some of the resulting compartmentation was used as auxiliary bunker space ('coal tanks'). This provided extra protection against shellfire but reduced the volume available for voiding the explosion of a torpedo warhead. As the latter were now typically 100kg (220 lb) of guncotton, a detonation would still cause huge damage as bulkheads were torn away, starting seams and rivets and fracturing pipes, causing slow, progressive flooding. Lacking a large stability range, an injured battleship would need to counter-flood to maintain a reasonably even keel. However, arrangements in British battleships were rudimentary and, with spaces often anything but void, pump inlets rapidly became clogged. The result was that five battleships of the above classes would succumb to capsizing after torpedo hits during the Great War.

Until the completion of the two Republique class battleships in 1906, French practice favoured four heavy guns, mounted singly forward and aft, and on either beam amidships. To enable the latter pair to fire axially they were sponsoned out over sides that were given exaggerated tumblehome. This feature necessitated an exceptionally shallow belt. To offset this, the designers bridged the upper edges of the belts with a protective deck, and the lower edges with a thinner, splinter deck. The two-metre space between was heavily subdivided to form a sort of armoured raft, able to contain flooding while preventing penetration by fragments to the spaces below. French constructors disliked 'soft' ends, the 'raft' being continued over the full length of the ship. As they also favoured high freeboard and good command for the

guns, the massive topsides were almost devoid of protection, defensive properties being completely subordinated to offensive. Tumblehome further decreased the damaged stability range, for very little extra buoyancy was submerged by a heel.

The three Charlemagne class, completed 1899–1900, adopted a main battery in twin turrets but retained a pronounced tumblehome for the benefit of their 139-mm (5.5-in) secondaries. Three of these older ships would be sunk by capsizing following damage by mine or torpedo.

American practice preferred a significant tertiary battery. Thus the three 10,250-ton Indiana class combined four 13-in (330.2-mm) guns, in twin turrets forward and aft, with eight 8-in (203.2-mm), in twin turrets at the superstructure 'corners', and four casemated 4-in (101.6-mm). This triple-layer armament persisted right up to the pre-Dreadnoughts, excepting only the Illinois and Maine classes, which adopted a more 'European' balance of four heavy guns and a homogeneous battery of fourteen or more 6-in (152.4-mm).

The term 'pre-Dreadnought' usefully defines ships with guns of an intermediate calibre capable of piercing a degree of armour protection . Thus the Virginia class, launched in 1904, were contemporary with the British King Edward VIIs, the one design having twinned 8-in guns at each corner, the other, single 9.2s. No doubt the American balance was the better, but improvements in gunnery practice had already made the tertiary battery concept obsolete. As a result, the Royal Navy's Lord Nelsons, a class limited to two ships, combined four 12-in with no less than ten 9.2s.

British construction imperatives looked now, no longer to a Franco-Russian coalition, but to the quickening

Below: Laid down in 1906, the *Danton* was the logical extension of the pre-dreadnought design: the secondary battery increased to 12 intermediate calibre guns. While other major powers built dreadnoughts, France perversely continued the Danton class to a total of six units, all completed in 1911.

pulse of the German Navy, not yet a threat, but becoming a cause for concern.

Below: The Danton class battleship *Condorcet* seen during World War I in the colour scheme adopted by some French warships: grey hull and upperworks with ochre-brown turrets. The Dantons are sometimes described as 'semi-dreadnoughts' but these anachronistic battleships were really out of date before they were completed.

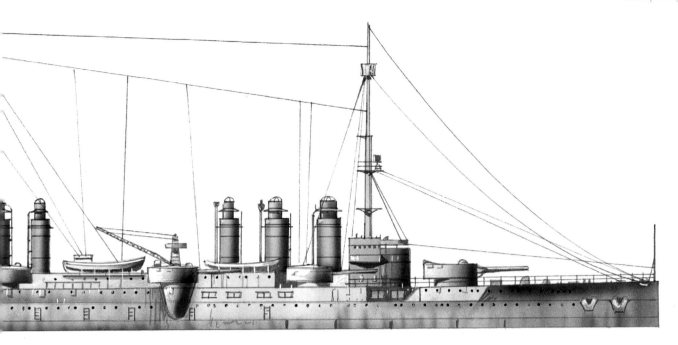

Danton class

data:

Displacement standard	18,360 tons
Length	481 ft
Beam	85 ft
Design draught	29 ft
Complement	921

Class: *Danton, Condorcet, Diderot, Mirabeau, Vergniaud, Voltaire.*

Armament:
4 x 12-in guns
12 x 9.4-in guns
16 x 75 mm guns
10 x 47 mm guns
2 x 18-in torpedo tubes

Machinery:
4 steam turbines, 22,500 shp
4 shafts
19 knots

Armour:

Belt	10 in
Ends	8 in
Main turrets	12.6 in
Barbettes	11 in
Secondary turrets	8.7 in
Deck	2.75 in

Below: The London class battleship *Bulwark* seen in 1907 when she was flagship first of the Mediterranean and then the Channel fleets. One of the pre-dreadnoughts assigned to the Channel in 1914, she was destroyed by an accidental explosion while taking on ammunition at Sheerness on 26 November 1914. Only 12 men out of 750 aboard survived.

Vickers Monoplane.

Floating Docks.
Floating Cranes.
Icebreakers.
Dredgers.
Turbines.
Steam, Oil, and Gas Engines.
Electrical Plant.

Group of Finished Guns, manufactured at Sheffield.

WARSHIPS
OF ALL TYPES.

Armour Plates.
Projectiles and Explosives.

Launch of H.M.S. "VANGUARD" at Barrow-in-Furness.

VICKERS LIMITED,
VICKERS HOUSE, BROADWAY,
WESTMINSTER, S.W.

Barrow-in-Furness. Erith. Dartford.
Sheffield. Birmingham. Crayford.

Above: Then, as now, *Jane's Fighting Ships* carried advertising from various manufacturers, some of which are still in business today. When Fred Jane was producing the early issues of the yearbook, Britain was the world's greatest shipbuilding nation, supplying warships to many foreign navies. When war broke out in 1914, three modern battleships being built to foreign accounts were immediately added to the Royal Navy.

H.M.S. "SENTINEL."
Built and entirely fitted out at Barrow-in-Furness.

Guns of all Calibres with their Mountings for Naval or Field Service.

Motors for Marine and Aerial Navigation.

Monoplanes.

Motor Cars for Military Operations.

Turbine Rotor, constructed at Barrow-in-Furness.

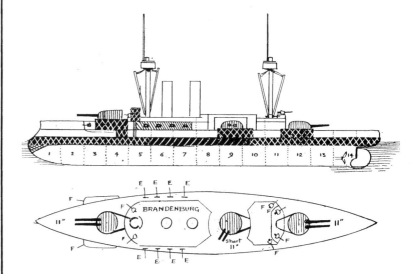

Above: From 1903 the yearbook added detailed line drawings showing the layout of guns and the varying levels of protection on each warship class. These were used in Jane's naval wargame: striker pins being stabbed against printed copies of these drawings to simulate gunnery while scale models manoeuvred on a gridded playing surface. The German Brandenburg class seen here were unusual in having six 11-in guns for their main armament.

Below: Battleships from Russia's Black Sea fleet survived the Russo-Japanese war because international treaties prevented them passing through the Dardanelles. The crew of *Kniaz Potemkin Tavritcheski* mutinied during the 1905 revolution and the ship, once recovered, was re-named *Panteleimon*.

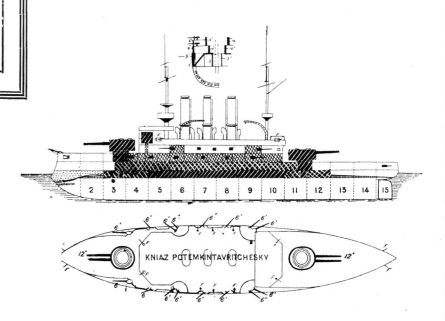

FRIED. KRUPP A. G.

GERMANIAWERFT
KIEL-GAARDEN.

Submersible "U 8."

BATTLESHIPS,

CRUISERS,

TORPEDO-VESSELS,

SUBMERSIBLES,

PASSENGER AND CARGO-BOATS.

OIL-MOTORS. STEAM-TURBINES.

STAHLWERK ANNEN
ANNEN (Westphalia).

Highest quality **Steel Castings** in Siemens Martin and Crucible Steel.

Steel Foundry. —— Rolling Mill. —— Steel Forge.

Large Turbine Drums cast of Siemens Martin Steel.

Specialities:—Cast Steel Stern and Rudder Frames.

Steel Castings for Steam Turbines and Diesel Motors.

Cast Steel Locomotive Wheel Centres and Crankaxles of highest reliability.

Toothed Wheels up to 6 meters diameter with cut straight or double helical teeth.

U. S. BATTLESHIP (16 knot).

IOWA (1896).

Displacement 11,410 tons.   Complement 486.

Length (*waterline*), 360 feet.   Beam, 72 feet.   *Maximum* draught, 28 feet.

Signal letter: L.   (Lower yard now removed, and top gallant mast fitted).

Torpedo Notes: Howell torpedoes ; broadside tubes, section 8.

Engineering notes: Designed speed reached on trial.

General notes: Laid down at Cramp's, August, 1893 ; completed 1897.   Cost *complete*, nearly £1,000,000.

105

Guns :
4—12 inch, I., 35 cal. (A).
8—8 inch, 30 cal. (F).
4—4 inch, (F).
22—6 pdr.
4—1 pdr.
4 Colts.
2 Field guns (3 inch).
Torpedo tubes (18 inch) :
3 *above water* (now removed).

Armour (Harvey) :
14″—11″Belt (amidships)*aa-a*
12″ Bulkheads .... *aa*
3″ Deck (flat on belt),
Protection to vitals is ... *aa*
14″ Turrets .... *aa*
5″ Turret bases .... *d*
5″ Lower deck side ...... *d*
6″ Secondary turrets .... *c*
8″ Barbettes to these .. *b*
10″ Conning tower ...... *a*

Ahead:
2—12 in.
4—8 in.
2—4 in.

Astern:
2—12 in.
4—8 in.
2—4 in.

Broadside : 4—12 in., 4—8 in., 2—4 in.

Machinery : 2 sets vertical inverted triple expansion.   2 screws.   Boilers : cylindrical.   Designed H.P. *forced* 11,000 = 16·5 kts.   Coal : *normal* 625 tons ; *maximum* 1780 tons.

Armour Notes :   Belt is 7½ feet wide by 200 feet long ; 5 feet of it below waterline ; lower edge is 9½″ thick amidships.   Main belt is reinforced by coal bunkers 10 feet thick.

Gunnery Notes :   Loading positions, big guns : all round.   Big guns manœuvred, hydraulic gear ; secondary turrets, steam.
Arcs of fire : Big guns, 265° ; 8 in., 135° from axial line.
Ammunition carried : 12 in., 60 rounds per gun ; 8 in., 125 rounds per gun.

Above: A facsimile page from *Jane's Fighting Ships 1906.* The style of the entries and the landscape format would endure until the 1950s.

Chapter 4 – The Drift to War

Kaiser Wilhelm II's appointment of Tirpitz in 1897, and the passing of the First Navy Bill the following year, signalled the opening of a new era. It was Wilhelm's avowed intention to enlarge Germany's suzerainty over Uganda and Zanzibar in return for control of Heligoland, now of strategic importance with the construction of the Kaiser Wilhelm (i.e. 'Kiel') Canal. Apparent British ease in expanding their Empire contrasted with Wilhelm's difficulties in the same direction, increasing further his feelings of enmity. Because Tirpitz's 'new' navy had been created virtually from scratch, its officers were largely from the middle-class created by the state's recent rise. Lacking the comfortable attitudes of the army, whose officers were usually of impressive lineage and family traditions of military service, it had much of the aggressive thrust of the state and a burning desire to prove itself.

The Kruger telegram of 1896 pledging German support for the dissident Afrikaners in the Transvaal, brought a hostile British reaction. Skilful and sustained propaganda by the German Navy League turned this to Anglophobia. Great Britain was portrayed as undermining any attempt by Germany to compete on trade, leading naturally to the mentality that defence was required against a hostile foreign force. Through the efforts of the Navy League and influential academics, the Navy gained both popular support and political leverage.

As mentioned above, the ambitious German Navy Bill did not cause undue British concern. Any worries centred on German expansion triggering building programmes in France and Russia, which, under the Two-Power Standard, Britain would be obliged to match.

Tirpitz skilfully made the most of German 'humiliation' on three counts; at having to play a minor role as American and British naval forces intervened in internal problems in Samoa and in the Boxer Rebellion, at the Royal Navy exercising its rights in stopping neutral shipping (including German) off the South African coast during the war there, and at the total defeat of the Spanish Navy at the hands of the Americans.

On a wave of public opinion, Tirpitz piloted a Second Navy Bill through a normally parsimonious Reichstag. It provided for nothing less than a doubling of the fleet funded by the earlier bill, but now apparently without financial limit. Bülow, the Foreign Minister, peddled the official line that the fleet was required for defensive purposes, but it was an open secret that Tirpitz viewed it as a deterrent, not against an attack on Germany, but against interference in German colonial objectives. A key point in his strategy lay in concentrating the fleet in the North Sea. It was surmised that the Royal Navy, with its worldwide commitments, would not be able to effect a similar concentration, and would never accept a battle where it would incur significant losses.

In January 1901, Queen Victoria died. Her successor, Edward VII, entertained a long-standing dislike for his nephew the Kaiser, and from this point Anglo-German relationships deteriorated steadily. Britain, with growing internal divisions over the South African War, had no real friend in Europe and was estranged from the United States. France, however, was at last realising that the British had no designs upon her and, with funds needed elsewhere, slowed warship construction. Italy was being gently wooed, it being pointed out that, if the Royal

Navy needed to be withdrawn from the Mediterranean to meet a threat elsewhere, the French fleet would have no counterbalance.

In the Far East the major European trading nations were involved in a scramble to gain privileged access to the lucrative Chinese market. Russia, in particular, was not only reinforcing her local naval presence but was considering transferring the Black Sea fleet almost en bloc. British naval strength on the station was already considerable, expensive to maintain, and required elsewhere. Japan was talking to Russia about their relative differences and Britain could see that time was not on her side. Acting swiftly, she agreed an alliance with Japan in February 1902. Initially to run for five years, it agreed that, in place of each seeking naval parity with a third party, their fleets would act in concert. A clause covered mutual support in the event of one being engaged in hostilities with more than one power, a Franco-Russian alliance being thought most likely. The hoped-for reduction in British naval commitments was, in fact, not realised, as Japan was thought to be using the alliance to defer expenditure on her own fleet.

China was seen by the Americans, too, as a vast untapped market, where the European powers were bent on creating enclaves and base facilities for use as springboards for later expansion. The United States thus encouraged, but could not enforce, an 'Open Door' policy, providing free access to all while safeguarding China's integrity. There was lofty talk of parallels with the Munroe Doctrine, but the countries who were seen as the major imperial predators, Great Britain and Japan, appeared satisfied for the moment with the status quo.

Below: While several other navies were planning 'all big gun' battleships, Admiral Jackie Fisher saw to it that the Royal Navy was the first to commission one. Constructed at astonishing speed, HMS *Dreadnought* was to lend her name to the generation of battleships that followed. The 'dreadnought race' had begun.

In 1902 Germany completed the first battleships provided for by the Second Navy Bill. Closely scrutinised by the British Admiralty, the Wittelsbach class was notable for limited endurance, cramped habitability, and with both gun calibre and speed apparently subordinated to battleworthiness – all pointing to use in near European waters rather than worldwide operation. Some at least of these characteristics were due to the limitations of dockyards and dredged approaches, but this aspect was probably played down for political gain.

Necessity sometimes creates strange bedfellows, and in 1902 British and German warships, accompanied by Italian, blockaded Venezuelan ports to enforce the repayment of huge defaulted loans. Recognising that state's delinquency, but also remembering the rebuff of 1895, the United States once again cited the Monroe Doctrine to support Venezuelan fundamental rights. Germany was not trusted because of her expansionist mood, while Britain might just take the chance to consolidate the western boundary of British Guiana. When the senior German naval officer began to behave in a high-handed manner (which also offended the British), the Americans sent their hero of the Spanish War, Admiral Dewey, with a squadron, obliging the Germans to back off and the Venezuelans to accept arbitration.

As yet a minor player in world terms, the US Navy was becoming a potent instrument of national policy in Central America and beyond. In view of their nation's powerful anti-colonialist stance, not a few Americans had ambivalent views regarding the territories gained through the recent successful war with Spain. Cuba, nominally independent, was occupied until 1902, following which the so-called Platt Amendment guaranteed American political control and commercial dominance. Puerto Rico was granted a somewhat ill-defined home rule, but under American protection. The remote island of Guam was seized and, along with Wake Island, was a potentially useful halfway house in the vastness of the Pacific. The Philippine Islands were at once a major prize and a major problem. Their considerable population wanted independence, not occupation by another Western power. Suppressing the ensuing three-year rebellion cost over 4,000 American casualties. The reward was a large group of islands that required administration and protection some 7,000 miles distant. Economic dependence upon the United States cost Hawaii part of its independence, followed during the Spanish War by full annexation. Finally, basing rights were granted by Samoa, leading to Great Britain and Germany demanding and receiving a similar concession. Such acquisitions were not unpopular with Americans at large, who viewed them as a natural corollary of gaining world status. They were also a major factor in the growth of the US Navy.

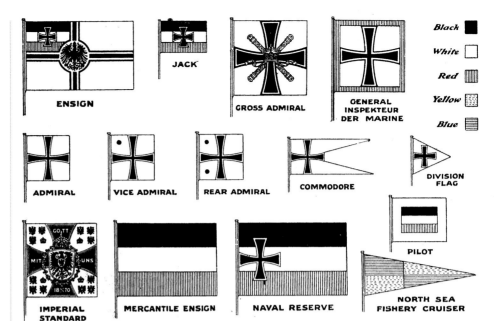

Imperial standard : Square ; yellow, with black cross ; Imperial arms in centre and in field.

Above: Flags of the German navy, the expansion of which did so much to bring about World War I.

Lord Nelson Class

data:

Displacement standard	16,090 tons
Length	443 ft
Beam	79 ft
Design draught	26 ft
Complement	809

Class: *Lord Nelson, Agamemnon*

Armament:	**Armour:**	
4 x 12-in guns	Belt	12 in
10 x 9.2-in guns	Ends	4 in
24 x 12-pdr guns	Deck	4 in
5 x 18-in torpedo tubes	Barbettes	12 in
	Turrets	12 in
	Secondary turrets	7 in

Machinery:
2 triple expansion engines,
  16,750 ihp
2 shafts
18 knots

Given both the instrument and the inclination, the United States began to intervene elsewhere. Between 1901 and 1903 there was involvement in events that led to Panama's secession from the state of Colombia, directly aiding the granting of a 99-year lease on territory which became the Panama Canal Zone (the canal itself being constructed by the US Army Engineers between 1907 and 1914). Before World War I the United States had become involved in Nicaragua, San Domingo, Haiti and Mexico, the last nearly causing them to become embroiled in the grim saga of the Mexican revolution.

Below: Admiral Stefan Makarov's flagship at Port Arthur, the *Petropavlosk* blew up after striking a mine in April 1904. Sistership *Poltava* and *Sevastopol* were also part of the Pacific fleet and both were sunk at the end of the war in 1905. *Poltava* was raised by the Japanese and served with the Japanese fleet as the *Tango*.

PETROPAVLOSK
7965

The Russo-Japanese War

February 1904 saw the commencement of hostilities between Russia and Japan. Although Japan was allied to Great Britain, neither the British nor any other third party was involved. Despite their trouncing of the decrepit Chinese war machine in 1894–5, the Japanese were still regarded as 'new boys', and their action against the unpopular Russians met with guarded international approval.

Numerically, the Japanese and Russian Far East fleets were not dissimilar, but the latter could be considerably reinforced from Europe. Japan's great advantage lay in her geographical domination of approaches to Russia's bases at Port Arthur and Vladivostok. Without declaration of war, Japanese destroyers attacked

Left: Agamemnon, last of the British pre-dreadnoughts, as she appeared in 1915 during the Dardanelles campaign.

Port Arthur and Dalny on the night of 8/9 February 1904. At the former base, two battleships and a cruiser were damaged by torpedoes, but an attempt the following day by Admiral Togo's heavy ships to complete their destruction was defeated by shore gunfire. On the same day, the Japanese used their local sea control to land a military force at Inchon, repeated a few weeks later at Port Arthur, where the force was to besiege the base.

Above: The light cruiser *Oleg* was not ready to join the major elements of the Baltic fleet sent to the Pacific in 1905. The *Oleg* served with the Baltic fleet during World War I, was taken over by the Bolsheviks and sunk by the British torpedo boat *CMB4*.

63

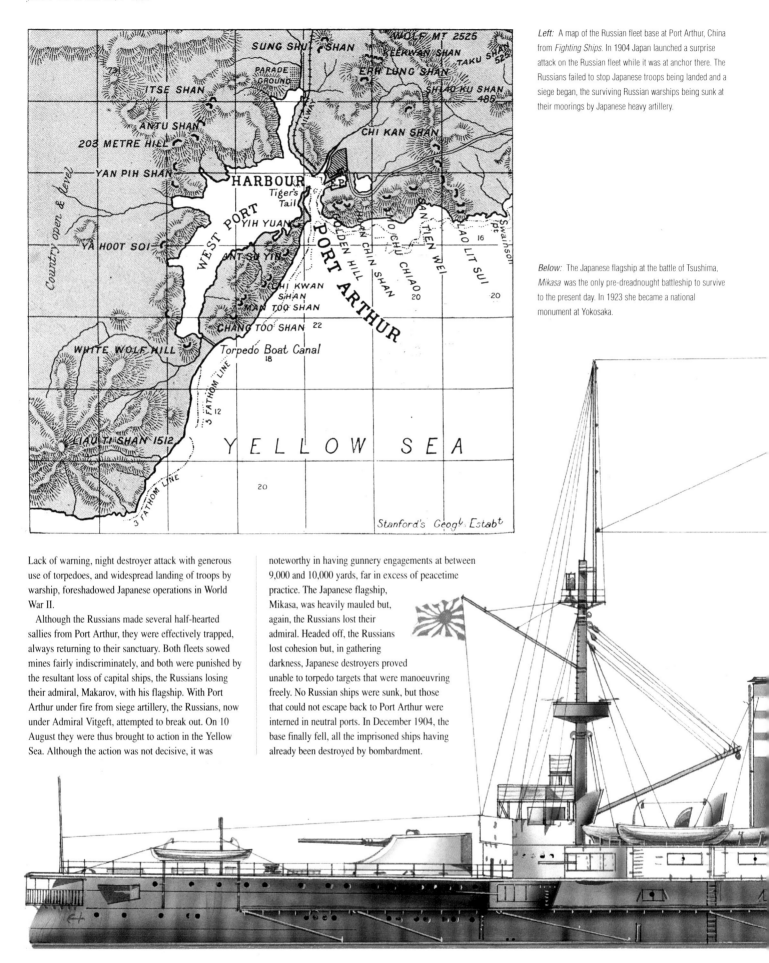

Stanford's Geogl. Estabt

Left: A map of the Russian fleet base at Port Arthur, China from *Fighting Ships*. In 1904 Japan launched a surprise attack on the Russian fleet while it was at anchor there. The Russians failed to stop Japanese troops being landed and a siege began, the surviving Russian warships being sunk at their moorings by Japanese heavy artillery.

Below: The Japanese flagship at the battle of Tsushima, *Mikasa* was the only pre-dreadnought battleship to survive to the present day. In 1923 she became a national monument at Yokosaka.

Lack of warning, night destroyer attack with generous use of torpedoes, and widespread landing of troops by warship, foreshadowed Japanese operations in World War II.

Although the Russians made several half-hearted sallies from Port Arthur, they were effectively trapped, always returning to their sanctuary. Both fleets sowed mines fairly indiscriminately, and both were punished by the resultant loss of capital ships, the Russians losing their admiral, Makarov, with his flagship. With Port Arthur under fire from siege artillery, the Russians, now under Admiral Vitgeft, attempted to break out. On 10 August they were thus brought to action in the Yellow Sea. Although the action was not decisive, it was noteworthy in having gunnery engagements at between 9,000 and 10,000 yards, far in excess of peacetime practice. The Japanese flagship, Mikasa, was heavily mauled but, again, the Russians lost their admiral. Headed off, the Russians lost cohesion but, in gathering darkness, Japanese destroyers proved unable to torpedo targets that were manoeuvring freely. No Russian ships were sunk, but those that could not escape back to Port Arthur were interned in neutral ports. In December 1904, the base finally fell, all the imprisoned ships having already been destroyed by bombardment.

Mikasa

data:

Displacement standard	15,140 tons
Length	432 ft
Beam	76 ft
Design draught	27 ft
Complement	830

Armament:
4 x 12-in guns
14 x 6-in guns
20 x 12-pdr guns
8 x 3-pdr guns
4 x 2.5-pdr guns
4 x 18-in torpedo tubes

Above: Azuma was one of a handful of Japanese warships built in France. Laid down in 1898, she was completed in 1900: a far quicker building programme than French yards were managing for their own navy. *Azuma* took part in the battle off Port Arthur in February 1904 and the battle of Tsushima in May 1905.

Machinery:
2 triple expansion steam engines, 15,000 ihp
2 shafts
18 knots

Armour:

Belt	9 in
Ends	4 in
Deck	3 in
Barbettes	14 in
Casemates	6 in

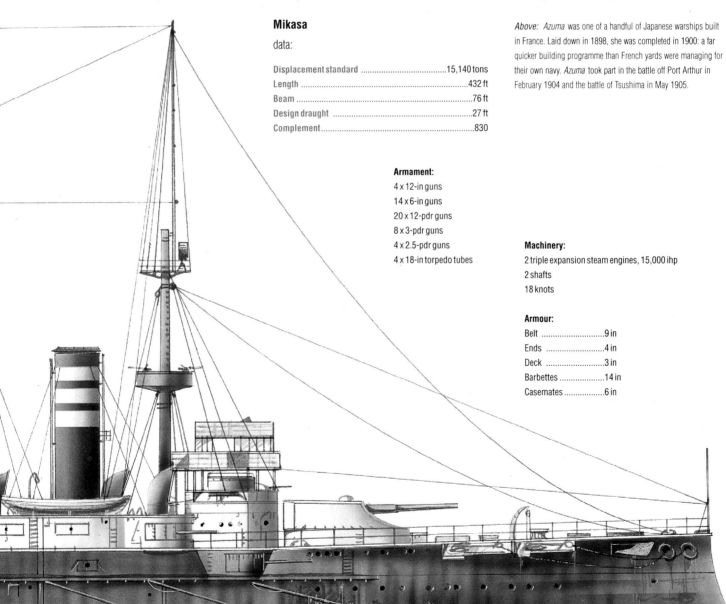

Since the previous October a large Russian reinforcement had been trundling eastward from the Baltic. An eclectic bunch of fighting and support ships, they were in dire need of mechanical overhaul, their crews stricken by tropical diseases and riven by political dissent. With Port Arthur fallen, their admiral, Rozhdestvensky, had to make for Vladivostok. Togo was lying in wait. The forces were again numerically similar, but that of the Japanese was fresh, battle-worthy and fully motivated.

Still some 500 miles short of his destination, Rozhdestvensky was intercepted in the Tsushima Strait on 27 May 1905. Togo paralleled the Russians' track, concentrating their fire on the head of the line and using superior speed to turn the Russians slowly off course. The manoeuvre culminated in a classic crossing of the Russian 'T' and as their flagship was pounded, their leader was severely injured.

Under their vice-admiral, Nebogatov, the Russians regrouped and tried to barge through on something like their original heading. Togo repeated his earlier tactics, wounding his adversaries sufficiently to be able to stand off at dusk to give his destroyers free rein throughout the night. By dawn there remained only Nebogatov and a group of older ships, several badly damaged. Surrounding him was Togo's comparatively unscathed fleet. Unable to fight or escape, Nebogatov surrendered.

Tsushima was one of the most complete naval victories of all time. For the loss of three destroyers, the Japanese sank six battleships and captured two. Of eleven assorted Russian cruisers and armoured ships, only three escaped; all of these were interned in neutral ports. The Russian fleet had virtually ceased to exist, while that of the Japanese was swollen by prizes.

Including the first 'real' engagements of modern times, the Russo-Japanese War taught some important lessons. As the British had observers aboard the ships of their protégé, they assimilated the lessons quickly. Only conservatism had prevented earlier discovery of the huge damage that could be inflicted by standard 12-in (305-mm) guns at ranges in excess of 10,000 yards (9,140 m). At the Yellow Sea action, Togo's flagship *Mikasa* had been heavily hit by a 12-in projectile at an estimated 14,000 yards. Its effect caused the Japanese admiral to hold off, and probably saved the Russians further loss.

British observers' reports stressed that the actions were decided beyond the effective range of secondary armaments. Critical to the result was the number of guns brought to bear, their rate of fire and the accuracy of their control. A margin of speed was essential to bring a reluctant enemy to action, to influence consequent manoeuvres and to decide the range.

When the war sputtered to an American-brokered halt in September 1905, the Russians had the will to continue, but were unable to do so because of the loss of their fleet, while the victorious Japanese had simply run short of ready cash. The Japanese fleet now assumed a new status. Discipline and sheer fighting ability elevated it by right to the ranks of first-class navies. From the peace agreement, Japan gained Port Arthur and a part of Sakhalin, together with control of Korea. Despite still having to acquire much materiel from Britain, Japan now sought eventual independence in warship construction.

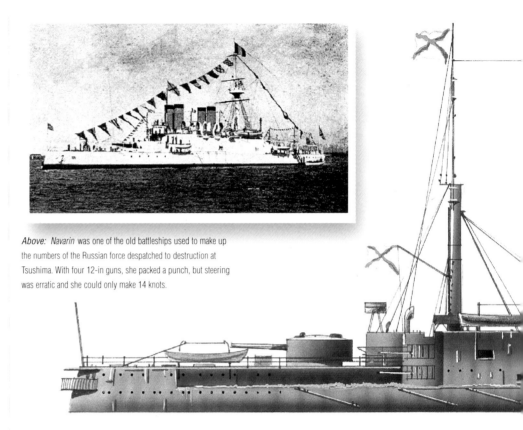

Above: Navarin was one of the old battleships used to make up the numbers of the Russian force despatched to destruction at Tsushima. With four 12-in guns, she packed a punch, but steering was erratic and she could only make 14 knots.

Askold

data:

Displacement standard	5,910 tons
Length	433 ft
Beam	49 ft
Design draught	20 ft
Complement	500

Armament:
12 x 6-in guns
12 x 76-mm guns
6 x 15-in torpedo tubes

Machinery:
3 triple expansion steam engines, 19,650 ihp
3 shafts
23.5 knots

Armour:
Deck ....2-4 in

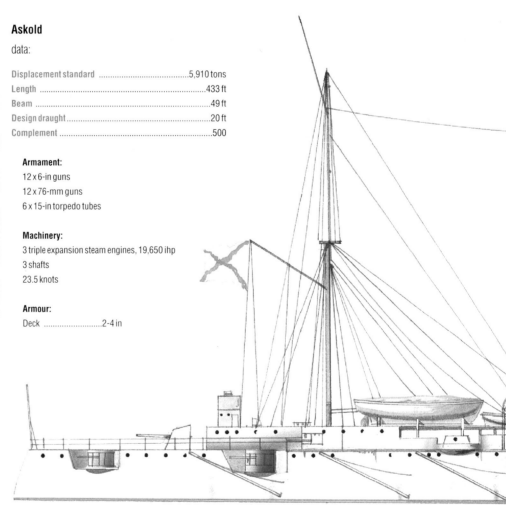

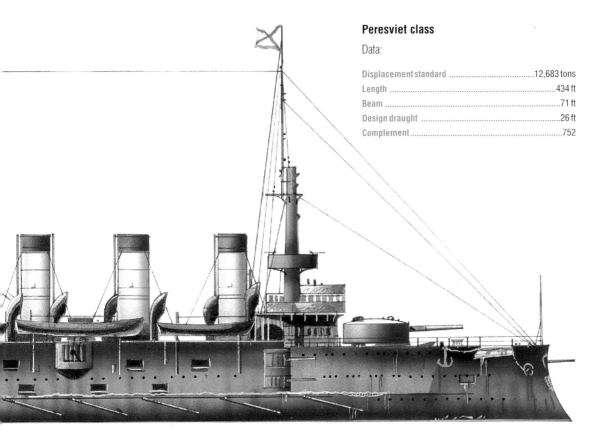

Peresviet class

Data:

Displacement standard	12,683 tons
Length	434 ft
Beam	71 ft
Design draught	26 ft
Complement	752

Class:

Peresviet, Osliabia, Pobieda

Armament:
4 x 10-in guns
11 x 6-in guns
20 x 12-pdr guns
20 x 3-pdr guns
5 x 15-in torpedo tubes

Machinery:
3 triple expansion steam engines,
  15,000ihp
3 shafts
18 knots

Armour:

Belt	9 in
Ends	5 in
Barbettes	8 in
Turrets	10 in
Deck	2.5 in
Casemates	5 in

Above: Osliabia was part of the Baltic fleet in 1904 and joined the force sent to the Far East that autumn. Her two sisterships were sunk at Port Arthur. *Osliabia* led the second division of the Russian fleet at Tsushima and was hit early in the battle, losing her forward 10-in turret. She capsized after several hits on the waterline.

Left: Askold as she joined the Russian Pacific fleet. She fought in both battles outside Port Arthur in February 1904 and in the battle of the Yellow Sea in August, after which she escaped to China. In 1915 under Captain Ivanov, the *Askold* impressed the British in the Mediterranean, raiding the Turkish coast and at Gallipoli, 'keeping up her reputation for smartness and exciting everyone's admiration by the neatness and accuracy of her salvoes', according to the British Official History.

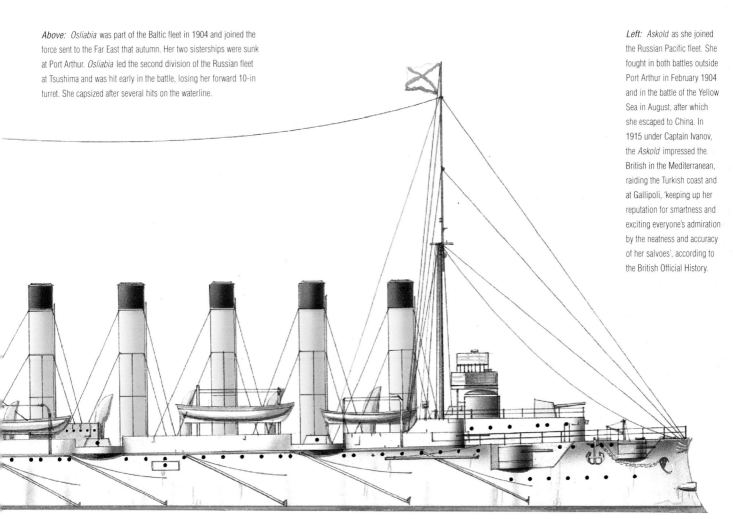

Below: Part of the Russian Pacific fleet, *Pobieda* was mined in April 1904, but repaired to fight at the Yellow Sea and was eventually sunk in Port Arthur by Japanese heavy artillery. Raised and repaired, she served in the Japanese fleet as the *Suwo* as did her sistership *Peresviet* which became the *Sagami*.

The Naval Race begins

Tied by alliance to a nation whose navy was very much their creation, the British could now confidently hope to withdraw heavy units from the Far East, a procedure which tacitly recognised the US Navy as being pre-eminent in the Pacific. The Americans, however, were concerned when, in August 1905, the Anglo-Japanese alliance was not only renewed for a further ten years but was also sharpened to cover attack on either party by just a single power. Careful re-wording emphasised the defence of territorial rights and 'special interests'.

Japan's crushing victory was not welcomed by the Americans. Now unchallenged in the Western Pacific, she was in an expansionist mood and a threat to the Open Door policy. It was thus in 1906 that the United States began work on what was to become Plan Orange, the war plan which, continuously up-dated, eventually provided the basis of operations in the Pacific during World War II.

These events were set against portentous developments in Europe. Germany's naval programme, and virulent Anglophobia over the South African War, aroused mixed feelings in Britain. Beyond the jingoism of the popular press, those in power were divided in opinion as to what German aims really were. The allusions of the 1900 Second Navy Bill to 'even the mightiest Naval Power' were tempered by explanations that the fleet was 'to provide security and defence for German commerce and enterprise'.

Bound by the Two-Power Standard, the British Prime Minister remarked that 'it is natural for us to take what steps we think necessary to protect our own interests'. Such mild utterances, conditioned by generations of supremacy, contrasted with those of the Kaiser himself: 'If naval reinforcements had not been refused me during the first eight years of my reign..... how differently affairs would have stood today! ..... If you had given me the ships I wanted, we could have had South Africa as a German market'. And, from Tirpitz: 'Other Powers must realise that it is more advantageous to them to come to terms with Germany than to make war on her'. Obviously, the fleet in preparation was to be an instrument intended for persuasion as much as deterrence. Well understanding the British position, the Germans had resolved to make her 'come to terms' and accept another major maritime power in close proximity. Unfortunately, the British were not bluffing.

Realising the Kaiser's ambitions rapidly increased the potential not only of the nation's shipyards but also that of allied industries, such as armaments, heavy armour plate and machinery. Progress was impressive but could not match the long-established lead of a British marine industry which could still claim to be supplier to the world. Even the British yards would have been better served, however, had the Government ordered in line with a coherent policy of expansion rather than when politically expedient.

The diagram on p69 charts the number of capital ships laid down by the leading maritime powers between the Naval Defence Act of 1889 and the outbreak of World War I. It demonstrates very erratic progress until, in the case of the European powers, after the 'post-Dreadnought pause'. The incoherent pattern of French construction followed the whims of successive Ministers of Marine. It was roughly shadowed by the Italians who required to build to at least 60 percent of the strength of the French, and to maintain a 4 to 3 margin over the Austrians. It will be noted that construction in the United States was relatively steady, not influenced by events in Europe. If there was any rivalry with Japan at this early stage it is very obvious that the latter really did not yet have the capacity to compete.

If, in the early years of the century, the world's fleet underwent radical change in technology, the Royal Navy went further, with an outwardly unobtrusive move to change the whole outlook of the Service. To a few men of vision it was apparent that the comfortable era of Victoria had died with her and that the Fleet needed to be cleared of outdated thought as much as outdated tonnage. The South African war was something of a watershed in not only unmasking Germany's unfriendly disposition but also in exposing the poor state of training of the Army and its lack of preparedness for modern war. Indeed this conflict actually did the British a service in teaching that lesson cheaply. To the Navy's thinkers it seemed that parallels could be drawn.

From 1899 to 1902 the British Mediterranean Fleet was commanded by Vice-Admiral Sir John Fisher. The Navy had always been fortunate in producing 'the man for the moment', but 'Jackie' Fisher was quite exceptional. Already 58 years of age, he arrived on the station with experience and a reputation. He was greatly interested in gunnery, having served as captain of the gunnery school, HMS *Excellent*, and as the Director of Naval Ordnance and Torpedoes, and had a burning ambition to improve the Fleet's shooting. As Third Sea Lord and Controller of the Navy he had greatly expedited the development of the destroyer and the universal adoption of the water-tube boiler.

A dynamo of a man, he descended on any of his ships, large or small, at minimal notice. Inspections, which had long been a formality, became a forenoon's whirl of activity, leaving the ship in total temporary disarray and its complement in a state of exhaustion. Their Admiral, however, had fully gauged their efficiency, and officers who did not measure up commonly found themselves drafted in short order to distant commands. One of his many unorthodox habits was the establishment of ad hoc committees to address specific questions. Fisher recognised that senior personnel were often not those

best-fitted to provide the answers, and he would elicit ideas from any he deemed worth listening to. His oft-stated ambition was to elevate both the Mediterranean and Channel Fleets to the permanent equivalent of war footing. He quickly discounted the French as a threat, as early as 1903 seeing the Germans as eventual enemies in that their growing interests conflicted everywhere with those of the British.

Twelve years Fisher's junior, Percy Scott transformed the Navy's shooting. After re-organising HMS *Excellent* in the early 1890s, he took command of the Mediterranean Fleet cruiser *Scylla*. He rapidly raised her shooting standards from the fleet average of under one hit in three to an astounding four hits in five. To do this he introduced 'continuous aiming', altering the elevation gearing on the guns to allow the layer to adjust continuously to keep the gun on the target rather than the old system of 'firing on the up roll'. He introduced telescopic sights, aligned to lead the target and mounted so as to be unaffected by shock and recoil forces. His 'dry loader' was an apparatus to enable practice to be

undertaken at any time. It incorporated a deflection simulator and a 'dotter' to mark 'fall of shot'. Frequent practice then resulted in the improvements mentioned. Fisher, taking over as C in C during Scott's service on *Scylla*, recognised the importance of these innovations, and had them installed throughout the fleet.

In 1900, Scott took over the cruiser *Terrible* in the Far East. Here, he met a young American lieutenant, William Sims, serving aboard the *Kentucky*. At this time, the US Navy looked upon even a 30 percent accuracy as phenomenal, and Sims was given permission to introduce Scott's methods to his own ship. Again, the results were striking, but lacking a Fisher the establishment was not enthused. Following two frustrating years, during which he got nowhere, Sims gambled his career and contacted the President directly. Theodore Roosevelt, a man of action, appreciated what he was hearing and installed Sims, still a lowly lieutenant, as Inspector of Target Practice. Ironically, this post pre-dated by three years the creation of one similar by the Royal Navy. Its first incumbent was Captain Percy Scott.

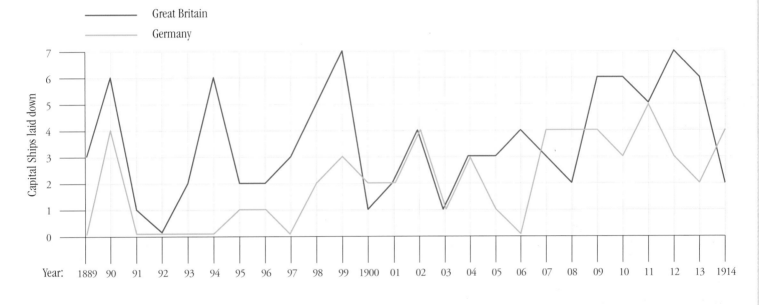

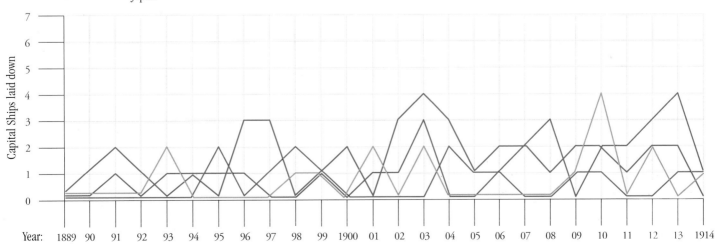

Figure 1: The Major Fleets. Capital Ships laid down to home account.

Gunnery Revolution

Naval gunnery was entering a new era. By 1903, i.e. even before the Russo-Japanese War proved the point conclusively, Fisher had demonstrated in the Mediterranean that engagements were quite feasible at 6,000 yards (5,484 m), and that contemporary guns could hit reliably at up to 8,000 (7,312 m). He knew also of French and Italian experiments at similar ranges. A stimulus to greater ranges was the torpedo, which already out-ranged the 3,000 yards (2,742 m) still used for 'battle practice'. Long-range fire required a change from the practice of 'smothering the target' to deliberate aim, using full salvoes. Gun-laying is accurate in bearing, but less so in range, the projectile being subject to a range of variables. As a result, a simultaneously fired salvo falls as a 'ladder', spread along an imaginary line joining firing ship to target. An observer, high in the ship, can apply corrections – up or down, left or right – until this ladder lays across the target, i.e. a 'straddle'. Once straddling, the firing ship has a fair chance of more than one hit per salvo – obviously an attractive proposition – and the immediate extension to this line of thought was to maximise the number of large-calibre weapons, beyond the customary four big guns on ships displacing up to 16,000 tons.

Such reasoning was not confined to any one person but was probably first publicly articulated by Vittorio Cuniberti, Chief Constructor to the Italian Navy. In 1903 he used Jane's own annual handbook to write on his theoretically ideal battleship. At 17,000 tons, little larger than the King Edward VIIs then building, his ship would accommodate no less than twelve 12-in guns. This was possible by the abandonment of smaller-calibre weapons which, he agreed, would be irrelevant as engagements would be decided at long ranges. Cuniberti believed also in speed (and had early introduced oil-burning to the Italian Navy), quoting 24 knots for his ideal in order to dictate the range of an engagement. This was a near five-knot increase on the speed of contemporary British

battleships and he did not make clear how he intended to double installed power within so modest a displacement.

Fisher claimed to have been working on the all-big-gun concept since 1900, his idea for incorporating a maximum number of faster-firing 10-in (254-mm) guns being changed by the Navy's preference for 12-in (305-mm). Weeks after being appointed First Sea Lord, in 1904, he established a joint civilian/service committee to define a battleship with the maximum number of 12-in guns, adequate protection and a size compatible with existing dockyard facilities. A second type of ship was also to be considered, a revolutionary 25-knot armoured cruiser, also armed with a 12-in main battery.

Aware of developments abroad, the committee worked rapidly. About one thousand tons heavier than Cuniberti's model, the resulting battleship proposal also mounted ten, rather than twelve, 12-in guns. Superimposed gun turrets were rejected in the belief that blast effects would render them mutually unworkable, but the final disposition was well able to satisfy Fisher's pre-occupation with end-on fire.

Existing battleships were limited to about 19 knots because of the increasing size of reciprocating machinery. As this type of engine was very unreliable for prolonged high-speed transits, a ship's quoted maximum speed was not a good index of real performance. The committee made the bold decision to specify Parson's steam turbine; 'bold' because it had been demonstrated successfully in only a few destroyers, and the main trials platform for this new machinery, the light cruiser Amethyst, was yet incomplete. Adopting a four-shaft layout, absorbing two-thirds more power than the Amethyst, a saving of over one thousand tons was made, while the compact nature of the engines permitted a more flexible disposition than was customary. The modest speed of 21 knots would have disappointed Cuniberti, but the overall weight saving (with an admittedly deficient scheme of protection) allowed for a freeboard adequate to fight the ship in adverse conditions.

Above: Temeraire was one of the three Bellerophon class battleships that were follow-ons from the pioneering *Dreadnought.*

Below: The problem with the later pre-dreadnoughts as typified by *Agamemnon* was that gunlayers could not distinguish between the shell splashes of the 12- and 9.2-in guns.

Right: Temeraire as depicted by a pre-war postcard. The 'all big gun' battleship simplified fire control by having only one calibre of main armament. However, the battles of World War I were conducted far beyond peacetime training ranges, and rangefinding equipment aboard British battleships was found to be inadequate.

Carrying the historic name of *Dreadnought*, the prototype was built in both secrecy and haste, being laid down by Portsmouth Dockyard in October 1905 and ready for initial sea trials a year and a day later.

Trends prior to this had been toward the provision of an increasingly powerful secondary armament; the tertiary, or anti-torpedo boat battery diminishing as a result. Germany, with a comparatively limited experience in warship design produced the five Braunschweig class and five Deutschlands, laid down between 1901 and 1905, with a combination of four 280-mm (11-in) guns and a homogeneous secondary battery of fourteen 170-mm (6.7-in). Cuniberti's four Regina Elenas of 1901–3 suffered a reduction of main battery to only two single 12-in in order to elevate the secondary armament to twelve 8-in (203-mm). Japan, also not bound by traditional ideas, built the *Satsuma* with four 12-in and twelve 10-in guns. Laid down in the same year, 1905, the British *Lord Nelson* and *Agamemnon* shipped a very similar armament of four 12-in and ten 9.2-in guns.

By experimenting with firing 12-in guns over the roof of a monitor's turret, the Americans proved that, subject to certain design restraints, superimposed mountings were perfectly feasible. Such an arrangement meant that fewer guns were necessary, owing to greatly improved firing arcs. Weight thus saved could be used to improve protection, offsetting the argument that to concentrate the armament increased the risk of losing several guns to a single hit. By combining eight 12-in guns, in superimposed twin mountings forward and aft, with twenty-two 3-in (76-mm), the Americans provided maximum hitting power with the extensive battery of anti-torpedo boat quick-firers which the Russo-Japanese War had shown to be desirable.

Thus configured, the *Michigan* and *South Carolina* were authorised early in 1905, actually being laid down before the *Dreadnought*. However, as they were not completed until 1909 they were overshadowed by the British ship which, in some respects, was their inferior.

Below: The first German battle cruiser, *Von der Tann* set the pattern for the rest: armed with lighter guns (11-in rather than the British 12-in) her armour protection was almost as good as a battleship.

Battle Cruisers

More revolutionary even than the *Dreadnought* was Fishers other creation, eventually to be called a 'battle cruiser'. Existing armoured cruisers had developed into ships so large and expensive that they were, effectively, at the limit of their evolutionary line. For instance, the Minotaurs of 1905 displaced 14,600 tons. Diminutives of battleships, they had 9.2-in (234-mm) guns forward and aft instead of 12-in, and 7.5s (190 mm) along either side in the waist in place of a battleship's 9.2s. To achieve a required speed of 23 knots, however, boilers and machinery demanded a hull l7 percent longer than the contemporary 16,500-ton Lord Nelson battleships.

Armoured cruisers needed both speed and firepower. Their function was reconnaissance in force, to close with the enemy to report on his strength and disposition. They were expected to support faster 'light' cruisers, doing much the same job on the flanks, and to finish off enemy units immobilised by a main engagement (but possibly still full of fight). As with battleships, foreign developments were pointing toward a 'super cruiser'. The Regina Elenas, mentioned above, accepted a

reduced level of armament and protection in exchange for a then considerable speed of 22 knots. With the two 13,750-ton Tsukubas of 1904, the Japanese took the idea . further with a battleship armament on a large cruiser's displacement, but with poor protection and a disappointing speed of only 20.5 knots.

Fisher was an apostle of speed and striking power. For him, speed was protection; it enabled a commander to choose his range and, if equipped with the largest-calibre guns, to destroy an adversary with impunity. A speed of 25 knots, a margin of just two knots over the latest armoured cruisers, required 41,000 shp, a 78 percent increase on the *Dreadnought*'s installed power. A large hull was required, both to accommodate the necessary thirty-one boilers and to obtain fine enough lines. To maintain speed in adverse conditions a considerable freeboard was necessary. Everything conspired to increase size and, with Fisher driving the project, the armament was maximised at eight 12-in guns to complement the speed but, inevitably, the scale of protection suffered. There was no way that the vast expanse of hull could be protected adequately, but in the event the ships made do with even less than an armoured

Above: The *Tiger* was the last of Admiral Beatty's
'famous cats' to join the battle cruiser squadron and
fought at Dogger Bank and Jutland.

Above: The Dominions of Australia and New Zealand each funded
a battle cruiser, and both *New Zealand* and *Australia* served with
the Grand Fleet in the North Sea during World War I. *New Zealand*
is seen here on her initial visit to the Dominions in 1913.

cruiser. A shallow, 6-in (150-mm) belt extended no
further aft than the after barbette, but continued forward,
tapered to four inches (100 mm). Turrets and barbettes
had just seven inches (175 mm) of protection. A one-
inch main deck gave a measure of splinter protection but
the protective deck proper was only 2.5-in (64-mm)
thick at best. Patches of 2.5-in plate were worked in
around the magazines.

Such a package equated to the proverbial heavyweight
with a glass jaw, a ship designed to dish it out but not to
'fight hurt'. Used as intended they would prove superb,
but as critics immediately pointed out, given the ship's
armament, an admiral would be tempted to add it to the
battle line where its speed would be of no value and its
deficiencies quickly exposed. Prophetic words.

The first trio, the Invincible class, were completed in
1908. Just fifteen months after the arrival of the
Dreadnought, they made a considerable impression,
particularly as once run in all comfortably exceeded
28 knots.

H. M. S. "Agamemnon" (Battleship 16500 tons.)

Left: Agamemnon was attached to the 5th Battle Squadron in the Channel in 1914, while sistership *Lord Nelson* became flagship of the Channel Fleet.

Right: The Kaiser class were armed with 12-in guns and retained the off-set midships turrets that allowed limited arcs for cross deck firing. Four of the five Kaisers fought at Jutland, *Kaiser Wilhelm der Grosse* serving as Admiral Scheer's flagship.

Preparing for War

Although the Royal Navy was acquiring its big guns, the science of using them efficiently was rather slower in development. Percy Scott's reforms really began to make progress only in 1904 when Fisher became First Sea Lord; another specialist, Captain John Jellicoe (later C in C, Grand Fleet) being appointed director of Naval Ordnance. Scott was his own worst enemy; wildly out-spoken and totally lacking in tact, he made few friends. He was convinced that hitting at long range demanded broadside or salvo firing, carefully spotting the fall of shot until the target was being straddled. Unfortunately, the Admiralty appointed two admirals, Custance and Lambton, to explore the best approach to long-range gunnery. Thousands of rounds later, their findings conflicted, the version of their report finally being promulgated still effectively allowing ships to use their individual systems. In consequence, standards of gunnery varied widely throughout the Royal Navy.

Below: Operating off the Russian coast, the German cruiser *Magdeburg* grounded herself at 15 knots just after midnight on 26 August 1914. She was destroyed by the Russian cruisers *Bogatyr* and *Pallada* whose boarding parties captured a set of German naval codes which the Russians passed to the British.

Uncovering the basic fact that the Fleet's gunsights were deficient, Scott appraised the Admiralty in his usual forthright manner but was fobbed off with platitudes and prevarication in place of action. Following promotion to flag rank in 1905, and acquiring the title of Inspector of Target Practice, Scott was able, with Jellicoe, to introduce more realistic 'battle practice'. This included requiring a ship, while manoeuvring, to fire all guns simultaneously at a towed target, five to seven thousand yards distant. 'Simultaneous' was a relative term, as ships still had only a single, short-blade rangefinder and a complex network of voice pipes and coordinating officers. In the US Navy, by contrast, Bradley Fiske was developing a system of electrically based communications to each gun position.

A useful interim aid in the Royal Navy was the 'Dumaresq', a type of plot invented by an officer of that name. It enabled the movement of own ship and the estimated course and speed of target to be plotted on a continuous basis, giving up-to-date range and deflection solutions.

Scott, in cooperation with the firm of Vickers, made the most fundamental contribution by the introduction of 'director firing'. This system exploited electrical loop control to allow all guns of a battery to be laid from a common point. The Director himself was sited high in the ship, theoretically above the smoke nuisance, continuously receiving and updating range, bearing, speed and heading of target. Once every position indicated 'guns ready', the director fired them simultaneously with a single switch, observing the fall of shot to correct for the following salvo.

Almost symptomatic of the new mood in the Navy was the abandonment in 1902 of the ships' bold Victorian paint scheme. As the Army was forsaking its bright uniforms for khaki, so the Fleet turned to a uniform colour, known universally as 'crabfat grey'. Its function was to make it more difficult for an enemy gunner to estimate range and heading.

Fisher, meanwhile, had made a wholesale clearance of the Navy's antiques in order to concentrate resources where it mattered. Seventeen battleships were among the 154 warships retired. This radical action sprang from the confidence engendered by Britain's following the 1902 alliance with Japan by an entente with France, agreed two years later. These agreements, together with the virtual elimination of the Russian fleet at Tsushima in 1905, enabled the First Sea Lord to drastically reorganise the disposition of the Royal Navy. For several years he had viewed the Germans as the most likely future opponents, and now, with the Mediterranean and Far Eastern waters dominated by fleets of friendly powers, he could safely build up the Home Fleet to a pre-eminent position. Through shrewd diplomacy, the British were thus able to effect the concentration in home waters that Tirpitz had gambled on them not being able to do due to worldwide commitments.

British naval bases reflected the requirements of earlier wars in being concentrated in the south of the country. In view of the seriousness of the new threat from across the North Sea, a new first-class base was under somewhat leisurely construction at Rosyth, with anchorages and basic facilities being prepared at Cromarty and Scapa.

A re-organised Channel Fleet, with a core of twelve battleships, was based temporarily at Dover. From Gibraltar, four days' steaming distance away, a further eight battleships could be provided by the Atlantic Fleet. The strength at Malta fluctuated considerably but was greatly reduced.

The High Seas Fleet

German Anglophobia strengthened Fisher's arm, making his sweeping reforms the easier. Unconcealed British response, together with the 1907 Triple Entente with France and Russia, further inflamed German emotions, which fluctuated between bellicosity and apprehension. The completion of the *Dreadnought*, and the obvious preparedness of the British to continue building, left the Germans with a dilemma. Not only was their concentration strategy a shambles but the battleships under construction were effectively already obsolete. To rebuild to Dreadnought, standards would require resources obtainable only through robbing the Army; their sheer size would demand a major up-grading of the Navy's infrastructure and, worse, the British would be in no doubt regarding the challenge to their naval supremacy. The costs would be horrific and the results risking the catastrophic.

Tirpitz' planned battleships would have slowly been increased to about 16,000 tons displacement, representing dimensions compatible with the locks at Wilhelmshaven and the depth of the Kiel Canal. His

Above: Helgoland was the name-ship of the second class of German dreadnoughts. Both classes had reciprocating engines rather than turbines.

hand was now forced. The initial German crisis meeting was, however, held on 22 September 1905, ten days *before* the laying down of the *Dreadnought* herself. Costings were prepared for a planned building rate of three battleships and one battle cruiser per year. Accompanied by Tirpitz' theatrical threat to resign should it not be approved, the proposal was presented to the Kaiser early in 1906 and passed by the Reichstag as a Supplementary Bill in May 1906. Although the already large appropriations for the Second Navy Bill were now increased by some 35 percent, actual numerical increase involved only six more large cruisers and 50 percent more torpedo boats. The massively expensive upgrading of the battleship programme to Dreadnought standard would be explained by 'experience of recent years, and particularly by the Russo-Japanese War'.

Following a pause for rapid re-design, the first class of four Dreadnoughts, the Nassaus, was laid down in 1907. Shorter and beamier than the British ships, their standard displacement, at 18,870 tons, was greater. As steam turbines were not yet thought suitable for capital ships, 22,000 ihp triple expansion plant was fitted, considerably

influencing hull layout. An eight-gun broadside was required but, as the hull was too short for a Michigan-style arrangement, a hexagonal layout was adopted. The two wing turrets on either side could be accommodated because of the moderate dimensions of 280-mm (11-in) mounting and underdeck structure, but were a major factor in the increase in beam. A feature of the lower hull was its very thorough subdivision.

The first true battle cruiser, *Von der Tann*, was delayed to avoid repeating the mistake of the *Blücher*. Again, she was shorter, beamier and heavier than the exemplar, in this case the *Invincible*. Only 18 boilers were required, compared with the British ship's 31, and combined with the adoption of steam turbine machinery, this permitted a more flexible machinery layout. This in turn resulted in the positioning of the waist turrets to give greatly improved firing arcs. The *Von der Tann* thus had a genuine eight-gun broadside in contrast to the *Invincible's* virtual inability to train all eight guns on the beam. Only fractionally less beamy than the Nassaus, the battle cruiser had a 10-in belt, tapering to 4-in, compared with the British ship's 6-4-in scheme.

Anticipating that the Dreadnought's completion would trigger instant reaction abroad, the British Admiralty expected to lay down four ships annually. In the event, there was an initial hiatus as the implications were assimilated. Already enjoying numerical superiority, the Navy Board had to accept a politically imposed slowing in construction rates.

Dreadnought's hasty design showed, in one respect, in an inability to defend herself against torpedo boats. The following three Bellerophon class rectified this with a sixteen 4-in gun secondary battery and a continuous torpedo bulkhead. The smaller weapons did not mark a reversion to tiered armaments as they were meant purely for close-range defence. Marking the progress toward long-range spotting, the Bellerophons featured observation platforms on a pair of lofty tripod masts.

Few major changes were made in the three St. Vincents of the 1907 programme. Plating was thinned at the extremities in order to improve protection where it really mattered. Their 12-in main battery barrels were increased in length from 45 to 50 calibres, which increased muzzle velocity and penetration at the expense of reduced accuracy and increased rate of wear.

With only a limited industrial base for warship construction, the Germans found that estimates were being exceeded by considerable margins. Large crew were also expensive, and naval appropriations were rapidly soaked up. The 1906 Supplementary Bill provided for funding intended to last until 1911, but money was virtually non-existent for running the Service. Even the national budget was creaking under the strain, and political comment was frequently hostile.

A critical clause of the 1906 *Novelle* provided for the replacement of capital ships at twenty years of age, rather than the accepted twenty-five. This effectively increased the number of hulls already due for replacement, and Tirpitz, having achieved his aim to justify four keels per year, now had to find means to fund them. A whole new industry had developed, however. Wealthy, powerful and vociferous, it fed on political and popular misgivings, the construction programme acquiring a momentum, a life of its own.

Although apparently satisfied with smaller-calibre guns

than the British, the German Navy supported Krupps in the development of larger weapons. The second group of Dreadnoughts, the Helgolands, were the first with 305-mm (12-in) guns, but retained the outdated hexagonal layout, which gave a broadside of only eight of the twelve barrels carried. The five Kaisers which followed, laid down 1909–10, were increased in length sufficiently to superimpose the after pair of twin 305-mm guns. As the amidships turrets were echeloned in a large gap amidships, both could train on either beam, giving the ships a broadside of ten barrles from ten guns.

Germany's planned 21 Dreadnoughts by 1914 had become a long-term goal of 58 by 1920. In Britain, alarm set in as it was calculated (falsely) that parity could be achieved by 1912. Hotly opposed by the Treasury (led by the then Chancellor of the Exchequer, Winston Churchill), a popular 'We want eight and we won't wait' programme was initiated. The four Orions of 1909–10 reintroduced the 13.5-in gun, the ten-gun disposition following the lead taken by the Americans in the Delawares – an all-centreline layout with a single amidships turret and two superimposed at either end. Again the Germans followed suit with the four Königs, although the 305-mm gun was retained.

Britain's accelerated programme, despite political

resistance, was assisted also by growth in the Austro-Hungarian fleet. This service, too, was hard to justify, its functions vague. Ultimately hostage to whoever controlled the Strait of Otranto, it was effectively neutralised by hostilities with both Italy and France.

Still referred to officially as 'armoured cruisers' the Royal Navy's battle cruisers also adopted the 13.5-in gun. To maintain a two-knot advantage over the 25-knot German *Moltke*, the Lions were still significantly larger than battleships then building.

The era of the 13.5-in 'super-Dreadnought' was brief, extending only to the succeeding King George V and Iron Duke classes. In 1912, the *Queen Elizabeth*, first of the 15-in battleships, was laid down. Only four turrets of this size could be carried, resulting in a symmetrical two-forward, two-aft disposition. This jump in calibre was quickly equalled by the 380-mm (15-in) weapons of the two German Bayerns with some evidence that these were under consideration ahead of the British. Both classes were well designed and, as far as World War I was concerned, were the 'ultimate' battleships.

Below: The Italian dreadnought *Guilio Caesare* was completed in 1914. Use of double and triple turrets enabled her to carry thirteen 12-in guns supplied by Vickers.

British ships, with their guaranteed oil supplies, had completed their transition from coal-firing to oil, but the less-fortunate German fleet used fuel oil mainly for boost speeds. Diesel oil was also required to supply the cruising machinery at last entering service. The difference was significant, with British ships of similar size having complements some two hundred fewer, due to lower numbers of stokers. Most important was the two-knot speed advantage of the Queen Elizabeths, justifying the new term 'fast battleship'.

German opinion was inflamed by Churchill, who had been appointed First Lord of the Admiralty in 1911, describing the Kaiser's fleet as being 'in the nature of a luxury'. The latter word, in German, translates unfortunately as sumptuousness or extravagance, and the resulting furore lubricated the way for a further supplementary bill. This, by funding a further three capital ships, would have resulted in an eventual 61 capital ships. The Anglo-German naval race had dominated the period from 1906 until 1914, but as the diagram above shows, its influence resulted in a rise in construction elsewhere.

The French came late to the Dreadnought concept, doggedly laying down the six Dantons between 1906 and 1908. In 1911, when foreign fleets were commissioning all-big-gun battleships, the *Marine Nationale* was taking into service 19-knot coal burners, with a main battery of four 305-mm (12-in) guns.

Completed in 1913–14, the four Courbets carried six twin 12-in turrets for a ten-gun broadside. The three Bretagnes, which were accepted in 1915–16, had 340-mm guns, and were roughly comparable with the British Orions. Guns of this same calibre were then quadrupled in a bold move forward. Three such turrets were to be accommodated in the trio of Normandies, four in the following quartet of Lyons. Such ships would have had immense firepower on a reasonably limited displacement, but were destined never to be completed.

Triple turrets had been proven in Italian, Russian and Austro-Hungarian battleships, being adopted by the Americans also in the two Nevadas, launched in 1914.

Mere comparison of numbers is invidious, as characteristics varied so much. As war loomed in 1914, the Royal Navy was still debating the future of director firing, the handful of ships so fitted still very much experimental. The torpedo menace was certainly acknowledged, but as launched from surface craft rather than submarines, whose potential had yet to be realised.

On 24 November 1910 Eugene Ely, at the controls of a Curtiss biplane, launched himself from a temporary platform in the bows of the USS *Birmingham*, ushering in the era of airpower at sea. The British Admiralty showed immediate interest, launching from several battleships. As reconnaissance was seen as an aircraft's major task, however, the launch and recovery of seaplanes over the side was accepted for the moment as the most reliable and safe method.

Right: The Argentine dreadnought *Commodoro Rivadavia* seen off Rio de Janeiro, June 1918.

Opposite below: The Brazilian dreadnought *Sao Paulo* ready to join the Allies, June 1918.

Below: *Tegetthoff*, one of the four Austro-Hungarian dreadnoughts built on the eve of World War I.

Chapter 5 – World War I

Although World War I was indeed a 'world war', the issue at sea was decided almost entirely between the fleets of Great Britain and Germany. The relative importance of these forces differed considerably. The Royal Navy protected British shores from the threat of invasion and, almost as importantly, safeguarded the continuous flow of merchant shipping which imported the materials to sustain both the war effort and the population. To lose the fleet was to lose the war. Germany, in contrast, remained a continental power and, despite considerable population growth, was largely self-sufficient. An anticipated brief war would be decided by military means; the loss of both fleet and merchant marine would be serious but not necessarily fatal.

Admiral Jellicoe's Grand Fleet was tasked with establishing sea control, ensuring free British use of the sea while denying it to the enemy. Economic blockade would wither his trade, slowly reducing his capacity and will to fight. Military forces would be transported and supported in foreign campaigns.

Germany's only practical exit to the open ocean was through the 250-mile gap between the Orkneys and the Norwegian coast. Flanking this was the Grand Fleet's adopted base at Scapa Flow, whose bleak fastness was 'home'-to twenty-four Dreadnought battleships and battle cruisers and thirteen pre-Dreadnoughts. Having failed in his aim to effect a superior concentration in the North Sea, Tirpitz now faced a major confrontation in any attempt to leave it.

While the Russian fleet threatened the Baltic, its ability was not rated very highly by the Germans. Admiral von Ingenohl's High Seas Fleet was, therefore, concentrated on its North Sea base of Wilhelmshaven, whence it could quickly access the Baltic via the Kiel Canal if required.

At the outset, its major strength lay in its fifteen Dreadnoughts and eight pre-Dreadnoughts.

This disparity in strength, and the belief that the British would descend in force to 'Copenhagen' him, caused the Kaiser to urge extreme caution in fleet deployment. Following the planned brief war, he wanted the force intact, to act as a powerful bargaining chip at the peace table. Jellicoe, careful and prudent, would certainly take no chances that would jeopardise his margin of superiority over the High Seas Fleet, whose potential he fully respected. With neither Commander-in-Chief inclined to take risks, a major confrontation would thus occur only by accident.

The longer the war, the greater the German disadvantage. Already building thirteen battleships to Germany's five, Britain also appropriated three others building to foreign account. In battle cruisers, completed and working-up, the Royal Navy had an advantage of thirteen to five. Germany, however, better appreciated what would become the 'fast battleship', building three to Britain's one. For a while, von Ingenohl's policy was one of '*Kleinkrieg*', posing a continuous threat yet avoiding action except under favourable circumstances, and using ambush, mines and, increasingly, submarines to whittle away at British numbers.

Below: The importance of airpower at sea increased dramatically during World War I and by 1918 the Royal Navy was planning a mass airstrike on the German fleet, launched from its new force of aircraft carriers. *Argus* seen here, was converted from a liner left on the stocks since the outbreak of war. In 1918 her airgroup consisted of 18 Sopwith Cuckoo torpedo-bombers.

Left: Breslau was a German light cruiser accompanying the battle cruiser *Goeben* in the western Mediterranean when war was declared. The two slipped past several British squadrons and entered Constantinople, precipitating the Turkish entry into the war on the side of the Central Powers. She operated under Turkish colours until mined and sunk in 1918.

Not four weeks into the war, the Kaiser's worst fears were realised when Commodore Tyrwhitt's Harwich Force penetrated the Heligoland Bight . With just two light cruisers and a couple of flotillas of destroyers, Tyrwhitt was targeting the many minor German units usually active in the area. Jellicoe, on learning of the raid, despatched three further battle cruisers under Vice Admiral Sir David Beatty, supported by a light cruiser squadron. Of these late reinforcements Tyrwhitt knew nothing, as he was already beyond radio range.

In the Bight there were patches of thick haze and, with a force of over 30 destroyers proving impossible to control, the sweep degenerated into a series of unconnected skirmishes. Although surprised, the Germans reacted strongly, quickly getting six light cruisers into the action. Tyrwhitt's own ship, *Arethusa*, was slowed by a hit and became a liability on the enemy's doorstep. Beatty, monitoring radio traffic, realised the danger to the Harwich Force and, with great boldness, waded in with his entire force. Three German cruisers were destroyed and Tyrwhitt's withdrawal covered.

The morale of the British public and the German fleet were elevated and depressed in equal measure. Yet it could so easily have ended in disaster: poor British staff work could have led to British submarines attacking their own capital ships, of whose presence they were unaware. Beatty's ignoring of the Bight's known mined areas was justifiable in the circumstances. His battle cruisers acquired the aura of the cavalry, but the action proved little about battle cruisers and much about leadership.

Although the practice was contrary to international convention, both sides took enthusiastically to mining open waters, each blaming the other for initiating the process. The most cost-effective means of maritime warfare, mines can be laid cheaply but cleared only expensively. The disruption thus caused is immense. As the major risk was to the minelayers themselves, auxiliaries were preferred to regular warships, which were displaced in turn largely by submarine minelayers.

Over the 51 eventual months of war, mines would sink 46 British warships, including five battleships, and destroy or disable over 1.1 million gross registered tons (grt) of merchant shipping. An early shock casualty was the modern battleship *Audacious* which foundered in heavy seas over twelve hours after striking a single mine. Damage control and the designing-out of leak paths were techniques yet in their infancy.

Fiasco at the Dardanelles

The Kaiser's 'six-week war' bogged down in Western Front stalemate. In the Mediterranean, Italy had opened hostilities against Austria, and Turkey had declared for the Central Powers. With the Turks pressing his troops hard in the Caucasus, the Tsar appealed for a diversion to distract them. Churchill, the First Lord, needed no further bidding and enlisted French support for a naval expedition to force the Dardanelles. By appearing in strength before Constantinople, it was reasoned, the Allies would quickly force Turkey out of the war. The

Royal Navy had twice before in history made an opposed passage to the strait, but now things were different.

Forty-odd miles in length, the Dardanelles are winding and, in places, very fast-flowing. Under German guidance, the Turks had heavily mined the waters and, using sound military principles, had installed modern artillery to cover the minefields. Before the mines could be swept the guns had to be neutralised. Without a military force, this task devolved to heavy naval guns – and history showed that ships rarely proved a match for fixed fortifications.

Fourteen pre-Dreadnoughts (four of them French), the two Lord Nelsons, the thin-skinned battle cruiser *Inflexible* (probably because of the presence of the German battle cruiser *Goeben* above the strait), and the brand-new *Queen Elizabeth* were assembled.

Commencing 19 February 1915, defences along the un-mined lower reaches were systematically reduced by gunfire and totally demolished by landing parties. By 1 March the Narrow defences came under attack but, for accurate gunnery, the ships needed virtually to stop and were hit repeatedly by heavy artillery.

Any attempt by converted trawlers to sweep the mines was defeated by a combination of searchlights and guns (specially modified destroyers were not used). Indirect fire from the *Queen Elizabeth*'s 15-in guns could hit the vulnerable reverse faces of the fortifications by shooting across the peninsula. This depended upon aerial spotting, however, which failed initially through poor communications, unreliable aircraft and inadequate organisation. However, with practice and the provision of

Left: Majestic was part of the second squadron of pre-dreadnoughts assembled for the Dardanelles and took part in the bombardment in March 1915.

Right: From her new base at Constantinople, the *Goeben* transported Turkish troops across the Black Sea and had several engagements with the Russian fleet based at Sevastopol.

Below: The officers and men of *E11.* Lt. Commander Nasmith won the VC for his daring raid into the Sea of Marmara during which he bumped his way through a minefield to penetrate the Turkish defences.

accurate gridded maps to both ship and aircraft, indirect fire became very effective. Paradoxically, it was the older pre-Dreadnoughts that proved to be best suited. Their short-barrelled 12-in (305-mm) guns had a low muzzle velocity and, therefore, a more arcing trajectory.

The Admiralty, looking for better leadership, replaced the Admiral with his deputy and ordered a maximum effort for 18 March. A rolling assault was making some progress, despite the attentions of numerous mobile field batteries, when disaster struck. In quick succession, two British and one French pre-Dreadnought hit mines and were lost, while the valuable *Inflexible* barely survived a further encounter. All attempts at minesweeping were again defeated.

Planning was commenced for a further attempt, but it was obvious that without military support ashore it would be fruitless. It would also be impossible to support any fleet that did succeed in breaking through. The way was now open for the beginning of the equally disastrous Gallipoli campaign.

This operation commenced with the yet-largest opposed amphibious landing in history but, in getting bogged-down, it required months of close naval support. The pre-Dreadnought battleship *Goliath* was torpedoed and sunk by a Turkish destroyer whilst engaged in a bombardment detail. Then the first U-boat arrived and quickly disposed of the *Triumph* and *Majestic*. All three had anti-torpedo nets deployed, but from this point the navy had to abandon the centuries-old principle of close blockade and conduct operations from Mudros.

Admiral Fisher, his every action 'circumvented' by the First Lord, Churchill, resigned in May 1915. With the formation of the coalition government that followed, Churchill himself was deposed by his many detractors. Two first-class brains, diminished by their being unable to work in harmony, were replaced by the former Prime Minister, Arthur Balfour, and Admiral Sir Henry Jackson. '[With the] philosopher wedded to the scientist...speed of action waited on cautious conviction...the fiery energy that drove the

Admiralty...suddenly vanished, and was succeeded by a period of sound, but lethargic, administration': not a prescription for the successful prosecution of a life-and-death struggle at sea.

Right: Anchored close inshore to provide fire support for the landings, *Majestic* was torpedoed by *U-21* on 26 May, capsizing in only nine fathoms so her keel was awash. Although she went down in seven minutes, most of her crew were able to escape.

Below: During the bombardment of 18 March, the French battleship *Bouvet* had suffered several hits while suppressing the Messudieh battery, setting fire to her bridge and steering compartment. Following the *Suffren* out of the narrows, she struck a mine which detonated her magazines. Only a handful of the 660 men aboard were rescued.

BOUVET

Von Spee's Odyssey

Tsingtao, the German enclave in China, was base to a small but potent squadron commanded by Vice Admiral Graf von Spee. It comprised the modern armoured cruisers *Scharnhorst* and *Gneisenau*, and three light cruisers. With Japan bound by treaty to support Great Britain, war would make Tsingtao untenable. Von Spee detached the cruiser *Emden* and two armed auxiliaries to work against commerce in the Indian Ocean and off Australia while, with the remaining units, he set out to return to Germany, half a world away.

Slow and erratic progress brought the squadron by the end of October 1914 to the west coast of South America. Between it, the Horn and a clear run home stood a scratch British squadron commanded by Rear Admiral Cradock. Anxious to intercept von Spee, Cradock neither waited for an armoured cruiser that had been despatched to his assistance nor concentrated on the old battleship *Canopus*, whose big guns would have offered a degree of protection. On 1 November the two squadrons clashed off Coronel in Chile. Two large British cruisers were lost with all hands in the Royal Navy's first defeat for over a century. Neither could fight its much-criticised lower-casemated guns in the heavy seas, while the two ponderous 9.2-in (234-mm) guns of Cradock's flagship were ineffective against the sixteen 8.2s (208 mm) of the German armoured cruisers.

While Cradock's ships were inferior, his impetuosity overrode the sound military principle of concentration.

Concentration, however, would probably have meant Cradock's survival and von Spee's declining action. Such a course was out of keeping with the Royal Navy's offensive ethos. Although the outcome was a sharp blow to British prestige, the alternative was unthinkable.

Fisher acted quickly, robbing the Grand Fleet of three battle cruisers, of which two were despatched to the South Atlantic. Further dispositions covered the eventuality of the Germans doubling back into the Pacific, transiting the new Panama Canal or making for South Africa. In the event, von Spee decided to raid the Falklands, probably to complete with coal for the long haul northward. Approaching in clear weather on 8 December he found there Vice Admiral Sturdee with the two battle cruisers and five cruisers.

Von Spee's only hope lay in flight, but his ships had fouled hulls through being so long out of dock. The intention of the armoured cruisers was to distract the British heavy units, leaving the cruisers to scatter and escape. Sturdee, however, had sufficient ships, although nominally slower, to pursue them.

In textbook fashion, the British battle cruisers stayed just beyond their opponents' secondary 150-mm (5.9-in) gun range and, with no shortage of ammunition, slowly pounded them into oblivion. There were few survivors. Of the remainder, only one light cruiser, *Dresden*, escaped to temporary freedom, and one auxiliary to internment.

The Battle of the Falklands showed that, used as intended, the battle cruiser was outstanding, although lack of damage was at the expense of an enormous ammunition cost.

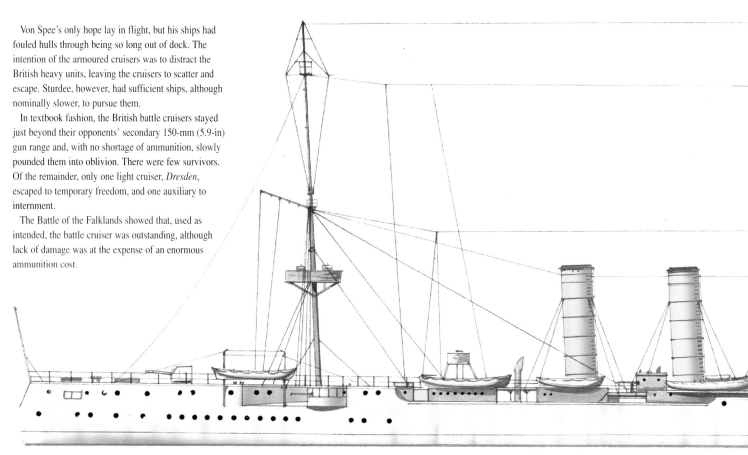

Below: Built by Thames Iron Works as a central battery ironclad for the Turkish navy 1871-3, *Mesudiye* was reconstructed in 1903 but had been partly disarmed and anchored as a guardship off Canakkale in 1914. The British submarine *B11* broke through the Turkish minefields to torpedo her on 13 December 1914.

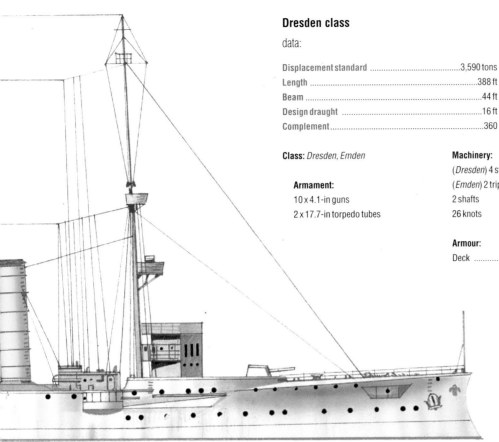

Dresden class

data:

Displacement standard	3,590 tons
Length	388 ft
Beam	44 ft
Design draught	16 ft
Complement	360

Class: *Dresden, Emden*

Armament:
10 x 4.1-in guns
2 x 17.7-in torpedo tubes

Machinery:
(*Dresden*) 4 steam turbines, 10,800 shp,
(*Emden*) 2 triple expansion steam engines, 14,500 ihp
2 shafts
26 knots

Armour:
Deck ....2 in

Left: The light cruiser *Emden* as she appeared on the Pacific station 1909-14. Admiral von Spee detached her to raid into the Indian Ocean, while he led his squadron across the Pacific. *Emden's* raid tied up a large number of British warships until her destruction by HMAS *Sydney* in November.

Below: Nurnberg took part in the German victory at Coronel but was overhauled and sunk by the old armoured cruiser *Kent* at the battle of the Falklands after a chase lasting most of the afternoon. Many of her crew made it into the water but only seven survived the intense cold before they could be rescued.

Above: Glasgow survived the defeat at Coronel to take part in the battle of the Falklands, helping to sink the *Leipzig.*

Dogger Bank

In hope of expediting his attrition of the Royal Navy, Admiral von Ingenohl decided on 'hit and run' raids against the English east coast. Hipper's battle cruisers had the speed to be in and out before the Grand Fleet could react. Public outrage would demand the transfer of a battlecruiser force to prevent such forays and these, it was hoped, could be lured into an ambush by the High Seas Fleet. Fisher claimed to have anticipated such tactics, but his prescience may well have owed much to the activities of the Admiralty's Room 40 which, in possession of many German ciphers, was becoming adept at determining their shifting order of battle and their operational intentions.

At daybreak on 16 December 1914 Hipper duly bombarded Hartlepool and Scarborough as a distraction from a minelaying operation. Laying back, mid-way across the North Sea, much of the High Seas Fleet lay in support. Foreknowledge, however, enabled the British to have Beatty, reinforced by a battle squadron, positioned to cut off Hipper's retreat.

In the pre-dawn darkness, the opposing light forces tangled indecisively, but the skirmish was sufficient to persuade von Ingenohl to turn back. Hipper, ripe for an unsupported interception, escaped due to a sudden sharp deterioration in weather conditions and a woefully ambiguous signal from Beatty's flagship, which caused his light cruisers, already in visual contact with the fleeing Hipper, to turn away.

Justifiably disappointed, the British Admiralty chose to criticise personal performance rather than poor procedures. In practice, however, the former would improve with experience, while the latter needed tightening up. Little appreciating the fact, the popular press predictably raised the cry 'Where was the Navy?'. Germany claimed that the towns were defended and, therefore, legitimate targets. This could not explain the 560 civilians killed or injured. Neither would the episode be the last of its kind.

Another fine opportunity was squandered on 24 January 1915, when Hipper attempted an offensive sweep of the south-eastern Dogger Bank. He was supported by light forces, but one of his battle cruisers had been replaced temporarily by the hybrid cruiser *Blücher*. Again, intelligence allowed the British to make a perfect interception by light forces. As the smoke from Beatty's five battle cruisers came over the horizon, Hipper assumed them to be a battle squadron and turned south-eastward under easy steam. All too soon, the *Blücher*, at the tail of the German line, recognised the truth and Hipper increased to the full 23 knots of which she was then capable. With a four-knot advantage, the

British line slowly overhauled their enemy from the starboard quarter. The day was brilliantly clear. Hipper was far from home and without the support of the High Seas Fleet.

Fire was opened at nearly 20,000 yards, an unheard-of range a bare decade earlier, and it was naturally the British leaders and German tail-enders that bore the brunt. It took 35 minutes for Beatty to close to 17,500 yards, where all his ships were in range. He had the advantage of five ships to four, and signalled 'engage corresponding ships in the enemy line'. This was ambiguous, with individual commanders reckoning from the head and the rear of Hipper's line. The upshot was that the number two, *Moltke*, was not fired on at all. In company with the flagship, *Seydlitz*, she began to punish Beatty's *Lion*.

Nonetheless, the battle was going to the British, with a battered *Blücher* ablaze and obviously slowing, and the *Seydlitz* heavily hit. (A 13.5-in shell had pierced a barbette, causing enormous damage. She was saved only through the flooding of the after magazines.) The *Lion*, however, had been hit in a feed tank. As water contaminated her fuel, her port engines stopped. Progressively she also lost generating power and fell out of line.

Hipper, however, was still in mortal danger when, at 10.54, Beatty 'personally' saw a submarine periscope. Fearing a trap, he ordered his line (now two miles ahead) to turn together eight points to port. This caused the

range to open rapidly and Hipper, leaving the *Blücher* to her fate, saw the chance to escape. Beatty, now well distant, saw the action disintegrating. Having no power for signal lamps, he indicated cryptically by flag hoist that his remaining four ships continue to engage the rear of the enemy line. This was taken literally, the hapless *Blücher* being despatched as Hipper's three battle cruisers disappeared to the south-east. An incandescent Beatty transferred to a destroyer but, by the time that he

closed his squadron, resumption of the pursuit was beyond question.

Hipper had been in error by substituting the makeweight *Blücher* for a first-line unit although, paradoxically, it was to be her gallant sacrifice that permitted his escape. To the British, the outcome was seen almost as a disaster, with more signalling errors compounded by a total lack of initiative on the part of Beatty's second-in-command. A valuable lesson, as yet

unlearned, was the need to contain flash fires consequent upon hits on turrets or their lower structures. The Kaiser despaired further as the British margin of superiority increased yet more. Von Ingenohl was relieved of his command, being replaced by Admiral von Pohl.

Below: Jellicoe's flagship *Iron Duke* leads the starboard line as the 4th and 2nd battle squadrons take part in a sweep a few months after Dogger Bank.

Above: German
sailors moving
ammunition aboard
the battle cruiser
Moltke. Requiring a
higher temperature to
detonate than British
propellant, the relative
stability of their
ammunition saved
several German
warships from
destruction.

Right: By the time of
Jutland, the British
had a squadron of fast
battleships with 15-in
guns, out-matching
anything in the
German fleet.

A BATTLESHIP'S 15-INCH GUNS AT WORK.

Canadian Official

Jutland

The Dogger Bank action was followed by a considerable period in which there were no major fleet engagements to stir the public imagination. In the war's early months the Royal Navy was continually in the news, but the year of 1915 was marked by its absence. Popular opinion did not appreciate that the very lack of activity represented ascendancy over a compliant enemy and that the stress of the maritime war was already moving toward the campaign against commerce.

As the Balfour-Jackson era consolidated, however, the struggle elsewhere was not going well. The then military way of war generated an insatiable demand for manpower, reducing the quality and choice of the naval intake, and slowing ship construction through the drafting of shipyard workers, often skilled. At the same time, rumours abounded of 'super ships' under construction in Germany. With the war on the Western Front atrophying and Zeppelins roaming English skies, the call was renewed: 'Where *was* the Navy?' The public still had expectations of a cataclysmic Nelsonian action that would put the enemy totally out of contention. People required news of victories, not quiet assurance that the situation was being contained. As the nation's efforts were diverted elsewhere, the overall policy had the appearance of going on the defensive.

This was neither accurate nor fair. Within the strictures imposed upon them, the opposing C-in-Cs continued to pursue strategies that they hoped would bring an opposing force to battle on terms unfavourable to it. Both camps fretted under their limitations, manifested in Britain by moves to reinstate Admiral Fisher and, in Germany, by the replacement of the Chief of Naval Staff following a difference of opinion over the conduct of the controversial submarine campaign.

Following the sudden death of von Pohl early in 1916, Admiral Reinhard Scheer succeeded to the command of the High Seas Fleet. He immediately set about gingering-up its operational policy to give it a more offensive edge. In this he had the reluctant support of the Kaiser, who recognised that a more positive approach would improve the morale of both fleet and nation.

An unenterprising sortie in March 1916 was followed on 25 April by a bombardment of Yarmouth and Lowestoft. Again, this was tasked to the battle cruisers, the bulk of the fleet being held to the west of the Texel. Gambling that the Grand Fleet was stationed too distant to interfere, Scheer hoped that smaller British forces would be drawn up from the Nore and the English Channel, and caught between the two German groups.

Tyrwhitt's Harwich Force reacted quickly, encountering the battle cruiser force at first light. Greatly inferior in strength but undeterred by the enemy's 12-in salvoes, the British light cruisers and destroyers used their greater speed to weave, probe and threaten with torpedo attack. Boedicker, deputising for Hipper, was unnerved. Concerned at his proximity to the English coast, and that heavier forces would come to Tyrwhitt's aid, he withdrew at high speed. The Grand Fleet was indeed heading south but, impeded by heavy seas, had no hope of an interception .

Scheer had succeeded in his objective of bringing to action an inferior British force but, on the day, his commander on the spot lacked the resolve to destroy it. There were furious recriminations from Beatty, who maintained that he might well have caught Boedicker but for an inexplicable three-and-a-half hour delay in the Admiralty's ordering him to sail. Public indignation at the raid caused the First Lord to promise Parliament that measures would be taken to guarantee severe punishment to future perpetrators.

This, of course, confirmed to the Germans that their goading strategy was working. To maintain the pressure, Scheer decided on a raid against Sunderland at the end of May. Deliberately closer to British bases, there was a far higher chance of significant response. To cover the Grand Fleet's likely tracks, Scheer despatched fourteen U-boats and further minelaying submarines. Ten Zeppelins were available for reconnaissance.

Prolonged heavy weather delayed the operation and, as the Zeppelins were unable to fly, Scheer changed the operation to a large demonstration along the west coast of the Jutland peninsula. The fleet sailed at maximum strength early on 31 May 1916. Hipper, with his full reconnaissance forces, was some fifty miles ahead of Scheer as they approached the latitude of the Skagerrak. Unsuspected, Beatty's battle cruisers, supported by the fast Queen Elizabeths of the 5th Battle Squadron, were approaching from the west. Some seventy miles astern was Jellicoe with the whole Grand Fleet. They had sailed on the basis of intelligence, untroubled by the submarine trap, which had lost cohesion through being too long at sea.

Again it was Beatty's and Hipper's light forces that made first contact, sighting each other at 14.20, the day well advanced. Hipper's clear duty was to lure the British battle cruisers back onto the advancing Scheer. Beatty, remembering the failure at the Dogger Bank, needed no encouragement. With six heavy units to his opponent's five, and leaving the 5th Battle Squadron behind, he took off after his quarry.

There followed the first phase of the Jutland action, the so-called 'Run to the South', with the two lines exchanging punishing fire at up to 18,500 yards. The first casualty was the British *Indefatigable*, which blew up after absorbing two full successive salvoes. Straining every nerve, the Queen Elizabeths were able to get into the action, opening fire with their 15-in guns from 19,000 yards. Heartened, Beatty pressed in yet more closely, only to lose the *Queen Mary* to a second catastrophic explosion. Under heavy fire from Beatty's four remaining ships and, now, four modern battleships, Hipper still faced disaster.

Below: British destroyers surge ahead of a battle squadron. Both sides launched mass torpedo attacks at Jutland, leading to a whirling melee of torpedo craft.

Below: An unfortunate signalling error led to the British aircraft carrier *Campania* missing the battle of Jutland. Her battle station was on the disengaged side of *Iron Duke*; she was intended both to launch scouting aircraft and to fly a captive observation balloon.

Below: The German battlecruisers' heavy armour and stout construction were severely tested at Jutland. *Von der Tann* survived despite heavy damage and a period during which none of her guns were functioning.

Below: HMS *Queen Mary* blows up at 4.30 pm, 31st May 1916 while under fire from German battle cruisers *Seydlitz* and *Derfflinger*. A shell detonated the forward magazines, separating the hull before the ship vanished in this catastrophic explosion. Two of her crew were captured by the Germans, seven rescued by the British and 1,266 were killed.

Pressure was relieved somewhat by a confused mêlée of light forces between the lines, and then at about 16.30 the situation changed dramatically. The light cruiser *Southampton*, out ahead, suddenly came in sight of the whole High Seas Fleet on a reciprocal course. Hipper had done his job well, delivering Beatty into Scheer's arms.

With the situation suddenly reversed, Beatty turned sixteen points, inexplicably delaying the order to the 5th Battle Squadron, which suffered unnecessary punishment as a result. There began phase two, the 'Run to the North', it now being Beatty's task to entice both Hipper and Scheer onto an as yet unsuspected Grand Fleet, which was observing radio silence. At all costs, Hipper had to be prevented from sighting Jellicoe in time to warn Scheer off.

In deteriorating visibility the German admiral dogged Beatty but, in being drawn away from the High Seas Fleet, took mounting damage. Just after 17.30, Hood's 3rd Battle Cruiser Squadron. probing ahead of Jellicoe's battleships, linked with Beatty, but its intervention met with disaster as its flagship, *Invincible*, blew up on being hit. Hipper's battered force was, nonetheless, headed off to the east, preventing its sighting of the advancing Jellicoe, who came into sight from the *Lion* just before 18.00. The third phase of the battle, the fleet engagement, was now a matter between the opposing C-in-Cs.

Jellicoe had known of Scheer's approach since *Southampton's* sighting at 16.38. The Grand Fleet was in cruising order of six parallel columns, each of four ships. To engage the enemy it would need to adopt a single line formation, deploying on the port or starboard wing column depending upon the bearing of the High Seas Fleet. This last vital piece of data was not yet known to the admiral, with relative and absolute positions of individual ships and groups uncertain.

He took a typically calm decision to deploy on the port wing. It was the last minute and there was no room for error. A formation of this size took nearly twenty minutes to complete such an evolution and, even before its completion at 18.40, individual ships had commenced firing on the head of Scheer's line. In text book style, Jellicoe had crossed the Germans' 'T'.

Below: Known as the 'five minute ships', because that is how long they thought they would last against British dreadnoughts, six pre-dreadnoughts were included in the German fleet, led by *Deutschland* flying the flag of Admiral Mauve.

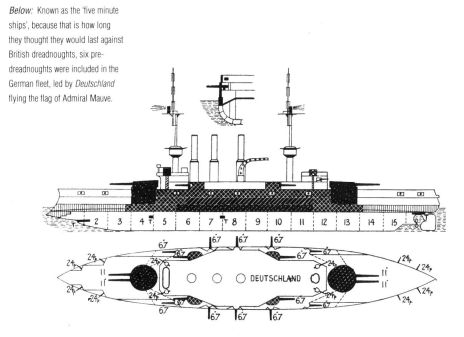

Below: Flying the broad pennant of Commodore Goodenough, *Southampton* pressed perilously close to the battleships of the High Seas Fleet to warn Admiral Jellicoe that the long awaited clash of dreadnoughts was imminent.

Above: This view of the 'R' class destroyer *Satyr* shows how exposed the crews of the lighter craft were, both to enemy fire and to the elements. The 975 ton 'R' class were turbine-powered and had a designed top speed of 36 knots.

Jellicoe's decision had been the correct one and a dismayed Scheer suddenly found his 'T' crossed in classic style. In line ahead, and with few guns bearing, he faced a barrier of gun flashes which arced across his track, almost from horizon to horizon. Of the British ships themselves, there was little sign in the poor visibility.

With the head of his battle line walled by splashes, Scheer reacted instinctively, ordering a 16-point 'battle turnaround'. The British gunners saw the German line turn as one and melt into the haze in reverse order, at 18.45. Jellicoe, suspicious, altered more to the south to get across the enemy's line of retreat. Beatty, believing his task completed, had placed his force ahead of the line in accordance with his battle instructions. Again, however, he was charged with establishing visual contact, and again it was Goodenough's light cruisers that proved equal to the demand.

At about 19.00, with the Grand Fleet echeloned to his port side, Scheer inexplicably ordered a turn, which again found his line with its 'T' crossed. Immediate heavy punishment dictated a second 16-point turn. To cover this potentially hazardous manoeuvre Hipper's sorely tried battle cruisers were ordered to charge the British line. This 'death-ride' was the sort of battle madness on which traditions are founded, and that he survived at all was due to a near-simultaneous lunge by all available torpedo craft. Faced by over a score of running torpedoes, Jellicoe ordered a turn-away, subsequently much criticised because a 'turn towards'

S. M. S. „Seydlitz" nach der Skagerrak-Schlacht
mit schweren Treffern in der Schleuse zu Wilhelmshaven.

would have been as effective. Contact was again lost and, in the fading light, the fleet turned onto a heading which converged slowly with the retreating German line.

Scheer was now bent on disengagement, his course homeward. With half an hour to sunset, Beatty was still in touch, but pleas to his C-in-C to follow him went unanswered. As the sun dipped, the opposing battle cruisers again had a sharp exchange, but the Grand Fleet was not practised in nocturnal engagements and Jellicoe went to night cruising stations with the intention of getting across Scheer's line of retreat, to resume the action at first light on 1 June.

With his opponent having four available routes through the heavily mined bight, Jellicoe had to guess which would be taken. Throughout the night there were vicious little skirmishes as light forces made chance contacts, but the British C-in-C was poorly served by his captains, as vital information went uncommunicated. He, himself, ignored an Admiralty signal at about 23.30, which clearly indicated Scheer's intentions, course and speed. The final phase of Jutland was thus anti-climactic, with Jellicoe surveying an empty sea as day broke.

The battle was over; the Grand Fleet would never get a further chance. With almost the sole exception of the light cruisers, British signalling had been abysmal, with Jellicoe often unaware of important events obvious to a commander on the spot. More individual initiative was urgently required and less rigid adherence to established procedure. Important knowledge gained, however, was that when pressed to the limit the German fleet would

opt for survival rather than a fight to the finish.

British battleships, particularly the Queen Elizabeths, had proved well able to absorb punishment with, for instance, the *Warspite* surviving fifteen heavy-calibre hits. As predicted, battle cruisers were vulnerable when unable to exploit their speed and firepower. In fairness, their survival appeared something of a lottery in being a function of 'where' they were hit rather than the number of times. Each of the three that were sunk had been struck by no more than half a dozen 11- to12-in projectiles whereas, of the survivors, the *Tiger* had received no less than fifteen hits, the *Lion* thirteen and the *Princess Royal* nine.

Of Hipper's battle cruisers, the *Lutzow* was scuttled as she lay foundering from the cumulative effect of 24 hits, many by heavy 13.5- or 15-in shells. *Seydlitz* survived 22 hits and the *Derfflinger* 21. 'Soft' ends proved to be a liability when heavily damaged, causing problems in trim, progressive flooding and, ultimately, stability. British ships scored about 20 percent more heavy-calibre hits than they suffered, yet incurred far heavier material loss and casualties.

In his anxiety to avoid a defeat, Jellicoe lost the chance of a victory. With the war going badly, the British people demanded a Trafalgar, and Jellicoe, despite his obvious competence, was never forgiven for not providing one. Apologists for the disappointing outcome sometimes give the impression that the High Seas Fleet never again contested possession of the North Sea. It sortied, however, on three further occasions, twice in 1916 and

Above: Hit by some 23 heavy shells at Jutland, the German battle cruiser *Seydlitz* limped past British destroyer squadrons during the night. Shipping over 5,000 tons of water, her draught forward reached 46 ft and she was listing eight degrees to port. Steaming astern at 3 knots, she could barely stem the tide off Wilhelmshaven. Repairs took until mid-September.

once in 1918. None resulted in an action, and this low level of activity was insufficient to prevent a slide into a mood of disillusionment and, ultimately, open rebellion. Scheer had pointed out to the Kaiser that, in the absence of a fleet powerful enough to defeat the Royal Navy decisively, the only alternative was an all-out war against commerce. His gloomy assessment was reinforced by the arrival in December 1917 of an American battle squadron to join the Grand Fleet. Future, and ultimately, German success would now depend on the submarine.

War against merchant shipping

While, throughout history, wars have usually been decided by military occupation, nations with maritime dependencies have proved highly vulnerable to blockade and cruiser warfare. Throughout World War I each side sought to strangle the other's trade, to reduce both the will and the ability to pursue hostilities. The opposing fleets adopted very different methods.

Below: The Caledon class light cruiser *Calypso* lays a smokescreen, giving some idea of how quickly visibility deteriorated during a fleet action.

Below: Off Bahia, Brazil, the German gunboat *Eber* arms *Cap Trafalgar*, 1 September 1914. *Eber's* captain had been ordered to take over the liner as a naval auxiliary to attack British merchant shipping. British warships were already searching the south Atlantic for the German cruisers *Dresden* and *Kahlsruhe.*

Above: The German navy began its war on merchant shipping early, sending the *Königin Luise* to lay mines off the Dutch coast. Intercepted by the British cruiser *Amphion* she was sunk on 5 August 1914 within 24 hours of Britain's entry into the war. In a tragic irony, *Amphion* ran on to the German mines and sank – taking 151 of her crew and most of the German prisoners from *Königin Luise* with her.

Below: The wreck of the *Invincible* seen from the battleship *Benbow* at about 7.00 pm on 31 May 1916. Just as *Invincible* inflicted mortal damage on the *Lutzow* she was hit herself and destroyed by a magazine explosion.

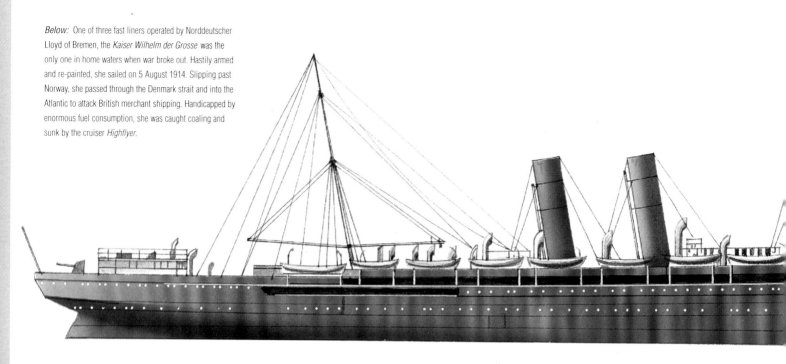

Below: One of three fast liners operated by Norddeutscher Lloyd of Bremen, the *Kaiser Wilhelm der Grosse* was the only one in home waters when war broke out. Hastily armed and re-painted, she sailed on 5 August 1914. Slipping past Norway, she passed through the Denmark strait and into the Atlantic to attack British merchant shipping. Handicapped by enormous fuel consumption, she was caught coaling and sunk by the cruiser *Highflyer*.

SMS Kaiser Wilhelm der Grosse

data:

Displacement standard	24,300 tons	
Length	650 ft	
Beam	66 ft	
Design draught	28 ft	
Complement	584	

Machinery:
2 triple expansion steam engines, 28,000 ihp
2 shafts
22.5 knots

Armament:
2 x 4.1-in guns
2 x 37 mm guns

Right: Only completed in March 1914, *Cap Trafalgar* sailed between Germany and South America and was in Buenos Aires when war was declared. Painted to resemble a Cunard liner, she had the misfortune to meet a real one (*Carmania*) armed as a merchant cruiser. *Cap Trafalgar* lost the ensuing gun duel off Trinidad island.

German surface raiders

Recognising during the 1870s that Britain was too powerful at sea to be defeated in pitched battle, Admiral Aube's *Jeune école* advocated virtual abandonment of the French battle fleet in favour of fast cruisers to ravage the trade routes (as demonstrated successfully during the recent American Civil War) and 'swarms' of torpedo craft to defend home waters and defeat attempts at close blockade. Tirpitz, initially, had supported this strategy, but it was that of the weaker maritime power and was overtaken by the ideas of Mahan, whose power-based arguments had vastly more appeal for the burgeoning new state of Germany. By definition, war against commerce was slow throttling, while the Kaiser planned a rapid decision. Despite his intermittent enthusiasms for submarines, therefore, his Secretary of State kept the submarine force starved of funds to further the visions of a mighty battle fleet. Tirpitz also had the will and the power to destroy any with conflicting ideas.

Modern cruisers existed in numbers sufficient for fleet use but not for pursuing a trade war. The submarine, allied to its natural weapon, the torpedo, had been demonstrating considerable potential in exercises. Plans existed by 1912 for an eventual force of 72 U-boats, but only 28 were operational in August 1914. Even their inclusion in fleet exercises had been on an almost surreptitious basis, to avoid the all-seeing eye in the Navy Office. Admiral von Pohl, later C in C of the High Seas Fleet, was an enthusiastic supporter of submarine warfare but initially, a major consideration was the fear of violating international law.

The few cruisers that the Germans did deploy against

SMS Cap Trafalgar

data:

Displacement standard	23,640 tons
Length	610 ft
Beam	72 ft
Design draught	27 ft
Complement	319

Armament:
2 x 4.1-in guns
4 x 37-mm guns

Machinery:
2 triple expansion steam engines
2 shafts
18 knots

the trade routes caused disruption out of all proportion to the successes that they achieved. It was British policy to convoy only important shipping such as troop movements, using smaller and older cruisers to patrol main shipping tracks, particularly in the vicinity of focal points. Ships thus travelled much as in peace time and, while they were thus easy prey to any sudden foray, any such attack immediately triggered a concentrated hunt for the raider. Far from dockyard resources, unable to replenish ammunition, and dependent upon captures for fuel supplies, the raider usually enjoyed a short

existence. Considerable reliance had to be placed on supply ships for replenishment but the British quickly learned to remove these from circulation at an early opportunity.

The first raider was the armed 24,300-ton liner *Kaiser Wilhelm der Grosse*, whose theoretical speed of 22½ knots made her immune to interception. Her commander operated with a punctilious regard for international law, allowing two passenger liners to proceed unharmed. His 'bag' was just two merchantmen when his ship's great thirst for bunkers drove her to a rendezvous with colliers

in the territorial waters of a remote Spanish enclave in West Africa. Here she was discovered and destroyed by a British cruiser. Totally unsuitable for the task, her career had lasted three weeks.

Regular cruisers fared rather better. As noted earlier, the *Emden* had been detached by von Spee to work against commerce in the Indian Ocean. Sweeping first along the Ceylon-Calcutta track, then Ceylon-Aden, Captain von Müller netted 21 prizes before eluding the inevitable hunting groups by heading eastward to Penang. Here, in an audacious raid, he surprised and

destroyed a small Russian cruiser and a French destroyer. His progress suggested, however, that he might be tempted to destroy the strategically important cable station on the Cocos Keeling Islands. The assumption was correct. Early in November 1914 von Müller's men were actually engaged in cutting the cables when their ship was caught offshore by the Australian cruiser *Sydney*. The German's 105-mm (4.1-in) guns proved no match for *Sydney*'s 6-in (150-mm) guns and, fought to the end, the *Emden* was run on the reef at North Keeling to prevent her foundering.

A similar record of 68,000 grt sunk was achieved by the *Karlsrühe*. Shipping out of the Caribbean in August 1914, she operated in the focal area north-east of Brazil. Like the *Emden*, she caused disproportionate disruption until November 1914, when she was destroyed at sea by an internal explosion.

The older *Königsberg* took an early prize off the Arabian coast and then went to ground until 20 September 1914, when she suddenly appeared off Zanzibar, surprising and destroying the 2,200 ton protected cruiser *Pegasus*. To the concern of those responsible for running the large Indian troop convoys, the *Königsberg* again disappeared. Plagued with mechanical problems, she had retired into the delta of the Rufiji river. In this silt-choked, jungle-clad wilderness she was beyond the reach of the deeper-draught British cruisers that finally located her. Blockaded for months, she was despatched by shallow-draught monitors brought especially from Great Britain. As at the Dardanelles,

Above: The Cunard liner *Carmania* was armed, painted grey and sent to join Admiral Craddock's North Atlantic command in August 1914.

HMS Carmania

data:

Displacement standard	19,524 tons
Length	650 ft
Beam	72 ft
Design draught	28 ft
Complement	not known

Armament:
8 x 4.7-in guns

Machinery:
3 steam turbines, 21,000 shp
3 shafts
18 knots

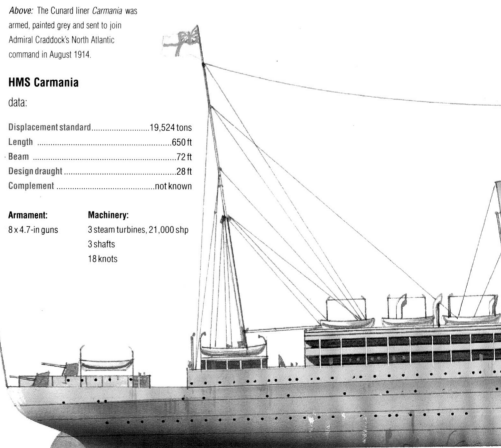

Above: The AMC *Calgarian* served with the 10th cruiser squadron, enforcing the British blockade of Germany by patrolling the northern entrance to the North Sea.

Below: *Carmania* served as an AMC for another two years after sinking the *Cap Trafalgar* but returned to commercial service in 1917.

aircraft proved very useful in spotting for indirect shooting.

These three valuable light cruisers, together with their crews, had been expended in exchange for under 150,000 grt of Allied shipping. Their main contribution had been in disruption and the tying-down of many other warships in largely futile hunting.

Following the disastrous choice of the *Kaiser Wilhelm der Grosse*, the Germans enjoyed better fortune with smaller mercantile conversions that could cruise economically and adopt innocent-looking disguise. Typical of the first-wave were the *Kronprinz Wilhelm* and the *Prinz Eitel Friedrich*. Both given a light armament on foreign stations at the outbreak of war, they were able to cruise for about eight months, accounting for 26 prizes. Both careers ended in internment, enforced by increasing mechanical problems.

A further batch of raiders was sailed late in 1915. Small ships, of non-distinctive appearance, they were converted and armed in home yards. Most successful was the *Möwe* which, despite her modest 4,800 tons, carried four 150-mm (5.9-in) and one smaller gun, and a pair of torpedo tubes. Her innocent appearance allowed her to lay a minefield in the Pentland Firth, hard by the Grand Fleet base at Scapa Flow. This accounted for the pre-Dreadnought battleship *King Edward VII* and a couple of merchantmen. Depositing the remainder of her mines off French Atlantic ports she then embarked on a cruise which netted fourteen prizes, totalling nearly 50,000 grt. She returned safely after about nine weeks at sea, during which she had accomplished more than expensive regular warship raiders.

Two other small conversions, *Greif* and *Wolf*, fared less well, although the former exposed the vulnerability of British Armed Merchant Cruisers (AMC) in sinking the *Alcantara* before herself foundering from damage received. A later *Wolf* undertook the war's longest cruise, nearly 15 months, between November 1916 and February 1918. She disposed directly of about 38,000 tons of shipping, laying mines that accounted for a further 76,000 tons. She was the first to carry a small seaplane with which to extend her horizon.

SMS Möwe

data:

Displacement standard	9,800 tons
Length	406 ft
Beam	47 ft
Design draught	24 ft
Complement	235

Armament:
4 x 5.9-in guns
1 x 4.1-in gun
2 x 19.7-in torpedo tubes
500 mines

Machinery:
1 triple expansion steam engine, 3,200 hp
1 shaft
13 knots

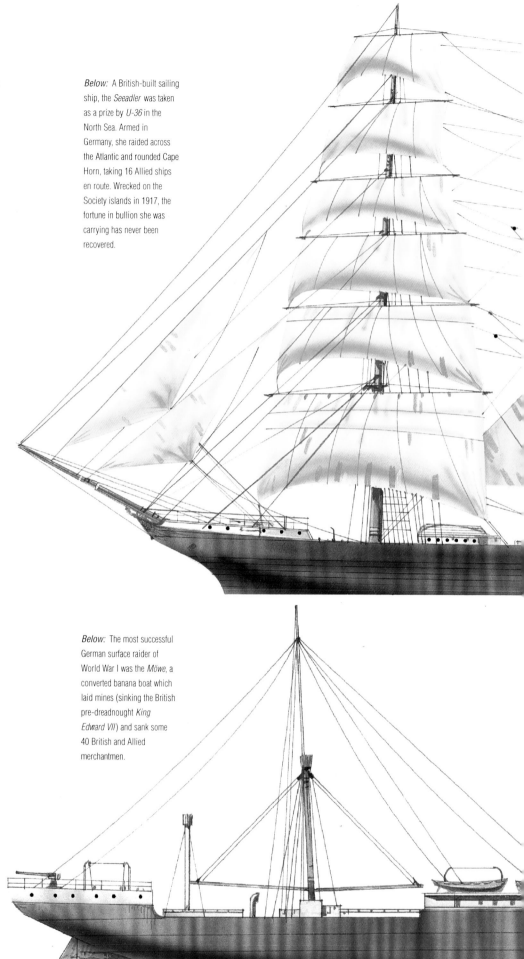

Below: A British-built sailing ship, the *Seeadler* was taken as a prize by *U-36* in the North Sea. Armed in Germany, she raided across the Atlantic and rounded Cape Horn, taking 16 Allied ships en route. Wrecked on the Society islands in 1917, the fortune in bullion she was carrying has never been recovered.

Below: The most successful German surface raider of World War I was the *Möwe*, a converted banana boat which laid mines (sinking the British pre-dreadnought *King Edward VII*) and sank some 40 British and Allied merchantmen.

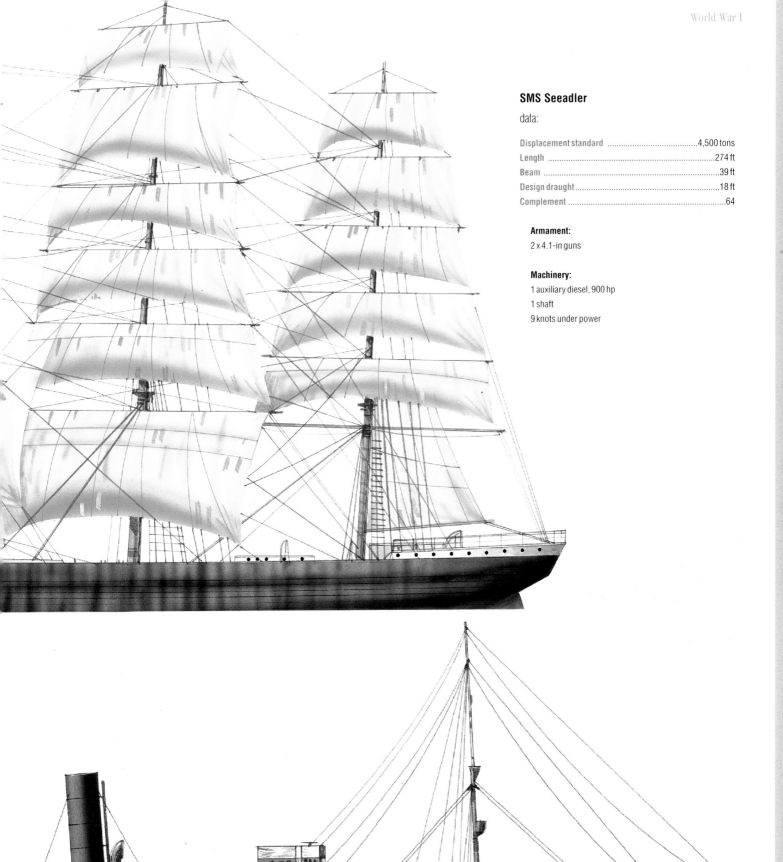

SMS Seeadler

data:

Displacement standard	4,500 tons
Length	274 ft
Beam	39 ft
Design draught	18 ft
Complement	64

Armament:
2 x 4.1-in guns

Machinery:
1 auxiliary diesel, 900 hp
1 shaft
9 knots under power

The U-Boat campaigns 1914–18

While surface raiders continued to cause disruption and apprehension, their achievements were small when compared with the destruction caused by submarines. Pre-war studies had examined commerce warfare employing submarines, but there were no formal plans, while the opposition of Tirpitz resulted in only two dozen deep-sea U-boats being available in August 1914. Aggressive application of mercantile blockade by the British, and their offensive mining of the southern North Sea provided a legal excuse for retaliation by submarine warfare along the British coasts.

Despite exercises having shown the staying power of submarines, and their ability to successfully attack defended anchorages, it came as a profound shock to the British to lose the three Bacchantes (*Hogue*, *Aboukir* and *Cressy*) in September 1914, followed by the cruisers *Hawke* and *Hermes* the following month. On New Year's Day 1915 the pre-Dreadnought *Formidable* was sunk off Portland. The impression created by the enormous loss of life (about 2,200 in these sinkings alone) was matched only by the apparent impunity with which the submarines carried out their attacks.

While the British viewed such warship sinkings as cowardly and underhand, their legality was never disputed in international law. Unarmed merchantmen were a different matter. Under accepted 'prize rules', a warship, before destroying a capture, had to check its particulars, allow adequate time and make provision for the abandonment and survival of crew and passengers. Even for a surface raider this was time-consuming (and merchantmen were beginning to carry wireless apparatus, which could compromise its position), but for a submarine it courted disaster. A submarine's defence was its invisibility, which had to

be abandoned if prize rules were to be observed. Submarines carried no weapons for graded response, being designed only to destroy. They carried no spare personnel for prize crews, nor space and provisions for accommodating survivors. A submarine's options were stark: either ignore a target or endeavour to sink it.

Operating at the outset within the rules, U-boats accounted for only ten ships of 20,000 grt in six months.

Within the naval establishment there emerged a powerful lobby pressing for operations without restriction. The British actually assisted their cause through an extensive programme for defensively arming merchantmen and a widespread chartering of neutral vessels. A final impetus was in Admiral von Pohl's appointment as C in C following the Dogger Bank action of January 1915. He convinced first the Chancellor, then the Kaiser, that

UB 1 class

data:

Displacement surfaced	127 tons
Displacement submerged	142 tons
Length	92 ft
Beam	10 ft
Design draught	9 ft
Complement	14

Class: *UB-1 to UB-8*

Armament:
2 x 17.7-in torpedo tubes
(four torpedoes)
1 machine gun

Below: Breaking through the channel became increasingly hazardous for U-Boats as the Dover Patrol was strengthened. *U-8* became entangled in anti-submarine nets in March 1915 and British destroyers detonated explosive sweeps, bringing the submarine to the surface stern first and at almost a vertical angle. Her crew surrendered and were rescued.

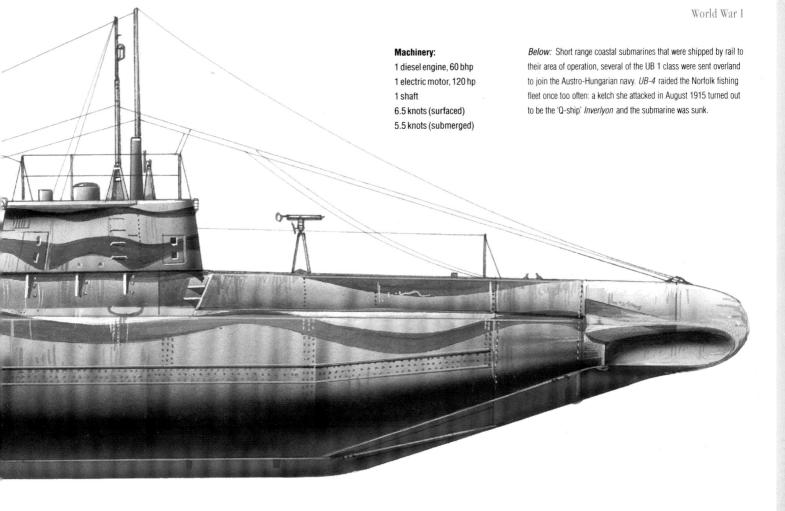

Machinery:
1 diesel engine, 60 bhp
1 electric motor, 120 hp
1 shaft
6.5 knots (surfaced)
5.5 knots (submerged)

Below: Short range coastal submarines that were shipped by rail to their area of operation, several of the UB 1 class were sent overland to join the Austro-Hungarian navy. *UB-4* raided the Norfolk fishing fleet once too often: a ketch she attacked in August 1915 turned out to be the 'Q-ship' *Inverlyon* and the submarine was sunk.

restraint was counter-productive. On 4 February 1915, therefore, the Germans declared the waters surrounding the British Isles a war zone. From the 18 February 'every merchant ship met with in this War Zone will be destroyed'. The concomitant danger to life and neutral tonnage was emphasised.

The neutral United States protested formally that, without declaring a blockade, the German action was

illegal. They also remonstrated with Great Britain over the use of neutral flagging, a legitimate ruse de guerre.

U-boat commanders were instructed that the safety of their boats was paramount. Surfacing was not advised, even if the suspected target appeared to be neutral: 'Its destruction will therefore be justifiable unless other attendant circumstances indicate its neutrality'. To pursue this, often shallow-water, campaign the building of the

small 127/142-ton UB type was commenced. These were joined by the slightly larger UC minelayers. The UBs' two 450-mm (17.7-in) torpedo tubes were not particularly effective against larger ships and, although both classes operated efficiently, their loss rates were comparatively high as A/S (anti-submarine) defences were more effective in littoral waters.

Their task was considerable. British-flagged ships

Below: The U-151 class were designed as submarine cargo boats to import strategic materials from the neutral USA. Able to carry some 350 tons of cargo, the *Deutschland* made a highly publicised voyage but the second boat *Bremen* disappeared. After the USA declared war, these large submarines were armed and sent on long range missions to the central Atlantic.

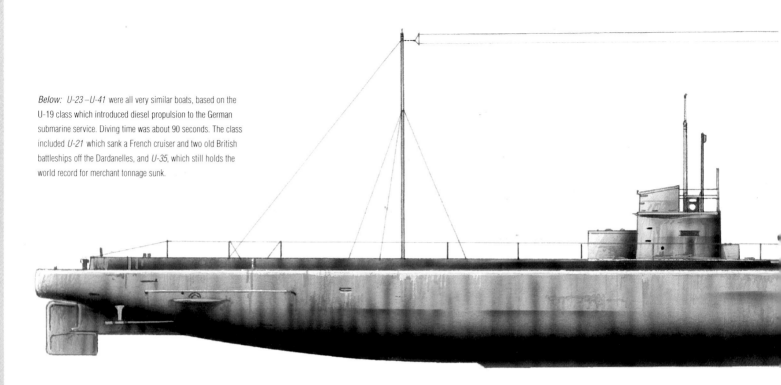

Below: U-23–U-41 were all very similar boats, based on the U-19 class which introduced diesel propulsion to the German submarine service. Diving time was about 90 seconds. The class included *U-21* which sank a French cruiser and two old British battleships off the Dardanelles, and *U-35*, which still holds the world record for merchant tonnage sunk.

alone amounted to a total of 4,068 of 17,517,000 grt at the outbreak of war. To offset losses, the annual capacity of British shipyards was 200 new ships, of nearly one million tons. Statistically, and ignoring the use of neutral tonnage, Britain could afford to lose 80,000 grt monthly without a reduction in capacity. The scale of such losses in human terms was, however, horrifying.

Starting from scratch, countermeasures were fairly basic. Across the much-used Dover Strait was installed a net barrier. Sown with explosive charges and tightly patrolled by auxiliary craft, some with powerful lights, the barrier was a considerable obstacle to small, low-powered submarines. Deep minefields were also laid, innocuous to surface craft but deadly to submerged submarines. Trawlers towed explosive sweeps and even, on occasion a small submarine (usually a C-boat), to which it was linked by telephone and which could be slipped to deliver a counter attack.

Then there were the controversial 'Q-ships'. Stemming from the concept of arming patrol trawlers with concealed guns, selected merchantmen were converted, from the end of 1914, to carry an elaborately disguised armament. Proceeding independently, they offered an attractive target for destruction by a submarine's guns. Once accosted, they feigned abandonment, inducing the U-boat to surface to save a torpedo. Hidden gun crews, on what was often a burning and sinking ship, patiently awaited the chance to drop their screens and fire on their attacker. Although the activities of Q-ships have been much romanticised, they accounted for several submarines at a time when other countermeasures had little success.

Scientific detection of submarines, using underwater microphones, or 'hydrophones', began with the outbreak of war. It showed promise but, as a brand-new technology, required a huge amount of effort before it could be made practical. The converse was also true for, by remaining silent, a hydrophone-equipped submarine could detect potential targets at considerable ranges.

Left: British sailors aboard the German coastal minelayer *UC-5*, captured in April 1916 and exhibited in London. The UC 1 types were 14-man, 168 ton boats equipped with six mine tubes.

Right: U-35 and U-41 rendezvous in the Mediterranean where the *U-35* sank a total of 224 merchant ships during World War I, a grand total of over half a million tons of shipping that has never been exceeded since.

With the commencement of unrestricted warfare, losses to submarine attack quickly escalated. Within six weeks came the first incident involving large-scale loss of life, when 104 died in the *Falaba*. A new era of frightfulness had, however, obviously dawned when, on 7th May 1915, the White Star liner *Lusitania* was sunk without warning in broad daylight. As 128 of the 1,200 fatalities were American, the incident attracted powerful

diplomatic protest. A German undertaking not thereafter to attack large passenger liners was soon broken when in August the same company's *Arabic* was destroyed. Again, American casualties were involved, and the ensuing diplomatic storm resulted, on 30 August, in the Germans abandoning unrestricted attacks and the partial withdrawal of U-boats. It also resulted in the replacement of the German Chief of Naval Staff.

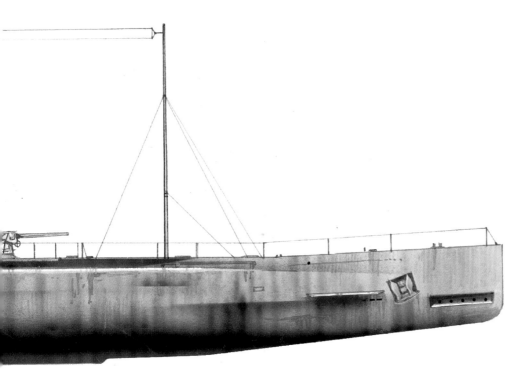

U-23 class

data:

Displacement surfaced	669 tons
Displacement dived	864 tons
Length	212 ft
Beam	21 ft
Design draught	11 ft
Complement	35

Class: *U-23 - U26*

Armament:
4 x 19.7-in torpedo tubes
(2 bow, 2 stern)
6 torpedoes
1 x 88-mm gun

Machinery:
2 diesel engines, 1,700 bhp
2 electric motors, 1,200 hp
15 knots surfaced
9 knots dived

This was all a relief to the British, whose monthly loss, exceeding 80,000 grt in both May and June 1915, had risen to an alarming 148,000 grt in August. Although shipyards were keeping pace with the average rate of loss, shortages were still apparent because of the huge volume of tonnage used by the government in direct support of the fighting services.

Until September 1916, the Germans observed restrictions, except in the Mediterranean where American interests and citizens were rare. The new Chief of Naval Staff, von Holtzendorff, was fretting at the enormous effect on the German war effort of the hobbling of the U-boat force. He was advised that little further effort would be required to commence a haemorrhage of British tonnage, whose losses, even in the 'quiet' year of 1915, were averaging 70,000 grt monthly. Windfalls of sequestered tonnage were a one-off, and a wasting asset. Shipyard production was falling off as workers were drafted to assuage the limitless demands of the military.

Following irreconcilable differences with the Kaiser, Tirpitz resigned in March 1916. His successor, Vice Admiral Capelle, and Admiral Scheer, who had recently taken command of the High Seas Fleet, were both greatly in favour of resuming a robust submarine campaign. Barring passenger ships, all vessels, armed or not, would be liable to be sunk if inside the declared war zone. With the U-boat strength at 52 boats, and 38 building, it was calculated that the British would sustain losses at a level that would enforce them to sue for peace terms within six months.

Opening on 4 March 1916, the new offensive again quickly caused a clash with the United States when the French cross-channeler *Sussex* was torpedoed off Dieppe. Dismissing claims that the U-boat commander thought that she was a troopship, the Americans threatened to break off diplomatic relations. Again the Germans backed down, and British losses, totalling a worrying 140,000 grt in April, declined sharply.

Anti-submarine escorts now deployed a practical depth charge but, yet lacking any means of detecting and tracking submerged submarines, the combination was still ineffective. There was, however, a steady trickle of U-boat losses, mostly to mines, explosive nets and stranding. Limited submerged endurance caused many to be surprised on the surface, destroyed by gunfire or ramming. Defensive arming of merchantmen was a powerful deterrent as, even without restrictions, submarine commanders preferred to economise on their few torpedoes by attacking with a deck gun.

Priority given to U-boat construction increased the number in service to 119 by October 1916, which figure remained fairly constant, despite losses. Much larger areas could thus be patrolled and, combined with virtually unrestricted operations in the Mediterranean, British losses again climbed, averaging over 150,000 grt for each of the last four months of that year. The Royal Navy was now devoting immense resources to the task, but escorts were simply not finding and sinking U-boats. Repercussions at the Admiralty saw Jackson step down as First Sea Lord. He was replaced in December 1916 by Admiral Jellicoe, who viewed it as a demotion. Beatty took over as C in C, Grand Fleet.

One of Jellicoe's first actions was to form an Anti-Submarine Division at the Admiralty. Its brief was to examine, recommend and coordinate measures to meet the U-boat threat. For their part, the Germans once again pondered the unleashing of unrestricted submarine warfare. The case for this was set out in the lengthy Holtzendorff Memorandum, circulated widely as Jellicoe took office. It argued that observing the prize rules prevented submarines from destroying sufficient shipping to effect a quick decision to the war. A total effort would probably cause the United States to be drawn in but, it was argued, this would be of little consequence as long as the same U-boats prevented their shipping supplies and manpower to Europe. The paper

reflected Germany's desire to finish the war in Autumn 1917 in order to reach the peace table in a strength sufficient to guarantee the fulfilment of her war aims.

Early in 1917 Germany's political leaders committed themselves to the gamble. Scarce labour and materials were given over to submarine construction, now of higher priority than even capital ships. Logic demanded that the latter could not be completed, nor would be required, in the six to nine months that it would take Holtzendorff's proposals to work. It was already an irony that, following the huge investment in battle fleets, the war would effectively be decided by the struggle between submarine and merchantmen.

On 1 February 1917 restrictions on U-boat operations were again lifted. Two days later President Wilson, his patience exhausted, severed diplomatic relations. Between February and April, over two million tons of shipping were sent to the bottom, more than half of it British. As the memorandum had predicted, neutral-flag shipping was increasingly intimidated into remaining in port and a crisis in tonnage quickly developed. On 6 April the United States declared war on Germany.

British methods of tightly patrolling shipping routes and instituting A/S patrols were ineffective, due to the enormous areas involved and a lack of means of detecting submerged U-boats. Defining the problem helped. As ships needed to be made available at a higher rate than they were being sunk, skilled labour for their construction was released from its obligation for military service, and a programme for simplified, standard designs instituted. Home food production was increased to relieve the pressure on shipping, while the latter acquired a Controllerate to optimise its effective employment. Over two million tons were involved in military support: as some had to be released, it may be said that the U-boat had an effect on military campaigns. Sinkings, however, still far outstripped acquisitions, and by the late spring the Allies faced a crisis.

Below: One of the German passenger liners converted to raiders, *Berlin* laid 200 mines off Lough Swilly before fleeing to Norway and internment in November 1914. Not until after the war did the German navy learn that these mines had sunk the new dreadnought battleship *Audacious* in October 1914.

For a while the Admiralty seemed minded to commit itself to a huge new escort construction programme, but it was obvious that a quicker solution was required. Over centuries, experience had showed that a system of escorted convoys reduced losses, and there had been numerous proposals for its re-introduction. Dissent ruled, however. Extra time for re-routing and assembly of convoys would exacerbate the shipping shortage. The speed of the slowest would be the speed for all, producing more delay. Arrival of a convoy would cause massive port congestion. Merchant captains were not skilled in close-formation manoeuvring. There were insufficient escorts to institute a network of convoy routes: and so on. Many in the Royal Navy itself felt that the convoy concept was 'defensive', and at variance with the offensive ethos inculcated into all levels of the Service.

Convoys were, in fact, already running to Scandinavia and to the Netherlands, to safeguard and to re-assure neutrals. Convoys ran to France to cover the continuous shipments of coal upon which French industry depended. The notion persisted, however, that these were 'special cases' and that Atlantic convoys would serve only to present U-boats with bigger targets.

Nonetheless, it was decided that convoying would be given a trial – once the question of escorts was settled. It was believed that ocean escort could be provided by two larger warships but, once in the more dangerous littoral zone, a convoy should be covered by destroyers on a scale of one to one. The Americans were asked to make good the shortfall in destroyers. Not only could they not (although 36 were eventually assigned to the duty), but they were dismayed to discover, for the first time, that Great Britain was actually threatened with defeat.

Above: The British H class submarines were built in Canada and the USA and made their way across the Atlantic, the second ten being held up until the US declaration of war in 1917. Single-hulled 364 ton boats, they had a crew of 22 and carried six 18-in torpedoes.

The then Prime Minister, Lloyd George, subsequently claimed credit for forcing convoying on a reluctant Admiralty with a virtual ultimatum of 'act or go'. This was hotly disputed, but it is apparent that his direct involvement expedited matters.

A convoy committee was formed to coordinate movements with known intelligence on enemy dispositions and intentions. Late in May 1917, a first 12-ship convoy arrived safely from the United States, having cost only one ship, a straggler. A 16-ship convoy from Gibraltar arrived without incident. Earlier fears proved to be largely unfounded.

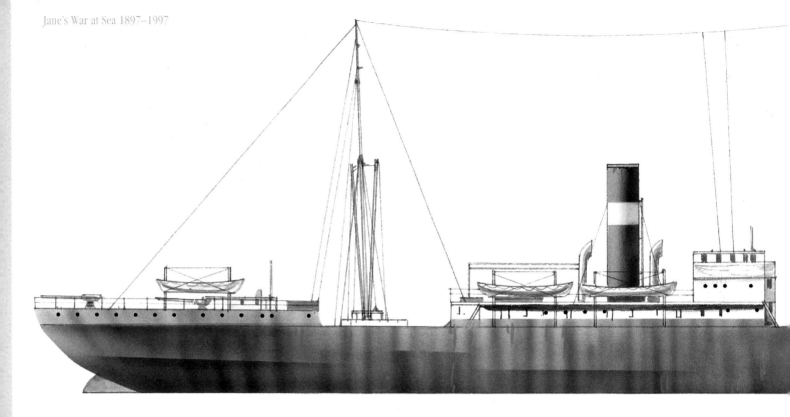

Convoys grew rapidly in both size and frequency as the network was extended. Destroyer escort was indeed under strength but this was more than offset by the extra difficulties experienced by U-boat commanders. Prevented from using their chosen weapon, the deck gun, they were given a maximum of one shooting chance by torpedo. Their slow submerged speed militated against achieving an ideal firing angle, while the greater expenditure of torpedoes reduced patrol periods. With more time thus spent in transit, this reduced the number of boats on station at any time.

The crash programme was seeing the entry into service of the first of what would be 111 Flower-class sloops, 24 Racehorse-class sloops, 75 P-boats (600-ton corvettes) and 40 Kil-class patrol gunboats. The Kils and the Racehorses were given a symmetrical, 'double-ended' profile to make difficult the estimation of their course. The 1,250-ton Flowers were designed with a deliberate mercantile appearance, as were some of the P-boats, which acted as Q-ships.

A further innovation, which deserves more recognition than it gets, was the introduction of the first anti-submarine submarines. The Royal Navy's R-class boats had a very clean profile for the day. They were small and agile, with a 15-knot submerged speed and a six-tube torpedo battery forward. They were ahead of their time, however, in that sensors were, as yet, inadequate. They also appeared too late in the war to be properly evaluated in service.

Hydrophones and 300-lb (136-kg) depth charges were now in general use, but noise interference rendered the

Below: Hired paddle steamers proved successful as minesweepers so the Royal Navy ordered some 26 purpose-built vessels of the Ascot class in 1916. They proved good sea boats, if prone to lose speed in a sea way as the paddle boxes became choked with water. Several were lost on mines and *Ascot* herself was torpedoed by *UB-67* on 10 November 1918, the last full day of the war.

Left: German U-boats often surfaced to sink merchantmen with their guns, conserving their torpedoes whenever they could. The British countered with 'Q-ships': merchant vessels manned by naval crews and fitted with hidden guns. In August 1915 *Baralong* sank *U-27* and a German boarding party found aboard the *Nicosian* was summarily executed in revenge for the *Lusitania.*

U-142s, whose size far exceeded that of even the big American boats used in the Pacific campaign of World War II. Their theoretical endurance exceeded three months, and their armament emphasised the gun rather than the torpedo.

Although convoying drastically reduced losses, it did not magically eliminate them, the U-boat commanders ever probing to discover weaknesses. One such was the vulnerability of 'independents' sailing to or from convoy assembly and dispersal points. Sinkings fell, however, from 881,000 grt in the horrific month of April 1917 to 512,000 in August. By the year's end it was down to 399,000 grt.

Seeing his main chance faltering, Scheer formed the U-boat Office to coordinate operations and building programmes. Huge new orders were placed, but the hour had passed and they would never be completed.

During most months between March 1918 and the armistice in November, the British acquired more mercantile tonnage than they lost, and the battle was won. The scale of the sacrifice remains shocking, with 1,764 ocean-going ships, totalling some 7.3 million grt, going to the bottom. Offset by a considerable amount of new building, the final overall tonnage of 14.4 million represented a decrease of about 3.1 million grt.

Counting small craft, submarines had accounted for a staggering 6,386 vessels of over 11.9 million grt. Of warships, they had sunk ten battleships, thirteen assorted cruisers and 21 destroyers, a total far in excess of that for the battle fleet. In exchange, improving A/S measures imposed a toll of 178 U-boats.

former ineffective for anything but zero speed or a flat calm. Surprisingly, by the end of 1917, A/S ships were already towing hydrophones in streamlined bodies to reduce the noise problem. By using matched hydrophones, and comparing relative signal strengths, a degree of directionality was possible. Before the war's end, it had been demonstrated that sound pulses could be used to produce an echo from a submerged submarine. A further innovation, which would also be developed in the future, was the A/S bomb thrower. Capable of hefting a 200-lb (91-kg) projectile out to 1,100 yards (1005 m) it, for the moment, out-stripped a ship's powers of detection.

To meet the extra problems posed by attacking convoys, U-boats were increased in size as well as in numbers. The U-117 type were of 1164/1512 tons, and capable of carrying 48 mines as far as the eastern seaboard of the United States. Of 1512/1875 tons, the larger U-151s were designed to be used also as cargo carriers. Both types were eclipsed by the 2158/2785

Below: A British destroyer is torpedoed by a submarine in the Mediterranean. Destroyers attacked submarines with primitive depth charges and explosive sweeps, but had no effective means of tracking a submerged U-boat.

Left: A boarding party from the Arethusa class light cruiser *Undaunted* aboard a German merchant ship captured in the North Sea. The blockade of Germany caused severe shortages of military equipment and brought the German civilian population to the brink of starvation.

The British blockade

Since the British had successfully exercised blockade during the French Revolutionary and Napoleonic Wars it had become increasingly regulated by international law. To differentiate it from common privateering, an 'effective blockade' needed to be declared. Definitions of 'neutral' and the Right to Capture Private Property at Sea loomed large. The Declaration of Paris, which went far to clarify matters, had never been signed by the United States. In 1909, the Declaration of London made a further attempt, but became too complicated for the participating nations to ratify.

As early as 1906 the Committee of Imperial Defence (CID) had been working on the means by which economic warfare could be imposed on Germany. By August 1914 the plans for blockade were mature, emphasising 'commerce prevention', i.e. the shutting down of trade, rather than 'commerce destruction', as preferred by the enemy. An anticipated bonus was that a relentless squeeze on trade would force the Germans to seek a decisive fleet action.

Goods being transported by sea in wartime were divided by the London Declaration into three categories: Absolute Contraband comprised materials of purely military use; Conditional Contraband covered those items suitable for both military and non-military purposes; Free List items were such as multi-purpose raw materials. By law, the first category could be seized, but the second category only if it could be proved to be destined for a military or government end-user. The third category should be immune from seizure. Unfortunately, goods could rarely be categorised in exact terms, while

the Declaration defining them was, itself, not ratified.

The British proclaimed a State of Blockade from the outset of hostilities. Within weeks, a further Order-in-Council tightened it by removing certain items from the Free List. This procedure went further, giving the Germans some moral and legal justification for their unrestricted submarine campaign. They argued that foodstuffs were for public consumption but, as they could never prove that none would go for military needs, the British increasingly impounded them. The Germans objected to war by starvation being waged on the populace.

Britain's geographical situation was key to successful blockade. By extensive mining in the Dover Strait, shipping was impelled to follow specific tracks. The Northern Patrol was a different matter, with a requirement particularly to police the 250-mile Scotland-Norway gap.

German-flag shipping disappeared quickly, subjected to inactivity in home ports, internment abroad or seizure. Early attempts to run the blockade furnished Britain with a useful 612,000 grt, in prizes, while the subsequent idleness of their residual shipping robbed the Germans of 'invisible' income.

Enforcement of the blockade demanded a degree of circumspection when dealing with neutral ships, whose cargoes could be for innocent home consumption or, covered by falsified paperwork, for onward shipment to belligerents. As the blockade tightened its grip, the benefit of the doubt was never given, cargoes being impounded until such times as an overloaded Admiralty Court decided between confiscation or enforced purchase. Although neutrals were hugely inconvenienced by the system, they also made enormous profits

freighting for the warring parties. Genuine neutrals, with neutral cargoes, could always follow inshore routes prescribed by the Germans, but here they were liable to be overtly attacked by the British.

As the ground war degenerated to apparent stalemate, Germany put military needs before those of her populace, who began to suffer shortages. Harvests, experiencing already a period of below-average yields, diminished further for want of bulk fertilisers.

In 1916 Britain turned the screw further with the formation of a Ministry of Blockade. Fodder was targeted, so that shortage of grain was matched by that of meat and dairy products, making rationing essential.

Operations in the English Channel were tedious and repetitive but, with a powerful naval presence exercised by the nearby Dover Force, they could be enforced by auxiliary craft. The Northern Patrol was a different matter, maintained in savage weather, biting cold and prolonged darkness. Larger ships were required here; ships able to defend themselves without support against armed raiders or warships. In addition there was the ever-present threat of a submarine torpedo.

Although reinforced from time to time by other units, it was the 10th Cruiser Squadron that bore the brunt of this patrol. It comprised initially eight obsolete cruisers of the Crescent and Edgar classes. As Scapa was too distant, their operation came to be based primarily on Lerwick in the Shetlands and the Orkney port of Kirkwall.

The cruisers proved poorly suited to the task of boarding and searching. They had little spare accommodation for the extra personnel necessary to form armed guards or prize crews. Mechanically, they were not fitted for weeks of low-speed patrols in often adverse conditions. They were wet and uncomfortable, inevitably reducing the efficiency of those aboard.

Within weeks, therefore, arrived the first of what proved an effective substitute, the Armed Merchant Cruiser (AMC). Medium-sized passenger liners, these were everything that the regular cruisers were not, offering a comparatively high degree of comfort and endurance. By November 1914, two dozen AMCs had taken the place of the regular cruisers. They were supported by smaller Armed Boarding Steamers. Actual boarding in northern seas could be a hazardous operation and most crews were selected Newfoundland fishermen, all superlative seamen.

The number of ships intercepted was very much a function of the weather. In the long, calm days of summer it might be at a rate of seventy per week, dropping perhaps to thirty in the black, howling gales of

winter. About one in three or four was sent in for examination. In terms of tonnage, the total was immense and, despite the obvious inference that more got through in the winter, the cumulative effect on the German war effort was soon damaging. Unfortunately, the work attracted no glory and no headlines; though contributing significantly to the war's final outcome, it went little-recognised by the British people.

Aircraft at sea

Although observation balloons have been used for military observation since the American Civil War, it was the French who pioneered their use at sea. At the forefront of submarine development, the *Marine Nationale* experimented also with the aerial detection of

submerged boats. Surprisingly, the Minister of Marine decided that the work showed, not the future of aviation at sea, but its lack of promise, and shut it down.

The first decade of the new century saw a worldwide enthusiasm for aviation and, by 1910, several navies had an air branch of sorts, although with little idea regarding final objectives. In Britain, a CID sub-committee was formed in 1908 to report on 'Aerial Navigation' and its applications. As a result, a rigid airship was ordered in 1910, only to be wrecked before it ever flew. This was the year in which Eugene Ely made the first flight from a warship's deck, but British naval officers who wanted to fly were still doing so at their own expense.

Below: Sopwith 2F 1 Camels on the flying off deck of HMS *Furious*. Seven Camels were flown off *Furious* to attack the German airship base at Tondern in July 1918.

At the sub-committee's recommendation, the Royal Flying Corps (RFC), with both naval and military wings, was formed in February 1912. The Naval Wing was formed at Eastchurch, on the Isle of Sheppey, and provided the nucleus of pilots which, as the Royal Naval Air Service (RNAS), was fully integrated into the Royal Navy in February 1914.

In the United States, Bradley Fiske (then a Captain) was enthusiastic about aircraft to the point where, in 1912, he proposed that they should be used to defend the Philippines, obviating the need for a defending fleet. The Navy Board gave the proposal a predictably frosty reception but, undaunted, Fiske (a Rear Admiral in the following year) went on to look at the prospects for air-dropping torpedoes. In 1914, the US Navy founded its first air station in an abandoned yard at Pensacola, Florida

With no satisfactory means yet developed for flying from ships' decks, the seaplane (or hydro-aeroplane, as it was then called) attracted much attention from enthusiasts such as Denhout in France, Curtiss in the United States and the Short Brothers in Britain.

The Shorts had, by late 1914, produced the 'Folder', which was able to safely drop torpedoes. As the name implied, its wings folded for shipboard stowage and, as such, it was put aboard the modified cruiser *Hermes* in 1913 for evaluation. Take-offs, both at anchor and under weigh, built on earlier ad hoc work carried out on the battleships *Africa*, *Hibernia* and *London*. A string of naval air stations was also established, primarily along the east and south coasts.

Above: The German navy pioneered the use of airships as long range naval reconnaissance aircraft. The commander of their airship service was an enthusiast for strategic bombing and eventually lost his life aboard L70 shown here, shot down by Major Edgar Cadbury and Captain Robert Leckie in a de Havilland D.H.4 in August 1918.

Among aviation-minded fleets abroad, the Germans were the most innovative. Ferdinand Zeppelin had developed the rigid airship to a point where, complete with observers and radio communication, it could stay aloft for hours. For fleets ever-dependent upon reconnaissance, such craft promised the redundancy of large and expensive cruiser forces. By 1912 the German Navy's first 'Zeppelin' had made a continuous flight of some 30 hours, travelling a then unheard of distance of about 900 miles.

It was in countering such airships that the Royal Navy found the impetus for the pioneering work that, by 1918, produced the first through-deck aircraft carrier. Gravity runways for aircraft launch detracted from a ship's fighting value, although the Americans had produced a practical catapult by 1915. The British thus converted a mercantile hull to the *Ark Royal* seaplane carrier, whose seven aircraft used the water for both take-off and landing.

As, with the outbreak of hostilities, the RFC was used mainly in army support, the RNAS found itself responsible for home defence in addition to fleet work.

For this it acquired forty conventional fighters and fifty flying boats. Seven airships were used for patrolling littoral waters.

The term 'flying boat' was, for much of the war, virtually synonymous with the Curtiss H4 and H12, known popularly as Small and Large Americas. Their role developed with the requirements of the war. Surprisingly, for an aircraft weighing over four tons at take-off, the Large Americas could prove quite agile. With an endurance of over six hours they were able to surprise Zeppelins deep into the Bight, twice with fatal results. They also boasted a useful bomb load, which enabled them to dispose of four coastal U-boats, one a minelayer.

Left: *Furious* was modified in November 1917 and a flight deck added aft, here occupied by a submarine scout airship. The latter proved effective long endurance submarine hunters across the North Sea.

Left: Shorts supplied seaplanes to the Royal Navy throughout the war. The Short N.2B two-seater appeared at the end of the war and was capable of 92 mph at sea level. It had an endurance of over 4 hours.

Above: A Sopwith Pup fitted with skids lands on the aft deck of *Furious* during her trials in early 1918.

Zeppelins, on sighting a hostile fighter, usually dumped ballast, which invariably enabled them to out-climb it. Small, land-based aircraft were most successful in catching them. Incendiary bullets proved deadly in igniting the hydrogen upon which the airships depended for their buoyancy, but on occasion fighters also used 20-lb (9-kg) bombs.

Even before the *Ark Royal* entered service, the Admiralty was converting the venerable 18,000-ton ex-Cunarder *Campania*. Her size permitted a long, sloping flying-off deck forward which, with her 22-knot speed, enabled an aircraft to get airborne without the need for hoisting it over the side. For this purpose, seaplanes used wheeled trolleys beneath their floats, the trolleys falling away to be recovered, if possible, by an escorting destroyer. In heavy seas, the two escorting destroyers were also tasked with steaming at high speed to make a 'slick' to facilitate seaplanes to land.

A series of converted cross-channel packets followed, with a substantial hangar added aft to accommodate three seaplanes and the cranes with which to handle them. Typical were the *Engadine*, *Riviera* and *Ben-my-Chree*, which ships proved remarkably versatile.

On Christmas Day, 1914, three of them launched a pioneer raid on Cuxhaven. Only seven aircraft were serviceable and thick fog frustrated their efforts. Four had to be 'ditched' on the return trip. This 'first' was matched by another, equally unsuccessful, when the returning British warships were subjected to their first air attack.

These small conversions operated extensively during the Dardanelles campaign, with resourceful personnel seeking employment beyond their normal roles of observation and reconnaissance. Just days before

hostilities began, one of the ubiquitous Short 184 seaplanes had successfully air-dropped a torpedo. During August 1915, three such attacks were made against Turkish shipping. Due to the surprise element, all were successful, although the hitting power of a 14-in (356-mm) torpedo left something to be desired.

The 184 was also used for bombing, notably on the German battle cruiser *Goeben*. This *bête noire* grounded briefly in the Strait, but although she was hit by numerous bombs these failed to make any impression on her protective upper deck. During 1916 it was another 184 which flew from the *Engadine* at Jutland to make the first-ever successful reconnaissance flight from a fleet in action.

Freely manoeuvring ships were also being successfully attacked from the air. In September 1916 the French submarine *Foucault* was bombed and sunk by Austrian aircraft while, on the 11 August 1918, a group of six British CMBs (Coastal Motor Boats) were riddled and disabled by machine-gun fire from German aircraft off the Dutch coast.

The Royal Navy preferred kite balloons to airships for observation and spotting but these, often lofted from converted merchantmen, were difficult to deploy in high winds or at significant speed.

The Royal Navy had a sneaking regard for the enemy's Zeppelins ('worth two light cruisers'), and high-performance land aircraft operated from shipboard were needed to counter them. The Sopwith 2F.1 Camel was particularly suitable in this context, lifting easily in an airflow of 30–35 knots from platforms on the foredecks of light cruisers or on the turret roofs of capital ships. Flights terminated in ditching alongside a suitable ship, depending upon flotation bags to keep afloat long

enough to be hoisted clear by a boat boom. Inevitably hazardous, the procedure cost many pilots and aircraft.

Ever inventive, the Harwich Force experimented with planing 'sleds', which could be towed at high speed by a destroyer. An aircraft lofted from one of these accounted for the L.53, which, on 19th August 1918, was the last Zeppelin to be destroyed in combat.

As the problem of recovering aircraft was greater than that of launching them, it was obvious that a 'landing-on' deck was required. One of Fisher's more spectacular failures were the three 'tinclads' of the Glorious type, giant 'light cruisers' destined for the still-born Baltic project. The third of these oddities, the *Furious*, was designed to mount two 18-in (356-mm) guns in single turrets. Even before commissioning, she had the forward mounting removed and a 228-ft (69.5-m) flying-off deck fitted. She entered service in July 1917, and in the following month her senior flying officer, E.H. Dunning, sideslipped his Sopwith Pup around her bridge to make the first-ever landing on a moving ship. With no arrester gear, he relied on a deck crew grabbing the aircraft which, at stalling speed, was moving scarcely faster than the ship. A few days later he was killed trying to repeat the manoeuvre.

His successor, F.J. Rutland, requested a full-length flight deck, but conservatism won, and a 284-ft (86.6-m) landing-on deck was added in lieu of the after turret. The superstructure separating the two decks caused such turbulence that the after space was unusable. Even limited to flying-off, however, the *Furious* made history when, on 19 July 1918, she launched seven bomb-armed Camels to attack the Zeppelin sheds at Tondern. Achieving complete surprise, they destroyed a pair of the hated airships, and ushered in a new age of carrier strikes.

Right: A Sopwith Camel flies over *Argus* prior to attempting to land. Carrier landings were extremely hazardous in these pioneering days of naval aviation.

Above: Oberleutnant Friederich Christiansen's Hansa-Brandenburg W.29 floatplanes caught the British submarine *C-25* on the surface off Harwich on 6 July 1918. The hull was pierced and the CO and five crew killed.

Below: The unfortunate *Campania* was lost in the last week of World War I. Stationed in the Firth of Forth, she dragged her cables during a gale and collided with the battleship *Revenge*.

Stung by widespread criticism of the increasingly passive role of the Grand Fleet, Beatty had encouraged a hugely ambitious plan which was cancelled due to lack of resources. Eight picked merchantmen would have been modified to carry a total of 120 Sopwith Cuckoo torpedo aircraft. Escorted by Large Americas flown directly from Britain, three waves of forty aircraft each would hit the High Seas Fleet's heavy units anchored in Schillig Roads. A plan that would have pre-dated Taranto by 22 years foundered on Admiralty objections, firstly that the necessary secrecy could not have been maintained and, more significantly, that all available resources should be directed at defeating the U-boat. In effect, the huge investments in battle fleets were already an irrelevance.

The complex gestation of the *Furious* was, fortunately, paralleled by the building of the *Argus* and *Hermes*. Converted from a half-constructed liner, the former was designed originally with two 'island' superstructures flanking a through-way which connected the forward and after flight decks. As completed, however, she was devoid of superstructure, with funnel gases being trunked right aft. The *Hermes* was the first designed from keel up as an aircraft (originally seaplane) carrier, but took a starboard-side island superstructure to simplify uptake layout and ship control.

While the *Argus* was actually complete by September 1918, the *Hermes* had been commenced only the previous January. By this time a third, and larger, hull had been taken in hand. This was the 28,000-ton battleship *Almirante Cochrane*, ordered to Chilean account but on which work had been suspended. Renamed *Eagle* she, like the *Hermes*, was completed eventually long after the cessation of hostilities. Perhaps, in retrospect, it is surprising that three ships so ill-matched in characteristics should have represented the Royal Navy's first through-deck carriers.

Germany had also converted ships to seaplane carriers, had experimented with carrying a floatplane on the casing of a U-boat, and had equipped the raider *Wolf* with a small seaplane to extend her horizon. Very late in the war came a proposal for a pair of through-deck cruisers, converted from passenger liners. It was not pursued.

The US Navy also had seaplane carriers in service and had a proven catapult in production, but torpedo aircraft and through flightdecks were still at the assessment stage. Its Flying Corps could already field over two thousand aircraft but these were deployed from shore bases on either reconnaissance or bombing missions. The first sketch proposal for a flightdeck carrier dated from June 1918, at a point when the Americans were greatly influenced by British practice and seconded personnel.

The end of the High Seas Fleet

For four years the High Seas Fleet avoided major confrontation except on its own terms. It faced a Royal Navy not only numerically stronger but also heir to a tradition of maritime superiority. The British never doubted that they would come out on top, but their opponents, if they ever believed it possible, gradually had any such belief eroded by the Kaiser's 'minimum risk' requirements.

By the autumn of 1918 the Triple Alliance was crumbling. In September Bulgaria sought an armistice, followed in October by Turkey and Austria-Hungary. Already evacuating their long-held lines in Flanders, the Germans, concerned at the daily increasing American military presence, persuaded their Kaiser to seek terms for ending hostilities. Before any negotiations could commence, responded President Wilson, all U-boats would need to be recalled. They were.

Scheer thus had an unexpectedly large number of U-boats available for fleet support. They were sailed on 20 October to set up a barrier, behind which, ten days later, the fleet would sortie, with the objective of inflicting on the British a blow sufficient to materially affect the peace terms.

Fully appraised by intelligence, the Grand Fleet stood ready, but its final hope of a showdown was dashed. Enlisted men in the German navy had endured considerable privations, serving in an organisation that encouraged little rapport with their officers. Their families at home were suffering real shortage, the news from the front deteriorated daily and a general war-weariness had set in. As the fleet was prepared to sail on 29 October, many saw themselves as being sacrificed in a useless climax that would solve nothing.

Since the previous July, agitators, allied to the communists who had seized power in Russia the previous October, had succeeded in fomenting large-scale disobedience in a variety of fleet units. This simmering unrest broke suddenly into open revolt, the situation being controlled only by threat of summary torpedoing of the ships involved, followed by the fleet being separated between its bases. It remained quiescent as Germany itself degenerated into a revolutionary state that was arrested only by the armistice, agreed for 11 November.

A condition of the armistice terms was the internment of a major portion of the fleet, pending a decision on its ultimate disposal. By the end of the month ten battleships, six battle cruisers, eight light cruisers and fifty destroyers had been steamed to the Firth of Forth, thence to Scapa Flow, where they were anchored with reduced crews. There they lay, deteriorating as the Allies argued interminably, extending the armistice month by month.

With rumours hardening that his ships would be seized, Admiral von Reuter authorised long-matured plans for a mass scuttling. On 21 June 1919, the great ships settled and disappeared into the quiet waters of the Flow, salvaging some honour for the German Navy and relieving the Allies of a considerable headache.

Below: Salvage work begins on the *Baden*. The destruction of the major units of the High Seas Fleet was a blessing in disguise for the British, ending the wrangling over which Allied navy would receive which German ships as war reparations.

Right: NS ('North Sea') non-rigid airships were used from 1917 to hunt U-Boats in the North Sea. Crewed by ten men and equipped with bombs and machine guns, one set an endurance record of 4,000 miles in 101 hours in 1919. Two NS ships were part of the British force that accepted the surrender of the High Seas Fleet in 1918.

Chapter 6 – **Between the Wars**

World War I resulted in a major shift in the relative strengths of Great Britain and the United States. While the British had been seriously debilitated, the Americans enjoyed a four-year spell as arsenal to the allied powers. Demand was virtually limitless; industry prospered and expanded as never before. Although not given a chance to prove itself, the US Navy was considerably enlarged. Its four new Colorado class battleships were probably the equivalent of the British Queen Elizabeths, their lower speed offset by the firepower of their 16-in (406-mm) guns.

The US Navy's main contribution had been in anti-submarine (A/S) escorts where, to provide the numbers required, the advantages of series production was early recognised. Destroyer programmes ran to hundreds of hulls, mostly flush-decked 'four-pipers', which would provide the backbone of the fleet's escorts for the next decade and more.

At the armistice, the Royal Navy was still by far the larger force, and at an operational level relationships had been excellent. American views on the British use of the fleet as an instrument of political policy differed somewhat, while British methods and technology were not universally admired. Still firmly entrenched among some senior American officers was a perception of Britain as 'the old enemy', and the call of 'second to none' began to be heard more frequently among those who urged further naval expansion.

As the terms for the ultimate Peace Treaty were thrashed out, Britain wanted future German naval power greatly diminished, and it was mainly at her insistence that its post-war strength was fixed at just six pre-Dreadnoughts, six light cruisers, twelve each of destroyers and torpedo boats, and definitely no submarines. Replacements could be built only when each unit achieved a specified age, their displacement limit being tightly capped.

Neither the United States nor Britain had need for any of the interned High Seas Fleet. The former was pursuing the capital-ship programme that had been delayed by the priority placed on escort construction, while the latter,

with a fleet now grossly over-large for peacetime use, was preparing a programme of mass disposal. Neither power wanted to see the existing balance shifted and France's continuous demands for a significant share of the tonnage were an embarrassment. Interminable argument was closed abruptly by the mass scuttling of June 1919.

As American military intervention had been decisive in determining the outcome of the war, so the policies of President Wilson shaped the peace. His greatest goal was to form a League of Nations, providing a forum in which issues could be settled other than by war. His support for naval parity with Great Britain was based on an altruistic desire that no one nation should be dominant. He was, however, equally aware that British commercial power had historically been based on an ability to crush her rivals at sea - Spain, the Netherlands, France and, now Germany. American trade, wealth and influence had expanded mightily due to the late war and, with precedents all too apparent, an ultimate clash with Britain was fully on the cards. This could begin in the Far East, where an aggressively expansionist Japan had increased her fleet during hostilities and was still bound in alliance with Britain.

It was for this reason that the President had supported the resumption of the 1916 capital-ship building programme. The British, assuming that a League of Nations would result in a reduction in armaments, were puzzled. Contemplating the traditional response of out-

building the new threat, they soon realised that this was no longer possible. From an inferior bargaining position, the best that the British could hope for was agreement to bilateral discussion to avoid an acrimonious naval race. In retrospect, both nations were wrong in assuming that superior naval power vested in the one should necessarily pose a threat to the other.

Britain had some cause for concern. Comparing front-line capital ships only, the British advantage over the Americans in 1919 was a comfortable 42 to 16. If the British proceeded with their disposal plans and the Americans continued with their approved 1916 construction programme, the balance by 1924 would be 30 to 27. If, as mooted, the Americans extended their building plans, and the British responded in kind, the 1924 ratio would be about 43 to 35. Second-line naval powers would react accordingly. France and Japan's reckonable strength of 7 and 14 respectively in 1919 would increase to 16 and 22 in 1924. From the American viewpoint, this would give the Anglo-Japanese alliance an advantage over them of 65 to 35.

One week after the scuttling of the High Seas Fleet, the Allies concluded the peace with the Treaty of Versailles. France and Italy were each allowed five modern cruisers and ten destroyers from the remaining German strength, but President Wilson felt (correctly) that other claims were extortionate. Disillusionment and resentment in Germany would result in another world war 'within a generation'.

Below: The US Navy had expanded rapidly during World War I: these destroyers are seen at Queenstown in 1918, where US escorts for Atlantic convoys were based.

Above Building in Britain in 1914, the Chilean battleship *Admiral Latorre* was bought for the Royal Navy and, as HMS *Canada* fought at Jutland. In 1920 she was returned to Chile.

Many in the US Navy, including Admiral Benson, the Chief of Naval Operations (CNO), had believed in Germany's being allowed to retain a significant fleet, mainly as a further means of off-setting British naval power. The German action at Scapa had precluded this, simultaneously damaging their credibility in giving the impression that any German political undertaking was, ultimately, hostage to the military.

The 1920 American presidential elections returned the Republican Warren Harding. Perspectives now changed, not least through the departure of the Secretary of the Navy, Josephus Daniels, an ardent supporter of a fleet 'second to none'. President Wilson had not only re-commenced the suspended 1916 capital ship construction programme but had asked Congress in 1919 to double it. His wish was to exercise a commanding naval superiority in the Pacific and in the Atlantic a 'defensive superiority'. The Panama Canal would allow reinforcement of the one from the other.

Great Britain, with traditional lack of sentiment for the ships that had served her so well, quickly scrapped two million tons, including forty capital ships and nearly ninety cruisers. Advances in war had made them obsolete in any case, but any savings possible through their disposal were offset by the continuing construction programme, which, like the American, had commenced under war conditions. Even in 1919-20 the British were sounding out the possibilities of an accommodation with the Americans to limit their relative naval strengths., In August 1919, the British Government also adopted the notorious 'Ten Year Rule'. Renewable annually, this would assume that Britain would not be involved in a major war within a decade, and could limit defence spending accordingly.

A complication was Japan. Her involvement in the war had contributed little, but she had gained considerably. Territorial gains under the peace settlement, including mandate (north of the equator) over the extensive Pacific island groups that had been German colonies, worried Australia and New Zealand particularly. True, Japan and Britain were in alliance, but there was very little evidence of a protective Royal Naval presence in the Far East. Newly confident, Japan was powered by a strong militarist lobby. Now self-sufficient, it pushed through the Diet (Japanese parliament) approval in 1920 for an 'Eight-eight' fleet, based on eight battleships and eight battle cruisers. The first two battleships were already being built as part of the war programme. These, the *Mutsu* and *Nagato*, were 26-knot, 33,800-tonners with the world's first 16-in (406-mm) guns. It was small wonder that the Americans took seriously the challenge from across the Pacific.

Their response comprised initially the six 43,200-ton South Dakota-class battleships and the six Lexington-class battle cruisers. Within the design constraints imposed by the Panama Canal locks the former mounted

Below The British balloon ship *Canning* seen off Salonika in 1920. The Royal Navy was very active in the eastern Mediterranean from 1919-22 after Lloyd George allowed the Greeks to invade Anatolia.

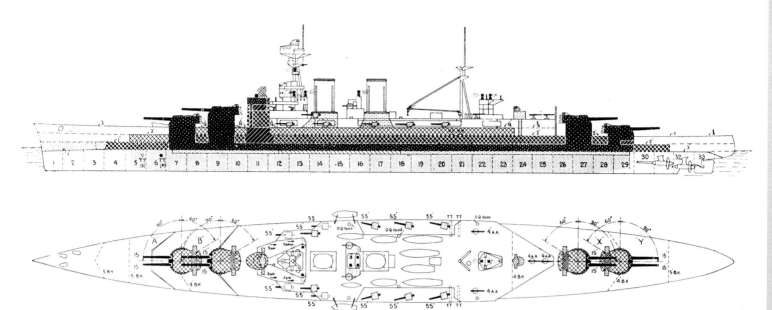

Above A *Fighting Ships* line drawing of *Hood*, completed in 1920. Work on three sisterships had begun in 1916 but was abandoned before the end of the war as the German capital ship building programme had ceased.

a twelve 16-in main battery, while the latter had a projected speed in excess of 33 knots. As both outclassed the 36,300-ton Hoods, then building, the British Admiralty responded with larger ships.

Fisher's dictum of 'speed equals protection' had overlooked that warships could not choose the style of battle in which they became involved. In these ships, three triple turrets were grouped tightly about a compact bridge structure, both to improve protection and to increase the number of main battery guns. The armour thus had minimum area and maximum thickness. A pronounced inclination was given to the main belt, improving its effectiveness by increasing the obliquity of an incoming projectile. Four 16-in gun battle cruisers were to have been followed by four 18-in (457-mm) gun battleships of much the same layout. Both groups would probably have displaced 48,500 tons.

Funding was approved only by the Admiralty's agreeing to reduce the number of commissioned capital ships to only sixteen, fourteen more being in reserve. Manpower was to be severely pruned and lesser dockyards, such as Pembroke and Queenstown, eyed for closure.

Orders were placed in October 1921, but there was an element of political bluff in appearing to be responsive to developments abroad while avoiding provoking foreign powers to go a step further. The term 'One Power Standard' was now current and the objective was to avoid losing naval superiority. An unspoken hope was that the funds need not be spent at all, and one month after the orders were placed, work was suspended.

The reason for this manoeuvring lay across the

Below: The Royal Navy supported Allied operations against the Bolsheviks, sinking several Russian warships in a torpedo boat attack on Kronstadt in 1919. The torpedo school ship *Dvina* (formerly the cruiser *Pamiat Azova*) was one of the vessels sunk.

Atlantic, where the Republicans were openly revolting against spending vast sums to meet hypothetical threats. To forestall a proposed British forum on Pacific and Far Eastern affairs, a resolution was tabled in Congress in December 1920 for an international disarmament conference. This would be held in Washington, where the Americans could retain the initiative. Opening on 12 November 1921, the conference comprised delegates from the five greatest naval powers of the day - Great Britain, the United States, Japan, France and Italy - with observers from other interested powers.

The Washington Conference

The American Secretary of State came straight to the point. The United States would scrap fifteen capital ships under construction, and fifteen pre-Dreadnoughts, a total of nearly 850,000 tons. In return, Great Britain would abandon its new buildings and dispose of nineteen existing capital ships, a total of about 580,000 tons. Japan would halt construction on seven, abandon plans for eight more, besides scrapping ten pre-Dreadnoughts, totalling some 450,000 tons. The immediate result would be a line-up of 22 British capital ships (604,000 tons), 18 American (501,000 tons) and ten Japanese (300,000 tons).

No capital ships would be built for a further ten years and, when built, would be limited to 35,000 tons apiece, with guns no larger than 16-in. An eventual ceiling of 525,000 tons apiece for Great Britain and the United States, and 315,000 tons for Japan was the aim, a ratio of 5:5:3. France and Italy would each be allowed 175,000 tons.

Below: Furious, the third and most idiosyncratic of Fisher's light battle cruisers was completed with her forward turret replaced by a flying off platform for aircraft.

Surprisingly, the proposals were eventually adopted. The US Navy had achieved theoretical numerical equality with the Royal Navy and, because of the age of the ships involved, would have technical superiority. Japan, unhappy at being accorded semi-permanent secondary status, was mollified by the powers agreeing not to fortify their Pacific territories. France had demanded twice her allocation but agreed eventually, only on the condition that no limits were imposed on other types of warship. This particularly included submarines, on which Britain, rather optimistically, had proposed a total ban.

Certain 'adjustments' were necessary, Japan being allowed to retain the near-complete *Mutsu* and Britain to build two new ships (to the new limitations), on whose

Above: While the British scrapped 40 capital ships after World War I, some of those earmarked for the post-war fleet were modernised. The battle cruiser *Repulse* was reconstructed from 1919-22, her clearly inadequate armour belt thickened to a still vulnerable 9 inches.

completion the four King George Vs would be scrapped. The British establishment, while deploring this final abrogation of maritime superiority, recognised the economic futility of trying to maintain it. For their part, many Americans were displeased at having to wait an interval before achieving equality.

Capital ships, taken as the yardstick of maritime strength, dominated the deliberations of the conference, but two other important classes of warship were affected.

Other than capital ships and aircraft carriers, no 'vessel of war' would, it was agreed, exceed 10,000 tons nor mount guns exceeding 8 in (203 mm) in calibre. This affected cruisers directly, and no ceiling was put on numbers.

The conference had an immense effect on the rise of aviation at sea. The through-deck carriers already being operated by the Royal Navy had impressed the Americans with their potential to the extent that five alternative types were being evaluated to establish that best-suited to the needs of the US Navy.

Washington had limited both the United States and Great Britain to a total of 135,000 tons of carriers apiece, Japan to 81,000 tons, and France and Italy to 60,000 tons. No new carrier was to exceed 27,000 tons, but two (only) might displace a maximum of 33,000 tons if converted from existing hulls that would otherwise have been scrapped. This clause applied specifically to the ex-battle cruisers *Saratoga* and *Lexington*, whose size would remain unchallenged for many years. Their great capacity and speed taught the US Navy very early of the advantages of large carriers.

An unwritten aim of the Americans was to terminate the Anglo-Japanese alliance, soon due for renewal. Hostilities with Britain remained unlikely, but there remained the possibility of a Pacific altercation with the Japanese getting out of hand, with British involvement under political obligation. The Americans were secretly intercepting and decoding all signal traffic between the various conference delegations and their respective governments, which accounted for much of their shrewd bargaining.

It was well appreciated by the British that the alliance was a source of friction. This was side-stepped simply by asking the Americans to join, along with the sensitive French, another considerable Pacific power. The

Right: With the 12-in and 13.5-in gun battleships now obsolete, the post-war fleet was based around the ten 15-in gun battleships completed during the war. *Queen Elizabeth*, seen here, commissioned in December 1914 and took part in the bombardment of the Dardanelles forts. To the frustration of her crew, she was refitting at Rosyth at the end of May 1916 and thus missed Jutland.

Below: Two of the five Japanese Kaba class destroyers that served in the Mediterranean 1917-18, one (*Sakaki*) surviving a torpedo hit from the Austro-Hungarian submarine *U-27*. The Japanese navy wished to continue its alliance with the British, but the USA succeeded in dividing them and the Anglo-Japanese treaty was not renewed.

resulting Four-Power Treaty provided for mutual 'consultation' if any of the signatories were threatened by an outside party. While this political fudge caused much relief in the Commonwealth and, indeed, in Great Britain, it was recognised by the latter that the only power which could challenge her Far Eastern interests had been converted from an ally into a potential rival. Officially amenable, privately bitterly resentful, the Japanese changed their perception of the British. Moderate opinion in the Japanese Navy was badly undermined, although its ultimate effect on the origins of World War II is difficult to quantify. To Britain, it meant simply that her position in the Orient would possibly need to be defended. Plans were already afoot to build up Singapore as a major fleet base; the outcome of the Washington Conference only made their fulfilment the more urgent.

The Americans had achieved virtually their every conference objective.

Airpower at sea

Early in 1920, the US Navy conducted explosion trials against the veteran battleship *Indiana*. Results indicated that such ships could be disabled by large air-dropped bombs. Largely because of these tests, ex-German ships, allocated as war reparations, were designated bombing rather than gunnery targets. Commencing July 1921, Army and Navy aircraft conducted a graduated series of attacks, closely monitored by observers. Moored submarines and destroyers were sunk easily, while the light cruiser *Frankfurt* was effectively destroyed by a single 600-pounder, a near miss, whose concussive effect blew in a large section of shell plating.

The Navy was interested particularly in the results of bombing on armoured ships, and the final tests, against the fairly modern battleship *Ostfriesland*, called for detailed inspection following each hit. Unfortunately, the Head of the Army Air Service, Brigadier-General William ('Billy') Mitchell, was more intent on demonstrating his force's expertise to support his arguments for its expansion. Flagrantly disregarding trials procedure, his bombers sank the battleship with one-and-two-thousand pounders. As the ship had been stationary, and without crew or damage control, the result proved little. Far from being censured, however, Mitchell was enabled to repeat the performance soon afterward on the old battleship *Alabama*. While unconvinced of the Army's claim that the day of the battleship was done, the Navy was left in no doubt of the potential of air attack, which explains the interest shown in carriers at the Washington Conference, soon afterward.

Above: Fleet Air Arm torpedo bombers practise against the battleship *Warspite* in 1932. Britain lost its lead in naval aviation during the 1930s and went to war in 1939 with obsolete aircraft aboard its carriers.

The US Navy's first true carrier was the *Langley*, converted from a fleet collier shortly after the conference. Slow at 15½ knots, she had a useful 523-ft (159.4-m) through flightdeck, unencumbered by an island. Her most notable contribution was the development of arrester gear, to slow and stop aircraft safely on touch-down.

With, as yet, no effective yardstick for carrier size, the arrival of the two converted Lexingtons in 1927 was a

Below: Japan's purpose-built carriers were lightly-built, carried large air groups and were very fast. *Hiryu*, built 1936-39 carried up to 73 aircraft and was capable of 34 knots.

radical step forward. To keep them within even the 33,000-ton special clause limitation required some very creative calculation and definition. Their vast 866 x 106-ft (264 x 32.3-m) flightdecks would not be eclipsed until World War II, while their 33.25-knot speed set a standard for later American carriers.

The US Navy made a fortunate choice in appointing William A. Moffet as Rear Admiral commanding the new Bureau of Aeronautics (Bu Aer). He succeeded in keeping naval aviation under Navy control, in contrast to the British who, since 1918, had been centralising all aerial activity into one service. Bu Aer believed in the offensive potential of the carrier, and worked particularly at the rapid launch of fighters and torpedo aircraft.

Most of the Lexingtons' 80 aircraft comprised fighters, bombers, torpedo bombers and scouts in almost equal numbers. 'Bombers' bombed not so much in level flight but by the still-developing techniques of dive-bombing. Resulting mainly from the lack of a reliable bombsight, the method had scored 21 hits from 44 bombs dropped against a ship target during the 1921 trials, and showed considerable promise.

The Lexington conversion involved the hangar walls and the flight deck becoming integral components of hull strength, reducing the stowage available for aircraft. It was soon discovered, however, that the size and proportions of the flightdeck would determine the size of

Below: The French *Béarn* was laid down as a Normandie class battleship in 1914 but completed as an aircraft carrier, 1923-27. Forty aircraft were embarked, but she still carried eight 6-in guns and even four submerged torpedo tubes.

Above: A 1,100 lb bomb hits the old battleship *Virginia* during tests in 1923. Such early trials showed that battleships could indeed be sunk by air attack, but they were moored, undefended and had no damage control parties. Advocates of the battleship remained unconvinced.

an air wing. Considerable area was devoted to the island, the huge stack, and four twin 8-in (203-mm) gun turrets, but the pair convincingly demonstrated the advantages of space and began the arguments relating to the relative merits of large and small carriers; arguments which have raged ever since.

In Great Britain, the RNAS and the RFC were amalgamated on 1 April 1918 to form the Royal Air Force (RAF). The unified organisation reduced the duplication and confusion caused by the demands of two similar services, but put what became known from 1924 as the Fleet Air Arm into steep decline. A major reason was the loss to the Navy of the enthusiastic pioneers who had been behind the spectacular progress during World War I. The Admiralty Board even lost the post of Fifth Sea Lord, whose brief had included responsibility for naval aviation.

Once the wartime stopgaps were discarded, the Royal Navy was left with the new *Argus*, developing doctrines suitable for through-deck carriers, and the *Furious* (and possibly *Vindictive*) awaiting full reconstruction. The *Eagle* commenced trials in 1920, but debate about her

County class

data:

Displacement standard	9,825 tons
Length	633 feet
Beam	66 feet
Design draught	21 feet
Complement	660

Class: *Berwick, Cornwall, Cumberland, Kent, Suffolk, Australia, Canberra, Devonshire, London, Shropshire, Sussex, Dorsetshire, Norfolk.*

Armament:
8 x 8-in guns
8 x 4-in guns
8 x 21-in torpedo tubes

Below: The 'County' class cruiser *Norfolk* as she appeared during 1943

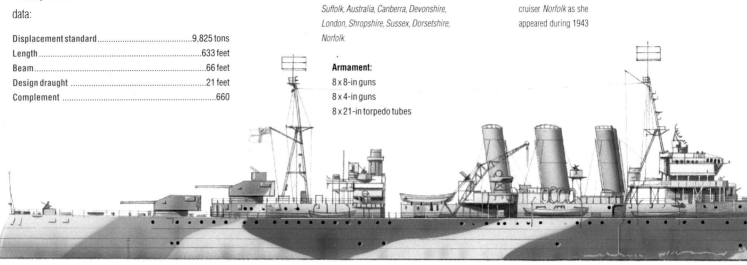

Above: Frobisher was disarmed and used for training in the 1930s, but was re-armed and served during World War II. The 200 lb shells fired by her 7.5-in main armament were hand-loaded.

superstructure delayed her actual commissioning until 1924. Also completed in 1924 was the *Hermes*, the first British carrier designed as such from the outset. Her modest 10,850-ton displacement and 25-knot speed proved to be limitations to her usefulness. *Eagle's* flightdeck was a useful 652 feet (198.7 metres) in length but her 21 knots was inadequate. The range of carriers available to the Royal Navy were thus all too small or too slow to acquire the experience available to the Americans.

An improvement was the 22,450-ton *Furious*, which rejoined the Fleet in 1925. Her narrow-gutted 'fast cruiser' form had required the addition of bulges to improve her stability, but she could still manage 30 knots. This did not place limitations on fleet speed, and guaranteed an adequate wind-over-deck speed for flight operations. Her 52-odd aircraft comprised various mixes of fighters, torpedo bombers and spotter/reconnaissance aircraft. Her upper hangar deck was continued out over

the forecastle, allowing aircraft to fly off directly from both this level and the flightdeck, reducing the time necessary to launch an air strike. It was to be 1928 and 1930 before her sisters *Courageous* and *Glorious* were completed as carriers.

During the 1920s, carrier aircraft were adequate in quality but few in numbers, only 128 in total by 1924. By the 1930s, design had begun to fall behind. This was due partly to a cash-strapped RAF, but was not helped by Admiralty indecision on what it really wanted in necessarily multi-role aircraft.

Still much influenced by British practice, the Japanese had also not been slow to introduce aviation at sea. Their 7,500-ton *Hosho*, completed in 1923 from a newly-commenced oiler, did not qualify as a fleet carrier but yielded valuable experience. Aircraft were usually home-built to foreign design. The treaty also allowed the Imperial Japanese Navy a pair of capital ship conversions. Selected were the hulls of the *Amagi* and *Akagi*, two of the 41,200-ton battle cruisers of the 'Eight-eight' plan. When the former was damaged during construction by an earthquake, the battleship *Kaga* was substituted. They entered service in 1927/8.

With original thinking typical to the Japanese, the *Akagi* had a short flightdeck, used only for landing on. The *Furious* concept was taken a stage further with both upper and lower hangar decks being continued forward for the purpose of flying-off. *Kaga* had only one such level. Like the British, the Japanese later abandoned the lower level take-offs, extending the shell plating and flight deck to the full usable length. Although they spent much of their careers in company, they were an ill-matched pair, the 32.5-knot *Akagi* being a full six knots faster than her consort.

Operating mainly in the confines of the Mediterranean, covered by coastal air stations, the Italians considered a carrier an unnecessary luxury, but the French thought it worthwhile to convert the hull of the battleship *Béarn*. Although the only all-turbine unit of the cancelled Normandie class, she had been laid down in 1914 and was already obsolete. On a displacement of 22,150 tons, she could carry only 25 aircraft, and her 21.5 knots were completely inadequate. Surprisingly, the French Navy showed no interest in third-generation ships until the late 1930s.

Even by the late 1920s, the 'major' fleets well appreciated that the aircraft carrier was a rising force, although the 'big-gun' faction was still supreme.

Treaty cruisers

As noted above, 'vessels of war', other than capital ships and aircraft carriers, would be limited by treaty to 10,000 tons and 8-in (203-mm) guns. This applied directly to cruisers, the parameters being based on the 9,750-ton 'Improved Birmingham' (or Hawkins) class, then being built by the British. These were unusual ships, ahead of their time, built specifically to counter surface raiders. Their size and endurance were exceptional, as were their 30-plus knots and seven 7.5-in (190-mm) guns. However, they were completed too late to meet the German wartime threat. By the end of World War I, the Royal Navy was concentrating on smaller cruisers, better suited to operations with the Grand Fleet and its large destroyer flotillas.

As size was critical to long-range Pacific operations,

Machinery:

Geared turbines, 80,000 shp

4 shafts

32 knots

Armour:

Belt ....5 in

Ends ....3 in

Deck ....1.5-4 in

Turrets ....2 in

Barbettes ....1 in

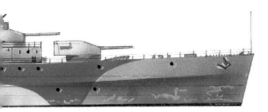

the Americans readily accepted the proposed limit, a sketch proposal for a cruiser superior to the Hawkins class having already been prepared. Within four months, the Japanese had completed their own draft design for a class of four.

For fleet cooperation and commerce protection the Royal Navy needed large numbers of cruisers of no great size. Ships built to a 10,000-ton limit would be required only for reconnaissance in force, independent operation, or as foreign station flagships. For these there was a limited requirement but, faced with the prospect of foreign cruisers of such a size, Britain had also to consider them. A new race was on.

Although the 10,000-ton 'standard' displacement excluded fuel or reserve feedwater (whose inclusion would have unreasonably restricted endurance), it proved a teasing limitation for designers seeking 'to pour quarts into pint pots'. While the British were not viewed seriously as potential adversaries by the Americans, British construction was something of a yardstick. Japan caused most concern but, in the Far East, with plenty of bases, the British could opt for low endurance. For the US Navy, the nearest guaranteed base was Hawaii, or the yet-to-be-built Guam.

Pursuing a 'fighting scout' concept, the Americans examined various options within the displacement limit. With negligible protection, it was possible to combine twelve 8-in guns with 33.5 knots. To armour on a scale to defeat destroyer gunfire cost two knots. Reducing the main battery to ten barrels gained 0.8 knots, to eight barrels 1.6 knots. The late war had highlighted the dangers of plunging fire, so deck protection, with its greater areas, could not be skimped to thicken the belt. Boiler spaces needed to be well spaced for survivability, while topside space was required for the catapult for the scout plane vital to the ship's function.

The result was the pair of Pensacolas, notable for a low freeboard and a unique ten-gun disposition, with triple turrets superfiring twin turrets. This layout, together with fuel tanks sited low for protection, did nothing for their tendency to roll, a problem which later needed correction.

Follow-ons sacrificed one gun for a more compact arrangement of three triple turrets. Weight saving was addressed so strictly that they actually came out under-weight, a characteristic that would not continue.

With little justification, the British produced their own 10,000-tonners in the County class, of which seventeen were requested. With even less justification, the gun-calibre was increased from a well-tried 7.5 to an 8-in. Projectile weight went up from 200 to 250 lb (91 to 114 kg), requiring the provision of power handling, whose complexity caused endless trouble.

By accepting an eight-gun armament and a moderate, but sustainable, 31-knot speed, the designers produced a longer ship with high freeboard and excellent habitability. An external bulge improved survivability but, with great problems in designing down to displacement, protection was limited to magazines and machinery spaces, with no contingency margin. At a time of economic stringency, the Counties were considered expensive, and a six-gun diminutive was proposed. These displaced only 8,400 tons, but their shorter hull required just as much power to meet the required speed. Only two, York and Exeter, were built.

In every respect, the most impressive of the 'Treaty Cruisers' were those of the Japanese. The first four, the Myoko class, set the style of being designed along the lines of diminutive capital ships. They had the slender form required for the demanded 35-knot speed, comfortably exceeded on trials. Habitability, already sacrificed to accommodate the 130,000 shp of machinery, suffered further with the late inclusion of twelve 610-mm (24-in) torpedo tubes within the after hull, together with stowage for 36 rounds. Ten 8-in guns were carried,

Below: USS *Wichita* was one of two new heavy cruisers allowed to the US Navy by the 1930 Treaty of London. She was part of a US Task Force sent to the aid of the British Home Fleet in 1942.

Above: Brooklyn was the first of a 9-strong class of cruisers armed with 15 rapid-firing 6-in guns that used new semi-fixed ammunition.

unusually, in five twin turrets. Capital ship-style protection was worked in, including both bulges and longitudinal bulkheads. Belt armour was steeply inclined and arranged to contribute to longitudinal strength rather than being supported on the hull. It could resist oblique hits from 8-in projectiles and direct hits from 6-in. There were peculiarly Japanese features. The conspicuously-trunked funnel casings reduced weight by combining two uptakes, while removing smoke nuisance from the bridge structure. The odd sheerline was a further weight-saving measure, the undulating freeboard reflecting the necessary depth of hull girder to counter the stresses that varied along its length.

The secret of this ambitious package was simply that the Japanese designers regarded 10,000 tons as a guide, a curb on unrestricted growth, rather than an absolute limit. They were, therefore, considerably overweight.

The French Navy emerged from World War I in poor shape. It had lost heavily, including four battleships and five cruisers. Its newest battleships were obsolete and its latest cruiser dated from 1908. As the world's second colonial power and with a coastline that bordered three very different maritime theatres, a capable fleet was necessary. However, France had no identifiable maritime opponent and a battle fleet was an expensive luxury for a nation repairing the enormous damage inflicted by the war. The German and Austrian ships ceded under the peace terms were a windfall. As these included five cruisers, ten torpedo boats and ten submarines, there was little enthusiasm for building further.

It was under the 1924 Programme that the French procured their first pair of Treaty Cruisers. They opted for a moderate, eight 8-in main battery but, to obtain a continuous speed of 33 knots, protection was virtually non-existent. These, the Duquesne class, were followed by the less extreme quartet of Suffrens. For a penalty of only one knot, these sacrificed about 16 percent in power in exchange for a thin protective deck and internal 'bulges'.

The one-off *Algérie* continued this trend, her 31-knot speed offset by a 110-mm (4.3-in) belt and a 76-mm (3-in) protective deck. Even this level of protection meant that armour accounted for over a quarter of the permitted standard displacement.

With yet poor communications, Italy's long peninsula made for an extended and vulnerable coastline, difficult to defend except by sea. In many respects, much of the nation had the characteristics of an island. Her colonial interests centred on North Africa, while there was a strong awareness that her forces could be confined to the Mediterranean by the foreign powers which controlled all its exits.

The Italian Navy's obsession with speed, therefore, not only reflected the dash of the national character but was also the means by which virtually any point in the Mediterranean could be reached in 24 hours. The long rivalry with the neighbouring French was accentuated by their being bracketed together at Washington. Italy's attitudes were those of a rising dictatorship, once Mussolini was made Prime Minister in 1922. Various provocative incidents culminated in the bombardment of

Above: One of the four Sendai class cruisers was cancelled under the Washington Treaty, but the other three were built 1922-5 and were all lost in action during the Second World War.

The initial class of Treaty Cruisers of the major powers, as built, compared as follows:

Nation:	Great Britain	United States	Japan	France	Italy
Class:	Kent	Pensacola	Myoko	Duquesne	Trento
Length overall:	630.0 ft/192.0 m	585.5 ft/178.5 m	668.5 ft/203.8 m	626.6 ft/191.0 m	646.3 ft/197.0 m
Maximum beam:	68.3 ft/20.8 m	65.3 ft/19.9 m	62.3 ft/19.0 m	62.3 ft/19.0 m	67.6 ft/20.6 m
Main battery:	8 x 8 in (203 mm)	10 x 8 in	10 x 8 in	8 x 8 in	8 x 8 in
Secondary battery:	4 x 4 in (100 mm)	4 x 5 in (127 mm)	8 x 5 in	8 x 75 mm (3-in)	16 x 100 mm (4-in)
Torpedo tubes:	8 x 21 in (533 mm)	6 x 21 in	12 x 24 in (610 mm)	6 x 550 mm (21.7 in)	8 x 21 in
Main belt:	Patches	4 in (100 mm)	4 in	Nil	70 mm (2.75 in)
Protective deck:	Patches	1 in (25 mm)	2.5 in (64 mm)	Nil	50 mm (2 in)
Shaft horsepower:	80,000	107,000	130,000	120,000	150,000
Continuous speed (knots):	31	32.5	33.5	33	35
Standard displacement (tons):	10,000	10,000	11,150	10,000	10,510

Greek Corfu by Italian warships. The League of Nations, far from condemning the Italians for an outrage, actually blamed the (probably uninvolved) Greeks. In doing so, it set the tone for the appeasement of dictatorships that played so great a part in the origins of World War II.

Unsurprisingly, Italy's armed forces were over-large for what might be considered normal commitments. Her fleet was of a size with that of the French, but totally reliant on land-based air.

Myoko class

data:

Displacement standard	13,380 tons
Length	662 feet
Beam	68 feet
Design draught	21 feet
Complement	780

Class: *Myoko, Nachi, Haguro, Ashigara*

Below: The Myoko class heavy cruiser *Haguro* as she appeared in 1944.

Armament:
10 x 8-in guns
8 x 5-in DP guns
8 x 25-mm AA guns
16 x 21-in torpedo tubes

Machinery:
Geared turbines, 130,000 shp
4 shafts
33.5 knots

Armour:
Belt	4 in
Deck	2.5-5 in
Turrets	1.5 in

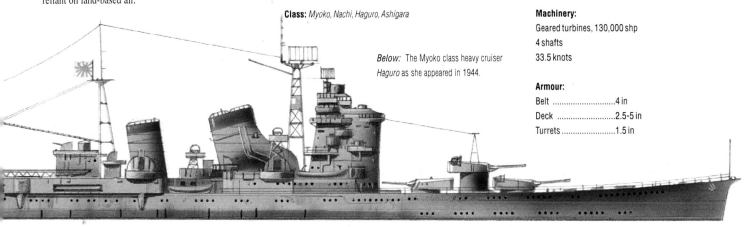

Le Fantasque class

data:

Displacement standard	2,570 tons
Displacement full load	3,350 tons
Length	434 feet
Beam	40 feet
Design draught	160 feet
Complement	210

Class: l'Audacieux, le Fantasque, le Malin, le Terrible, le Triomphant, l'Indomptable

Armament:
5 x 5.4-in guns
4 x 37-mm guns
9 x 21.6-in torpedo tubes

Machinery:
Geared turbines, 74,000 shp
2 shafts
37 knots

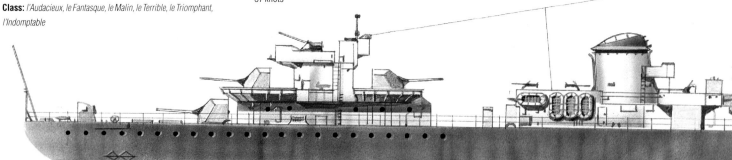

Italian cruisers were impressive ships. Immaculately kept, they gained much from the national flair for good proportion and style. While they are commonly castigated for having very light scantlings, this would seem to be based on misinformation or propaganda. The three Trentos had 75-mm (3-in) belts and 50-mm (2-in) protective decks, while the four following Zaras had 150-mm (5.9-in) belts and 70-mm (2.6-in) decks. All could dispose of an impressive 150,000 shp, returning trials speeds in excess of 35 knots and continuous speeds of some 32 knots. Again the main battery was a moderate eight 8 in, but the displacement limit was still breached, the Trentos being up to 500 tons overweight and the Zaras as much as 1,700 tons.

Destroyers

War experience showed that a destroyer's guns were more likely to be used than her torpedoes, but the latter were a potential threat that an opponent could not ignore. Displacement increased rapidly as successive classes acquired the size and power to stay with the fleet in poor conditions. Large flotillas proved difficult to control.

With large numbers of the various V and W classes available, the Royal Navy did not build again until the two Amazon 'specials', completed in 1926. The Modified V&W effectively defined the standard features of future British destroyers - superimposed 4.7-in (119-

mm) guns at either end, two banks of torpedo tubes on the centreline, and a raised forecastle for accommodation and seakeeping.

For comparison purposes, the two Amazon prototypes were built by separate destroyer specialists, Thornycroft and Yarrow. They were, essentially, small improvements on the existing design, except in their machinery where superheaters and improved boilers enabled an improvement of some three knots in maximum speed. During trials, *Amazon* achieved 38.7 knots.

Flotillas were reduced to a manageable eight boats plus

Below: The Akitsuki class destroyers were ordered in 1939. *Hatsutsuki* was launched in 1942 and sunk in 1944.

a leader. Commencing with the 'A' class in 1929, the construction rate was roughly a flotilla per year, with design remaining remarkably consistent through to the 'I' class of 1936. Quadruple torpedo tube banks were introduced with the 'A's, quintuples with the 'I's. For rapid manhandling of 50-lb projectiles, gun trunnions had to be limited in height, the resulting elevation being only 40 degrees.

The dominating parameter for American war-built destroyers was speed. For a given size, a hull was stronger for being flush-decked, without the discontinuity at the break of the forecastle. A high forward freeboard thus decreased in a long sheerline, making for a wet ship with a rather high centre of gravity. By completely freezing design detail, the Americans could employ successful and rapid series production, using a minimum numbers of yards configured for the task. The resulting 'four-pipers' had hull numbers running from DD69 to DD347, with very few cancellations. They were designed for 35 knots at a displacement of 1,150 tons and, while

The rapid development in opposing destroyers 1914-18:

	Completed by		Launched in	
Year:	1914	1914	1918	1918
Nationality:	British	German	British	German
Class: K	V25	Mod.	V&W	S131
Displacement:	1,072	975	1,500	1,170
Guns:	3 x 4 in (100 mm)	3 x 88 mm (3.5 in)	4 x 4.7-in (119 mm)	3 x 105 mm (4.1 in)
Torpedoes:	2 x 21 in (533 mm)	6 x 500 mm (19.7 in)	6 x 21 in	6 x 500 mm (19.7 in)
Speed (knots):	30.5	36.3	33	33.5

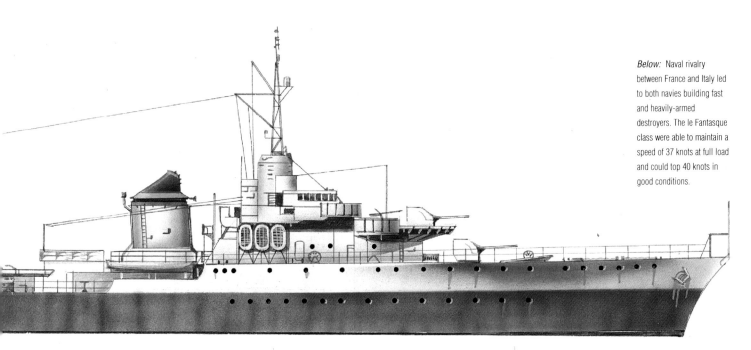

their four 4-in gun armament was unremarkable, their four triple 21-in torpedo tube banks emphasised their role as perceived by the US Navy.

Destroyer construction was resumed only in the early 1930s. The eight Farraguts could just about manage their five 5-in guns, eight tubes and machinery for 36.5 knots on their 1,400-ton displacement. The eighteen Mahans that followed began an over-ambitious trend. Maintaining the dimensions, they accepted a deeper draught at a further one hundred tons displacement in order to ship a further four torpedo tubes.

Low resulting stability margins were manifested in their being unable to accommodate heavier dual-purpose armament. Even the splinter shields were left off the after gun mountings. Later modifications only exacerbated the problem. They became very tender when operating with slack tanks, as extended operations in World War II obliged them to do. This contributed largely to the loss of three destroyers (and narrow escapes for several others) when the Third Fleet hit the typhoon of December 1944.

Having built fewer destroyers during the war, the Japanese continued in the early 1920s. Within a decade they progressed from 1,215-tonners, with four 4.7-in guns and six 21-in tubes, to 2,090-tonners with six 5-in and nine 24-in torpedo tubes. All capable of high sustained speed, they proved to be formidable fighting ships.

Subsequent to the Washington Treaty, the Japanese were keen to try out new lightweight construction techniques. The result was the one-off, 2,890-ton *Yubari* which, with her heavy armament, was really an example of the 'super destroyer', with which all the major navies exercised their minds at one time or another.

Part-leader, part scout-cruiser, the *Swift* had been

Below: The British K class destroyer *Kipling* seen shortly before her loss in 1942. Note the twin 4.7-in turrets and quadruple 2-pdr pom-pom AA mount abaft the funnel.

Maass class

data:

Displacement standard	2,230 tons
Displacement full load	3,160 tons
Length	390 feet
Beam	37 feet
Design draught	12.5 feet
Complement	315

Class: Z1–Z22

Armament:
5 x 5-in guns
3 x 37-mm guns
6 x 20-mm guns
8 x 21-in torpedo tubes
60 mines

Machinery:
Steam turbines, 70,000 shp
2 shafts
38 knots

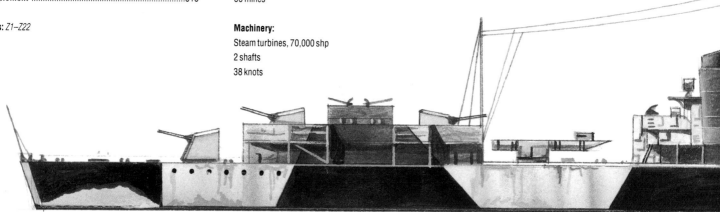

Soldato class

data:

Displacement standard	1,830 tons
Displacement full load	2,460 tons
Length	350 feet
Beam	33 feet
Design draught	12 feet
Complement	219

Class: Alpino, Artigliere, Ascari, Aviere, Bersagliere, Camicia Nera, Carabiniere, Corazziere, Fuciliere, Geniere, Granatiere, Lanciere

Armament:
4 or 5 x 4.7-in guns
1 x 37-mm gun
6 x 21-in torpedo tubes
48 mines

Machinery:
Steam turbines, 48,000 shp
2 shafts
39 knots

Above: Sparrowhawk was one of over 50 'S' class destroyers ordered by the Royal Navy in 1917. Completed in 1918, she served until 1931.

Below: The first group of the Soldato class were launched 1937-8 and were typically fast Italian destroyers, so lightly-built that *Lanciere* was overwhelmed by heavy seas during the battle of Sirte.

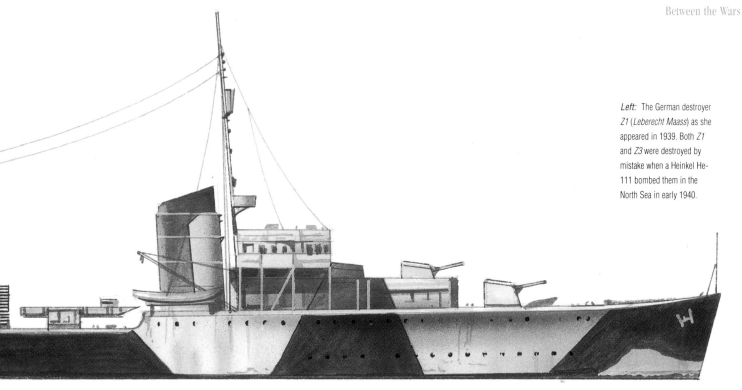

Left: The German destroyer *Z1* (*Leberecht Maass*) as she appeared in 1939. Both *Z1* and *Z3* were destroyed by mistake when a Heinkel He-111 bombed them in the North Sea in early 1940.

completed by the British as early as 1907. She combined the new, steam turbine drive with a 2,170-ton displacement, large for the day. She mounted 4-in guns, when 12-pounders were the norm, later taking a single 6-in forward. Together with four, slightly smaller, leaders of the Faulknor type (compulsorily purchased from Chilean account), she proved difficult to integrate into the fleet organisation. The concept was not pursued but was useful in defining any advantage accruing from larger dimensions.

In 1916 the Germans commenced several groups of 'large torpedo boats', displacing about 2,400 tons full load. With a 34.5-knot sea speed, they would have been a notable advance, carrying four 150-mm (5.9-in) guns and four torpedo tubes of an enlarged, 600-mm (23.6-in) calibre. Of the dozen planned, only two were ever completed, due to priorities being switched to submarine construction. Both were ceded to France in 1919 and may

Above: Destroyers of the Royal Navy's Harwich flotilla at sea, 1918.

have been the origin of the French interest in the super-destroyer. These beautiful ships were built in a continuous, evolutionary series from 1922 until 1940. With adequate size, freeboard and power, they could well maintain their speed, while their 130-mm (5.1-in) guns (later 138-mm/5.4-in) and large 550-mm (21.6-in) torpedo tubes made them a match for any destroyer afloat.

Submarines

Submarines were also passing through a period of experiment, nowhere more so than in the Royal Navy, which required a boat with a surface speed sufficient for it to accompany the Fleet. As the 19.5 knots of the short series of 'J' boats proved insufficient, a large steam-propelled design was the only current option. The French, with poorly developed diesel experience, had built several types of low-powered steam boats, but the British 'K' class were far larger. Completed, for the most part, in 1917 they were of 1,980/2,566 tons displacement. With two funnels to be closed off and a steam plant to shut down a 'K' took five minutes to dive. Their endurance under steam was poor, and their armament idiosyncratic, with three 4-in (102-mm) guns spaced along the extended casing but with only light (18-in/457-mm) torpedo tubes, four forward and four firing transversely amidships.

Four of the series became the experimental 'M' class. All were intended to operate with a short-barrelled 12-in (305-mm) gun, faired into the forward end of the

K1 class

data:

Displacement surfaced	1,980 tons
Displacement submerged	2,566 tons
Length	339 feet
Beam	27 feet
Design draught	17 feet
Complement	594

Class: *K1–K17*

Armament:
2 x 4-in guns
1 x 3-in gun
10 x 18-in torpedo tubes

Machinery:
Geared steam turbines, 10,500 shp
1 diesel, 800 bhp
2 electric motors, 1,440 bhp
2 shafts
24 knots surfaced (steam)
9.5 knots surfaced (diesel)
8.5 knots dived (electric)

M1 class

data:

Displacement surfaced	1,594 tons
Displacement submerged	1,945 tons
Length	296 feet
Beam	25 feet
Design draught	16 feet
Complement	64

Class: *M1, M2, M3.*

Armament:
1 x 12-in gun
1 x 3-in gun
4 x 18-in torpedo tubes (M1, M2)
4 x 21-in torpedo tubes (M3)

Machinery:
2 diesels, 2,400 bhp
2 electric motors, 1,600 hp
15 knots surfaced, 9.5 knots dived

Top: K2, served 1916-26
Above: K16 served 1917-24

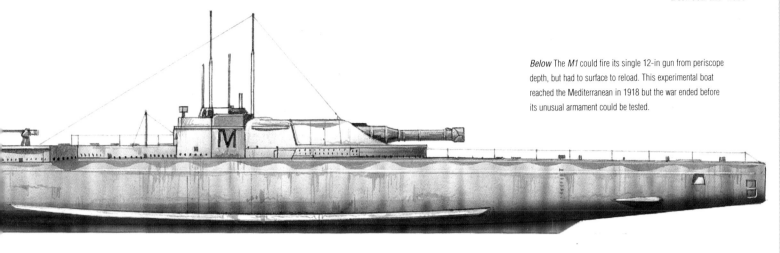

superstructure, but eventually only M1 retained it. Capable of being elevated to 20 degrees, the weapon was fired with the muzzle and upper tower awash. Fifty 850-lb (386-kg) projectiles sounded a fair exchange for the usual torpedo outfit, but the shot had to hit first time because the submarine had to be surfaced to reload. Never tried operationally, the concept was overtaken by the Washington Treaty , which banned any submarine gun superior to 8-in (203-mm) calibre, which limitation resulted directly in the French building the 3,304/4,218-ton 'corsair' submarine *Surcouf*, with two 8-in guns and a scouting aircraft.

The *Surcouf* was pre-dated by the *M2*, which had a small aircraft whose pressurised hangar opened onto a catapult laid into the forward casing. Her sister, *M3*, was rebuilt into a large minelayer. Her 100 mines were stowed in the casing and laid over the stern, the system providing useful experience for the design of the Porpoise-class minelayers. The *M4* was cancelled.

Also pre-dating the *Surcouf* was the 'cruiser' submarine *X1*. Completed in 1925, she was a 2,780/3,600-tonner with a twin 5.2-in (132-mm) gun mounting at either end of the superstructure. Her purpose remains obscure. Where the *M2*'s single 12-in (305-mm) gun was unlikely to hit anything, the *X1*'s four guns should have been quite effective. But against what? A single 4-in gun was adequate to sink merchant ships and no submarine commander would have been foolish enough to surface for a gunnery duel with a warship.

British submarine development then followed more

Above: The French 'cruiser submarine' *Surcouf*, lost in collision with a US merchant ship in 1942.

orthodox lines with the 'O', 'P' and 'R' classes, starting in 1927. Classed as 'overseas patrol submarines', their design was not inspired, and by 1939 they were obsolete. Unfortunately, their greatest employment was in the Mediterranean, where their considerable size and mediocre performance resulted in a high loss rate during World War II. Their shortcomings were, however, matched by the opposing Italian boats, which were

technically poor, over-large with a bold silhouette, and slow-diving.

In the US Navy, requirements for 'fleet boats' to actually work with the fleet were soon dropped, but the term remained, becoming synonymous with 'large boat'. Five diverse designs, grouped together as the 'V' class, were evaluated during the Twenties, leading the way to the successful Porpoise class (not to be confused with the British Porpoises). This type was intended to work in either ocean, but were of a size with the British 'O' class, and considerably smaller than the 1,850/2,723-ton Thames class, the last British attempt to build a submarine for direct cooperation with the fleet.

British attempts to outlaw the submarine were defeated at the Washington Conference by French objections. Germany, although barred by the Versailles Treaty from operating submarines, appreciated that a future remained to them and resolved to maintain design expertise. Several foreign countries had requested consultancy services, and in 1922 a specialist bureau was established in the neutral Netherlands. By 1925 this was being fed official funding, channelled through dummy firms set up by the German Navy. With the appointment in 1928 of

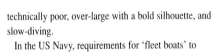

Below: The K class submarines were great technical achievements, but the idea of a steam-powered 'fleet submarine' was unsound.

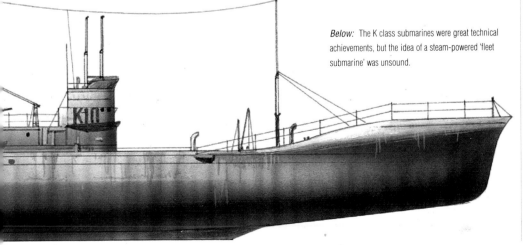

Olympus class

data:

Displacement surfaced	1,781 tons
Displacement submerged	2,038 tons
Length	283 feet
Beam	30 feet
Design draught	14 feet
Complement	53

Class: *Odin, Olympus, Orpheus, Osiris, Oswald, Otus*

Armament:

1 x 4-in gun
8 x 21-in torpedo tubes

Machinery:

2 diesels, 4,400 bhp
2 electric motors, 1,320 hp
2 shafts
17.5 knots surfaced,
9 knots submerged

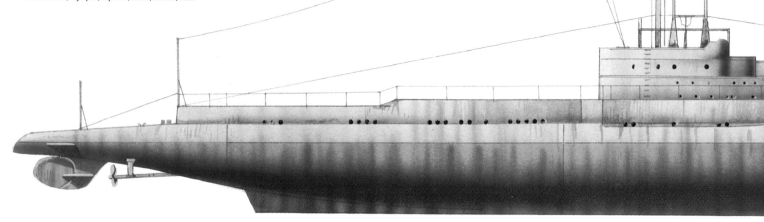

Left: A 'U' class submarine returns to base in World War II, flying the 'Jolly Roger'.

Admiral Raeder as Supreme Commander of the German Navy, things speeded up. Submarines, which were effectively prototypes for the first two types of new U-boat, were built in Spain and Finland under German supervision. Extensive 'trials' for their owners provided hands-on experience for German personnel.

The re-birth of the German Navy was signalled in 1925 with the launch of the *Emden*, built to a light cruiser limit of 6,000 tons. Two years later, detailed plans were formulated for a properly balanced fleet, to include sixteen submarines, but shortly afterwards, burdened with Allied reparation demands which far exceeded its capacity to pay, Germany dissolved into financial chaos. Having endured a lost war, the populace was losing its life savings. In the resulting widespread discontent lay fertile ground for extremists. The rise to power of Adolf Hitler and his National Socialists was linked inextricably with the state of the nation. On promises of a new, classless society, national unity and an end to the squabbling, self-interest of the other political parties, Hitler became Chancellor in 1933.

Japan, feeling slighted at Washington, resolved secretly in 1923 on a fleet expansion programme. Within a decade the Imperial Japanese Navy would comprise ten capital ships, four carriers, forty cruisers, one hundred destroyers and seventy submarines. Allowed 315,000 tons of capital ships and 81,000 tons of carriers (*Hosho* was excluded as 'experimental'), and with no agreed ceiling on the other classes, the plan was both feasible and legitimate. It was, however, hard to justify, and even employing secrecy subterfuge and circuitous funding, Japan's activities were obvious enough.

Left: Operating with surface ships at high speed, several 'K' class submarines were lost in collision. *K3* survived to be sold in 1926.

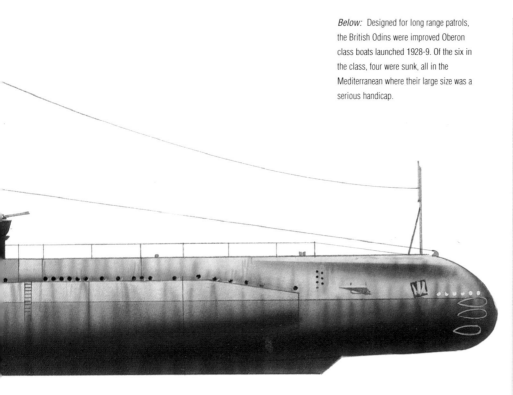

Below: Designed for long range patrols, the British Odins were improved Oberon class boats launched 1928-9. Of the six in the class, four were sunk, all in the Mediterranean where their large size was a serious handicap.

The London Naval Conferences

Concerned about general proliferation, President Coolidge called a further limitation conference at Geneva in 1927. This collapsed in disagreement between the two main parties. The United States proposed 300,000 tons of cruisers each, but Great Britain needed 600,000. Britain, in turn, wanted 8-in gun cruisers limited to 15 each but America, with an eye to developments across the Pacific, wanted 25.

The London conference of 1930 was thus called to rectify the omissions in the Washington agreements, due to expire in 1936. It began the separation of cruisers into 'heavy' (with guns of greater than 155-mm/6.1-in calibre) and 'light'. Individual destroyers were limited to 1,850 tons, with guns not exceeding 130-mm/5.-in calibre. Not more than 16 percent of total destroyer tonnage should comprise units exceeding 1,500 tons. Excepting those already in service, submarines should not exceed 2,000 tons surface displacement, nor have a gun exceeding 130 mm (5.1 in) in calibre. 'Tons', as ever, referred to imperial measures of 2,240 lb (1016 kg). These new limitations would play a significant role in the evolution of these warship types, and the total agreed ceilings may be summarised as follows:-

	United States	Great Britain	Japan
Heavy cruisers	180,000	146,800	108,400
Light cruisers	143,500	192,200	100,450
Destroyers	150,000	150,000	105,500
Submarines	52,700	52,700	52,700

The cruiser totals reflected the US Navy's greater need for heavy cruisers and the Royal Navy's for numbers of smaller light cruisers. Actual numbers of heavy units were fixed at eighteen, fifteen and twelve. The latter figure suggests that Japanese ships were to displace an average of no more than 9,000 tons, far from their actual 11,000 tons and more. With respect to capital ships, the London Conference extended the new construction moratorium until 1936, with France and Italy still free to proceed with tonnage already agreed. Invoking a clause from the Washington Treaty, signatories could increase the displacement of existing ships by up to 3,000 tons to improve their protection against air or torpedo attack.

Because of otherwise excessive obsolescence, Britain was permitted by the Washington agreement to build two new battleships, on the completion of which the four Iron Dukes were to be scrapped. Completed in 1927, the *Nelson* and *Rodney* were diminutives of the aborted 1921 battle cruisers. By concentrating nine 16-in (406-mm) guns into three triple turrets, and close-grouping these with a compact, tower-like bridge structure, the maximum thickness of armour could be spread over the minimum area. The result was a new 'engines aft' appearance, with the secondary 6-in (150-mm) battery sited in six twin turrets, also mounted aft. Their main weakness was their poor 23-knot speed. As their unit displacement was under 34,000 tons, higher-power machinery could have been included.

The Versailles Treaty permitted Germany to replace each of her pre-Dreadnoughts twenty years after its launch date. New 'armoured ships' were, however, restricted to only 10,000 tons. Not wishing to be perceived as a fleet without capital ships, the German Navy looked at various options to combine a realistic armament with useful speed and protection, but on a restricted displacement. Thus was born the concept of the 'pocket battleship', the keel of the *Deutschland*, the first of a planned six, being laid in 1929. The design was ingenious, concentrating a heavy main battery of six 280-mm (11-in) guns into two triple turrets. Eight single 150-mm (5.9-in) guns were mounted in shields to save weight. Extensive welding, a new technique, saved much hull weight. Diesel propulsion proved to be heavier than anticipated, but the four nine-cylinder engines made lower volumetric demands than steam propulsion. The 26-knot designed speed could be exceeded and, by taking units off-line, very great fuel economy could be achieved for cruising.

News of the Deutschlands stimulated the French to proceed with their long-delayed pair of new capital ships. Knowing something of the German ships' characteristics, they aimed to build to a design that would, to a pocket battleship, have the same relation as a battle cruiser had to an armoured cruiser. The two Dunkerque class were designed on the 'all-or-nothing' principle, similar to that of the Nelsons but with eight 330-mm (13-in) guns concentrated in two quadruple turrets, both forward.

Below: The Washington treaties allowed Britain to build two Nelson class battleships.

H.M.S. NELSON

Below: Japan re-constructed its Kongo class battle cruisers between the wars, converting them into fast battleships. The *Kirishima* accompanied the Pearl Harbor strike force in December 1941 and was sunk off Guadalcanal by the battleship *Washington* in November 1942.

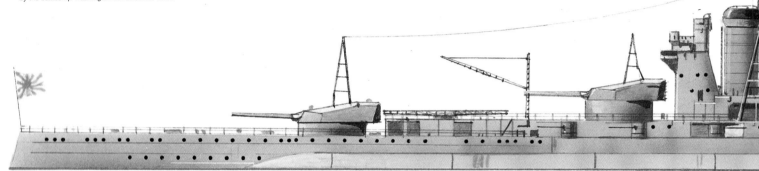

Beautiful ships, they bought their 29.5-knot speed at the expense of a long, unarmoured forward end. Too slow for battle cruisers, too weakly protected to be battleships, they were difficult to categorise.

This latter armament is valid also for the two German Scharnhorst class that they inspired. With the Dunkerques an obvious and effective response to the Deutschlands, the Germans cancelled the last three of the planned six, substituting the two larger Scharnhorsts. These, at 31,850 tons and with nine 280-mm (11-in) guns, were able to be built because of a rapprochement with the British.

Germany in the early 1930s began to find her voice again. As part of a general push for larger forces, Admiral Raeder drafted a 'naval reorganisation plan', effectively a five year expansion programme, for completion in 1938. Hitler, on becoming Chancellor, told Raeder that the most likely future enemy would be France and that he sought no war with the maritime powers. Because of this, he wished to agree with Britain a fixed ratio of fleet strengths, which would allow

Germany to build openly, without incurring foreign suspicions. With Raeder, he suggested seeking a ratio of 100 to 35.

When Hitler took over as President in August 1934, attitudes hardened. Having, with Japan, resigned from the League of Nations the previous year, Germany now took the gamble of unilaterally declaring the Versailles Treaty a dead letter.

Mussolini opened his carefully engineered hostilities against Abyssinia in December 1934. It drew condemnation from the democracies, but little else. There was a need for a firm stand in the Mediterranean but the British Admiralty was beginning to have fears of having eventually to wage war against three dictatorships simultaneously. With the Royal Navy in a run-down condition, this was no time for confrontation but for agreement and buying time.

The Anglo-German Naval Agreement was signed in June 1935. To German surprise, the British accepted that there was no longer a practical way of curbing construction, accepting the 35 percent proposal. More

surprising, submarines were also agreed. It was, in any case, *fait accompli*, for twelve small boats were already under construction, with a further twelve planned. The British actually agreed a 100:45 percent ratio in submarines, felt not unreasonable as British submarine strength was not great. But, and a big but, it was further agreed that the Germans could built to parity in submarines if they thought it necessary. A triumphant German government rammed the message home by announcing that, by 1942, the planned construction programme would result in six capital ships, 44,000 tons of carriers, eighteen cruisers, 37,500 tons of destroyers and 17,500 tons of submarines.

Against this sombre background, a Second London Naval Conference was held in March 1936 to mark the expiry of the Washington Treaty. It effectively removed the earlier ceilings which had curbed unfettered expansion.

Japan, already building strongly, demanded parity with the United States and Great Britain. When this was refused she withdrew from the conference. Italy also ignored it as a gesture against the sanctions placed upon her due to her invasion of Abyssinia.

A major decision by the delegates was to retain the 35,000 ton limit for individual capital ships. As the British believed that a satisfactory 16-in (406-mm) gun ship could not be designed under 40,000 tons, a maximum gun calibre of 14 inches (356 mm) was agreed. Should, however, any of the 'big five' fail to formally agree this by 1 April 1937, then the limit should stand at 16 inches. As the Japanese maintained their boycott, 16 inches it was.

It will be recalled that the first London Naval Treaty of 1930 had extended the moratorium on capital ship construction except for that yet unbuilt allowed to France and Italy. The signatories embarked, therefore, on ambitious modernisations of existing ships. Horizontal protection was improved to resist bombs and long-range gunfire. This increase in topweight was offset by the addition of bulges, which added beam and stability to

RODNEY.

M. & Co.   H.M.S. RODNEY.   311

Battleship. Built 1922-1927. 702 feet long, displacement 33,900-tons. Turbine engines 45,000 h.p., speed 23 knots. Burns oil fuel and has a compliment of 1,314.

Left: The modest size of the Nelsons left inadequate room for machinery and their speed was a disappointing 23 knots.

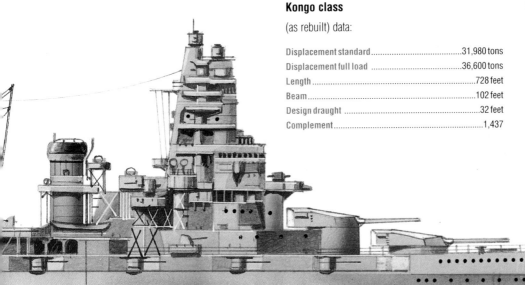

Kongo class

(as rebuilt) data:

Displacement standard	31,980 tons
Displacement full load	36,600 tons
Length	728 feet
Beam	102 feet
Design draught	32 feet
Complement	1,437

Class: *Kongo, Hiei, Kirishima, Haruna.*

Armament:
8 x 14-in guns
14 x 6-in guns
8 x 5-in guns
20 x 25-mm guns

Armour:
Belt	8 in
Ends	3 in
Turrets	11 in
Deck	4.75 in

Machinery:
Geared steam turbines, 136,000 shp
4 shafts
30.5 knots

increased protection from torpedo attack. Greater beam decreased speed, so in the case of Italian and Japanese rebuilding the hull was lengthened to restore something like the original lines. Loss of speed was generally limited as the replacement modern machinery and boilers required less space, so that power could be uprated. Superfluous space could be devoted to bunkerage for higher endurance. Main batteries were, in general, retained but re-engineered for increased elevation and range. In the case of the Italian Cavour class the guns were re-bored to increase calibre from 305-mm (12-in) to 320-mm (12.6-in). As these improvements often resulted in an overall reduced displacement, the secondary batteries could be upgraded. Heavy casemates with low-angle guns were replaced by turret-mounted, dual-purpose weapons of smaller calibre, but able to cope with the slow-moving aircraft of the day. Superstructures were enlarged, but in compact masses that supported separate fire control systems, with redundancy, for both main and secondary armament. Space had also to be found for catapults and hangars for several aircraft.

Such re-modelling undoubtedly produced effective fighting units, but at a cost that would have been better invested in new ships.

The limited achievement of the Second London Conference of 1936 and the non-involvement by two important players effectively signalled the end of the era of voluntary limitation of armament. The dictatorships were already building ambitiously and it was time for the democracies to respond. A measure of how much those involved actually adhered to the rules is given by a

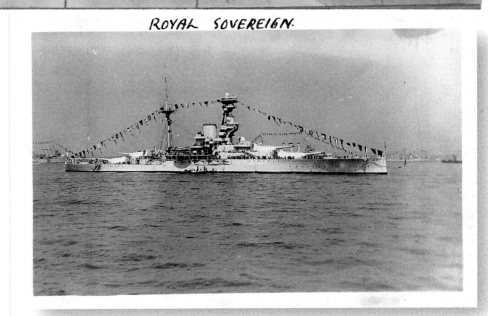

ROYAL SOVEREIGN.

comparison of contemporary battleships (see below): All except the four Yamatos, which were constructed in great secrecy, had an 'official' standard displacement of 35,000 tons. Even Great Britain and the United States relaxed the limits after 1936 and, from June 1938, 'legalised' a new limit of 45,000 tons. The King George Vs, even at 3,000 tons overweight, had their planned armament reduced by two barrels and their forward

Above: The British Royal Sovereign class were not significantly altered between the wars.

freeboard reduced, to the detriment of their seakeeping. Only the British proceeded with the 14-in calibre, which they had tried to introduce as a maximum. The Richelieus were built in response to both the Italian Vennetos and the Anglo-German Naval Agreement.

Nation:	Great Britain	United States	France	Germany	Japan	Italy
Class:	King George V	North Carolina	Richelieu	Bismarck	Yamato	Vittorio Veneto
Commenced:	1937	1937	1935	1936	1937	1934
Displacement:	38,000	38,000	38,500	41,700	65,000	41,150
Length overall:	745.0 ft/227.1 m	728.7 ft/222.1 m	813.0 ft/247.8 m	823.5 ft/251.0 m	826.9 ft/263.0 m	780.2 ft/237.8 m
Main battery:	10 x 14 in (356 mm)	9 x 16 in (406 mm)	8 x 15-in (380 mm)	8 x 15-in	9 x 18-in (457 mm)	9 x 15-in
Secondary battery:	16 x 5.25 in (133 mm)	20 x 5 in (127 mm)	9 x 6-in (150 mm)	12 x 5.9 in	12 x 6.1 in	12 x 6 in
Speed (knots):	28	28	30	29	27	30

Above: The Russian Gangut class battleship *Marat* seen in 1937 after her extensive refit.

From the beginning of 1939 the two Bismarcks were subsumed under a massive naval expansion known as the 'Z Plan'. That this programme would take at least a decade to realise suggests that Hitler really did not intend any immediate brawl with a major naval power. Such a time scale would have seen history repeat itself with a further naval race, as the objective was an 800-ship fleet, spearheaded by ten large and twelve smaller capital ships. Envisaged strategy saw convoys being savaged by not only 250 submarines but also by a wide variety of surface raiders, so powerful that convoys would need to be escorted by task groups, which were thus open to attack. The remaining strength of the Royal Navy would be tied to home waters by German 'fleet-in-being' tactics. Hitler's aggressive foreign policy thus worked against him in provoking a premature maritime war, for which his fleet proved inadequate.

It will be recalled that the Washington agreements allowed 135,000 tons of aircraft carriers each to the Americans and British, and 81,000 tons to Japan. These totals included those converted from existing hulls, and no additional units could exceed 27,000 tons. Japan was particularly circumscribed in that the *Kaga* and *Akagi* had already absorbed about 53,000 tons. The first purpose-built, *Ryujo* laid down in 1929 was therefore of

only 10,600 tons. She was a failure in attempting too small a displacement, so the next, the *Soryu*, consumed the remainder of the outstanding allowance, some 17,300 tons. A sister, *Hiryu*, laid down in 1935, exceeded the treaty ceiling. Japan's long conflict in China in the 1930s taught her the value of aircraft carriers in military cooperation. It improved the quality of her aircraft and trained a core of naval pilots with live battle experience.

The 66,000 tons of the Saratogas also bought up half of the US Navy's carrier allowance. Following many studies, the *Ranger* was built at under 14,000 tons to evaluate the merits of a small carrier. Where her larger consorts incorporated hangar walls and flight deck into the overall strength of the hull, the *Ranger* pioneered the approach of saving weight by making the hangar deck the strength deck, with hangar, flightdeck and forecastle being relatively light structures built on top. This 'open hangar' concept was to remain typical of American carriers until late in World War II. Despite her being significantly smaller, the *Ranger* was able by this approach to have a hangar some 25 percent larger than that of the Saratogas. The remaining tonnage was divided between the two 20,700 ton Yorktowns and the one-off 14,700 ton *Wasp*. Higher displacement allowed the Yorktowns a useful 32.5-knot maximum speed, but the Wasp reverted to the 29.5 knots of the *Ranger*.

Behind the 'open hangar' concept was the belief that adequate protection was not possible on a design limited to 20,000 tons. Better to accept a light structure and to use the displacement thus freed to carry extra aircraft, which, in turn, would reduce the likelihood of being hit.

In contrast, the first British third-generation carrier, *Ark Royal*, was of 'closed hangar' construction. Her resulting reduced aircraft accommodation was offset by her having two hangars. This, in turn, gave a good height to the flightdeck but, to keep the displacement to a desired 22,000 tons, only the vitals were armoured, not the flightdeck nor hangar walls. Completed late in 1938, she could stow sixty aircraft.

Before the *Ark Royal* was even in the water, the failure of the Second London Naval Conference had highlighted the differences between the main naval powers. Aware of its lack of modern carriers, the Admiralty included two in the 1936 Programme. At 23,200 tons, the Illustrious type just breached the agreed maximum displacement, but differed significantly from the *Ark Royal* in accepting an aircraft capacity of only 36 aircraft in a single hangar, in exchange for a 3-in armoured flightdeck and 4.5-in walls. Four of this type, with two derivatives, were eventually built.

Below: The Japanese *Nagato* as she appeared in 1944 with radar aerials on the mainmast and atop the bridge structure. Her two funnels were replaced by a single unit during her second reconstruction, 1934-36.

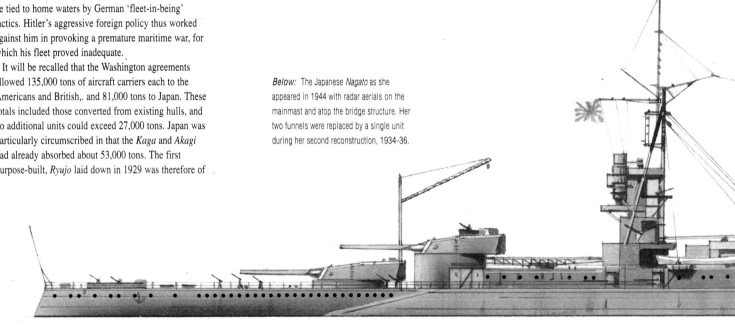

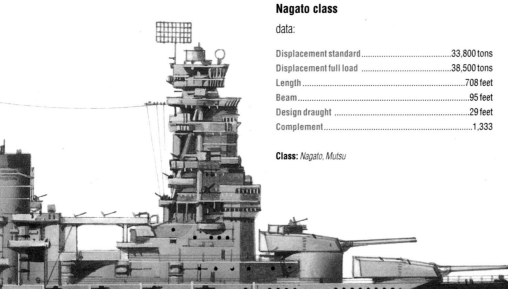

Nagato class

data:

Displacement standard	33,800 tons
Displacement full load	38,500 tons
Length	708 feet
Beam	95 feet
Design draught	29 feet
Complement	1,333

Class: *Nagato, Mutsu*

Above: USS *Wyoming* after her 1925-7 reconstruction. Under the terms of the London Treaty she was converted to a training ship, with two turrets and her armour belt removed.

Armament:
8 x 16-in guns
20 x 5.5-in guns
3 x 3-in guns
8 x 21-in torpedo tubes

Armour:

Belt	12 in
Decks	up to 3 in
Barbettes	12 in
Turrets	14 in
Conning Tower	12 in

Machinery:
4 Geared steam turbines, 80,000 shp
4 shafts
25 knots

Ark Royal

data:

Displacement standard	22,380 tons
Displacement full load	27,520 tons
Length	800 feet
Beam	95 feet
Design draught	28 feet
Complement	1,630

Class: *Ark Royal.*

Armament:
16 x 4.5-in guns
4 x 8-barrelled pom-poms

Aircraft:
36

Machinery:
Steam turbines, 103,000 shp
2 shafts
31.5 knots

Armour:
Sides	4.5 in
Hangar deck	3 in

Below: Ark Royal became famous for her role in Force 'H' at Gibraltar. Her ageing Fairey Swordfish damaged the *Bismarck*, enabling the British Home Fleet to intercept her. *Ark Royal* was torpedoed and sunk in November 1941.

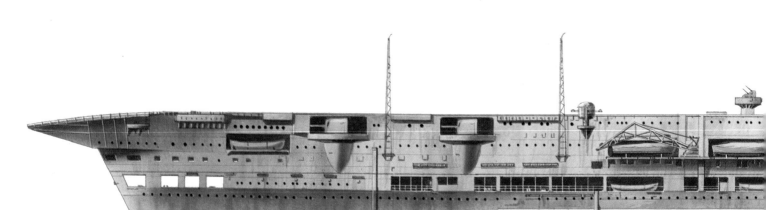

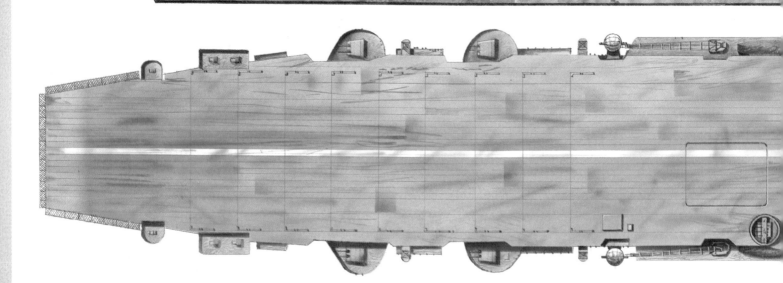

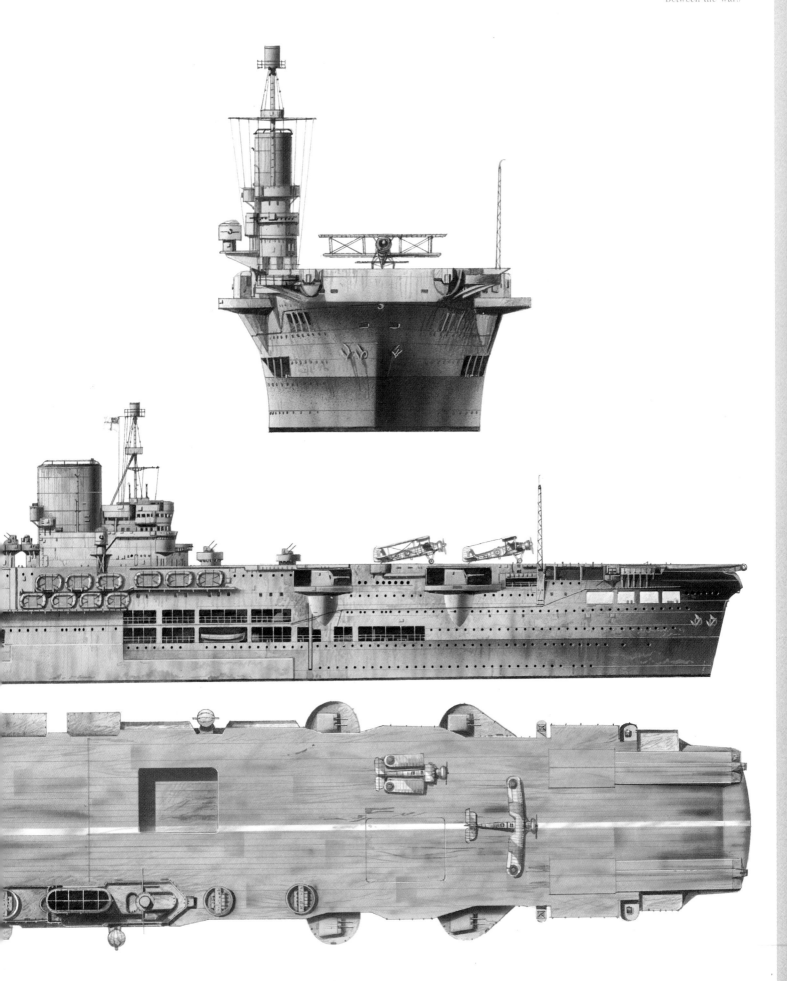

Chapter 7 – World War II

On 30 March 1939, in the face of continued and aggressive German expansion, France and the United Kingdom guaranteed Poland's frontiers. Heedless of this implicit warning, Hitler abrogated the Anglo-German Naval Agreement on 28 April. In June and August the keels of the first two of six planned 56,200-ton battleships were laid down, part of the ambitious Z-Plan, which would take a near decade to realise. This was not the action of a state bent on hostilities with a major naval power. The Führer expected that his ambitions in continental Europe would be achieved militarily, and Britain, faced with a fait accompli, would seek an accommodation rather than wage an impossible war. If necessary, hostilities with the British would follow in the late 1940s.

Germany's Axis partner, Japan, was following a similarly aggressive path. By 1941, with France and the Netherlands occupied by Germany, and Britain still facing defeat, their rich and extensive Far Eastern colonies were ripe for seizure. The United States feared for its interests in Guam, and the Philippines decided to freeze Japanese assets and trade. This was in July 1941. Thus cut off from her major oil supplies, and with stocks for only 18 months on a war footing, Japan was forced into making her move.

Occupation of territory owned by militarily beaten European powers would probably not bring the anti-colonial United States to war. Taking the Philippines was a different matter. It was just possible that a 'peaceful' occupation of the islands (which the Americans were known to regard as indefensible) could be undertaken if the USA could be persuaded that a war to reclaim them would be unrealistic. Unfortunately, the security of the Philippines was underwritten by the powerful element of the US Pacific Fleet that was based in Hawaii. With the Japanese Navy fully committed, it was vital that this force did not interfere. This was achieved by the pre-emptive strike against Pearl Harbor but, far from America accepting the situation, it was outraged by the act. Japan was not equipped for protracted war, her industrial capacity small in comparison with that of her adversary. Unless the Americans could be persuaded militarily to accept some sort of accommodation, Japan's ultimate defeat was certain.

The Battle of the Atlantic

Considering that, just 25 years earlier, the United Kingdom faced defeat from an unrestricted submarine campaign against her commerce, it seems odd, with hindsight, that neither the British nor the Germans made greater efforts to prepare for a similar campaign in World War II.

Between 1930 and 1935, British shipping had endured its worst-ever slump. Even in 1938, home shipbuilding was at only half the pre-1914 level. Many famous yards and companies had ceased trading or had cut back drastically. In 1937 British-controlled tonnage, at 20.4 million gross registered tons (grt), was at about the same strength as in 1914. As the world fleet had grown, however, the proportion of British tonnage had declined from 47.6 to 32.5 percent. Because the number of tankers had increased considerably and individual ship size had also increased, the number of dry-cargo carriers had dropped significantly.

Left: Aircraft carriers were the true capital ships of World War II. At the battle of the Coral Sea in 1942 the issue was decided by airstrikes alone, the surface ships never making visual contact. Here *Enterprise* steams at high speed with an escorting cruiser to starboard during the decisive battle of Midway.

Above: German submarines had come dangerously close to defeating Britain in World War I. They did so again in World War II, largely because of the lack of effort devoted to anti-submarine warfare in the 1930s. Here a Type VIIC U-boat is re-launched after maintenance.

Defeat in 1917 had hinged on the crude equation of new tonnage exceeding sinkings. The answer, as shown already by the Americans, was series construction of 'no-frills' standard ships. Facing a new conflict, the British did not set up the mechanism for such programmes and, when further orders began to filter through, it was the more lucrative warship contracts that were sought by the shipyards. Fortunately, the Americans had already acted. Congress wished to re-vitalise a moribund shipping industry but, with domestic building costing some 60 percent more than European construction, considerable intervention was necessary. In 1936, therefore, the US Maritime Commission (USMC) was established and in 1938, with a target of fifty hulls annually, placed its first contracts. By September 1939, it was already in a position to increase its target figure four-fold. Only standard designs were considered, involvement spreading quickly from seven to nineteen yards.

In the United Kingdom, the approach was less sharply focused. The Ministry of Shipping (later Ministry of War Transport) operated through its Directorate of Building, placing contracts to its own account and, still, that of individual companies. The latter, nonetheless, had to be to a yard's standard design and conform to wartime restrictions.

In September 1940, with the loss rate already spiralling, a British Technical Merchant Shipbuilding Mission was despatched to Canada and the United States. An initial order for sixty ships stimulated the Americans to create two completely new yards, each with seven slipways. Twenty-six similar vessels were ordered from the Canadians.

Below: Fifty US 'four stacker' destroyers built at the end of World War I were transferred to the British for use as escorts.

The British requirement was for a simple freighter that could shift 10,000 tons of cargo at 11 knots, with a low-powered (2500 ihp) reciprocating steam engine. The Americans needed to be persuaded of the advantages of building so basic a ship. Its virtual prototype existed already in the Sunderland-built *Empire Liberty*, and the American yards adapted it quickly for assembly from modular welded units. Initially, the Canadians followed British practice of framing-up and riveting. Undoubtedly, the timely creation of the USMC was one of the events critical to the eventual outcome of World War II.

In July 1935, following the signing of the Anglo-German Naval Agreement, Captain Karl Dönitz was

Above: German aircrew celebrate further successes against Allied merchant shipping.

given responsibility for the German Navy's U-boat arm. Dönitz was single-minded in his belief in submarine warfare but had to acknowledge the Agreement's re-emphasis on a Submarine Protocol. Submarine construction was slowed by the requirements for an overall naval expansion.

Nonetheless, by September 1939, he had overseen an expansion to 56 boats; almost numerical parity with the Royal Navy. They were of smaller overall displacement but all modern designs. Over half were the little Type II,

for use only in the North Sea and around British coasts. There were eighteen Type VII, capable of working the Eastern Atlantic, and a handful of Type IX, large enough to work farther afield. The latter two types went on, through continuous improvement, to provide the backbone of the force.

With the outbreak of war, the Z-Plan, with its projected 250 U-boats by 1948, was abandoned. Dönitz wanted 300 boats for an all-out assault on British shipping. Work was abandoned on all capital ships not actually launched, but absolute priority for submarine construction was forthcoming only in July 1940, when it was obvious that Britain was not going to be intimidated into a negotiated peace after the fall of France. The Germans had lost a further ten valuable months initiating a programme of twenty submarines monthly. Assuming a 10 percent loss rate, this was calculated to give a force of 300 operational boats by the spring of 1943.

So acute was the shortage of convoy escorts in the early days that it may be overlooked that the British Admiralty had devoted considerable time to their development. Until 1927, the Royal Navy operated sloops built under various World War I programmes. The 1,045-ton Bridgwaters were then introduced, evolving quickly through the successive classes of Halcyons, Grimsbys, Bangors and Algerines. They were, specifically, minesweeping sloops, which could land their sweep gear for anti-submarine (A/S) operations. It is worthy of note that the Halcyon-class *Seagull* was the Royal Navy's first all-welded ship. A derivative of the above line of development was the Kingfisher/Guillemot type. Configured for coastal convoy escort, the design proved to be unsuitable but re-introduced the category of 'corvette' to the fleet.

For ocean convoy work, a strong anti-aircraft (A/A) armament was wisely deemed necessary. The Stork prototype of 1934 led to the various sub-classes of Black Swans. These sloops were expensive but highly effective in both A/A and A/S roles. Despite their value, however, they were still expected to convert easily to a minesweeping role.

The 19-knot Black Swans had to be built to full naval standards but, in the interests of series production, design changed to those suitable for construction to good mercantile practice. Simplicity in design reduced construction times; simplicity in operation reduced the standard to which crews needed to be trained to achieve competence.

A second exception to this rule were the Hunt class destroyers, first cousins to the 'torpedo boats' of the German and Italian fleets. Their extra speed and armament made them suitable for the escort of hotly contested convoys, such as those to Malta, but they were equally at home on the English east coast. They came on-line when most needed, as did the first of the larger corvettes. These, the famous 'Flowers', were intended originally for coastal work, and their simple design, related to that of the then common whale catcher, made them particularly suitable for construction in small, basically equipped yards. Many stemmed from Canada, whose contribution was outstanding. Because they could be built and manned in numbers, the Flowers found themselves deeply involved with the so-called Battle of the Atlantic, where there was extreme urgency and with which they have become inseparable. Of these two groups alone, 86 Hunts and 135 Flowers were completed.

Plans for trade protection had long been finalised and the Admiralty assumed control of all British shipping a week before hostilities commenced. A huge programme was instituted to arm merchantmen defensively from the enormous stockpile of weapons retained after the warship scrapping spree of the 1920s. Gunners had also to be trained. To give an idea of the scale of this effort, the British merchant fleet then comprised about 3,000 deep sea ships and 1,000 coasters.

Within the Naval Staff, the Admiralty Trade Division organised the convoy system, its routing and provision of escorts. From the outset, coastal convoys ran at frequent intervals to link major ports and assembly points, the timetable synchronising with the cyclic nature of the ocean convoys. Major long-distance routes were to and from Halifax and Sydney, Nova Scotia, and to and from Gibraltar and Freetown, Sierra Leone. Routes quickly multiplied.

Above: The Germans converted a number of Focke-Wulf FW200s to long range maritime patrol aircraft that attacked convoys and vectored in the U-boats.

An initial acute shortage of escorts on the North Atlantic service was eased by escorting a convoy only for the first few hundred miles, after which it remained as an unescorted group for a day or two more before dispersing.

Given earlier experience, it is surprising that many had to re-learn the lesson that the best place for A/S ships was with a convoy. Many in authority saw this as 'defensive' and supported the formation of 'offensive' hunting groups. These rarely stumbled across a U-boat in the vastness of the Western Approaches. Convoys, of course, attracted the very U-boats that they sought but, while 'killing' submarines was laudable, the primary objective of a convoy escort's senior officer was the safe and timely arrival of the convoy.

The assault on commerce involved mining, submarines and surface raiders, and aircraft. Mines could badly disrupt the vital coastal convoy timetable. Laid by aircraft, destroyers, submarines or S-boats, mines were countered only by the patient, dangerous and endless task of sweeping designated safe lanes.

Initial havoc was caused by magnetic mines. Their principle was known to the British, who had also built them, but the provision of an antidote had to await the recovery of a specimen so that its polarity could be established. Steel-hulled ships could then be 'wiped' to give a measure of immunity by temporary de-magnetisation or, by means of on board generators and a heavy cable girdling the hull, permanently 'degaussed'.

Of the other modes of attack, submarines and surface raiders were effective from the outset, but aircraft needed to await the availability of forward airfields.

With much shipping capacity consumed on government service, strict economy was necessary and neutral charters were essential. Rationing in the United Kingdom reduced imports from the usual 60 million tons to 47 million.

It remained a temptation to route faster ships independently, rather than delay them in convoy, but

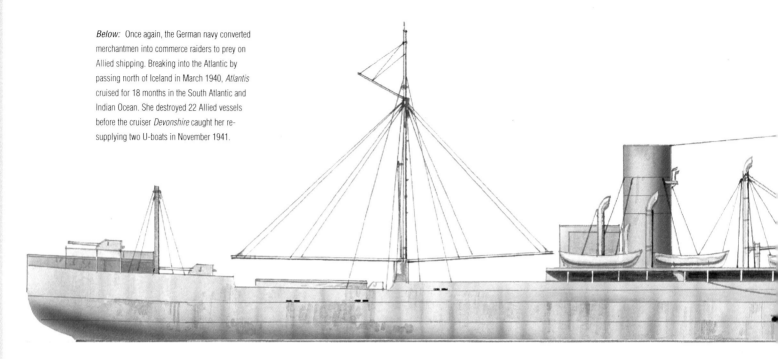

Below: Once again, the German navy converted merchantmen into commerce raiders to prey on Allied shipping. Breaking into the Atlantic by passing north of Iceland in March 1940, *Atlantis* cruised for 18 months in the South Atlantic and Indian Ocean. She destroyed 22 Allied vessels before the cruiser *Devonshire* caught her re-supplying two U-boats in November 1941.

from the outset the loss rate of 'independents' was higher. In the first four months of war, to the end of December 1939, submarines sank 114 ships, totalling over 421,000 grt. Only four of these had been sunk while in convoy.

By July 1940, with the end of the so-called 'phoney war', the whole of the continental European coastline, from North Cape to the Spanish border, came under German control. French Biscay ports now sheltered U-boats, greatly reducing transit times to and from their operational areas. From French airfields flew the big FW 200 Condors, which located convoys, zeroed in the U-boats, and attacked any stragglers.

Admiral Dönitz, himself an ex-submarine commander, had long theorised on the benefits of attacking in coordinated groups. However, with U-boat losses and the building programme still getting into its stride, he still had only 28 operational boats in July 1940. Only in early summer 1941 did numbers become adequate, and the general adoption of 'wolf-pack' tactics came to the British as an unpleasant surprise. The essence of the concept was that the first boat to sight a convoy kept contact and acted as a beacon to attract others. Group attack was then by night and on the surface. A U-boat's small silhouette made her almost invisible in darkness, and made it simple to penetrate the escort screen. Surfaced submarines were faster than most escorts and the latter's Asdic (sonar) apparatus was useless against other than submerged targets. Until the defences' tactics evolved to meet the threat, they were sometimes overwhelmed to the extent that voices once again questioned the viability of convoy. Cold, long-term statistics, nevertheless, correctly supported its continuance.

Admiral Dönitz's priority was to sink merchant ships, and he resisted any attempt to divert his submarines to other tasks. Any pretence at observing prize rules went by the board within weeks. (In fairness, restrictions on Allied submarines were virtually lifted in home waters,

and in the Mediterranean totally, from February 1941.) U-boats were met with in the Caribbean, attracted by the tanker traffic, and were always in evidence in the Mediterranean. Other than on the Atlantic convoy routes, however, their greatest success was along the US Eastern Seaboard during the first six months of 1942. The Americans at this time lacked both convoy system and A/S measures, and the Germans sank so much shipping, and with so little retribution, that they dubbed it, with grim humour, their 'Happy Time'.

Although the German Navy was more ready than in 1914-18 to commit heavy fleet units to commerce warfare, and caused considerable disruption by doing so, the results barely justified the means. In November 1939, both Scharnhorst-class battle cruisers broke out into the Atlantic but their six days at sea resulted in the sinking of just one ship, the armed merchant cruiser (AMC) *Rawalpindi*. During December, the 'pocket battleship' *Admiral Graf Spee* allowed herself to be outfought by three British cruisers, and sought refuge in the neutral River Plate. Faced with no prospect of ever getting out, her captain scuttled her. Her total 'bag' had been only nine ships, totalling some 50,000 grt. Her sister, *Admiral Scheer*, and the heavy cruiser *Hipper* netted a further 150,000 grt. In the face of the level of threat, the Admiralty began to incorporate, where possible, an old battleship into a convoy's defence. Several large convoys were spared when a raider sheered off rather than risk damage in a gun action. Ironically, no such gun action ever occurred and, despite the obvious risks, no battleship was ever lost on this duty.

In May 1941, the new German battleship *Bismarck* was lost after the dramatic chase which followed her sinking of the British battle cruiser *Hood*. Her objective, however, as that of her consort, the heavy cruiser *Prinz Eugen*, had been commerce destruction. Between them, they had accounted for not a single merchantmen.

On the last day of 1942 the *Hipper* and *Lutzow* (ex-*Deutschland*) were badly worsted by lighter British

forces covering a convoy near North Cape. Hitler's illogical response was to demand the de-commissioning of all heavy fighting ships, which 'irrevocable' decision led to the resignation of Grand Admiral Raeder. Then, on Boxing Day 1943, the *Scharnhorst* was destroyed by the British battleship *Duke of York* and several cruisers as she tried to intercept the convoy that they were covering.

German surface warships waged their campaign against British commerce until the U-boat arm had been built up to strength. This same period was used to convert selected merchant ships (twenty-six were planned) for duty as auxiliary cruisers. They carried a near-standard armament of six 150-mm (5.9-in) guns and four torpedo tubes, all carefully concealed. Within the cargo spaces were carried a pair of seaplanes, a large number of mines, extra fuel and workshops for self-maintenance.

Auxiliary cruisers completely out-gunned British AMCs, with which they should not be confused. The *Thor*, for instance, sank one and engaged two others without being brought to book. The *Kormoran* was intercepted by the cruiser HMAS *Sydney* off Western Australia, resulting in a duel which ended in both ships being sunk. Cruising for periods of up to five months, these raiders were far more successful than regular warships, in terms of shipping sunk and disruption caused, not least by their laying of small minefields at unlikely points.

Allied shipping losses reached crisis point during 1943. In spite of losses, U-boat strength increased from 250 boats in early 1942 to over 400 by mid-1943. About 50 percent were operational at any time. Evasively routed slow convoys took over a fortnight to cross the Atlantic and the running battles took on, for crews involved, a nightmarish quality.

March 1943 saw one of the biggest encounters, when two eastbound convoys in close proximity were savaged by forty submarines. Twenty-one ships were lost for only one U-boat.

Atlantis

data:

Displacement standard	17,600 tons
Length	489 feet
Beam	61 feet
Design draught	28 feet
Complement	351

Armament:
6 x 5.9-in guns
1 x 75-mm gun
2 x 37-mm guns
4 x 20-mm guns
4 x 21-in torpedo tubes
92 mines
2 aicraft (HE 114s)

Machinery:
2 diesel engines, 7,600 bhp
1 shaft
16 knots

Surprisingly, the balance shifted soon afterward. The 'killing ground' of the mid-Atlantic air gap was closed by long-range aircraft, assisted by the new escort carriers and A/S groups that could respond to emergencies. The early U-boat 'aces' were mostly dead, and the defences gained slowly in strength and technical superiority. During April and May 1943 alone, 56 U-boats were lost, mostly without survivors. In the July, the steeply rising curve of shipbuilding output overtook losses for the first time. Output kept rising as losses flattened out. For the second time in a generation, a submarine-led *guerre de course* had been defeated by the narrowest of margins.

Once again the key to success or failure, the merchant fleets had lost heavily. Over 5,000 Allied and neutral ocean-going ships, grossing over 21.5 million tons, were destroyed in the course of the war, of which 68 percent were sunk by submarines.

Below: After the fall of France, German U-boats were based on the French Atlantic coast, greatly increasing patrol times. These giant concrete shelters protected them from air attack.

The war against the U-boat

Successful outcome of the war against Germany depended upon the steady flow of ship-borne supplies from the New World to the Old, and the importance of beating the U-boat was paramount. A gross error on the part of the Royal Navy between the wars was the generally held assumption that technology had totally solved the problem.

Underwater ranging by the use of sound pulses was well established before the end of World War I, with British scientists building on the work of the French. Known by its acronym 'Asdic', the system remained experimental during the 1920s, its potential being explored in a couple of destroyer flotillas. Given the problems that were highlighted - false contacts, extraneous noise, water temperature variation, operator error, etc., it is surprising how quickly complacency set

in in high places. For the destroyer men knew better. Asdic 'beams' were highly directional and, because of their limited angle of depression, the operator lost contact with a submerged target on the run-in. This 'dead time', combined with the spell that it took depth charges to sink to the required depth, allowed an astutely handled submarine time to haul off to a safe distance. An ahead-throwing weapon, capable of engaging a contact still fixed by the beam, was introduced as early as 1930. The 3.5-in (89-mm) stick-bomb thrower, ancestor of the spigot mortar, could fire a projectile about a half-mile, adequate for the detection range of Asdic at the time. Its further development was abandoned on cost grounds. It would be resurrected at a later date, along with tactics involving two A/S vessels, one holding the target while the other attacked.

Admiral Dönitz knew well of Asdic and its limitations, which contributed to his enthusiasm for night attack on the surface. German surface ships were also fitted with

passive hydrophones, to detect both distant shipping and incoming torpedoes.

Despite all experience in the earlier war, there remained a body of opinion in the Fleet that forming merchantmen into convoys merely presented a submarine commander with an unmissable target. In truth, the immensity of the ocean was such that a group of ships was hardly more visible than a single ship. Where a given number of 'independents' would suffer a percentage intercepted and destroyed, the same number gathered in convoy could well get through unobserved. Independents could not be given individual escort. Attacking a protected convoy, on the other hand, left submarines open to counter attack by A/S defences that had not needed to waste effort in futile search.

Initially, the number of necessary escorts was over-estimated. It took time to realise the simple truth that the periphery of a defended circle increases only linearly with an increase in radius, whereas the area increases as

Flower class

data:

Displacement standard	940 tons
Displacement full load	1,160 tons
Length	205 feet
Beam	33 feet
Design draught	11.5 feet
Complement	85 max

Armament:
1 x 4-in gun
1 x quadruple 2-pdr
40 depth charges

Machinery:
Steam engine, 2,750 ihp
1 shaft
16 knots

Below: Adapted from a design for a whalecatcher, the Flower class corvette was pressed into service as an escort vessel. Over 250 were built in Britain and Canada.

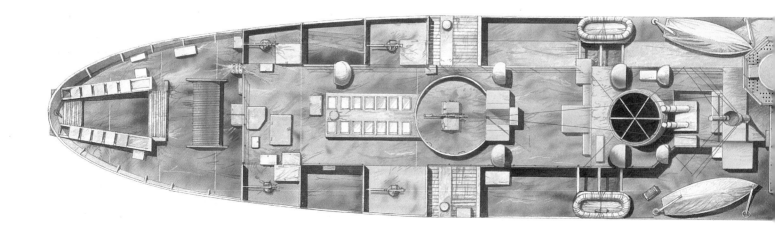

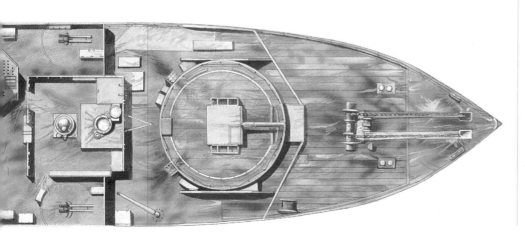

Above: The Type IXA long range submarine *U-42* being commissioned. She was an early loss, sunk in October 1939.

its square. For a given escort spacing, therefore, a large convoy was far more efficient than a small one, in terms of numbers of escorts to ships being protected.

Air power was a major factor in A/S warfare. In 1937 the Royal Air Force relinquished its responsibility for naval ship-borne aircraft and crews, although the relationship overlapped for some years following. In the same year, RAF Coastal Command was committed to maritime support. Then, in 1941, although remaining an element of the RAF, Coastal Command was placed under Admiralty operational control. The command was woefully short of effective aircraft. American-built Lockheed Hudsons and the indigenous Short Sunderland were being procured for medium- and longer-range operations but, by September 1939, only three squadrons had received modern aircraft. Coastal convoys might enjoy standing air patrols and the ability to call up additional air support when threatened, but outward-bound convoys soon passed beyond most air cover, a situation eased later by the establishment of air bases in Iceland and the Faeroes. Aircrews, in any case, had still received only minimal training in A/S tactics and still lacked a suitable weapon. As submarines had low speed and endurance when submerged, the presence of an aircraft to force them down usually meant that they lost touch, but carrier-borne aircraft for this purpose had to await the introduction of the Escort Carrier, late in 1941.

Following the fall of France, Admiral Dönitz moved his headquarters to Lorient. His policy of operating U-boats in loose groups, and his requirement for routine reports, generated considerable radio traffic. The British capitalised on this by developing an efficient high-frequency direction-finding ('Huff-Duff') set. One intercept allowed an A/S escort to run along a line of bearing to catch the unwary transmitter. Two intercepts gave a fix on the submarine's position, with both range and bearing: so an escort commander could quickly make the decision on whether or not to divert his ships for an attack.

U-boats attacking at night on the surface were first met with only starshell and gunfire. In early 1941, however, the first shortwave radar sets capable of detecting such small targets were coming into service. An important next step was to miniaturise them to make them aircraft-compatible. In parallel were developed powerful flares and then a wing-mounted searchlight, known as the Leigh Light.

By March 1942, RAF Bomber Command was able to transfer twin-engined aircraft, such as the Wellington, to Coastal Command. Carrying both radar system and weaponry, these could range over the Bay of Biscay to catch U-boats transiting on the surface at night. With what seemed agonising slowness, these marauders were joined by four-engined aircraft, such as modified B-24 Liberators and the ubiquitous Sunderland.

Type XXI

data:

Displacement standard	1,621 tons
Displacement submerged	1,819 tons
Length	251 feet
Beam	22 feet
Design draught	20 feet
Complement	57

Armament:
4 x 20-mm guns
6 x 21-in torpedo tubes
23 torpedoes

Machinery:
2 diesel engines, 4,000 bhp
2 electric motors, 5,000 hp
2 'creeping' electric motors, 226 hp
2 shafts
15.5 knots surfaced
16 knots submerged
3.5 knots 'creeping' submerged

Below The Type XXI U-boats were a dramatic improvement over earlier German submarines. With high underwater speed and advanced sonar equipment, they would have posed a serious menace to Allied shipping but the war ended before they could enter service in quantity.

Left: The German submarine campaign was centrally directed by Admiral Karl Dönitz. He continued to send his boats to attack in 1943 after the Allies' technological superiority led to a steep rise in U-boat losses. His son was one of the casualties.

Right: Its enormous battery capacity enabled the Type XXI to travel underwater at the same speed as some escort vessels, as the lack of paint on this boat's fin and stemhead testify. Active and passive sonars were carried, so the Type XXIs could achieve a firing solution without raising the periscope.

Corvettes, which had performed valiantly in the deep ocean on tasks for which they had not been designed, were gradually replaced by frigates. These were larger and faster, with greater endurance and depth charge capacity. Importantly, they also improved crew comfort, vital for high efficiency.

Initially ad hoc groups of available ships, escort forces were increasingly built around designated 'Escort Groups'. Ideally consisting of eight ships, these trained as a team, staying together to refine their skills and to develop methods of quick and effective response. A major force in such policies was Admiral Sir Max Horton, an ex-submariner, who was appointed to head

the Western Approaches Command in November 1942.

By early 1943 convoys enjoyed escort for the whole of the North Atlantic crossing. At meridian 26 degrees West, the responsibility changed from British to American and Canadian escorts.

Obliged by increasing aircraft patrols to transit submerged, U-boats had their time on operations severely curtailed. A first response was to modify the topsides for an enhanced A/A armament. Such modifications made a boat difficult to handle, while the guns were not reliable due to water ingress. Most importantly, they did not guarantee immunity. Radar detectors were next introduced, which gave warning of

an approaching radar-equipped aircraft. From early 1942, however, radars moved from metric to centimetric operational wavelength, for which the receivers were useless. Suspecting that their own equipment was radiating sufficiently to act as a homing beacon, the Germans compounded their problems by switching it off. Only early in 1943 did they acquire the answer in a shot-down British aircraft, which contained a nine-centimetre H2S set.

This discovery resulted, in turn, in new types of detector, and the introduction of decoys and radar-absorbent materials. At no time did the Germans seem to suspect that their routine radio traffic monitored by

Above: The Type 3 Hunt class escort destroyer *Derwent* pulls away after refuelling at sea.

'Huff-Duff' was a major source of their discomfiture. With the availability of escort carriers, fixes on transmitting U-boats could be followed up swiftly by aircraft, allowing escorts to remain in the screen.

Then there was 'Ultra', high-grade intelligence gleaned from the breaking of German cyphers, which allowed countermeasures to be more precisely targeted. Bombing the U-boats 'at source' was singularly unprofitable. Hulls were assembled in building yards, using component sections constructed in plants scattered around the country. All the French Biscay ports, and some assembly yards, were by now equipped with bomb-proof pens, which survived intact despite enormous collateral bomb damage inflicted on the local population and their cities. In the first five months of 1943, 266 bombers were lost in such unproductive raids.

The climax of the convoy war came in Spring 1943, with large-scale battles in the mid-Atlantic gap where air patrols were still thinnest. May was a disaster for the U-boats, with 41 destroyed, some 30 percent of the available strength at sea, and Dönitz temporarily withdrew his forces. They were left in no peace, however, with Allied aircraft now conducting an all-out effort in the Bay of Biscay. Allied escort carrier and hunter-killer groups also made their appearance. Their 'nose' for finding U-boats, seemingly uncanny at the time, can be attributed to Ultra.

Frigates increased the lethality of their attacks by dropping patterns of ten to fourteen depth charges. Despite their extra capacity, they often had to transfer further supplies from selected ships in their convoy. As fewer weapons would be required if fired when the target was still fixed by the Asdic, ahead-throwing mortars were again introduced. 'Hedgehog', which fired a near-instantaneous pattern of twenty-four 30-lb (14-kg) projectiles, began development in 1940, going into production in the autumn of 1941. Its bombs exploded only on contact with the target.

Asdic (soon to be re-named 'sonar') had now been refined to give range, bearing and depth, though with an accuracy dependent upon conditions and, often, the skill of the operator. By 1944, in the later corvettes and frigates, it was married to the Squid mortar, whose three fast-sinking projectiles each contained 200 lb (91 kg) of explosive. Fused automatically from the Asdic output, they could tackle deep-diving targets. A final wartime development was the 'Double Squid'.

Where U-boats had earlier avoided attacking escort ships in order to sink the higher-priority merchantmen, the escorts could no longer be ignored. The *Zaunkönigelectric* torpedo homed acoustically onto a frigate's characteristically high-revving propellers, typically blowing off the stern. Acoustic counter-measures were introduced to counter them, mostly crude clanging-pipe devices which simply saturated the torpedo's hydrophones.

Dönitz's boats also began to receive rubber-based anechoic coatings, to absorb the energy from a sonar pulse. In good conditions they could attenuate a reflected pulse by 75 percent, drastically reducing Asdic range.

The Bay of Biscay air offensive showed that U-boats were in greatest danger when caught on the surface and trying to dive. Surface transits under diesels were faster, and enabled batteries to be charged. To enable a diesel to be run in the submerged condition the Germans developed *Schnorkel* (or 'Snort') gear. Patented ten years earlier by the Dutch, it comprised a mast (later retractable) for the induction of air and the exhaust of diesel gases. Snort-fitted boats still made slow progress when submerged and greatly fatigued their crews. Radars, endlessly improved, could also now detect the small target of the snort masthead in reasonable conditions.

As the merchant navy crews had stuck to their task during the dark days of 1940 to early 1943, so now the U-boat men addressed theirs. In June 1943, seventeen boats were lost. In July, thirty-seven. By the year's end, another eighty-seven. The 'Happy Time' was definitely over.

Some U-boat commanders cheated the air patrols by using Spanish territorial waters, others by operating in less heavily patrolled areas. To extend their endurance, specially fitted re-supply submarines operated at pre-arranged rendezvous. 'Ultra' usually got wind of these, however, and they were especially targeted.

Facing total defeat, the U-boat itself had to change. Two major new concepts emerged. The revolutionary Type XXVI had, as auxiliary machinery, the Walter turbine. By burning diesel oil in an atmosphere of hydrogen peroxide a powerful combustion process was possible without the need of air. The gases thus formed drove a turbine. Sufficient hydrogen peroxide was carried for six hours' running at 25 knots. As most A/S escorts could manage no more than 20 knots, the submarines could both evade them and gain a required attacking position on the convoy. In practice, the process proved to be unstable and dangerous, and no satisfactory submarine design was ever based on it.

To achieve high underwater speed all external detail needed to be enclosed, retractable or removed. This was true also of the other major departure, the Type XXI *'Elektroboote'* and its diminutive, the Type XXIII. These utilised the conventional technology of large electric propulsion motors powered by a very large battery capacity. Where diesels were still used for snorting and battery charging, the stored energy was sufficient, in the case of the Type XXI, for running submerged for 10 hours at 12 knots, or in the attack mode for 90 minutes at 18 knots. Additional small motors were fitted for slow, silent running.

Following Grand Admiral Raeder's resignation in January 1943, his successor, Dönitz, raised submarine construction priorities by every means. Despite growing losses, strength was maintained at between 400 and 450 boats from mid-1943 until the close of hostilities. It was fortunate for the Allies that the new technologies came on line too late to be of consequence. Of about 1,160 commissioned U-boats, total losses from all causes equalled 784, with most of their crews.

Mention should be made of the various types of miniature submarine known collectively as 'Small Battle Units'. Their purpose was to target offshore shipping engaged in amphibious landings and to deny use of the large estuaries. They ranged from the *Marder* and *Molch*, which carried one, or two, close-range torpedoes, to the advanced two-man Type XXVII variants of *Hecht* and *Seehund*. Over 300 of these were built, with some crews showing considerable fortitude in operating as far afield as the English East Coast. While the small battle units proved to be a nuisance off Normandy and in the Scheldt approaches to Antwerp, the Japanese-style overwhelming of the amphibious forces' defences never materialised. Losses, as much to lonely, unmarked disappearance as to the attentions of patrolling warships, did not justify the considerable resources devoted to them.

Below: A US destroyer is refuelled by the cruiser HMS *Norfolk* while escorting an Atlantic convoy.

The submarine war against Japan

Above: The Gato class submarine USS *Sea Dog* prepares for her last war patrol in the Pacific, 1945.

By Spring 1942 the new Japanese empire stretched from Burma in the west, along the Malay peninsula and the great islands of the Dutch East Indies to New Guinea. Thence it swept via the Solomons and Gilberts northward into the unmarked wastes of the Pacific, somewhere in the near 4,000-mile gap that separated Japan proper from the nearest American outpost at Hawaii. Grimly, Australia and India awaited their turn but, for the moment, the Japanese stayed their hand.

Japan now had access to all the raw materials that she required; her vulnerability lay in their being scattered over thousands of islands up to 3,000 miles away from Japan. Like the United Kingdom, Japan was dependent upon her merchant marine - outward to support a hundred garrisons, homeward with basics for her industry and war machine. Yet the Imperial Japanese Navy had paid scant heed to commerce protection, which it regarded as 'defensive'. Resources had been concentrated on fighting ships, in pursuit of the planned 'short' war. There were no real plans for convoys and few available A/S escorts. Japanese submarines were trained to sink warships; it was expected that foreign boats would do the same.

In December 1941, when she went to war, Japan possessed some 6.1 million grt of merchant shipping, immediately swollen by a further 0.8 million grt of prizes. Over four million tons of shipping were needed to service her scattered conquests. The large population of the home islands could rely on few indigenous natural resources. Oil imports alone required nearly five million tons annually and even rice had shipped in from Indo-China. Home shipbuilding potential, already limited, was poorly organised and subject to shortfalls in raw materials and skilled manpower. It was as obvious to the Americans, as it had been to Admiral Dönitz, that a sustained submarine assault on the enemy merchant fleet could be decisive.

American naval forces in the Pacific were split between the West Coast, Hawaii and the Philippines, the latter group designated as the 'Asiatic Fleet'. With the deteriorating situation immediately pre-war, the bulk of the Pacific submarine force was moved forward to Manila. At the outset there were here 23 'fleet' submarines and six old 'S'-boats. Lacking air-conditioning, the latter were ill-suited to tropical operations, the crew living and working in almost

Right: American shipping was protected from Japanese submarines by new classes of DEs like the *Rudderow*.

Above: By 1945, Japanese shipping was also attacked from the air. Here one of the escorts of a convoy sinks off Indochina.

unbearable levels of heat and humidity.

With the Japanese quickly winning air supremacy, the Asiatic Fleet's surface units were obliged to pull back, leaving only the submarines to continue the fight. Older boats formed a defensive screen around the northern Philippines, while the sixteen best submarines were organised into deployed and reserve strike forces. Their achievements were disappointing. Japanese ships abounded, but the aerial reconnaissance necessary to direct the American effort was no longer available. By later standards, submarine skippers were relatively old and, by training and by orders, over-cautious. They were also plagued with the beginnings of the great torpedo problem.

With the remorseless Japanese advance, the Asiatic submarines also had to fall back, first on Java, then on Freemantle/Albany in south-western Australia, the latter an inconvenient 1,500 miles from the nearest enemy. A measure of the disarray into which the Allies had been plunged is that, of the US Navy's 111 operational submarines, no less than 73 had been shared between Manila and Hawaii. From day one they had been ordered to operate without restriction yet, so far, only 50,000 grt of Japanese shipping had been destroyed, for the loss of four submarines. Fortunately, a further 73 were under construction.

S class submarines

data:

Displacement surfaced	854 tons
Displacement submerged	1,065 tons
Length	219 feet
Beam	21 feet
Design draught	15 feet
Complement	42

Armament:

1 x 3-in or 4-in guns
4 or 5 x 21-in torpedo tubes
12 torpedoes

Machinery:

2 diesel engines, 1,200 bhp
2 electric motors, 1,500 hp
2 shafts
14 knots surfaced
11 knots submerged

The theatre in south-west Asia was so large that one force, mainly old 'S'-boats, operated under Rear Admiral Ralph Christie from Brisbane on Australia's east coast. The remainder stayed at Freemantle, with Rear Admiral Charles Lockwood in command. A noted optimist, he revitalised a dispirited service. One of his first actions was to lease two hotels for crew rest and recreation between patrols. Then he looked into the question of delinquent torpedoes. Representations to the Bureau of Ordnance (BuOrd) that they were running deep were met with angry rebuttals, and assertions that the complaint was merely a cover for poor marksmanship. Lockwood arranged for specimen weapons to be fired through a strung fishing net, which proved the point conclusively.

It would be another year before their reluctance to explode was explained. Magnetic exploders were very effective in causing a torpedo detonation below a target's keel but proved in service to be over-sensitive (geomagnetic strength varies greatly worldwide). Their unreliability had caused the Americans, like the British and Germans before, to abandon them for contact devices. Lockwood's basic experiments involved dropping sample torpedoes on their noses. Those that didn't explode were then (carefully) dissected. It was quickly established that the firing pin assembly was of faulty design and, ironically, the squarer the impact, the less likely it would be to fire. By now, many crews had risked life and limb to tote around dud torpedoes, and there were many enemy ships that, by rights, should have been on the bottom.

Applying their usual methods of standardisation and series production, the Americans commissioned 35 new boats in 1942, 55 in 1943 and 53 in 1944. By the end of the war in the Pacific there were 169 submarines in the theatre, about one-third of which were in their patrol areas at any time.

Left: US submarines carried heavy gun armaments, sinking smaller ships with shellfire to conserve torpedoes.

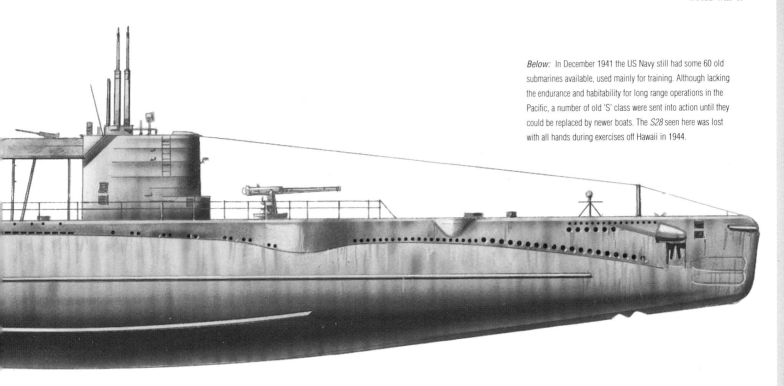

Below: In December 1941 the US Navy still had some 60 old submarines available, used mainly for training. Although lacking the endurance and habitability for long range operations in the Pacific, a number of old 'S' class were sent into action until they could be replaced by newer boats. The *S28* seen here was lost with all hands during exercises off Hawaii in 1944.

Their dimensions effectively defined by the pre-war Salmon class, American boats increased very little in size. However, habitability and endurance were gradually improved, along with hull design, and steel quality and thickness. Boats were thus able to dive deeper and better able to survive depth-charging. Above-water profiles were cut down to reduce radar cross-section. Larger, low-speed motors were developed, which could drive propulsion shafts directly without the requirement for noisy, expensive and space-consuming reduction gears.

The ultimate group, the Tench class, were 1,570/2,415 ton boats, capable of 75-day patrols. In size 311.7 x 27.3 ft (950 x 8.3 m), they could dive to 400 ft (122 m). For the ten torpedo tubes, six forward and four aft, 28 torpedoes could be carried. Mines, commonly laid in Japanese waters, could be substituted at a rate of two mines for each torpedo. Two 5-in (127-mm) guns could be mounted to economise on torpedoes. The crew totalled 81.

American electronic research was well ahead of that of the Japanese. Good sonar (as American Asdic was termed) was soon complemented by air search radar, to give early warning of prowlers. The really valuable addition was surface search radar. Its antenna mounted on an extendible mast, it allowed precision attacks to be made at night, when the Japanese observed few precautions.

Over the first twelve months of the submarine war, the Japanese lost some 700,000 grt of shipping, mostly offset by new acquisitions. New building, however, came a poor second to be demands of the army and navy, who controlled all policy. Their plan for a short war concentrated on the salvage and repair of casualties rather than the construction of replacements. This economised on raw materials and saved time, but resulted in a rapidly deteriorating stock, of which an

Right: Seen through the periscope of SS 309 *Aspro*, another Japanese merchant ship slips below in 1944.

ever-increasing proportion awaited repair.

While the Japanese instituted a formal convoy system only in early 1944, ad hoc escorted groups were running as early as 1942. American submarines were still operating singly and, although they were undoubtedly hurting the enemy, it is a feature of the period that claims of sinkings were considerably overstated, and not borne

out by post-war records.

One top-scoring boat was the Brisbane-based *Silversides*. She sailed on the last day of 1942 on a fairly typical patrol, to operate around the Japanese fleet base at Truk and then to proceed to Hawaii for refit. While they were still short of their objective, a 22-year old pharmacist's mate had to perform an emergency

'Gato' class submarines

data:

Displacement surfaced	1,525 tons
Displacement submerged	2,415 tons
Length	312 feet
Beam	27 feet
Design draught	15 feet
Complement	80

Armament:

1 x 3-in gun
10 x 21-in torpedo tubes
24 torpedoes

Machinery:

4 diesel engines, 5,400 bhp
4 electric motors, 2,740 hp
20 knots surfaced
8.5 knots submerged

Below: A 'Gato' class submarine of late 1942. Officially capable of diving to 300 feet, successive variants could dive even deeper. Late war 'Gato' class boats were operating at 450 feet with a crush depth of 750 feet.

appendectomy on a sick crew member. It was successful. Hours later, *Silversides* attacked an enemy destroyer which, unscathed, retaliated with hours of depth-charging. It called up an aircraft, whose accurate bomb pattern sent the submarine spiralling downward. Control was regained well below safe depth and *Silversides* pressed on for Truk. She fired at a Japanese fleet submarine and claimed it as sunk, but this was not confirmed post-war. A 10,000-ton tanker, however, exploded very satisfactorily. A full six-tube bow salvo was then launched at a convoy of four freighters, escorted by two frigates. Five ran satisfactorily, sinking a creditable three ships, totalling 17,800 grt. Elation was short-lived, however, when it was realised that the sixth torpedo was stuck halfway out of its tube. Once the rumpus died down, *Silversides* surfaced, went full astern and gave the recalcitrant 'fish' a further blast of compressed air. To the relief of all, the torpedo disappeared. As the skipper was unable to observe the effect of his attack on the convoy, he was credited with only one ship. His 'confirmed' bag from the patrol was thus a submarine, a tanker and a freighter. His actual score was a tanker, three freighters and no submarine, illustrating the overall difficulties in making intelligence assessments.

In August 1943, in the face of spiralling losses, the Japanese High Command finally ordered that all merchant ships would be escorted. A General Escort Command was established and a crash building-programme for utility diesel frigates initiated. Over 150 were built in a series of sub-groups that reflected the growing crises in the supply of materials and skilled labour. Unprepossessing, straight-line ships they were, but they carried a respectable 120 depth charges, a weapon which, like the torpedo, the Japanese expended generously. A 3-in (76-mm) army trench mortar was an ingenious substitute for a Squid-type stand-off A/S weapon.

Left: USS *Salmon* before the war. She survived a prolonged depth-charging by Japanese destroyers in 1944.

Above: Top-scoring US submarine, USS *Tautog* seen in 1945 with full scoreboard painted on her sail.

American response to convoy was 'wolf-packing'. Initially boats were paired, but co-ordinated attacks were difficult as the boats were forbidden to speak with each other, direction coming from Brisbane in the same way Dönitz controlled his boats from ashore. Resulting radio traffic was disliked for the same reason. Commencing in October 1943, the three-boat 'packs' were initially not popular. Skippers, selected for self-reliance, objected to a divisional commander exercising close control. Communications still needed improvement, with the ever-present risk of a 'blue-on-blue' encounter. Nonetheless, the Japanese lost over 1.8 million grt in 1943, and managed to replace only 0.8 million grt of it. Fifteen Pacific Fleet boats were sunk however, victims of improved countermeasures and the risks attendant in penetrating increasingly constricted and shallower waters.

During 1944 Allied advances in the Pacific theatre allowed submarines to operate from tenders (i.e. depot ships) in forward zones. Transit times shortened, thirty more boats were operational, and the Japanese-controlled zone was shrinking. Convoy routes, so tardily established, were having to be abandoned. Oil, in desperately short supply, had to be hauled from the far south of Japan's island empire. Tankers were given high priority as targets and, by the year's end, the Japanese were forced to station their major fleet units where oil supplies were available.

Submarine packs, sporting unofficial labels such as the 'Mickey Finns', 'Blair's Blasters' and 'Clarey's

Crushers', scoured the diminishing enemy fiefdom for targets. As the fleet carriers were freed from covering major amphibious operations, their aircraft joined in the slaughter. Convoys hugged the coasts and the ten-fathom line in vain as submarines took increasing risks in shoal water. Nineteen boats were lost in 1944, but the Japanese suffered more - nearly 3.9 million grt sunk against 1.7 million grt replacement.

By March 1945, the enemy had abandoned the south China Sea. The convoy network collapsed, a monument to failure to foresee the obvious or to learn from history. Most surprising was the lack of air cover, which could have been mounted from the various islands. Aircraft had been a decisive factor in the defeat of the U-boat, but it was not aircraft that the Japanese lacked, it was front-line aircrew.

History's most effective blockade had, by June 1945, reduced the Japanese population to the beginnings of starvation. They had lost air and sea supremacy, and the dropping of two nuclear bombs only speeded up the inevitable surrender.

American submarines, of which fifty were lost in the theatre, accounted with their allies for 60 percent of the eight million grt of Japanese shipping destroyed. They also sank over two hundred warships.

Below In 1943 Japan began to build the austere Matsu class destroyers instead of the extremely well-equipped pre-war types.

Amphibious warfare

With command of the sea comes the ability to put ashore an invading force on a defended coast. This may take the form of a raid, with limited objective like Zeebrugge in 1918 and Dieppe in 1942, or a large-scale landing with a view to conquer. For a raid, temporary air and sea control will suffice until the force is withdrawn, but the situation in a major landing is different. Once a successful beachhead has been established, much of the amphibious force may be withdrawn, but the forces ashore will require to be supplied in bulk, and by sea, for as long as is required. Air and sea control must, therefore, be maintained.

World War II's first major opposed landing was in April 1940, when Germany firmly terminated the 'phoney war' by invading Norway. This nation's geography is unusual, with most of the population concentrated in a few major coastal towns, connected by comparatively few lines of communication. Taking enormous risks in the face of the strength of the British Home Fleet close by, the German Navy committed much of its strength in penny packets, which used surprise to great advantage to simultaneously land military forces in the heart of the half dozen most populous areas.

The plan worked admirably but British reaction, though very slow, cost the Germans many useful ships,

Below: US landing craft head for the Normandy beaches on D-Day, June 1944.

Above: Australian troops are landed at Lae, New Guinea by US LSTs, 1943.

which they could ill afford to lose. The losses had a considerable bearing on Operation ' Sealion', the plan to invade the United Kingdom which, postponed by stages, was eventually quietly abandoned.

In June 1940 the last British forces had been ignominiously expelled from mainland Europe via Dunkirk. Strangely, at a time when mere survival was the priority, there were some who directed their thought at a eventual re-conquest of Europe. The Germans in Norway

had used established port facilities, but it had to be assumed that these would not be available 'next time'. An assault would need to be truly amphibious, undertaken and supported over the beach.

Following their experiences at Gallipoli, the British had decided in 1924 to develop a doctrine for future

Above: Obscured by shell bursts, Mount Suribachi looms over the invasion beaches on Iwo Jima, 1945.

seaborne assault. The so-called 'Landing Craft Committee' was formed to consider the design and numbers required of craft suitable to land troops and armour on a hostile coast. Specialised craft had been built during World War I for Admiral Fisher's aborted Baltic project but had been used at Gallipoli. Some of these X- and Y-lighters still remained and formed the basis for the MLC1 of 1926. Of simple design, capable of series production, this craft could transport one hundred equipped troops or their equivalent weight. For use in shallow water, it was water jet propelled.

The MLC1 had a hoisting weight of twenty tons, so that it could be stowed aboard ship. It had already been recognised that there would be two major categories of amphibious vessel. Minor types, later grouped together as Landing Craft, would undertake the inshore tasks involved in the actual assault, but larger vessels, Landing Ships, would be required to assist if a prior substantial sea crossing was involved. Several marks of MLC were built during the 1930s, establishing essential features such as the forward lowering ramp, and hull form designed to take and leave the beach in a kindly fashion.

Completing its brief in 1938, the Landing Craft Committee was disbanded in favour of an Interservice Training and Development Centre. This produced, among others, a useful 10-ton Assault Landing Craft, or ALC, to be slung under the davits of a converted merchantman known as a Landing Ship, Infantry, or LSI. By 1939 the British, although hardly boasting an amphibious capability, had laid the groundwork and had taken the first steps toward 'Combined Operations'. The first application of these fledgling techniques was in Norway in 1940, but their usefulness was largely lost in the general opprobrium heaped upon what was a rushed and ill-considered campaign.

In the United States, also, much work had been done. As early as 1918, the possibilities of war with Japan were being assessed. There was the paradox of accepting that the Philippines were effectively indefensible, while identifying the need for forward fleet bases far from the West Coast and Hawaii. The prospects of seizing defended islands had to be considered.

At this point, the US Marine Corps succeeded in persuading the authorities that they were the ideal force

Left: The 283 ton LCTs were the smallest US landing craft to receive numbers. LCT 1179 is seen here off Sicily, 1943.

Above: Landing on remote islands, the US amphibious forces had to land vast quantities of supplies over open beaches.

to develop amphibious warfare doctrines. Exercises tested their theories and, in 1934, they published the 'Tentative Landing Operations Manual'. This milestone document identified six factors vital to a successful amphibious operation:

1. Organisation and Command.
A naval attack force would be responsible for transporting the landing force to the point of application. The senior officer of the naval attack force would also be responsible for the landing force until the completion of the assault phase, when the landing force commander would assume authority over his own force.

2. Naval gunfire support.
While recognised as vital to the success of the assault, naval gunfire's weakness lay in not being able to engage targets on reverse slopes. Practical test showed also that the appearance of a naval barrage was more impressive than its actual results. Trained observers were required to be put ashore to spot fall of shot and to target gunfire to respond quickly to the needs of troops on the spot.

Above: Ancon was the first of several dedicated amphibious command ships converted from merchant hulls.

3. Aerial support.

Later of critical importance, this was best supplied by the Marine Corps' own pilots, who well understood the problems on the ground. Such support, however, required Marines to fly from carriers and this, at the time, they did not do.

4. Ship-to-shore movement.

Even by 1940 this was still based on the Higgins boat. A hard-chine 18-knotter, it could survive in surf but accommodate only thirty troops and was not suited to heavy equipment. A valuable innovation was the tracked amphibious vehicle (LVT). The vehicle's tracks gave traction ashore and in the 'swimming mode'. With twenty equipped men aboard it could negotiate the offshore reefs common in the Pacific and, importantly, cross the beach to put its complement ashore under better cover. Although growing in size and weight, the LVT developed into a miniature landing craft cum light tank, equipped with both forward ramp and a turret-mounted cannon.

5. Securing the beachhead.

With the assault troops ashore, the operation entered a critical phase, their holding still shallow and covered by enemy gunfire. It was identified as vital to put ashore, under the cover of naval guns, dedicated 'labour units' to prevent bottlenecks developing on the beach as vehicles, light artillery, fuel, ammunition and stores were brought in. Such parties came under the control of the beachmaster, who directed the movement of craft and their discharge. As amphibious operations grew in size, this area of the organisation required great resource and flexibility.

6. Logistics.

This blanket term covered the provision of suitable ships and craft, and who or what was shipped by which. It included the measures necessary to sustain a beachhead to the point of breakout. The principle of 'combat loading' was evolved, so that materiel arrived ashore in the order in which it was required. This meant 'last aboard' was 'first ashore', and often conflicted with the preferred loading plans of the ships' first officers, who were accustomed to putting the stability of the ship before the convenience of the cargo arrangements.

Above: A wrecked US LCM and Japanese landing ship on Iwo Jima beach, 1945.

The Tentative Manual enshrined experience to date but was subject to continuous revision as each operation taught new lessons.

American interest in amphibious warfare between the wars was not unconnected with the experience being acquired by the most likely enemy, Japan, which had been developing techniques since the early 1920s. Here, it was the army's task to make the assault but, as inter-service friction was normal, there was competition for resources. Doctrines were for the application of limited force in a carefully considered manner. Extensive previous war-gaming was undertaken to examine various options and to anticipate likely response from the defences. Landings were preferably to be undertaken at night, and at numerous points to wrong-foot the defence. Troops were to be landed in self-sufficient units, able to fight independently down to platoon level. The Navy was responsible for the overall protection of an operation

Left: An LST heads to the Sicily invasion beaches laden with M3 half-tracks.

Above: Japanese destroyers contested the waters off Guadalcanal in a series of bitter night actions.

were surrendering to much smaller groups of invaders. Because they had carefully gauged the level of opposition, the Japanese did not need the enormous paraphernalia of amphibious war that the Allies would require to reclaim the territory.

After World War I Japan had received mandate for the vast Pacific island groups that had formed part of the German empire. Including the Marshalls, Marianas and Carolines, their strategic value was apparently lessened by the Washington Treaty clauses that forbade their signatories to fortify territories in the theatre. By restricting access to the area, the Japanese excited American suspicions, but there is little evidence to prove that they contravened the agreement to any degree before war became inevitable. Once fortified, however, and held by resolute garrisons, the islands became the scenes of bitter dispute and some of the war's hardest fighting.

So vast was the theatre that two major commands were created, each subordinate to Admiral Chester Nimitz, C in C Pacific. General Douglas MacArthur's forces were to advance along the 'southern perimeter', from New Guinea to the Philippines. The direct route across the Pacific to Japan was given to Vice Admiral Robert Ghormley, soon replaced by Vice Admiral William Halsey. This was a leap-frogging campaign, with head-on assaults at those islands that could not safely by bypassed. The objective was to advance sufficiently close to Japan to mount a heavy bombing offensive, following which would be actual invasion.

MacArthur's major contribution was to make the

until the beachhead was secure, but forces ashore were expected to fend for themselves in short order and to take losses as inevitable. Great stress was laid on local air and sea superiority, assault points being chosen with an eye to rapid seizure of airfields. With air superiority established, a working port was favoured, as landing barges were confined to LCA-sized craft.

As early as 1935 the Japanese had completed the 11,500-ton specialist landing ship *Shinshu Maru*, which operated with her ungainly successors in China. They had a conventional engines-amidships arrangement, but with a vast superstructure to house twenty of the ubiquitous Daihatsu landing craft. Pre-loaded, these

could be put afloat over a stern ramp. Returning, they were then reloaded through large side ports in the ship's side. Aircraft could be carried, but not operated directly by the ship.

The Japanese offensive in the south-west Pacific was effectively over in about ten weeks. Knowing that Allied forces in the theatre were weak and ill-coordinated, they conducted a brilliant campaign, using ships in small groups to stage landings at a bewildering number of locations in quick succession. As defences were weak, or non-existent, small forces sufficed. Few landings were truly amphibious, being conducted from warships or hastily converted transports.

Seeking to create confusion, they succeeded. Confusion bred an air of despondency and hopelessness in the defence, so that often quite large Allied forces

Below: USS *Fletcher*, name-ship of a 175-strong class of destroyers, seen here off New York in July 1942.

Above: US transports off Guadalcanal were just in range of Japanese shore-based bombers operating from Rabaul. Here, a formation of Mitsubishi G4Ms (Allied reporting name 'Betty') attack at low level through a hail of American anti-aircraft fire.

Right: One of the Japanese bunkers on Tarawa which proved impervious to anything but a direct hit from a heavy shell. After 1943 the Japanese tended to concentrate on defending inland, accepting that US naval firepower made it impossible to hold the beach.

Japanese divert vital resources to a campaign that did not directly threaten the Home Islands. Halsey's forces were pitted against fanatically motivated defenders, prepared to die to a man for the possession of a few acres of unremarkable coral strand.

America's assault troops were chosen from the Fleet Marine Force which, in three years of combat, expanded from two under-strength brigades to six divisions, organised in two corps.

The great initial Japanese assault faltered with their reverses at the Coral Sea and Midway in May and June 1942. Building on success, the Americans decided to block their progress down the Solomons chain. In August 1942 the 1st Marine Division landed on Guadalcanal in a deceptively easy ad hoc amphibious landing. This used LCAs working from attack transports, with later reinforcements run in by APDs, 'four-pipe' destroyers converted to high-speed transports for 200 troops. Foreshadowing things to come, it took six months of nightmarish close-quarter combat to persuade the Japanese to leave.

Future assaults involved larger forces and longer ocean passages. Critical to their timing was the availability of Landing Ships, Tank (LSTs). Over one thousand of these 3,700-tonners were built in the United States and a further 115, slightly larger, in the United Kingdom and Canada. With bow doors and ramp they were built to take the beach, supplementing the 370-ton Landing Craft, Tank, or LCT. Deliveries commenced in November 1942, the month of the North African landings, an operation which (like all others in the Mediterranean) was looked upon by the Americans as something of a side-show.

Ironically, the LST's value was, generally, not as a tank carrier. This became the province of the Landing Ship, Dock (LSD), a ship-fronted floating dock, whose floodable well could accommodate up to fourteen Landing Craft, Mechanised (LCM). Each of these could be pre-loaded with a medium tank, and floated in or out of the welldeck. The LSTs, of which there were never enough, became universal cargo carriers, packed with stores and a few trucks to shift them ashore. Troop transport and casualty evacuation was also the usual lot.

Assault fire support in the Mediterranean, where landings were usually conducted at night, was at a lighter level than the Pacific, scene of daylight landings against a fanatical enemy. Veteran battleships commenced a new career in this service, but precise follow-up support, in answer to demands from forward observation officers, was often best provided by destroyers. These proved vulnerable when working inshore, so smaller landing craft were modified for the duty, with tank turrets, elderly naval guns, or large numbers of the Army's 5-in (127-mm) rockets.

As early as October 1941, Admiral Lord Louis Mountbatten was given command of British Combined

Above: The LSD (Landing Ship Dock) *Ashland* seen during the landings in the Marshalls, March 1944.

Operations. The multi-service nature of the organisation was recognised by siting the senior officers of each service involved, their staffs and communications, aboard a single headquarters ship. Until 1943, this would be a warship, but converted merchant ships proved to be better suited. During an operation, conditions aboard could be bedlam, with possibly 100 signal staff coordinating several services, landing craft, aircraft direction, support fire and heavy naval forces offshore.

In under three years, the Americans alone built over 45,000 specialised landing ships and craft. They saw service in some of the war's most momentous operations, culminating in the Pacific at Iwo Jima and Okinawa and, in Europe, at Normandy.

Below: *LST-4* approaches 'Yellow Beach' during the landings in southern France, August 1944.

Above: Landing craft form up to head for the beach during the invasion of Iwo Jima. The LSTs in the foreground are *LST-787* and *LST-789*, the latter has *LCT-801* embarked.

Right: The battleship *Indiana* opens fire on a Japanese iron works 250 miles north of Tokyo, July 1945. At this date, plans were well advanced for an amphibious invasion of the Japanese home islands. Allied casualties were estimated at over 250,000 but the development of the atomic bomb rendered the operation unnecessary.

Aviation at sea

At the outbreak of World War II, the Royal Navy had six operational carriers but less than 220 aircraft deployed at sea. The still-neutral United States, in contrast, could field 2,000 Naval and Marine Corps aircraft, 1,000 more had been authorised, and these were entering service at a rate of 350 annually. British aircraft were also of low performance. The 245 mph biplane Sea Gladiator was being superseded as fighter by the even slower and ill-conceived Roc, a derivative of the Skua dive-bomber. For torpedo, reconnaissance and spotter duties, the much-loved Fairey Swordfish was carried. With a maximum speed of only 140 mph, however, it was very vulnerable in the face of an adequate defence.

With so few carriers available, each was of extreme value, yet their deployment in the early months of the war was highly questionable. The *Ark Royal* and *Courageous* were sent on anti-submarine patrols, with the result that the former was near-missed by a salvo of torpedoes and the *Courageous* was sunk with heavy loss of life. The war was scarcely a fortnight old. Later, carrier-borne aircraft would be highly effective against

U-boats, but circumstances would then be different.

The abortive Anglo-French campaign to halt the German occupation of Norway brought carrier reinforcements from the Mediterranean. Quite unnecessarily, the *Glorious* sailed back from Norway in June 1940 ahead of the main force. Compounding this error by having no patrol aloft, nor strike armed and ready, she encountered the two Scharnhorsts and was sunk by gunfire, a rare fate for a carrier.

It was fortunate that, by the end of 1940, the first two armoured-deck carriers (*Illustrious* and *Formidable*) were complete, and deliveries were beginning of the Fulmar fighter. The first American-built Grumman F4F Wildcats, known by the British as the Martlet, were also arriving.

In June 1940, Italy spread the war to the Mediterranean, a theatre for which the Swordfish was well suited. In the November, 21 aircraft from the *Eagle* and *Illustrious* struck by night at the Italian fleet base of Taranto. Arriving in two waves, they put three battleships on the bottom for the expenditure of eleven torpedoes and the loss of two aircraft. Only weeks later, the *Illustrious* was nearly destroyed by newly arrived Ju 87

Above: The US Navy received 16 Essex class fleet carriers between 1942 and the end of the war.

('Stuka') dive-bombers. Seven hits from heavy bombs, and severe damage to shell plating from the concussive effect of near misses, put her out of the fight for nearly a year. Repaired at Norfolk, Virginia, her powers of survival impressed the Americans to the extent that they revised the early construction plans for what were to become the Midway class.

Formidable, her replacement in the Mediterranean, operated Albacores, the intended successors to the Swordfish. In March 1941, *Formidable* mounted an air strike against a reluctant Italian force. Although the primary target, the battleship *Vittorio Veneto*, went unscathed, a torpedo brought a cruiser to a halt. A powerful cruiser and destroyer force sent back to assist and was then caught and destroyed in the nocturnal battle known as Matapan. Fortunes then swung again. During the heavily disputed battle for Crete, the *Formidable* was caught by dive-bombers and, with similar damage, joined her sister under repair at Norfolk.

With the carriers absent, Fleet Air Arm (FAA)

Left: Grumman Avenger torpedo bombers, Douglas Dauntless dive bombers and Grumman F6F Hellcats spotted forward on the flight deck of USS *Lexington* (CV 16) during strikes against Saipan, June 1944.

Below: Douglas Devastator torpedo bombers unfold their wings aboard *Enterprise* at the Battle of Midway, 4 June 1942. Only four of these aircraft survived the combat air patrols of 'Zero' fighters and defensive fire from the Japanese carrier group.

squadrons worked very successfully from Malta and North Africa, striking at Italian convoys to Tripoli and Benghazi, vital to the support of the Axis armies in the Western Desert. The elderly *Argus* and *Furious* found useful employment in running fighter aircraft to beleaguered Malta and to West Africa, for staged onward flight to the Middle East.

Poorly served by shore-based air support and reconnaissance, the Italians realised, too late, the value of aircraft carriers. Two large passenger liners were hastily converted, but technical difficulties prevented their ever entering service in time to be of use.

Germany had commenced two 23,000-ton carriers in 1937/8. These, the Graf Zeppelins, would have had an air wing of 42 aircraft, split one third dive-bombers, two thirds fighter/fighter-bombers. A powerful surface armament suggested that they could be used for independent commerce raiding, but their actual purpose is rather obscure outside the general context of an overall fleet expansion. Like the Italians, however, the Germans were starting carrier design from scratch. Problems were experienced particularly with arrester gear, catapults and suitable aircraft. Neither ship was ever completed.

A Graf Zeppelin accompanying the *Bismarck* in May 1941 would have given the Royal Navy a major problem.

As it was, the battleship had broken out into the Atlantic and had stunned the British by sinking the battle cruiser *Hood*, which had successfully intercepted her. From that point she was a marked ship. Swordfish from the Home Fleet carrier *Victorious* hit her with a torpedo, but the 18-in (457-mm) weapon caused little damage other than a persistent oil fuel leak. The *Ark Royal*, with the Gibraltar-based Force H, then hit her twice more, the second damaging the port shafts and jamming the port rudder. Slowed, the *Bismarck* was eventually destroyed by gunfire.

Malta's survival meanwhile, was essential to the outcome of the campaign in North Africa, but sustaining the island exacted a high price. Unlike Atlantic convoys, which were threatened mainly by submarine attack, those to Malta were under continuous air attack from airfields ashore, threatened by surface attack by the Italian fleet, and still plagued by submarines. The constricted geography of the Mediterranean allowed little deviation from set routes, making elaborate deception plans necessary.

This hard-fought series of operations climaxed in Operation Pedestal, the 'August Convoy' of 1942. In the course of this action, the veteran carrier *Eagle* was lost to submarine attack, while the new *Indomitable* suffered

Above: With sixteen 5-in guns, the Atlanta class cruisers came to be used as anti-aircraft escorts for US carrier groups.

two heavy bomb hits and three near misses, the cumulative damage taking six months to repair.

November and December of 1941 marked the nadir of the Royal Navy's fortunes during World War II. One loss was that of the *Ark Royal*, sunk by a single submarine torpedo on 14 November. As with the *Audacious*, 27 years before, the sinking provided many lessons for the design of later ships. A major problem with carriers was the necessity to run uptakes from the port boiler room across the ship beneath the lower hangar deck to the starboard side funnel. A quite moderate list could create a major leak path. *Ark Royal*'s auxiliary generators were also all steam-driven, resulting in a loss of power when the boiler spaces had to be evacuated.

Severe action damage took fleet carriers out of service for months at a time. Only the most important of convoys were thus able to get carrier cover. This had been foreseen pre-war, and a number of large, diesel-driven passenger liners were earmarked for conversion to auxiliary carriers. However, while they were being prepared, emergency measures needed to be taken to counter the long-range German aircraft used to 'snoop'

Above: A Douglas Dauntless dive bomber approaches Japanese-held Wake Island. Note the fuze extension fitted to ensure the bomb explodes on the surface, rather than burying itself in the ground.

Left: *Hornet* entered the China Sea in early 1945, attacking Japanese merchant shipping. Here a Curtis SB2C-3 Helldiver returns to the carrier.

Akagi

data:

Displacement standard	36,500 tons
Displacement full load	42,000 tons
Length	855 feet
Beam	103 feet
Design draught	28 feet
Complement	1,340

Armament:
6 x 7.9-in guns
12 x 4.7-in guns
28 x 25-mm guns

Machinery:
Steam turbines, 130,000 shp
4 shafts
31 knots

Aircraft:
63

Armour:
unknown

Below: Vice-Admiral Nagumo's flagship, the *Akagi* led the attack on Pearl Harbor and the subsequent raids against Australia and British targets in the Indian Ocean. She was destroyed at Midway by dive bombers from USS *Enterprise*.

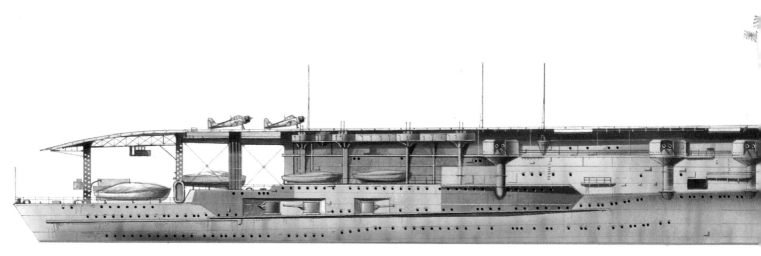

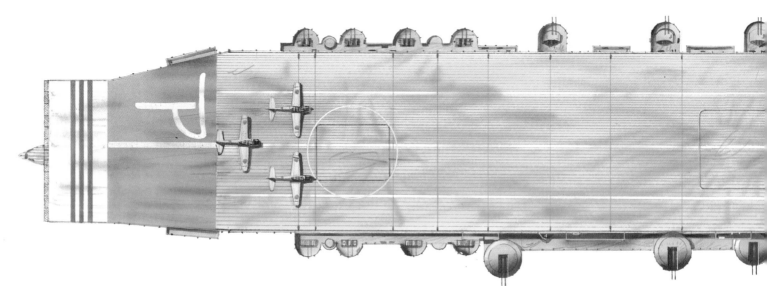

Above: Shokaku had a partially armoured deck, enabling her to survive dive-bombing attacks in 1944.

convoys and to pick off stragglers. The interim solution was the Catapult-Armed Merchantman (CAM), of which 35 were planned. These ships were able to carry a full cargo, but had a catapult fitted over the forecastle. Permanently ranged on it was an expendable Hurricane or Fulmar fighter, to be launched when a prowler made an appearance. Following an action, a CAM pilot needed either to ditch and hope to be picked up, or fly ashore if in range. Starting in January 1941, CAMs made over 200 voyages. Only eight launches were recorded but nearly every one resulted in a 'kill'.

More elaborate were the Merchant Aircraft Carriers (MAC). Either tankers or bulk grain carriers, their capacity cargoes could be handled by pipe, allowing a full-length flight deck to be fitted over. Most boasted neither hangar nor catapult. The flightdeck was between 400 and 500 feet in length, and the ship's 15 or so knots could not guarantee a reasonable wind-over-deck. Here the Swordfish, with its great lift and low stalling speed, came into its own. Four were permanently ranged on deck.

In the event, only the *Pretoria Castle* passenger liner was converted to an auxiliary carrier; liners proved to be too valuable as troopships and the yards were overloaded with work. Escort carriers (CVE) were needed in large numbers, effectively a production problem, and best left to the United States.

The pioneer CVE was the British ship *Audacity*, converted to minimum standards from a captured German merchantman. With no hangar, her mix of six Martlet fighters or Swordfish lived on deck. Her life was short but valuable.

In parallel, the Americans had commenced more extensive conversions of standard C3 ships ('C3' being the US Maritime commission code for a cargo ship of between 450 and 500 feet). The first were to British account but, recognising their potential, the US Navy began to retain some for training. In all, some 130 CVEs were built. Later units were designed as such from the

keel up. Others were larger, rebuilt T4 tanker hulls. Their immense contribution included A/S convoy escort, ferrying replacement aircraft, and operating in large groups to provide close air support for large amphibious landings such as Salerno and Leyte.

Also deficient in numbers of flightdecks, the Japanese made several elaborate conversions, varying from the two 11,260-ton Shoho types, rebuilt from naval ships, to the *Hiyo* and *Junyo*, 24,150-tonners remodelled from a pair of NYK passenger liners. In both regular and auxiliary carriers the Japanese made the mistake of wasting resources over too many classes. Series production arrived only with the 17,150-ton Unryu class. Ten were planned, but the programme started too late to see more than three of these 34-knot ships completed.

Accustomed to standardisation, the Americans did not make the same error, concentrating on the 27,500-ton Essex and 11,000-ton Independence classes, the latter built on the hulls of large light cruisers. Considered by the navy to be rather small, the Essex class design dated from the 1930s, reflecting the treaty-limited types that preceded it. Nonetheless, the class was highly successful, running to ten 'short-' and fourteen long-hulled units completed out of a planned 32-ship series.

Carrying only 45 aircraft (the Essex class carried 100) the nine Independence class could be recognised easily from the row of four stumpy funnels at the starboard deck edge.

Japan's assault on Pearl Harbor on 7th December ushered in a new era of maritime warfare. This was typified by large scale manoeuvre, featuring ships built around, and supporting, a core carrier force, which launched air strikes from ever-increasing ranges. To attack Hawaii, the Japanese mustered six carriers, deploying some 420 aircraft. With nothing to oppose it, such a concentration could wreak havoc.

Under its very able and aggressive commander, Vice Admiral Nagumo, the Japanese carrier squadron was left unchanged as far as possible, going on to strike at Darwin in February 1942, and at Ceylon and shipping in the Bay of Bengal in April.

Following the loss (to shore-based aircraft) of the battleships *Repulse* and *Prince of Wales*, remaining British naval forces were in inadequate strength to resist the rampaging enemy, falling back and effectively yielding control of the eastern Indian Ocean. The enormous scope of the Japanese advance meant, however, that their forces became ever more extended, risking groups of ships which depended for protection on local air superiority, i.e. carriers.

In May 1942 a typically complex operation began, with the objective of taking Port Moresby in New Guinea and establishing a foothold at the southern end of the Solomons. The invasion force was covered locally by the small carrier *Shoho* and, from a distance, by the two big Zuikaku class. Aircraft from USS *Lexington* and *Yorktown* found and sank the *Shoho*, causing the assault to be abandoned. A counter-strike from the enemy fleet carriers mistakenly attacked the American replenishment group but, next day, in improving visibility, the main

Below: The CVE *White Plains* was part of the light carrier group attacked by Japanese battleships off Samar in 1944.

Japanese carrier aircraft

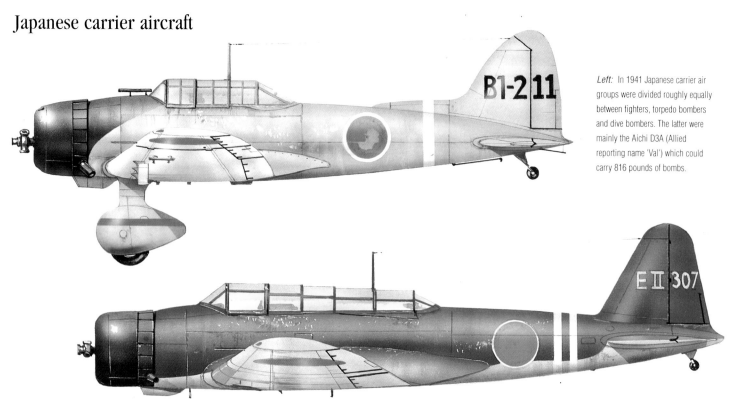

Left: In 1941 Japanese carrier air groups were divided roughly equally between fighters, torpedo bombers and dive bombers. The latter were mainly the Aichi D3A (Allied reporting name 'Val') which could carry 816 pounds of bombs.

Above: The Nakajima B5N (Allied reporting name 'Kate') was the standard Japanese carrier-based torpedo bomber in 1941.

Left: The Mitsubishi A6M (Allied reporting name 'Zeke', though often called the 'Zero') could out manoeuvre almost any Allied fighter in 1941 and had far greater operational range.

Essex class

data:

Displacement standard	27,208 tons
Displacement full load	34,888 tons
Length	820 feet
Beam	93 feet
Design draught	27 feet
Complement	2,682

Class: *Essex, Yorktown, Intrepid, Hornet, Franklin, Ticonderoga, Randolph, Lexington, Bunker Hill, Wasp, Hancock, Bennington, Boxer, Bon Homme Richard, Leyte, Kearsarge, Oriskany, Antietam, Princeton, Shangri La, Lake Champlain, Tarawa, Valley Forge, Philippine Sea.*

Armament:
12 x 5-in guns
32 x 40-mm guns
46 x 20-mm guns
91 aircraft

Machinery:
Steam turbines, 150,000 shp
4 shafts
33 knots

Armour:
Belt ....4 in
Ends ....2 in
Deck ....1.5-2.5 in

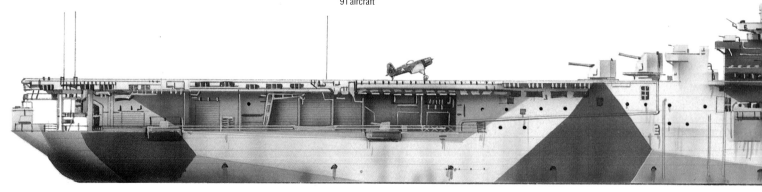

US carrier aircraft

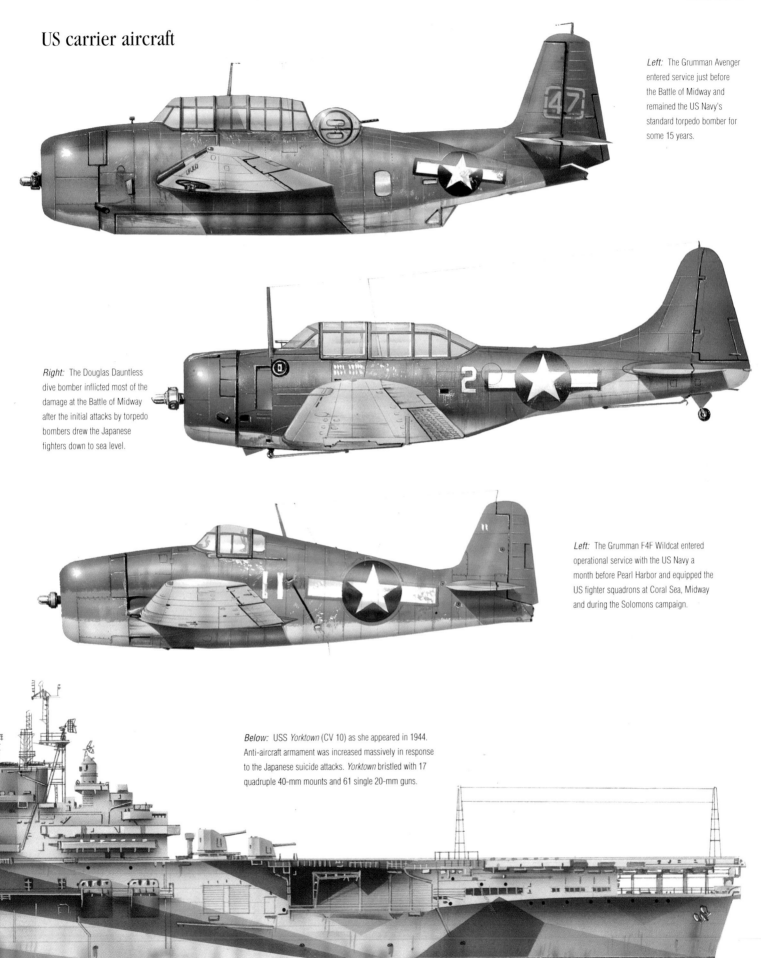

Left: The Grumman Avenger entered service just before the Battle of Midway and remained the US Navy's standard torpedo bomber for some 15 years.

Right: The Douglas Dauntless dive bomber inflicted most of the damage at the Battle of Midway after the initial attacks by torpedo bombers drew the Japanese fighters down to sea level.

Left: The Grumman F4F Wildcat entered operational service with the US Navy a month before Pearl Harbor and equipped the US fighter squadrons at Coral Sea, Midway and during the Solomons campaign.

Below: USS *Yorktown* (CV 10) as she appeared in 1944. Anti-aircraft armament was increased massively in response to the Japanese suicide attacks. *Yorktown* bristled with 17 quadruple 40-mm mounts and 61 single 20-mm guns.

Left: As a stop-gap measure to increase the number of carrier decks before the Essex class were completed, nine light cruisers were converted on the stocks into light carriers. The Cleveland class all commissioned in 1943.

Right: The sea plane carrier *Chitose* seen in the late 1930s. Converted to carry midget submarines before the war, she was converted into a light carrier after the Battle of Midway and sunk at the Battle of the Philippine Sea in 1944.

Below: A Japanese aircraft falls blazing towards a US carrier. Without self-sealing fuel tanks, most Japanese aircraft tended to catch fire if badly hit.

carrier groups located each other in the Coral Sea and struck almost simultaneously.

Shokaku survived three bomb hits but the *Lexington*, attacked from high and low level, was hit by two bombs and two torpedoes. The structural damage she would have survived but, as so often with fuel and munition-laden carriers, collateral fire and explosion proved to be fatal. On balance, the American loss was the greater but, for the first time, the Japanese had been frustrated in their intentions.

Japanese naval strategy still sought to draw the Americans into a single decisive battle, and in June 1942 they attempted this with an operation directed at the tiny island of Midway. This outpost was 1,100 miles west of Hawaii but, it was calculated, was too valuable for the Americans to ignore. The Japanese mobilised huge naval forces but, typically, spread them widely in a complex plan that included an attack on the Aleutians. As a result, only four out of the six available carriers threatened Midway. Only three decks were available to the Americans who, however, were fully appraised of Japanese intentions by virtue of code-breaking.

A first enemy air strike against the island did not sufficiently quell the defences and the Japanese admiral decided on a second. As his aircraft were re-arming aboard his ships, the American strike arrived, achieving complete surprise. The formations had become very fragmented but a low-level torpedo attack drew the Japanese fighter cover down, leaving the American dive-bombers unmolested. A devastatingly accurate attack hit three carriers, all of which were destroyed by fire. The fourth, however, got away a counter strike which sank the American *Yorktown* before she too was despatched. The main Japanese surface group was too distant to be of

any support and, again, the operation was abandoned.

Midway was of critical importance. The Japanese were never to be granted time to replace four carriers and their battle-hardened air wings before American production got into full swing. Coral Sea and Midway had set the pattern for the Pacific war. Many small and bitter actions were to be fought between surface groups but the major actions, upon which the course of the war depended, all pivoted on carrier forces.

From the Japanese aspect, American carrier strength grew at an alarming rate. On the last day of 1942 the new *Essex* joined the fleet. Within the next twelve months she was joined by six sisters and six CVLS. In November 1943 came the first of the giant strides across the Pacific, when Tarawa and Makin were assaulted to recover the Gilberts. Covering the operation, and suppressing every Japanese airfield within flying range, were 730 aircraft from six fleet carriers and five CVLs. For close support, a further 200 aircraft flew from eight CVEs. Both sides lost over one hundred aircraft, but only the Americans could afford to.

Two months later it was the turn of Kwajalein, in the neighbouring Marshalls. The fast carrier force was now organised in four groups and, in February 1944, these struck at Truk, the Japanese fleet base in the eastern Carolines. The fleet was absent but, in a huge attritional action lasting two days, 250 Japanese aircraft and over 137,000 grt of shipping were destroyed.

In June 1944 the circus moved on to the Marianas, where landings on Saipan and Tinian provoked major reaction by the Japanese fleet. It mustered five fleet and four light carriers, with about 430 aircraft, to attack the American covering force. However, this now included seven fleet and eight light carriers with twice as many

aircraft. In a do-or-die action the Japanese admiral, Ozawa, mounted four maximum strength air strikes from his carriers and nearby Guam. Spruance, his canny opponent had organised his defence in considerable strength, and waves of attackers were slaughtered. During what was officially the Battle of the Philippine Sea, but popularly termed the 'Marianas Turkey Shoot', the Japanese lost in the region of 400 aircraft, most with their aircrew. The loss rate was some 3 to 1 in the Americans' favour.

From this point the Japanese Navy had so few remaining aircrew that their carriers were virtually ineffective, and operations depended upon shore-based air cover. The last great effort for the fleet was in response to the American landing in the Philippines, at

Leyte Gulf in October 1944. Four separate encounters comprised the greatest naval trial of strength in history. By now the American covering forces could deploy over one thousand aircraft from eight fleet and eight light carriers. Ozawa's four remaining carriers could muster just 115 aircraft between them. For inshore support, 400 further American aircraft flew from no less than eighteen CVEs.

Not for the first time in history, shore-based air power proved to be inadequate to fleet requirements and, despite a dreadful lapse of judgement on the part of Halsey, the Japanese were roundly defeated. Leyte Gulf cost them four carriers, three battleships, ten assorted cruisers and eleven destroyers. As their fleet no longer constituted a threat to American progress, the Japanese

Above: Firecrews in action on the flight deck of a US carrier in 1944.

hit back with a new weapon, the *Kamikaze*.

It was during the battle off Samar that the Americans were disconcerted to find enemy pilots deliberately crashing their bomb-and-fuel-laden aircraft into the CVEs. It marked the beginning of a campaign, brought about by the lack of fully trained pilots which, in turn, had been caused by the introduction of proximity-fused A/A ammunition, which had greatly increased loss rates.

The Japanese home islands were already within range of B-29 bombers working from the Marianas but, in order to provide fighter escort, closer airfields were required. In early 1945, therefore, the islands of Iwo Jima and Okinawa were taken, following weeks of bloody, hand-to-hand combat. Amphibious vessels and the covering force alike were exposed to extended *Kamikaze* attack. Destroyer pickets, posted to provide early warning, themselves became targets. Anything, from carriers to landing craft, were chosen indiscriminately by the suicide pilots who, engaged on a one-way mission had effectively twice the normal range.

As the sea war in Europe was entering its final stages, the British built up an Eastern Fleet to fight alongside their ally. Four armoured-deck carriers, two battleships and five cruisers, which could have changed the course of the war had they been available a few years earlier, now formed but one further task group for the final act. The carriers' tough protection enabled them to shrug off *Kamikaze* strikes but a great limitation was that all units were designed for shorter-range operations, with access to foreign bases. As such, they required substantial support in the Pacific.

Considerable controversy surrounded the relative merits of American and British carrier design. On balance, it came down to numbers. With only a few decks, Britain could not afford to lose them, accepting smaller airwings as the price of survivability. For sheer offensive capability, the American approach, with large airwings and a ship designed to turn them around quickly, was superior.

In the event, the Midway class carriers, completed too late for the war, combined British experience with a large airwing, resulting in a ship of 45,000 tons standard displacement.

Above: Bunker Hill on fire after two *Kamikaze* aircraft crashed into her off Okinawa.

Below: USS *Yorktown* CV 10 during the landings on Saipan, June 1944.

The decline of the capital ship

It is interesting to speculate whether the capital ship era would have ended as quickly as it did had it not been for the long moratorium on construction imposed by the Washington Treaty. Most capital ships engaged in World War II were of World War I design, irrespective of subsequent modernisation. By the time the treaty restrictions were abandoned, war was already looming and few could be built in time. With the sole exception of four American Iowas, only those battleships laid down two years or more ahead of hostilities had any hope of being completed. Thus, the 45,000 ton British Lions (commenced mid-1939), the 55,400-ton German 'H' type (mid-1939) and the 41,000 ton French *Clemenceau* were abandoned for higher priority work.

Even the invaluable British King George V class experienced construction spans that increased progressively to over five years. Effective battleships could not be built smaller than their foreign peers, whereas effective aircraft carriers could. Carriers were also simpler to construct, with little requirement for armour plate and none for turrets and major ordnance, the production of which consumed major resources.

World War I had demonstrated that the capital ship was threatened as much by submarine torpedo as by heavy gunfire. By 1939, the aircraft had been added to the

Right: Prince of Wales as she appeared at the time of her loss in December 1941. The previous May she had engaged the *Bismarck* with the ill-fated *Hood*. Off Malaya she became the first modern capital ship to be sunk by air attack while able to manoeuvre and fight freely (unlike the battleships at Pearl Harbor).

threat list, although air-dropped torpedoes proved more effective than the anticipated bombs in actually sinking a ship.

Despite experience proving again that auxiliary cruisers were more effective commerce raiders, all of Germany's few capital ships were so employed at one time or another. This policy, which resulted directly in the loss of the

Bismarck, Scharnhorst and *Graf Spee*, stemmed from the original philosophy underlying the Z-plan. By menacing convoys with heavy raiders, the Germans would oblige the Royal Navy to cover them with task groups, which

Below: The German battle cruiser *Gneisnau* during the celebrated 'Channel Dash' back to Germany, 1942.

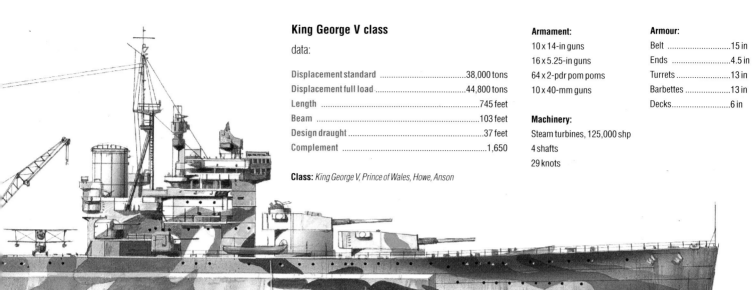

King George V class

data:

Displacement standard	38,000 tons
Displacement full load	44,800 tons
Length	745 feet
Beam	103 feet
Design draught	37 feet
Complement	1,650

Class: *King George V, Prince of Wales, Howe, Anson*

Armament:
10 x 14-in guns
16 x 5.25-in guns
64 x 2-pdr pom poms
10 x 40-mm guns

Machinery:
Steam turbines, 125,000 shp
4 shafts
29 knots

Armour:

Belt	15 in
Ends	4.5 in
Turrets	13 in
Barbettes	13 in
Decks	6 in

would themselves be vulnerable to attack by the planned 'super'-battleships. Premature war caused abandonment of the Z-plan, but available major units, *Scharnhorst*, *Admiral Scheer*, *Admiral Hipper*, et al, were still used to attack shipping. The British response, as predicted, was to use battleships to accompany convoys. This, however, was where the plan went awry for, in the absence of the German super-battleships, an old British vessel proved a quite adequate deterrent.

As the King George Vs and, usually, the Nelsons were retained in home waters, the Mediterranean Fleet had to make do with Queen Elizabeth class. Excellent in their day, these were now 25 years old and only three of five had been fully modernised. Pre-war Anglo-French planning had called for the Mediterranean to be primarily a French responsibility. As things turned out, the Queen Elizabeths were rarely allowed by the Italians to get within gun range so, again, their great value was in deterrence.

One of the earliest exchanges of fire was in fact with French heavy units when, in July 1940, their squadron at Mers-el-Kebir (Oran) had to be immobilised. The action was ordered at the highest level, but was deeply distasteful to the Royal Navy and considered nothing short of treachery by the French themselves. Immediately after Dunkirk, however, the British mood was desperate and major units not disposed to cooperation could not be allowed to fall into enemy hands.

Early encounters between heavy ships, such as those between the *Renown* and both Scharnhorsts (off Norway in April 1940) and between the *Warspite* and *Giulio Cesare* (off Calabria in July 1940), showed that even one or two major-calibre hits were sufficiently demoralising for a faster enemy to break off the action.

By the time that the *Bismarck* was brought to book, she had been damaged by torpedoes, was proceeding slowly and erratically, and unable to steer. The *Rodney* and *King George V* conducted the final act from very close range, within the theoretical immunity range of all three. Although the *Bismarck* was thus reduced to a wreck topside, she refused to sink by gunfire alone and had to be destroyed by torpedo.

When the Japanese hit Pearl Harbor in December 1941, it was the Americans' great fortune to have all their carriers elsewhere. The loss of elderly battleships, although of immense psychological impact, was not of great importance. From the outset, the Pacific war was one of grand manoeuvre and dominated by the aircraft carrier. In their then current state of modernisation they would have been no more use against the rampaging enemy than were the British 'R' class battleships in the Indian Ocean. As it was, most were salvaged and, as a matter of national pride, refurbished and brought up to a reasonably modern standard, being available for the vital task of fire support when they were most needed.

It is noteworthy that, at the Coral Sea action, no

Above: The World War I battle cruiser *Renown* seen in heavy seas from her Force 'H' consort *Ark Royal*.

battleships were present. Just weeks later, at Midway, the Japanese had no less than eleven capital ships in support. In either engagement, however, it was only the carriers that were involved in significant action, and it was the carrier casualties that really mattered. The enormous firepower of the Midway support groups remained quiescent, irrelevant to the outcome.

Six months of dispute over Guadalcanal resulted in a dreadful toll of ships. On the night of 14/15 November 1942 the new American battleships *South Dakota* and *Washington* encountered an enemy bombardment detail

C.W. Nimitz,
Fleet Admiral, USN

with two heavy cruisers and the 1915-vintage battle cruiser *Kirishima*. Throughout the Pacific war, the Americans enjoyed technological advantage but this tended to over-reliance, and sometimes rebounded. The *South Dakota* was hotly engaged with destroyers when, probably due to the shock of her own gunfire, her main circuit breakers dropped out, causing a total power loss. This lasted only three minutes but disrupted the vital radar plot. Out of touch with her senior ship, she blundered into the Japanese heavy units. Unencumbered, these smothered her with an estimated 42 hits, fortunately mostly 8-in (203-mm). The Japanese, however, were so intent on the unfortunate *South Dakota* that the *Washington*, all unsuspected, was able to suddenly engage the *Kirishima* at decisive range.

Shattered by nine 16-in (406-mm) and some forty 5-in (127-mm) hits, she blazed until scuttled about three hours later.

The action was significant in being one of only a handful in World War II where capital ships engaged each other at sea. Two of the others, those of the sinking of the *Scharnhorst* in 1943 and the Surigao Strait in 1944, were also fought in darkness and involved superior radar-laid gunnery.

By the latter half of 1942 the battleship's new status was already emerging. At the Battle of Santa Cruz in the October, the *South Dakota* kept close station on the carrier *Enterprise* through a series of determined air strikes. Although damaged, the carrier escaped destruction only through her consort's rugged defence,

Above: Texas exchanges shots with German shore batteries at Cherbourg, France, 1944.

which accounted for an estimated 26 aircraft.

Six British battleships were mustered to cover the landings in Sicily in July 1943. As at later operations at Salerno, Anzio and the South of France, their contribution was in fire support and distant cover, the major focus being on the amphibious attacks.

In September 1943 the Italians concluded an armistice with the Allies and their main fleet was sailed for Malta. En route it was attacked by German aircraft, using the new 'FX'-1400 glider bomb. This 1400-kg armour-piercing weapon could be steered by command link from its high-flying parent aircraft and on this occasion, sank

ROYAL OAK.

H.M.S. ROYAL OAK DISPLACEMENT 26,150 TONS

Left: The World War I battleship *Royal Oak* was torpedoed and sunk at the fleet anchorage of Scapa Flow by Gunther Prien's *U-47* in October 1939.

the new battleship *Roma* and damaged the *Italia* (ex-*Littorio*). Over the ensuing days, several ships were attacked off Salerno with the bomb. It tended to pass through most ships even including the veteran battleship *Warspite*, which was severely damaged by one which penetrated a boiler space and exploded at about the level of the double bottom. (The era of the air-to-surface guided weapon had, in fact, commenced some weeks before, when the *Luftwaffe* deployed the 'Hs' 293 against A/S forces working in the Bay of Biscay. The Hs293 was smaller than the FX-1400 but had small propulsion motors in addition to a command link. Its warhead was 500 kg.)

Experiences of fire-support battleships varied. At Casablanca, during the North African landings, the new American battleship *Massachusetts* duelled with the incomplete and immobile French battleship *Jean Bart*. At Salerno, gunfire was used to break up a massed armour attack ashore. In Normandy, enemy gun batteries were protected by several metres of concrete, while in the South of France the problem was massive, stone-built fortifications of the Napoleonic era. Under the innocuous-looking palms of Pacific islands were concealed intricate systems of interconnecting and mutually supportive strong points, difficult both to detect and to destroy.

After hammering its way through all of the major Pacific landings, the veteran American gunline had its hour during the Leyte Gulf actions of October 1944. The southern Japanese thrust against the landing zone was directed by night through the Surigao Strait. It had no hope of surprise, and doggedly pushed up the waterway, harassed by torpedo attacks from American destroyers and light units. At the northern end of the strait the old battleships were waiting, their column crossing the Japanese 'T' in classic fashion. Two enemy battleships and several smaller ships were sunk as the thrust was defeated.

Four of the intended six Iowa class battleships were completed during 1943-4. Retaining the standard armament of preceding classes, they had an upgraded protective scheme and a continuous high speed of a reported 33 knots. This last requirement was the primary cause of an increase in displacement to 52,000 tons from the South Dakota's 42,000. By the time of Leyte Gulf they were constituted as a fast battleship division, or Surface Action Group, operating as a complementary force to the fast carrier groups, rather than in their direct support.

One of the great unanswered questions of the Pacific War surrounded the likely outcome of a gunnery duel between an Iowa and a Japanese Yamato. The 18.1-in (460-mm) main battery of the 69,000-ton Yamatos was matched by well-thought-out and heavy protection. In a gun action, however, an Iowa's 5.5-knot speed advantage would have enabled her to dictate the range which, in a heavy-calibre exchange, is critical to survival. That the battleship's day was done, however, was underlined brutally by the loss of both Yamatos to carrier-based air attack. As scorpions succumb to a massed attack by ants, so did these super-battleships founder from the cumulative effect of scores of torpedo hits, bomb hits and near misses.

Below Japanese battleship *Yamato* with rudders hard over during a US air attack in the Inland Sea, March 1945.

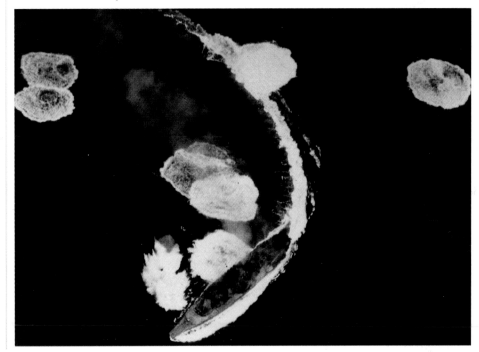

Chapter 8 – Navies in the Nuclear Age

Strategic nuclear weapons at sea

For most of the post-war era the naval scene was dominated by the Cold War confrontation of the USA and its allies facing the Soviet Union. By 1948 the wartime marriage of convenience between the two super-powers who had emerged from World War II had broken down. In Europe the Communist coup in Prague seemed to demonstrate that domestic Communism backed by the threat of Soviet invasion was an imminent and immanent threat. The Western Europeans formed a 'Western Union', predecessor of today's WEU, both to protect themselves and to demonstrate to the United States their alliance worthiness. Against the background of the Berlin blockade - dramatic witness to the breakdown of four power accord on Germany's future - the American senate paved the way to the signing in Washington in 1949 of the North Atlantic Treaty that bound the Europeans and Americans in an unprecedented formal peacetime alliance, the essence of which was the use of American nuclear power to balance the overwhelming power of the Soviet armed forces on the European mainland.

The essence of this confrontation was a maritime alliance versus a continental empire. Although the USA was developing a strategic bomber force that could strike the USSR directly from the Continental USA (the first component of which, the B36, had gained priority over the cancelled nuclear armed super carrier *United States* in the bitter post-war inter-service wrangles in Washington), the forward bases upon which American strategic nuclear power would rely for many years were dependent, like the forward bases of World War II, on America's ability to sustain them by sea. Moreover, when both the Soviet nuclear bomb in 1949 and the Korean War of 1950 proved the need for at least some corresponding Western conventional capability to match that of the East, this had to be projected and sustained by sea. As Korea opened the way to major re-armament, the Western navies were able to sustain themselves both as force projection assets in their own right and as enablers to maintain allied lines of communication against a Soviet submarine force that was growing in strength in quality and quantity to a worrying extent.

The centrepiece of allied naval capability for projecting force was the aircraft carrier. The Korean War had scarcely begun when Secretary of Defense Johnson, who had cancelled the *United States*, told the Navy that it could expect a similar super carrier when it wanted it; USS *Forrestal* was duly laid down in July 1952. In the meantime, existing ships of the Midway and Essex classes were deployed off Korea and in both Atlantic and Mediterranean to contain the Communist threat. In 1951 the arrival of a mixed group of P2V-3C Neptunes and AJ-1 Savage heavy attack bombers in Morocco marked the inauguration of a carrier nuclear strike capability. For operation from the first two nuclear capable carriers, *Coral Sea* and *Franklin D Roosevelt* of the Midway class, these aircraft were kept ashore for deployment aboard the ships in emergency. The bombs were 20-40 Kiloton Mk 4s with a weight of 10,800 lb (4903 kg) which required large aircraft for delivery. The Navy had developed an alternative strategic doctrine to that of the newly independent Air Force, with an emphasis on the attack of military targets rather than urban industrial centres. This combined with attacks on enemy naval and air bases to defeat the enemy maritime threat 'at source'. To enhance the threat to Soviet-hardened submarine bases, special nuclear weapons were developed, the Mk 8 deployed from 1952 and the Mk 9 from 1955. The shape of these weapons and their comparatively light weight allowed carriage in fighter and light attack aircraft that were part of the normal inventory of carriers. The general application of nuclear weapons was even more greatly enhanced by the introduction of the from 1952 the 1,700-lb (772-kg) Mk 7 with a yield up to 70 Kilotons. Now virtually any carrier aircraft was potentially nuclear capable. Heavy attack aircraft still remained in service, however, and from 1958 they were equipped with megaton range Mk 27 H-bombs. The latter were large

Below: From the mid-1950s US carrier airgroups included A-3D Skywarriors equipped to deliver nuclear bombs.

Above: France joined the exclusive club of SSBN operators in 1971 when *le Redoubtable* commissioned after a 30 month programme of trials.

Left: The development of submarine-launched intercontinental ballistic missiles profoundly affected post-war naval strategy. Here a Polaris missile breaks surface during a 1960s test launch.

and could only be carried in Skywarrior or Vigilante bomb bays. By the early 1960s, however, the one megaton Mk 43 gave even the smallest carrier-borne attack aircraft a potential thermonuclear punch.

Although carriers were included in the Single Integrated Operational Plan (the SIOP) to destroy the Soviet Union, there was tension between the requirements of a strategic strike and the general flexibility required from America's most mobile airfields. Meanwhile, an alternative mode of maritime delivery had become available to navies, the submarine-launched ballistic missile. Relatively crude ballistic and cruise missile systems were developed from 1954 by a Soviet Union anxious to find some means of retaliation against the USA. The US Navy was also interested in missile development and also pursued both cruise and ballistic missile options. Deployment of the former Regulus system was only limited, but the Polaris solid-fuelled submarine-launched ballistic missile entered service in 1960 in the first of 41 American SSBNs (nuclear-powered ballistic missile submarines). These submarines complemented the rest of the American strategic forces by providing an ultimate second strike capability - hard, if not impossible, to find but capable of wreaking havoc among Soviet urban industrial targets. The US Navy had

hoped to use Polaris as the basis for a policy of 'minimum deterrence', releasing funds from Air Force programmes for investment in maritime limited war capabilities, but in the event the SLBM force became part of a strategic triad with land-based bombers and intercontinental ballistic missiles. In 1962 the carriers lost their strategic role when they were removed from the SIOP. This had the effect of releasing these crucial ships to allow them to be used as both conventional and nuclear instruments of the more 'Flexible Response' that Secretary of Defense McNamara was trying to develop.

The threat of nuclear attack from the sea caused the Soviets to emphasise both anti-carrier and anti-submarine warfare in their missile development. For a time, the Soviet Navy lost a direct strategic strike role to the Strategic Rocket Forces, and the SLBMs were given an anti-carrier capability, but following the fall of Khrushchev the Project 667 ('Yankee') class submarines were developed as equivalents of the American Polaris submarines. Thirty-four of these units were built, based on the Polaris submarines of the USA. Unlike the

H.M.S. NELSON.

which the main duty of the rest of the fleet was to maintain the 'combat stability' of its 'PLARB' (SSBN) force.

The US, with its bases for forward deployment and its conviction that its SSBNs could hide safely from detection, first increased striking power rather than range. The Poseidon, with its 6-14 independently targetable warheads but with the same 2,500-mile range as the later Polaris A3, replaced Polaris in the 31 Lafayette class boats of the American fleet from 1969 to 1977. In 1979 the first conversion of twelve of these units to carry the 4,250-mile range Trident C-4 missile went to sea on patrol. The same year the first of the huge Ohio class submarines, specially built to carry the Trident weapon, was launched to enter service in 1981.

Other Western navies went down the SSBN route. In the United Kingdom the cancellation of the preferred American Skybolt air-launched missile system forced an acquisition of Polaris A3, something the Royal Navy would have preferred to keep to the next generation of strategic systems after its carrier replacement programme had been safely put in place. The Navy's worst fears were justified as an angry RAF asserted a monopoly for

Above: End of the battleship era: her guns removed, a forlorn *Nelson* awaits breaking up in 1948.

American submarines, however, these boats operated under severe operational disadvantages. The advent of the missile (and nuclear torpedo-firing) threat had changed the emphasis of US anti-submarine thinking away from defence of shipping to defence of the USA itself. By 1960 SOSUS (Sound Surveillance System) sonar arrays were operational off the US coast and the system was progressively extended into transit areas, notably the Greenland-Iceland-UK gap. Any submarine trying to get within D-5 (SS-N-6) missile range of the US coast (1,300-1,600 miles according to variant) was in serious danger of detection. The Soviets therefore pressed ahead with development of a longer-ranged D-9 (SS-N-8) with a range of over 4,000 miles. These were deployed in Project 667B ('Delta') class submarines from 1973. The advent of these longer-ranged missiles and their successors led the Soviet Navy to develop a 'bastion' concept of defending these submarines in

Above: Laid down in 1944, the Midway class carrier *Coral Sea* remained in service for nearly 50 years.

the provision of air power in limited war, a campaign that succeeded in obtaining the cancellation of CVA01, *Queen Elizabeth*, in 1966. The first of the four Resolution class SSBNs went on patrol two years later. France also chose the 'SNLE' (SSBN) as a component of a national strategic triad; *Redoutable*, the first of six boats entered service in 1971 with the 1,500-mile range M-1 missile.

The European navies with their Continental-shelf waters required their submarines to be covered by mine countermeasures forces, but in general in Western navies

Left: Originally planned to attack German targets on round-trip flights from the USA, the B-36 was Strategic Air Command's frontline nuclear bomber during the 1950s.

the SSBNs operated at a remove from the rest of their respective fleets. This was less so in the Soviet Union. Although the Project 941 Akula ('Typhoon') class monsters were apparently built to lose themselves for long periods under the ice as an ultimate strategic reserve, Soviet doctrine expected the Project 667 derivatives ('Deltas II to IV') to operate under protection. During the 1980s, Western maritime strategy was re-cast to reflect this preoccupation, the main war role of American and British attack submarines being the penetration of the Soviet bastions to tie Soviet forces down in a defensive battle. Thus Soviet forces, submarines in particular, would be prevented from surging out into the Atlantic and interdicting NATO shipping .

Associated with this concept was that of using carrier striking forces as far forward as practical to engage and destroy Soviet naval strike aviation, the other main component of the Soviet Navy's offensive power. This was a descendant of the old 'attack at source' concept, although there were some important changes. In its first decade NATO naval doctrine had emphasised nuclear strikes by the carrier striking fleet followed by a protracted period of broken backed hostilities. The British had used this thinking to sustain their carrier

programme in the early 1950s, but by the end of the decade they had begun privately to disagree fundamentally with this concept. They continued to pay lip service to it on grounds of NATO solidarity but increasingly saw their carriers (nuclear-armed from 1961) as instruments of limited war 'East of Suez'. There was, however, discussion of how the concept of conventional 'shield' forces operating beneath the nuclear threshold in the early stages of a confrontation might be used as instruments of crisis management. This thinking, pioneered on land by NATO's European command at the end of the 1950s became official doctrine in 1967 with the formal adoption of the 'Flexible Response' strategy by the Alliance.

The first study of the maritime implications of Flexible Response, completed in 1969, emphasised the role of maritime contingency forces to provide a controlled response and deter escalation. If, however, deterrence failed, the Alliance's forces, led by the Americans, would be used to pursue a conventional maritime campaign to contain and destroy Soviet submarines as far forward as possible, while carriers supported land and amphibious operations ashore. A theoretical Norwegian scenario was used with Allied carriers attacking Soviet forces ashore

and engaging Soviet land-based naval aviation. Most Soviet submarines were held back for defensive purposes and the barrier forces at the GIUK gap and convoy escorts were able to defeat those that were sent forward. By the late 1970s, however, the growth of Soviet maritime capabilities and the draw down in Western strength led to serious doubts about the viability of forward operations against the full might of the Northern Fleet.

There was, however, a re-affirmation of a forward maritime strategy both in NATO and national US thinking, for application both in the Atlantic and the Pacific in a war that would be kept as long as possible beneath the nuclear threshold. This was reflected in the definition in 1980 of a new NATO Concept of Maritime Operations, which stressed containment, defence in depth and keeping the initiative, and the drafting in 1982 of a new US 'Maritime Strategy', which emphasised forward operations and carrying the fight to the enemy. During the self-confident Reagan years these concepts were exercised, notably in the annual NATO Atlantic

Below: Coral Sea served throughout the Vietnam war and survived to operate F-18 Hornets during the 1980s.

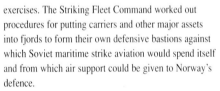

Above: The Iwo Jima class amphibious assault ship USS *Guadalcanal* (LPH-7) was delivered in 1994.

Left: The Thomaston class dock landing ship *Alamo* (LSD-33) was commissioned in 1956. As built these LSDs carried sixteen 3-in AA guns, later removed. Phalanx CIWS was added during the 1980s.

exercises. The Striking Fleet Command worked out procedures for putting carriers and other major assets into fjords to form their own defensive bastions against which Soviet maritime strike aviation would spend itself and from which air support could be given to Norway's defence.

A key component in this mature Western maritime strategy was the role of amphibious forces (which always formed an important component of the NATO Striking Fleet). After a period when, like carrier forces, their survival seemed to be in doubt, these became relatively much more important to the major navies in the Cold War period than they had been before. Not only did they have important roles in Alliance reinforcement but, as demonstrated at the Inchon landings in 1950 and in the deterrence of an Iraqi attack on Kuwait in 1961, they had key roles to play in limited war and naval diplomacy. World War II had seen the development of dock landing ships (LSDs) to give smaller landing craft full strategic mobility. These were enlarged into amphibious transport docks (LPDs) in the early 1960s. By that time an alternative method of getting troops ashore had appeared in the shape of the helicopter. The USA converted existing carriers into interim LPHs (amphibious transport helicopters) and then from 1960 launched purpose-built ships of this type, constructed over the rest of the decade.

Then the LPH and LPD concepts were combined into the LHAs of the 1970s and the LHDs of the 1980s and 90s. The latter ships, 40,500 tons full load are general purpose vessels designed not only for the operation of air cushion landing craft but short-take-off and vertical-landing fighters and ASW helicopters in a sea control role. This concept had been first trialled by an LPH in 1971. All the flat-topped amphibious ships are in fact capable of a range of roles, including acting as bases for close-support aircraft or minesweeping helicopters.

The United Kingdom followed America's lead but only after a decade in which the Royal Navy set its face firmly against an amphibious priority that would take resources away from forces designed to maintain command of the sea in the Atlantic. The growing emphasis on more limited contingencies and the promise of the helicopter changed things, and by 1956 two light fleet carriers *Ocean* and *Theseus* were used as LPHs operationally in the Suez landings. This led to the conversion of two larger and newer light fleets into LPHs, the first of which, *Bulwark*, was available for the emergency reinforcement of Kuwait in 1961. With British 'amphibiosity' thus vindicated, two LPDs were ordered the following year. The primary focus of these assets was East of Suez, but the simultaneity of the adoption of Flexible Response and the decision to

withdraw from East of Suez led to the almost immediate reallocation of the LPDs to a role on NATO's flanks (the LPHs were commandeered as interim ASW support carriers before being replaced by the Invincible class). By the 1980s amphibious shipping, somewhat scorned a quarter of a century before, was being regarded as

comprising some of the 'capital ships' of the Royal Navy, and at the end of the decade a new LPH was being considered to be one of the 'principal platforms' of the 1990s and beyond.

Although the Soviet Union used smaller landing ships to support her diplomacy and built two larger assault ships in 1978 and 1983, she did not put the same emphasis as the major Western powers on long-distance amphibious projection. Her forces were clearly primarily intended to support the strategic offensive on the maritime flanks of the Soviet ground forces.

Thus it was that a classic confrontation of the whale

Above: Seen on her sea trials, USS *West Virginia* was the eleventh Ohio class SSBN to commission.

and the elephant saw maritime power emphasise the capacity for force projection, made possible by new technologies. It was not, as we shall see below, that

Above: The Austin class amphibious transport dock USS *Dubuque* (LPD-8) enters Freemantle, Australia in 1984.

traditional naval operations were forgotten, but more that the instruments of power projection ashore became the key maritime assets. In some senses the Maritime Strategy of the 1980s was an attempt to use power projection forces to obtain the vital sea control that NATO needed to wage war for as long as possible beneath the nuclear threshold. The emphasis on forward operations also reflected the greater challenge that post-war naval technology posed to traditional methods of maintaining command of the sea.

The Post-war Naval Revolution

World War II had seen a revolution in naval warfare but the forces that emerged from it were soon to be made obsolete by two technologies in particular that were emerging by its end. The first was the high-speed submarine. The Germans had produced the Type XXI and Type XXIII boats, which had twice the underwater performance of their predecessors. This technology was available to the war's victors, including the Soviet Union. New ASW weapons now had to cope with speeds of 15 knots or more. This required a complete new generation of escort vessels equipped with new weapons and fire-control systems. The problem was similar to that faced by gunners in the early years of the century and the solution was the same: the combination of analogue

Left: The Soviet navy's nuclear strike force relied increasingly on the hump backed 'Delta' class SSBNs.

Above: The Lafayette class submarine *James Monroe* (SSBN-662) was commissioned in 1963. Built to carry Polaris, she was later modified to take Trident.

computer fire-control technology with advanced sonars that could cope with faster targets and with longer ranged ASW weapons. Classic answers to the new threat were the British Type 15 frigates converted from World War II fleet destroyers with Type 170 scanning sonar and Mk 10 Limbo depth-charge mortars; the sonar could track to 2,000 yards and the weapon engage at 1,000. With their very light gun armament these ships looked much less offensive in a traditional sense than they had done in original configuration but they were admirable ships for the new world of fast battery-driven U-boats (as the Royal Navy continued to refer to its underwater enemies for about a decade).

During World War II, a major distinction between frigates together with other escort vessels of similar role and fleet destroyers had been speed. The advent of the fast frigate, optimised to deal with submarine or air threats, rang the death knell of the traditional destroyer in most fleets. Either it grew into a light-cruiser-sized fleet escort (DLGs - classified as 'frigates' in the US and 'destroyers' in the RN) as this kind of size was required to do both ASW and AAW properly and keep up with the fleet. Or it was replaced by the frigate (in its British sense), which had sufficient gun power to cope with gunboat roles and which could devote the rest of its displacement to dealing with subsurface and air threats, often by the control of aircraft - an interesting example of the synergy of platforms.

The air threat itself was transformed by the high-speed jet aircraft, which posed a serious challenge to the early manual action information organisation techniques developed during the war. The British took the lead in the mechanisation of this, thus laying the foundations for the transformation of the management of naval operations in the subsequent decades of the century. From 1947, equipment was developed to provide a synthetic radar picture to quite literally keep track of the fast-moving and complex battle. An advanced analogue computer was added to the system to work out fighter interceptions. The result was the Comprehensive Display System (CDS), which in conjunction with the 984 three-dimensional radar made the interception capabilities of the two British carriers equipped with it in the 1950s the envy of the Americans. In 1958, 22 of the 23 US aircraft 'attacking' HMS *Victorious* in an exercise attack were deemed to have been shot down. In order to share the plot with escorts that were too small to have a 984/CDS of their own (none of the cruiser-type ships designed to have the system were built, and the smaller County class DLGs would have had to have dispensed with their guns to carry it), a 'Digital Plot Transmission' system was created, the first data link that went into service as Link 1.

This British technology was shared with the Americans who, as a result, began development in 1955 of their own Naval Tactical Data System (NTDS) to compile and distribute a comprehensive tactical picture throughout a

Left: Spruance class destroyer launches an ASROC missile from the Mk 41 Vertical launch system.

force. This first went to sea in 1961 and from 1966 started to become a standard fitting in larger destroyer-type ships (DLGs). A new improved Link 11 (corrupted from 'Link II') was developed by a joint Canada-US-UK committee. The British considered the latter too expensive for general use in their fleet and made do for a while with an inferior Link 10 (another corruption, this time from 'Link X'). The British developed their own digital computer-based systems, the complex ADA (Action Data Automation) fitted in the carrier *Eagle*, ADAWS (Action Data Automated weapons System) for the second generation DLGs and subsequent ships and the more austere CAAIS (Computer Aided Action Information System - less kindly 'Can't Automate Anything Insufficient Software') primarily for ASW ships. As these systems and their successors were adopted, naval warfare became increasingly interactive between platforms; each unit became a node in a network connected electronically. By the late 1980s the coming of systems such as JOTS was raising the automation of picture compilation from the tactical level to the operational and the strategic.

The challenge to ASW systems had increased dramatically with the advent in the mid 1950s of the nuclear-powered submarine. This made obsolete the latest ASW systems designed to cope with the fast battery-driven boat. New sonars were required to cope with fast-moving targets at long range as were new even longer-ranged means of weapons delivery, especially as many held that only nuclear firepower was the sure

Right: The Akula nuclear attack submarines are far harder to detect than previous Russian submarine designs.

answer to the menace of the SSN. Only in 1967 with the advent of the US Mk 46 did a lightweight torpedo enter service with sufficient speed to engage a nuclear-powered attack submarine. The British chose to emphasise the small helicopter as an anti-submarine weapons delivery device, a decision vindicated by the failure of the equivalent American Drone Anti-Submarine Helicopter (DASH) and the potential of the ship-borne helicopter as a logistical and surface warfare asset. The more successful American development was the ASROC missile system, with its alternative torpedo and nuclear depth-bomb capability.

The best answer to an SSN proved to be another SSN which shared its unique mobility in three dimensions and which could exploit sonar conditions to the maximum. From the early 1960s the ASW potential of nuclear-powered submarines began to be emphasised with improved quietening, sensors and weapons. The

Above: The 14,000 ton Oscar class SSGNs fire anti-ship cruise missiles with a range of 250 miles.

American Thresher and Sturgeon classes had their bows completely filled with a massive BQS-6 sonar transducer, which necessitated mounting the tubes for the torpedoes and 40-mile-range nuclear-armed SUBROC missiles amidships. Like surface ships, submarines suffered from shortcomings with their torpedoes, and not until 1971 did an adequate weapon enter service with the US Navy: the 35,000-yard-range, 50-knot Mk 48 - none too soon, given the move to 'Flexible Response' strategy. Coincidentally, this was the same year that the British finally completed the mating of her first generation wire-guided torpedo, the Mk 23, with its fire-control system. Until then British SSNs - for which an ASW role had always been paramount - had to do with the traditional unguided World War II Mk 8. These remained the boats'

primary armament against surface ships until the early 1980s, as demonstrated by HMS *Conqueror* in the Falklands war in the sinking of the cruiser *General Belgrano*.

Nuclear-powered submarines, with their unique combination of tactical and strategic mobility and stealth combined with sufficient striking power to deal with surface ships (and increasingly their own kind), made capital 'battlefleet' assets alongside carrier- and land-based strike aviation. In the Soviet Navy in the 1960s, the Project 675 ('Echo II') SSN was combined with anti-ship cruise missiles to provide a long-range anti-carrier capability. Land-based aircraft, later satellites provided target designation using a data links. These systems suffered from the launching submarines having to stay surfaced and the possibility of the target having moved too far from the previous datum to be acquired. Later SSGNs of the Project 670 ('Charlie') class were armed with much shorter-ranged missiles designed for autonomous use submerged. In the 1980s the Soviet Union began to replace the 675s with huge 12,500 ton Project 949 Antey ('Oscar') class submarines equipped with 24 long-range missiles capable of submerged launch on satellite data. Such submarines were as large as early twentieth-century battleships.

Western navies also began to enhance the missile potential of their SSNs by adding torpedo-tube-fired anti-ship missiles and Tomahawk land-attack cruise missiles, the latter in both nuclear and conventional variants. The Soviets replied to the extent of producing a missile similar in concept to Tomahawk and developed a submarine, the Project 971 'Bars' (confusingly called 'Akula' in the West) apparently to carry it. During the Cold War, such cruise missiles tended to be seen primarily as additional nuclear strategic systems.

The guided missile has played an enormous role in the post-war naval revolution. Already before the end of World War II, guided bombs had at last made it possible for high-level bombers to sink battleships at sea while air-to-surface missiles had sunk cruisers. The need to knock down aircraft at beyond missile release range increased the importance of air cover and also made accurate long-range AA systems mandatory. Attacking missiles spawned both electronic countermeasures and defensive missiles to destroy the launching aircraft at long range or the missile itself closer in. By the 1960s the main armament of the larger Western major surface combatants had ceased to be the gun but had become the large medium- to long-range surface-to-air missile, such as Terrier and Seaslug. Such armed the large destroyer/small cruiser DLG type ships built for carrier escort in Western navies. Smaller missiles began to rival the older and larger missiles in range, and this allowed fitting in smaller ships such a the British Type 42 destroyers. But these ships, like their predecessors, were limited in engagement to only a very restricted number of targets, the same number as the guidance radars carried.

The solution was to combine command guidance with auto pilots and semi-active terminal homing switched on only when the missile was close to the target. This allowed much greater target coverage, especially when combined with an advanced electronically scanned phased-array radar. Thus was born in the 1980s the Aegis cruiser with its remarkable capacity to engage as many

targets simultaneously as it can keep missiles in the air; the system is credited with the ability to engage 128 tracks at once.

The Soviet Union saw the missile as primarily an anti-ship asset for surface units of various sizes, the larger examples of which were fitted with surface-to-air missiles for self-defence. Soviet anti-ship missiles rocked the naval world when, in 1967, the World War II-type Israeli destroyer *Eilath* was sunk off Egypt by SS-N-2 missiles fired from a missile boat. This had the effect of both increasing the urgency of finding countermeasures - notably chaff rockets, close in weapons systems using rapid-firing guns and point defence anti-missile missile systems - and encouraging the development in the West of anti-ship missiles of various ranges in large part to take out enemy missile-firing craft. These Western weapons proved effective at disabling larger surface combatants in both the Falklands and the Gulf, but they are best delivered by aircraft and submarine rather than surface ships, which remain in the West primarily anti-air and anti-submarine assets. They have not restored to the surface ship its old pre-eminence as an anti-surface platform, although the deployment of Tomahawk on

American surface combatants does give enhanced potential in attacking surface targets at long range both afloat and ashore.

Modern surface ships tended to lose much of their aesthetic appeal as sensors, command spaces and bulky missile magazines took up space and top weight. A single-barrelled automatic gun capable of delivering ordnance as effectively as a battery of old usually suffices. The essential features of a ship's capability are hidden in data-handling systems and even the missile launcher has disappeared to be replaced by the vertical launcher, which makes little impact on the eye. No ship typifies the effects of the post-war revolution better than the Aegis cruiser. She is boxy and bare but her capacity to dominate the environment above, on and below the sea has never been surpassed. Such is the paradoxical result of the post-war naval revolution.

Right: A Charlie class SSGN patrolling in the South China Sea during 1974.

Below: HMS *Exeter*, a Type 42 Batch 2 destroyer equipped with Sea Dart surface-to-air missiles.

Chapter 9 – Modern Navies

The Western Powers Aircraft Carriers

The basis of Western surface fleets in the post-1945 era has been the aircraft carrier, a reflection of the predominance of the airborne platform for both reconnaissance and striking against all forms of potential target. The land-based aircraft – despite its institutional supporters – has never had the capability to exert maritime power with the same degree of effectiveness. The spiralling cost of carrying the ever heavier and higher-performance aircraft of the late twentieth century

has had the effect of restricting full carrier capability to one nation only, the United States. Only America has been able to afford the truly massive ships required to extend into this period the equivalent capability of the World War II fleet carrier.

The enormous development potential of the wartime Essex class ship stood the US Navy in good stead for maintaining an effective carrier force into the post-war period. The late completion in 1950 of the USS *Oriskany* to a revised SCB-27A design with stronger flightdecks and catapults presaged some 15 conversions which later adopted British technology, first the steam catapult and next the angled deck (as well as the closed in 'hurricane

bows') to operate improved aircraft. The British faced a more acute challenge in modernising their older ships, hence their pioneering technological breakthroughs but the Americans with their greater resources were able to capitalise on the British improvements to maximise the potential of their ships of all sizes.

The three completed Midways of almost 50,000 tons standard displacement, built to combine the striking power of US ships with the armoured resilience of British vessels, were the only US ships able to operate unmodified the new generations of aircraft. They were key assets in the immediate post-war fleet but even they had to undergo extensive modernisation along the lines of the Essexes. The size of the ships meant that a next round of modernisation could allow operations into the 1980s, but only one ship, *Midway*, was so treated; she remained active, operating out of Yokusuka, Japan, from 1982 until after the end of the Cold War. *Franklin D Roosevelt* did not receive the conversion and was stricken in 1977, but *Coral Sea* received a less extensive modernisation that kept her in service until 1990.

The full answer to the conundrum of the operation of modern aircraft was the super carrier of 60,000 tons standard displacement. After the false start with the cancelled *United States*, the US Navy laid down the *Forrestal* in July 1952. Another, *Saratoga*, was under construction by the end of the year and two more were begun in 1954 and 1955. Over a thousand feet long overall, these ships were robust armoured platforms for 90 modern aircraft and the almost 2,000 men required to operate, arm and support them. The ships themselves required almost 3,000 personnel, making the carriers

Above: Dassault Super Etendards of the French navy. This single-seat strike aircraft came to prominence during the Falklands war when a handful of Argentine Etendards posed a major threat to the British Task Force.

Above: The Spanish aircraft carrier *Principe de Asturias* has a ski ramp of the sort pioneered by the Royal Navy and her air group includes BAe AV-8Bs.

Left: Until the 1950s French aircraft carriers had been converted from other vessels or acquired from aboard, but the two Clemenceau class carriers were designed as such from the outset. *Foch*, seen here, was commissioned in 1963.

Above: The 13,500 ton Italian aircraft carrier *Guiseppe Garibaldi* commissioned in 1985.

effectively floating towns. A fifth ship *Kitty Hawk* was begun to a somewhat modified design in 1956, but the next carrier, *Enterprise*, marked a major step forward as she was nuclear powered and over 10,000 tons larger. Another conventionally powered ship, *Constellation*, was commissioned at about the same time as *Enterprise* and the McNamara Pentagon preferred similar oil-powered vessels as follow-ons, *America*, completed in 1965 and *John F Kennedy* in 1968. After that, however, the advantages of nuclear propulsion – range and endurance only limited by provisioning and aviation fuel requirements coupled with enhanced operational time between replenishments – saw the laying down of what became the definitive Nimitz class, the first of which was

laid down in 1968 and completed in 1975. Six more were in service by 1996 with another building and a ninth ordered. These ships have standard displacements of 73-74,000 tons and later ships displace over 100,000 tons full load. Although the Nimitz class carry the same number of aircraft as a Forrestal, they have provision for ninety percent more aviation fuel and fifty percent more ordnance.

The British had to pull out of the fleet carrier business after squeezing the maximum out of their World War II carriers. All British post-war carriers were laid down before the war ended and were of two basic groups; larger fleet carriers and medium-sized 'light fleet carriers'. Each group contained two generations of ships, the first built for wartime aircraft and the second built for the larger generation of piston-engined aircraft expected in the mid to late 1940s. The earlier fleet carriers were

the 23,000-ton Illustrious class and their derivatives, the later ships built with enhanced hangar space to carry more aircraft. Aircraft capacity was always a problem with these carriers due to the emphasis on armoured hangar protection in their design. It was planned to convert them to carry modern aircraft after the war, but only one ship, *Victorious*, was given the complete rebuild necessary to operate a limited number of jets (28 reducing to 23). The reconstruction took seven years and took up most of the labour in Portsmouth dockyard. *Victorious* saw service for another ten years, being decommissioned in 1968.

The little 13–14,000-ton light fleet carriers of the Colossus and Majestic classes proved to be cost-effective ships with the aircraft capacity of an original Illustrious on a much smaller displacement. They were the backbone of the Royal Navy carrier fleet in the

potential – but two of the former survived the inevitable post-war cancellations and were completed with the traditional carrier names of *Eagle* and *Ark Royal*. *Eagle* was commissioned in 1951 with a straight deck, but a partially angled deck and mirror landing aid were fitted in a 1954–5 refit. She always operated jets and her aircraft complement was just short of 60. From 1959 to 1964 she was given a complete rebuild to bring her up to *Victorious* standards of angled deck, steam catapults and radar; her action information organisation was more advanced. In her new configuration she operated 35 fixed-wing aircraft and 10 helicopters. The decision to phase out carriers and withdraw from East of Suez led to her decommissioning in 1972.

Her sister, *Ark Royal*, lasted a little longer. She was completed to a modified design with a partially angled deck in 1955. She was progressively modified further but was slated for relatively early disposal in the 1970s. The cancellation of her projected replacement (see below) led to a major refit in 1967–70 to operate F-4 Phantom-IIs,

decommissioned in 1966. *Hermes* herself was completed with fully angled deck, steam catapults ad 984/CDS as a reduced version of *Victorious* in 1959, the last traditional carrier to be commissioned by the Royal Navy. With her original air group of 28 aircraft, her capabilities were only marginally reduced compared to the larger ship. She had an active life in the 1960s before decommissioning to become an LPH in 1971. Before long, however, changes in policy had her rerated as an interim CVS (ASW Support Carrier) with Sea King ASW helicopters, and she was fitted with a ski-jump to operate Sea Harrier Short Take-Off-Vertical Landing (STOV/L) fighters. As such she was the flagship of the Falklands carrier task group. *Hermes* survives in the Indian Navy as *Viraat*, having been sold in 1986.

That there could be such a thing as a British carrier task group when the Falklands crisis broke out in 1982 was something of a surprise. In 1966 a momentous decision had been taken that Britain would no longer deploy aircraft carriers after the 1970s. The Royal Navy

immediate post-war years, with piston-engined fighter/ASW air groups that allowed them to participate in limited wars ashore and escort convoys at sea in potentially hotter conflicts. Plans to modernise them were curtailed, but they were widely loaned or sold to provide friendly navies with carriers. Some were modified to operate jets, and three – the Indian *Vikrant*, the Argentine *25 da Mayo* and the Brazilian *Minas Gerais* – lasted into the 1990s. Such vessels provided their owners with limited but at times significant organic air power.

The larger carriers of the wartime programme were intended into be of two kinds: one a 32,500-ton enlargement of previous British ships and the other of 47,000 tons based on American practice to optimise striking power. The latter ships were never laid down – a pity as they would have had the greatest development

which allowed her to survive as Britain's last carrier until 1978. By the end her aircraft complement had dropped to thirty-six.

Given the relatively limited air groups of the larger ships, the light fleet carriers could live up to their name. Indeed they were used effectively as small fleet carriers in the power projection roles that predominated in the Cold War era. The larger light fleet carriers formed the Hermes class, although, confusingly, the name-ship of the class was the last of the four to be completed. The first three, *Centaur*, *Albion* and *Bulwark* were completed in 1953–4 to a 22,000-ton design and carried over 30 aircraft, largely first generation jet fighters. The last two became LPHs in 1960–62 but *Centaur* provided a fifth attack carrier with about sixteen second-generation Sea Vixen and Scimitar jets plus four airborne early warning aircraft and eight ASW helicopters until she

Above: The Sea King was introduced as a stop gap AEW platform at the time of the Falklands war.

had tried in the early 1960s to obtain authorisation for a new class of medium-sized 50,000-ton attack carriers (CVAs) to replace existing ships, but with fierce inter-service competition from the RAF for the tactical air support role East of Suez, only one ship was authorised to replace both *Victorious* and *Ark Royal* to keep a three-carrier force in the 1970s. The Defence Review of 1964–6 put paid even to this ship, and HMS *Queen Elizabeth* (CVA01) was cancelled. Although this gave a limited new lease of life to *Ark Royal* it looked as if the days of the carrier as the centrepiece of the British fleet were numbered – a considerable crisis for the Royal Navy.

Help was at hand, however in the shape of the new

Above: HMS *Invincible* received Goalkeeper CIWS during her refit in the late 1980s.

Below: Discarded in 1978, *Ark Royal* was the Royal Navy's last conventional aircraft carrier.

Right: USS *America*, the third unit of the John F Kennedy class, seen in the Solent, 1991.

class of helicopter-carrying command cruiser. The
Italians had pioneered this type of vessel with their
5,000-ton Andrea Dorias laid down in 1958 and the
7,500-ton *Vittorio Veneto* begun in 1965. These ships
combined helicopter hangars and flightdecks aft with
surface-to-air missile batteries forward. The British had
similar ships in mind to accompany and supplement the
CVAs, and there was still a requirement for such vessels
in the amphibious/ASW task forces operating under
land-based air cover envisaged in immediate post-1966
planning. A 12,500-ton design on Vittorio Veneto lines
was prepared in 1967, and soon a 'through deck' was
found to be the optimal one for the operation of large
ASW helicopters in sufficient quantities. The first such
ship, the 19,500-ton HMS *Invincible*, was laid down in
1973, and two years later the decision to give her Sea
Harriers was finally confirmed. She entered service as an
ASW support carrier (CVS) in 1980. Two sisters were
already under construction, *Illustrious* and *Ark Royal*.
The first two were completed with a seven-degree 'ski
jump' to optimise the performance of their STOV/L
fighters, and this was increased to 12 degrees in *Ark
Royal*, completed in 1985; the other ships were later
brought up to this standard. The Invincible class ships

Above: An F-14 Tomcat shows off its long range air-to-air missiles designed for distant defence of US task forces.

Right: USS *John F Kennedy's* airgroup includes F-18 Hornets and F-14 Tomcats.

Above: The Breguet Alizé ASW aircraft has served the French and Indian navies since the 1960s.

Below: The French carrier *Clemenceau* seen at Toulon after returning from the Gulf War.

gave the Royal Navy a centrepiece for a force able to operate autonomously, either ahead of the main NATO Striking Feet as an ASW striking force, or in more distant waters against significant air opposition, as demonstrated in the Falklands. Their normal air group has grown to nine Sea Harriers, nine Sea King ASW helicopters and three Sea King airborne early warning helicopters (a key capability sadly lacking in the Falklands).

The USA considered building ships of broadly similar capability, if not similar ancestry, in the 1970s: there were plans for a 10,000-ton 'sea control ship', which later expanded into a 20,000-ton VSS (VSTOL Support Ship). None were built and the US Navy eventually decided to expand the capabilities of their large-deck amphibious vessels (see above) as supplementary smaller STOV/L carriers. Spain, however, took up the design to replace their old American built CVL and the result was the 16,700-ton (full load) *Principe De Asturias* completed in 1988 to operate around 20 Harriers and helicopters. Italy also expanded its Vittorio Veneto class into a small 10,000-ton through-deck carrier the *Giuseppe Garibaldi* commissioned in 1985, although inter-service problems kept Harrier type aircraft off her

until the early 1990s.

The other carrier power in the West in the post-war period was France, which has tried to stay with ships of more conventional layout. France obtained a British light fleet carrier in 1946 and two American light carriers in 1950–53 and used them with piston-engined aircraft in support of her operations in Indochina and at Suez. Plans for a 16,000-ton domestic design were abandoned in 1950 but resuscitated later in the decade; two rather larger 22,000-ton light fleet carriers *Clemenceau* and *Foch* being laid down in 1955 and 1957 respectively. They were completed in 1961–3 and have a maximum capacity of up to forty aircraft. The ships are too small to operate the most capable modern aircraft, but a group of 22 Etendard/Super Etendard attack aircraft, eight US built F-8N Crusader fighters and seven Alizé ASW aircraft has given some medium-power projection capability. The great weaknesses of the ships are their lack of organic AEW and an inability to operate their aircraft in rough weather, a sign of their small size for even the limited performance of the aircraft carried. A third carrier, for which a larger 35,000-ton design was considered, was abandoned in 1961.

In the 1980s France, rather overambitiously, decided to

replace *Clemenceau* and *Foch* with two new nuclear-powered medium carriers in the 35,000-ton class. The first, *Charles de Gaulle*, was laid down finally in 1989 and launched in 1994. She is due to complete in 1999. This prolonged gestation period reflects the fearsome cost of the project, and in 1996 it was decided that France can only afford one such ship at least for the time being. She will carry 35–40 aircraft.

Battleships

France was also one of the last countries to operate traditional battleships. One, *Jean Bart*, appeared at the Suez landings in 1956 for shore bombardment duties but was considered too powerful to use in the circumstances. By this time, Britain's last battleship, *Vanguard*, utilised despite a reduced complement as Home Fleet Flagship in the early 1950s, had been decommissioned. The US Navy had kept one of her high-speed Iowa class 48,000 tonners, *Missouri*, in service after the war as a training ship, and her three sisters were re-commissioned in 1950–51, the four to act as bombardment assets off Korea. After more use for training, the last ship, *Wisconsin*, was decommissioned in 1958 but, contrary to expectations, that was not the end. *New Jersey* saw effective service off Vietnam in 1967–9, and then in the 1980s all four were brought back into service to symbolise the Reagan naval build up and provide resilient platforms for both 16-in (406-mm) guns and Tomahawk cruise missiles as the centrepieces of surface action groups. Modernisation was kept very limited. They were useful status symbols but their one-

dimensional military capabilities were insufficient reason in the more stringent post-Cold War era to tie up even a reduced complement of 1,600 men. All were laid up by 1992 and were stricken three years later. Finally it does seem that the battleship has died.

Above: The modernised battleship *New Jersey* fires a harpoon anti-ship missile.

Below: The Spruance class DDG *Fife* alongside *New Jersey* before the latter finally decomissioned in 1991.

Below: The 16-in guns of the Iowa class provided naval gunfire support to operations ashore in Korea, Vietnam and the Middle East. Now these battleships have finally left service, work is underway to develop new guns and ammunition that will enable modern warships to fulfill the same role.

Cruisers, Destroyers and Frigates

The traditional gun-armed cruiser found utility in the first two post-war decades as a more economical major surface unit for flagship, presence and fleet screening and bombardment duties, as well as being some answer to the latest Soviet gun-armed cruisers. In Europe incomplete older ships were completed with new fully automatic 5 to 6-in gun (127 to 152-mm) armaments for anti-air as well as anti-surface unit warfare, but it was found in the UK that older ships could be used in unmodernised form as limited and Cold War assets in low-threat areas. The USA commissioned four classes of traditional cruiser in the late 1940s, the largest the battleship-sized 17,200-ton Des Moines class with nine fully automatic 8-in (203-mm) guns. They served, like their smaller cousins, as flagships, training ships and shore-bombardment units. By 1963, however, only two traditional gun-armed cruisers remained in service with the US Navy.

As described above, the surface-to-air guided missile was developed to deal with the developing air threat, and the bulky early types required volume and top weight intensive electronics. A stable platform was also necessary for missile guidance and fighter direction. The relatively large and roomy cruisers of the time fitted these requirements well. The USA began to convert cruisers into partially or fully missile-armed ships in the

1950s. For a time a large-scale conversion programme was considered, but in the end only six light and five heavy cruisers were converted. The British planned a huge 18,400-ton monster guided-missile cruiser to be equipped with the Seaslug missile, automatic 6-in (152-mm) guns and the 984/CDS sensor and command suite, but it proved too expensive and was cancelled in 1957.

Above: USS *Long Beach* was the world's first nuclear-powered warship and the first to have a guided missile main battery.

The Dutch, French and Italian navies each carried out one missile conversion of an existing light cruiser.

The problem with all these ships was their size and uneconomically large crews. As discussed above, the

Above: The Leahy class cruisers were the first US warships to carry surface-to-air missiles as their main armament. Modernised to carry SM2-ER Standard missiles, they provided air defence for carrier task forces from the early 1960s until the early 1990s. USS *England* was deleted in 1994.

Left: Displacing over 6,000 tons, the County class 'destroyers' were so-named to gain Treasury approval for their construction in the 1960s. They carried the first generation beam-riding Sea Slug SAM: an enormous missile that saw its first and only action in the Falklands. *Kent* seen here in 1977, retains both 4.5-in gun turrets, but four sisterships had 'B' turret replaced by four Exocet missile launchers.

best longer term solution was to enlarge the destroyer into a new form of light cruiser. It was in 1951 that the US Navy invented the term DL (Destroyer Leader, re-rated 'Frigate' in 1955) to cover the large destroyer-type ships laid down in 1949–50 either as a hunter-killer cruiser against the high-speed submarine threat (the USS *Norfolk*) or as large carrier task group escorts (the four ships of the Mitscher class). The latter 3,650-ton vessels built to remain operational at high speeds in rough weather looked under-armed with their two single 5-in (127 mm) automatic mountings and two twin 3-in (76-mm), but effectively their main armament was provided by the fighters of the carrier task force guided to their targets by a well-equipped Combat Information Center fed by a comprehensive radar suite. Their ASW capability was also not inconsiderable.

The Terrier missile made the Farragut class the first class of DLGs, commissioned in 1959–60, the weapons and sensor fit improvement (which included ASROC and improved sonar) dictated by the further improvements in strike aircraft and the threat of the nuclear-powered submarine. The AAW missile fit went double ended with the Leahys of 1962–4 but the successor 5,400-ton Belknaps went back to a single-ended configuration to provide the extra flexibility afforded by a 5-in gun mounted aft. Nuclear power seemed an obvious addition to the DLG type ship, especially given the recognition that escort endurance was perhaps the key factor in limiting carrier task force operations. The first attempt at a DLGN grew into a fully fledged cruiser, the 15,000-ton USS *Long Beach*, commissioned in 1961; but a more moderate 7,250-ton USS *Bainbridge* based on the Leahy class was already under construction and was

commissioned in 1962. The second DLGN, *Truxtun*, a variant on the Belknap theme (albeit at over 8,100 tons) was commissioned five years later.

Nuclear power was expensive and, hence, controversial, and only Congressional pressure kept the nuclear fleet escort programme alive into the 1970s. The result of the wrangling was the impressive but perhaps rather less than satisfactory *California* and *South Carolina*, completed in 1974–5, and the four improved Virginias commissioned between 1976 and 1980. Along with most of their conventionally powered cousins these DLGNs were re-classified 'cruiser' in 1975 – a much better term for ships of their size.

The British drew up plans for a rapid-fire 5-in gun armed cruiser-destroyer in 1949 both to act as a task force screen and to deal with Soviet cruisers. Nothing came of this but there remained a requirement for a fast fleet escort. It was found that Seaslug was compatible with a ship of relatively moderate size and the result was the 6,200-ton County class, built in two batches between 1959 and 1970. These combined the Seaslug area defence SAM with two point defence Seacat SAM mountings, two twin 4.5-in (114-mm) gun mountings for anti-surface and anti-shore work and a capable Wessex ASW helicopter for ASW. A combined steam and gas turbine plant gave a maximum speed of thirty knots. Rated destroyers, they were good looking cruiser substitutes and were referred to in the service as 'DLGs'. It was originally planned to give them a massive anti-cruiser punch by fitting them with two nuclear-tipped

Seaslugs for surface-to-surface use but this concept was abandoned in 1960. The four 'Batch Two' ships with their computerised command systems were fitted with the Exocet surface-to-surface missile in place of 'B' 4.5-in gun mounting before being decommissioned in the 1980s. France had two generations of DL type ship, one an AAW/ASW conversion of two Italian wartime cruiser/destroyers and the other a pair of fully fledged DLGs built to provide carrier escorts, the two Suffrens built in 1962–70.

By the end of their careers the earlier American DLGs were re-rated 'destroyers', a reflection of the growth in size of the classical destroyer of World War II era as it converted itself into a fast fleet escort that was smaller and cheaper than the fully fledged DLG. Destroyers were already getting bigger before the war ended, and when the Royal Navy completed (in the early 1950s) their eight 2,830-ton Darings, the first of which had been laid down just as the war ended, they referred to them as an intermediate type of 'Daring type ship' and ran them as cruisers. These ships were classical destroyer in layout, however, and carried six 4.5-in (114-mm) guns and ten 21-in (533-mm) torpedo tubes a Squid mortar provided ASW capability. The tubes disappeared as accommodation had to be improved for their large 300-man ship's companies and they had all been decommissioned by 1969 as they were not suitable for full modernisation.

France also built ships of around the same size as Surcouf class 'Squadron Escorts' with dual purpose gun

Left: The Italian Lupo class frigates carry both anti-ship and surface-to-air missiles.

Below: HMS Arethusa was converted to fire the Ikara ASW rocket-launcher system in 1977.

Above: The Belknap class cruiser Fox evaluated the Tomahawk cruise missile box launcher for the US Navy.

Above: The Type 42 Batch 2 destroyer HMS *Liverpool* commissioned in 1982.

Below: USS *Leftwich:* one of the 31 Spruance class ASW destroyers commissioned by the US Navy.

armament and ASW/anti-surface torpedoes. The Surcouf hull was just too small to be an effective fleet escort in both the anti-submarine warfare (ASW) and anti-air (AAW) roles and they were rebuilt as specialist command, AAW or ASW ships, while the follow-on Duperres were effectively radar pickets. Britain converted relatively modern destroyers to the radar picket role.

The trouble with DLGs was that they could not be afforded in large enough quantities, even by the Americans. In order to expand numbers of fleet escorts, the US Navy developed a 2,700-ton development of the classical World War II destroyer. Some 18 Forrest Sherman class ships were built in the 1950s armed with guns for AAW and torpedoes for ASW; they were later rearmed with missiles either as ASW or AAW assets. The latter ships carried the Tartar system specially developed for smaller ships and this was combined with the ASROC ASW missile and two 5-in guns into a medium sized 3,300-ton Charles F Adams class, 23 of which joined the US Navy in the early 1960s. Modified versions were also built for West Germany and Australia. The foreign vessels were equipped with computerised action information systems but only a few of the American ships were so fitted before the Cold War ended. Decommissioning of the American units began in

1989 and all had gone by 1992, but four have been leased to Greece and modernised with a Dutch combat data system.

The impact of the fast submarine on escort design was described above. Frigates now had to rival the speed of traditional destroyers, and the British answer was to both convert old destroyers into ASW frigates and build new steam-turbine-powered 29 knot Type 12 frigates, equipped with main armaments of ASW mortars and ASW torpedoes as well as twin 4.5 in guns for limited AsuW (Anti-Surface Warfare) and AAW (Anti-Aircraft Warfare). The same hull form was used for slower diesel-powered frigates with double the gun armament for anti-air duties and enhanced radar and command-and-control facilities for aircraft direction. However, these latter classes were only built in limited numbers, and the fast ASW design was modified as the general purpose Leander, the first of which was as well as completed in 1963.

Compared to the Type 12, the Leander had improved radar and air control facilities as well as modified sonar and a weapons delivery helicopter to give at least limited potential against nuclear-powered submarines. No less than 26 were built for the Royal Navy and the type was adopted by the Dutch, Indian and Chilean navies. A closely related River design was also built in Australia. These ships were flexible and cost-effective escorts, capable of all kinds of operation from fleet escort through convoy protection to gunboat diplomacy. Most of the older Type 12s were modified to Leander standard, and the Leanders themselves were modified either as specialist ASW ships with Ikara or the new towed array sonar or as improved general purpose frigates with Exocet missiles, improved helicopters and, in some of the later broad-beam 2,500-ton ships, Sea Wolf anti-air missiles. The Type 12/Leander formed the main component of the surface capability of the Royal Navy

from about 1965 to 1985, and the Indian Navy was still building an enlarged version in the 1990s.

The British themselves tried to enlarge the Leander into a full-scale fleet escort with the Type 82 projected in the 1960s to escort the new generation of carriers. The new compact Sea Dart SAM was placed aft instead of the helicopter, while ASW armament was provided by the Ikara torpedo-carrying missile system mounted abaft the new fully automatic single 4.5 in gun. Extra volume was, however, required for a full set of Olympus gas turbines, better access to machinery spaces and enhanced command and control spaces, and the new ship HMS *Bristol* came out as a 'destroyer' (effectively a DLG) displacing 500 tons more than the Counties. She remained unique, as the carriers she was designed to escort had been cancelled even before she was laid down in 1967. She was built largely as a trials ship for her new systems – Ikara fitted in modified Leanders and Sea Dart fitted in a new class of wholly gas-turbine-powered Type 42 ships (again numbered in the frigate series but because of their AAW capability rated destroyers). These moved Sea Dart forward abaft the gun and replaced Ikara with the more flexible Lynx helicopter. They were designed to the minimum dimensions and came out at a rather cramped 3,850 tons standard. Ten were built between 1970 and 1983 and four more in the early 1980s to a modified design with the originally designed length restored. The loss of two of these ships in the Falklands led to the enhancement of their close-in weapons capability.

Side by side with the Type 42s, the Royal Navy built two new classes of 'frigate'. The first was the Type 21 – a general purpose design built to provide Leander type capabilities in a more visually attractive gas-turbine-

Below: The Broadsword class frigate *Beaver* seen with her Westland Lynx ASW helicopter.

powered package designed with greater input from private shipbuilders. Hopes that these ships would be cheaper proved unfounded and their development potential proved disappointing, but they were always popular with their crews. Two were sunk in the Falklands and the other six sold to Pakistan in 1993–4.

The definitive Leander replacement was the Type 22, a 4,000-ton platform for an advanced active sonar (initially 2016) and two ASW/AsuW strike helicopters, the whole

protected by the advanced Sea Wolf point defence SAM; Exocet missiles provided extra anti-surface capability. The design was stretched after four units to incorporate the American Outboard long-range ESM/code breaking equipment to allow both strategic surveillance and long-range targeting. The programme would have been curtailed if it had not been for Outboard as the ships were considered rather large and expensive for their capabilities. The Falklands also gave the class a new

Above: The 46-strong Knox class ASW destroyers were later fitted with harpoon to give an anti-ship capability.

lease of life, and the last four of the fourteen ships of the type were built to a still further enlarged Batch 3 design with a gun for shore-bombardment.

The later Type 22s were fitted with towed array long-range sonars, although they were not the optimum platforms for this system in terms of quietening. The attempt was made in the 1980s to produce a quiet towed array tug that would be considerably cheaper than the Type 22. With Falklands experience this grew into a general purpose 3,500-ton Type 23 frigate, the first of which, *Norfolk*, was commissioned in 1990. These ships were built to be stealthy both in terms of sound and radar signature and carry both active hull-mounted and passive towed array sonars, Sea Wolf SAMs in their latest vertical launched version. Provision for a large helicopter and a gun completed the weapons suite. The only problem with these ships was that as their capability increased their combat data system could not keep pace and the original design was abandoned. Not until the end of the 90s was this problem being rectified.

By 1997 the Royal Navy's frigate and destroyer fleet provided a set of assets which could operate individually or in groups in a range of roles from naval diplomacy to sea control or power projection ashore. Although they were powerful escort vessels to merchant or amphibious

Left: The Oliver H Perry class frigate USS *Doyle* seen with her Sikorsky SH-60 embarked.

shipping, it was better to regard their role when operating with carriers as that of forming part of an integrated and dispersed force, each ship providing its own set of sensors, command and control and force projection capabilities.

The first American reaction to the need for fast anti-submarine ships was to modify some of their existing wartime destroyers as 'Escort Destroyers' (DDEs) with heavy anti-submarine armaments for use in ASW task groups. Later all the older destroyers were modified along rather similar lines as part of the Fleet Rehabilitation and Modernisation (FRAM) programme. There were varying degrees of conversion but a typical FRAM I conversion Gearing class had one twin gun mounting removed, leaving four 5-in (127-mm) weapons, an ASROC anti-submarine missile launcher added between the funnels, provision for a drone anti-submarine helicopter aft, lightweight ASW torpedoes, and less visibly an SQS-28 long-range hull sonar and improved command spaces. These ships were suitable for both convoy escort and fleet work in the ASW role while still retaining enough shore-bombardment capacity to be useful.

The Americans tried to increase the performance of their equivalent of the wartime British frigate the 'destroyer escort' (DE) to cope with faster submarines. To enhance the potential for mass production, single screw propulsion was a distinguishing feature of these ships, which, by the beginning of the 1960s, were being seen as replacements for at least some of the modified destroyers (despite a speed of only 27 knots). The Garcia (ASW) and Brooke (AAW) classes led to the controversial Knox class, no less than 46 of which were commissioned between 1969 and 1974. These were quite large 3,000-ton vessels, as the more compact power plants of their predecessors had proved unreliable. They were specialist ASW assets like the British Type 22s, but they always carried a gun and lacked the point defence AAW potential of the British ships; only later was a Sea Sparrow system installed. ASROC missiles forward and DASH drones aft comprised main armament, and the generous provision for the latter allowed easy conversion to carry a helicopter when the drone system failed. A guided missile AAW version was built locally in Spain. The DEs were re-rated frigates when DLGs became cruisers in 1975.

The Knox was not really suitable for fast carrier operations, which required a speed of 30 knots, and it was followed by a class of much larger 'destroyers' that were so capable both in terms of power and seakeeping. These huge gas-turbine-powered Spruance class vessels, which displaced 7,800 tons full load, had their origins in a planned anti-air warfare ships, but all the 31 hulls built for the US Navy were completed as ASW assets with a powerful sonar suite, ASW helicopter and ASROC. Two of the latest 5-in guns and a Sea Sparrow SAM added anti-surface and point defence AAW potential. These ships, like the Knox class, were criticised for lack of capability in anything but ASW, and later they were fitted with cruise missiles for land attack and long-range anti ship tasks, usually in a vertical launcher where the old ASROC launcher had been. Four additional ships were built for Iran in the AAW variant with SAM launchers fore and aft, and following the revolution in

Left: The Arleigh Burke class destroyers are constructed of steel, the result of lessons learned when the cruiser *Belknap* suffered a serious fire after colliding with the *John F Kennedy* in 1975. Here, the second unit of the class, DDG 52 *Barry* fires a harpoon anti-ship missile.

Below: The Suffren class guided missile destroyers were designed to defend the French navy's carriers against submarines and air threats. This view of *Duquesne* reveals their obvious recognition feature: the huge radome which provides target data for their Masurca semi-active radar-homing missiles.

Above: *La Fayette's* hull and superstructure are designed to minimise her radar signature.

Below: The Brooke class were modified Garcia type frigates, fitted with Tartar and then Standard SAMs.

that country they were taken into the US Navy as the Kidd class.

The definitive anti-air warfare variant of the Spruance was the Ticonderoga class, fitted with the Aegis system. Originally considered as an Aegis destroyer to supplement larger Aegis cruisers (an 18,000-ton 'Strike Cruiser' was projected in the 1970s), the Spruance based ships eventually became the primary Aegis platforms commissioned between 1983 and 1994. At almost 9,000 tons full load they were classified as cruisers alongside the former DLGs and represented the most impressive and powerful surface combatants of their day. To complement these ships, a rather smaller 8,315-ton Aegis 'destroyer' was designed in the 1980s to a completely new Arleigh Burke design. The first was completed in 1991, and in the late 1990s this was the only major surface combatant under construction in the USA. The Burkes were intended to cost two thirds as much as a Ticonderoga but have three quarters of the AAW capability They carry one 5-in gun as opposed to two, and almost all lack a helicopter hangar – perhaps their most serious defect.

Aegis ships were intended to form the 'high' end of the mix of capabilities of the US surface fleet: the low end would be a single-screw gas-turbine 2,650-ton 28.5-knot general purpose frigate, the first of which, *Oliver Hazard Perry* (FFG7), was laid down in 1975 and commissioned four years later. This was the first of 51 such ships built for the US Navy. They mounted a combined launcher for AAW and anti-surface missiles forward, had provision for two helicopters primarily for ASW, and mounted a 3-in (76-mm) automatic gun amidships. They combined remarkably effective three-dimensional capabilities in a cost-effective form and were purchased by the Australians (who consider them better than a British Type 42), Spain and Taiwan.

The high-low mix was also favoured by the French, who built a relatively small number of large fleet escorts to replace the older Squadron Escorts. They were in the 3,500- to 5,000-ton size bracket mainly in the ASW variant. These were originally classified as '*corvettes*' as they were smaller than the Suffren class DLG '*fregates*' but they were later given '*fregate*' designations also. There were only about a dozen of these ships, insufficient to maintain the global presence required by French foreign policy, and the small convoy *escorteurs* of the 1950s were supplemented and then replaced by *avisos* (probably best translated as 'sloops') of the 1,750 Commandant Riviere and the 1,100-ton D'Estiennes D'Orves class. The latter, of which 17 were built, had only minimal ASW capacity, and this was deleted completely in the rather larger (3,000-ton full load) Floréal class *Fregates de Surveillance* and the Lafayette class *Fregates Legeres* built in the 1990s; the former built to mercantile and the latter to warship standards. Both, however were more offshore patrol vessels than major surface combatants.

Two major navies who specialised in ASW in the post-war world were the Canadian and the Japanese. Both saw themselves as adjuncts of the USA and were unwilling respectively either to enter or stay in the carrier business.

Left: The Aegis cruiser *Vincennes* achieved notoriety in the Gulf by accidentally downing an Iranian airbus.

Hence both emphasised the use of the large helicopters from a relatively small hull. The Canadians first produced their own domestically designed variants on the British Type 12 theme, no less than eighteen of which entered service as escort destroyers (DDEs) between 1955 and 1963. They were armed with ASW mortars, but in the 1960s the Canadians began to fit hangars and flightdecks for large Sea King helicopters. Two similar ships were built new in this configuration, and in 1969 construction began of four larger DDHs of the Tribal class, each with provision for two helicopters. The Tribals had originally been projected as DDGs with AAW capability: this warfare discipline remained a considerable weakness in the RCN until the 1990s when the Tribals were rebuilt to carry the American Standard SAM system and the older ships finally began to be replaced by the modern general purpose frigates of the City class with Sea Sparrow point defence missiles. These ships, however, retain the capability to operate a large search/strike ASW helicopter.

The Japanese Maritime Self Defence Force first built frigate- and destroyer-sized vessels concentrating on ASW but with some ships intended for anti-air warfare cover with guns. The smaller vessels were intended primarily for coastal work with the regional district

flotillas, while the main fleet was to be made up of escort flotillas of modern destroyers, built up for 'sea lane' protection out to 1,000 nautical miles from Japan, an objective officially adopted in 1983. Each flotilla was to have its own air defence ships and Japan built its first DDG in the early 1960s – the 3,000-ton *Amatsukaze*. These were supplemented by three 3,850-ton DDGs of the Tachikaze class laid down in the 1970s, two 4,600-ton Hatakazes in the 1980s and finally the impressive Aegis-equipped Kongos, 7,250-ton variants of the American Arleigh Burkes. It was hoped to have eight of the latter vessels but this was reduced to four on grounds of cost.

For their ASW vessels, both large and small, the Japanese relied on ASROC and DASH (with which they did rather better than did the Americans), but in the 1970s the first large DDHs of the Haruna class were commissioned – 4,700-ton ships designed to lead escort flotillas and to provide a base for three Sea King helicopters. Two similar but improved Shiranes appeared in 1981–2. All four are equipped with 5-in (127-mm) guns and ASROC forward and a hangar and flightdeck aft. To replace older ships and to spread Sea Kings around the flotillas, no less than twenty destroyers of the Hatsuyuki and Asagiri classes were completed between

Above: Named after a Navy pilot killed over Laos in 1968, USS *Milius* is the latest Arleigh Burke class destroyer.

1982 and 1990. Of 2,850–3,500 tons they all mounted a 3-in (76-mm) gun forward, ASROC, Harpoon SSMs, ASW torpedoes, and a Sea Sparrow launcher together with a Sea King hangar and flightdeck. By the 1990s these were the backbone of the escort flotillas and were being supplemented by a new more general purpose Murasame class intended to be more capable in AAW, given the shortfall in numbers of Kongos.

By the 1990s most other major Western navies saw the general purpose frigate as its major surface unit. The Dutch built ASW destroyers as 'submarine hunters' in the 1950s and replaced them in the 1970s with the 3,000-ton Kortenaer class frigates – developed versions of what might be called the Leander paradigm, with air cover provided by four ships equipped with US Standard missiles. Two of the latter were larger Tromp class units built to replace the two older Dutch cruisers and two were Heemskercks, modified Kortenaers, that had to be much more specialist AAW ships on their reduced displacement. Beginning in 1993 some Kortenaers were replaced by slightly smaller and considerably more economical Karel Doorman class frigates, the older ships being transferred to Greece. The latter had begun their design as austere OPV type ships but, like the British Type 23s, grew back into general purpose combatants, albeit with reduced complements.

Italy built a pair of missile air-defence destroyers in the 1960s and again in the 1970s and replaced the older two with a new 4,500-ton pair in 1993, but the main component of the fleet in the 1990s was made up of the Lupo and Maestrale class frigates built from the mid 1970s onwards to replace older large and small destroyer type ships. The 2,500-ton (full load) former class, built with export in mind, had to be enlarged into the 3,000-ton Maestrale, which corresponds to the standard pattern 5-in gun, Sea Sparrow SAM, Otomat SSM, ASW torpedo tubes and helicopters.

Germany has also gone down the same route. In its early days the *Bundesmarine* (apart from the three Charles F Adams class DDGs mentioned above) went for destroyers and frigates with heavy gun armaments and short-ranged ASW rocket launchers. These fitted a Baltic anti-surface warfare orientation. By the 1980s, however, construction of the Bremen class (based on the Dutch Kortenaer) marked Germany's joining the post-war consensus in warship design. These were 3,700-ton vessels with three-dimensional capabilities, including helicopters. The older gun-armed destroyers were replaced by four rather larger German-designed Brandenburg class ships of similar capability in the 1990s. The latter vessels are variants of the MEKO family that Germany supplied on the export market to a number of countries: Greece, Turkey, Nigeria, Portugal and Argentina. The last named rated them as 'destroyers' as they replaced old American-built FRAM – a final demonstration of the merging of categories that has created such confusion in the post-war world.

Mine Countermeasures

Mines had been a major menace in World War II and the Soviets were known to be great proponents of mine warfare. This put an emphasis on mine countermeasures operations in many post-war Western navies, confirmed by the experience of the Korean war. Because of the importance of low-acoustic, magnetic and pressure signatures, post-war MCM (Mine Counter Measures) vessels had to be relatively small. The United Kingdom laid plans in its post-war fleet for a truly massive flotilla of coastal and inshore vessels. Although the programme was curtailed, some 118 360-ton coastal minesweepers of the 'Ton' class were built along with 94 smaller 120-ton 'Ham' class inshore minesweepers for use in estuaries. These vessels were diesel-powered with aluminium framed wooden planked hulls. The United States also built a new generation of minesweepers, in two sizes. The small Bluebird class coastal minesweeper (MSC) corresponded to the British Ton while there was a larger Ocean Minesweeper (MSO) of 735 tons full load. 184 of the Bluebirds were built, of which 60 were retained by the US Navy: of the Ocean Minesweepers, 93 were built and 58 were retained. The above four classes represented the standard Western minesweepers of the period, and as well as being exported they were copied for local construction.

These units were mine*sweepers*, i.e. they relied on sweeps of various kinds to explode the mines. This was not a satisfactory answer to increasingly 'intelligent' influence mines, but it took time for effective sonar to be introduced to allow effective mine*hunting*: finding mines on the seabed and disposing of them by diver or some mechanical device. The British had projected such 'mine

location vessels' in their post-war programme and actually built a few all-wood 'Ley' class inshore vessels, but these never got their intended sonars and were not very effective. A similar derivative of the 'Ton' was cancelled and it was not until 1964 that a standard 'Ton', HMS *Kirkliston*, was converted into a minehunter with a Type 193 sonar. Seventeen similar conversions followed for the Royal Navy. Similar conversion programmes on older 'sweepers were carried out by other navies, including the Belgian navy, which emphasised mine hunting and converted two of its American type MSCs and six of its MSOs. The French constructed the first class of purpose-built minehunters in the shape of the 510-ton Circe class launched in 1970–72. They also pioneered the use of PAP (*Poisson Auto Propulseur*), literally a remotely controlled 'fish' equipped with surveillance and demolition gear.

A new generation of minehunters was built using glass reinforced plastic as the hull material. This was trialled in a specially built Ton, HMS *Wilton* built in 1972, and was used in the larger 750-ton 'Hunts', 13 of which were built in the late 1970s and 1980s. These sweeper/hunters were complemented from 1988 by 480-ton Sandown class single role minehunters fitted with the 2093 variable depth sonar. As sweeping was not part of their role, signature reduction was less important and the platforms could be produced more cheaply. In addition to these technologically advanced assets, the British deployed a dozen simple 890-ton River class vessels in the early 1980s to tow a special deep-water sweep to deal with Soviet anti-submarine mines laid on the ocean floor. These were discarded or transferred to other duties

Below: Termoli is one of the Gaeta class minehunters recently commissioned by the Italian navy.

Above: The Sandown class minehunter HMS *Inverness* seen off Portsmouth in 1992.

with the end of the Cold War.

As their equivalent of the 'Hunt', the mainland Europeans developed a smaller GRP 595-ton 'Tripartite' design at the end of the 1970s, 35 of which were built collaboratively by the Dutch, the French and the Belgians. In the 1980s the Italians built their own 520-ton Lerici class, which was enlarged in 1990 into the Gaeta class of almost 700 tons.

The Americans neglected mine countermeasures in the 1960s and 70s. A technique of sweeping using large Sea Stallion helicopters carried in LPH for strategic mobility was developed, but this was unsatisfactory except as a precursor measure for surface MCM vessels. The US Navy was forced to rely on European allies in the late 1980s when a mining threat became a serious consideration in the Gulf during the Iran-Iraq war. Construction of a new class of fourteen wood/GRP 1,300-ton MCM vessels had, however, begun and the first, *Avenger*, was commissioned in 1987. The design was advanced with variable-depth sonar but the vessels proved prone to teething troubles. It was originally hoped to supplement the larger ships with air-cushion coastal minehunters, but instead an 895-ton derivative of the Italian Lerici/Gaeta class was chosen for a new Osprey class of a dozen units, the first of which commissioned in 1993. The US Navy, however, remains much less experienced in MCM operations than its associate navies.

Another major MCM operator has been Japan. Minesweeping kept Japan's maritime forces alive in the post-war era, first using small 130–240-ton small wooden craft left over from the Imperial Navy; these vessels served off Korea in 1950 as the only MCM assets in theatre. Many passed to the Maritime Self Defence Force on its creation and MSCs were supplied from the USA. A family of coastal wooden minesweeper/hunters

Right: The latest French nuclear powered ballistic missile submarine (SSBN) S 616 *le Triomphant.*

was started in 1960 with the 360-ton Kasado class, enlarged in 1969 into the 380-ton Takami and further into the 440-ton Hatsushima in 1978 and the 490-ton Awashima in 1989. Two of each of the latter classes went to the Gulf to help clear up after the 1991 war. Three 1,000-ton ocean MCM vessels, also wooden-hulled, were built in the 1990s.

Other more original types of mine countermeasures platform have been developed post-war. The Germans have used three small drone minesweepers under the control of a mother ship as the 'Troika' system. The Norwegians have deployed surface effect craft and the

Australians catamarans, but it is significant that the latter were forced to return to a more conventional MCM craft (based on the popular Italian Gaeta) after problems with the more novel platform.

Submarines

During the Cold War years, the *anti*-submarine role has tended to predominate in submarine tasking, and the designator SSK, originally coined for specialist ASW boats, has come to be applied generally to conventional diesel-powered submarines. Western submarines soon copied the high-speed characteristics developed by the Germans during World War II. Attempts were made by the British to tame Hydrogen Peroxide (HTP) as an air independent propulsion system with the commissioning of a German boat as HMS *Meteorite* and the building of two HTP submarines *Excalibur* and *Explorer* as high-speed targets and trials vessels. They all proved to be very troublesome and dangerous and development work was stopped when it seemed that nuclear power offered the better option.

The best solution in the immediate post-war years was to adopt the less radical German technologies of streamlined hull form, high capacity batteries and snorkels. This provided revolutionary enough. The advanced German boats themselves had not been designed for a long life. They also had mechanical problems and the major Western navies considered it better, rather than copying them, to modify existing submarines along the lines of the German boats and build new improved boats of similar general concept. The Americans found their large fleet submarines eminently suitable for conversion under the GUPPY

Left: The French navy acquired Agosta class conventional submarines during the 1970s. A further four were built for the Spanish navy and two for the navy of Pakistan.

Right: Known to NATO as the Delta III type SSBN, this distinctive 'hump backed' submarine represented a major improvement in Soviet nuclear capability. These deep-diving boats continue to serve with the Russian navy in the late 1990s.

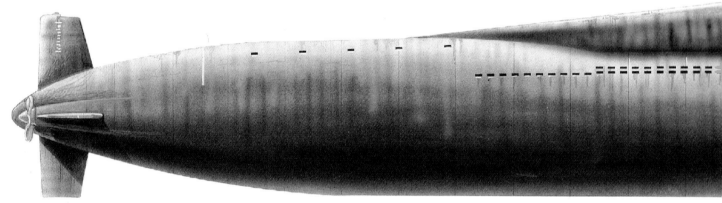

Delta class

data:

Displacement standard	9,000 tons
Displacement submerged	11,000 tons
Length	510 feet
Beam	40 feet
Design draught	28 feet
Complement	140

Armament:

16 x SS-N-18 SLBMs
6 x 21-in torpedo tubes
4 x 450 mm (17.7-in) torpedo tubes

Machinery:

2 nuclear reactors, 4 steam turbines
2 shafts
20 knots surfaced
24 knots submerged

(Greater Underwater Propulsive Power) into boats even faster than the German Type XXIs. Fifty boats were converted and sixteen others were partially modified. These submarines were widely distributed to Allies and some lasted into the 1990s. A new class of submarine, slightly smaller than the Guppy, was produced in the early 1950s. Six of these Tang class boats were to be followed by three enlarged Darters but two of the latter were reconfigured to carry the Regulus strategic cruise missile.

In 1953 an important experimental submarine was commissioned: the USS *Albacore*. This pioneered a teardrop hull shape, which, when combined with massive battery capacity, gave an underwater speed of 33 knots. The hull form was put into production in the 2,146-ton Barbel class, three of which were commissioned in 1959; but these proved to be the last diesel submarines in the US Navy, the decision being taken to go to an all nuclear force, to which the new hull shape was also applied.

The British also converted older boats to a greater or lesser degree, both 'T' and 'A' Class boats being treated. A new 1,565-ton Porpoise design was built in the late 1950s: this class proved very successful and was developed into the Oberon class that was built in the

Left: SSKs like the Agosta class have been fitted to fire Exocet or sub-harpoon anti-ship missiles.

1960s. The latter boats were very quiet and deep-diving and were exported to Australia, Canada, Brazil and Chile. They were retained in service by the Royal Navy until the early 1990s. Plans to replace ten of them with a new 2,400-ton Upholder class were abandoned in 1991 and the decision taken to follow the Americans to an all nuclear submarine force.

France decided to follow the same route in the middle of the 1990s having pursued an active conventional

submarine programme over the previous half century. She came closest to copying the type XXI in the shape six Narvals of the late 1950s and also built a small hunter killer type for ASW operations in the Mediterranean – the Arethuse class. The latter was developed into a small general purpose type with the

Below: S 803 *Dolfyn*, the second of the Royal Netherlands Navy's new Walrus class SSKs.

export market in mind, the Daphnes, eleven of which entered French service, eleven of which were delivered to the French Navy in 1964–70 and fourteen more to Portugal, Pakistan, South Africa and Spain (where they were built). At the same time as France began nuclear attack submarine construction in the 1970s, four 1,500-ton conventional boats (the Agostas) of similar streamlined-hull form were built, and this design again

did quite well on the export market.

Both the Netherlands and Japan have maintained capable ocean-going conventional submarine forces of their own construction. The former considered nuclear propulsion in the late 1950s, but instead a streamlined diesel design of novel triple hull form was continued, four boats entering service in the 1960s. The American Barbel was used as the basis for the 2,400-ton Zwaardvis

Above: The latest type of US attack submarine, SSN 21 *Seawolf* on her first at-sea trials, July 1996.

design, two of which were built in the 1970s. It was planned to replace all six of these boats with a new, advanced Walrus design based on the Zwaardvis. Again nuclear propulsion was considered but rejected. Considerable problems were faced in building the first pair, which took a decade to complete, but four were in service by 1994. In 1989 it was decided to limit the Dutch submarine fleet to four boats and the two last Walruses were cancelled.

Nuclear propulsion was even more clearly ruled out for Japan who commissioned her first post-war submarine, *Oyashio*, in 1960. The first boats were small, but in 1965 the first of a more capable 1,650-ton Oshio class was built. The teardrop hull form appeared with 1,850-ton *Uzushio* in 1971, and the design has been incrementally improved to the 2,700 tons of the Harushios laid down in the mid 1990s. As new boats were delivered on the basis of one a year, older ones were withdrawn from front line service to keep an operational flotilla of sixteen boats.

Once she was allowed to build submarines again, Germany became a very successful producer both for

Left: Australia ordered the Collins class to replace the ageing Oberon SSKs. Here, the *Waller* is seen approaching Sydney's famous opera house.

herself and on the export market. The designer of the revolutionary submarines of the wartime years, Ulrich Gabler, designed a new 200 series, which after some serious teething troubles proved very successful. The smaller versions of 400–450 tons with a crew of 21 became almost a NATO standard coastal submarine (SSC) in service with Norway (who also bought a larger version) and Denmark as well as Germany. The larger 1,000-ton type 209 was procured by Greece, Turkey, Indonesia, Argentina, Ecuador and Peru, and larger boats still of related design were adopted by India and Argentina.

Germany's main competition in the export market began to come from Sweden which salved a Type XXI and developed domestically from the 1950s a series of progressively improved classes of large SSC in the 1,000-ton class. One of the three Nackens of 1980–1 was modified in 1987–8 with an air independent Stirling engine to increase underwater endurance to two weeks, and the Gotland class under construction in the mid 1990s is being fitted with the same system. The Australians adopted a Swedish design for their rather larger (2,500 ton) Collins class boats that began delivery in 1995.

In the west only the three major navies have operated nuclear-powered submarines. These have included both attack and ballistic missile boats. The development of these has been touched on above. In the 1950s a series of experimental boats were built in various roles along with the first production class, the Skates, reduced Nautiluses with a similar shape hull. The Albacore hull was applied to the Skipjacks, the first of which commissioned in 1959 and which provided the basis for the first SSBNs. The definitive production SSN did not appear till the beginning of the 1960s with the 4,000-ton Thresher/Permit/Sturgeon classes, no less than 53 of which were commissioned between 1962 and 1975. Effectively anti-submarine hunter killers as described above, they were succeeded by the faster 6,000-ton Los Angeles class commissioned from 1976 to 1995. Built with double the power of their predecessors to support fast carriers, these boats found their true vocation in quiet submarine v submarine 'combat' with their Soviet counterparts during the Cold War and cruise missile power projection operations after it.

The British relied on the USA for the design of the power plant of their first SSN, HMS *Dreadnought* built 1959–63. Her modified Albacore hull shape was reproduced in slightly larger form in the 4,000-ton British reactor-powered Valiants, five of which were completed 1966–71, production being delayed for the construction of the related Resolution class Polaris SSBNs. A modified Swiftsure class was built in the 1970s, and after six of these the still larger (4,700 ton) Trafalgars were commissioned from 1983 to 1991. Twelve SSNs (five S class and seven Ts) formed the RN submarine force of the mid-1990s.

As dictated by its strategic doctrine, France emphasised the SSBN in its construction programme. Not until the first four of the six Le Redoubtable SNLEs (*Sousmarins, Nucleaire, Lance, Engins*) were completed in 1976 (the first was laid down in 1964) was an SNA laid down. A 4,000-ton attack version of the *Redoubtable* had been projected in the 1960s but rejected on grounds of cost. The new SNA 72 was a very different boat, unlike the

US/UK model in being, in effect, a nuclear enlargement of a conventional submarine. Displacing 2,670 tons submerged, the Rubis class only had a 9,500 hp power plant and was limited to 25 knots. Completed in the 1980s, the main purpose of these relatively noisy boats was anti-surface warfare, a capability enhanced by the fitting of submerged-launched Exocet missiles. To improve ASW potential, the follow-on Amethyste class was designed to be quieter, the class name standing for *Amelioration Tactique, Hydrodynamique, Silence, Transmission, Ecoute*. Only two of the new boats were competed (in 1992–3) instead of the planned four, but the Rubis class was taken in hand for conversion to the same standard. With the revisions in French defence policy announced in 1995–6, these six SNAs will form the entire French attack submarine force in the new century. Meanwhile, the SNLE force is being partially modernised with a new 14,200-ton (submerged) Le Triomphant class.

Auxiliaries and Reach

Navies are much more than warships. In the Pacific during World War II, the US Navy operated for sustained periods far from shore bases relying on a fleet train of replenishment ships. This restored to navies something of the autonomy they had lost when sail gave way to steam

Above: The RN's four brand-new Upholder class SSKs have been up for sale since 1995.

in the mid-nineteenth century. After 1945, this 'reach' was sustained by the US Navy and acquired by other Western navies, notably the British, who had faced great difficulties in matching American capabilities in the Pacific when the Royal Navy returned in strength to the region in 1945. Ships of wartime construction were replaced by a new generation of auxiliaries. In the US the demands of super carrier operations saw the construction in the 1950s of a new generation of oilers and ammunition ships of increased capacity. Then in 1959 a requirement was issued for a Fast Combat Support Ship (AOE) to be able to dispense fuel, ammunition and food in a high-speed hull. This resulted in the huge 53,600-ton *Sacramento* and *Camden*, powered by turbines intended for a cancelled Iowa class battleship. These 26-knot ships carried helicopters to add vertical replenishment to the established underway replenishment capabilities by hose and cargo line. Two more, *Seattle* and *Detroit* were completed by 1970. A new Mars class of combat stores ship (AFS) was also built, as was a smaller Wichita class replenishment oiler (AOR), used to supplement the Sacramentos and for less demanding task group operations. The early 1970s saw delivery of a new type of ammunition ship (AE), the Kilauea class.

Under Congressional pressure in the 1980s, the US Navy tried to increase the flexibility of its auxiliary fleet by making all its ships capable of delivering both fuel and solid stores. A new class of Cimarron class fleet oiler (AO) delivered in 1981–3 was taken in hand for lengthening to carry ammunition, and in 1989 construction began of a follow-on to the Sacramentos in the shape of four gas-turbine-powered Supply class AOEs, commissioning 1994–8 to replace the Wichitas. Auxiliaries also began to be transferred to the civilian-manned Military Sealift Command to save on costs of operation. In 1996 only the AOEs, five AOs and four AEs remained Navy operated.

The British always left their auxiliaries civilian-manned, flying the Blue Ensign and designated Royal Fleet Auxiliary (RFA). New construction began in the 1950s with the Tide class, capable of carrying both fuel and stores. After four of these, the last completed in 1963, came three more enlarged 'Ol' class ships (36,000 tons full load) completed in 1965–6. The mid-1960s saw

Right: The Fort Victoria class fleet replenishment ship A 388 HMS *Fort George.*

heavy investment in RFAs to give the fleet the reach it required for its East of Suez role. Two 22,800-ton Resource class fleet replenishment ships were built for ammunition and stores as were three smaller Ness class stores support ships. The larger tankers and replenishment ships were given helicopter hangars, which allowed the operation of helicopters, not only for replenishment but for ASW also.

After the decision to concentrate on operations in the North Atlantic, the small fleet tankers of the Rover class were delivered during 1969–70. The two new Fort Grange class Replenishment ships of the late 1970s were larger than *Resource.* In the 1990s two even larger

Above: The fleet oiler USS *Wichita* conducts underway replenishment operations with the Arleigh Burke class destroyer *Paul F Foster.* Note the latter's bulbous bow clearly visible below the water.

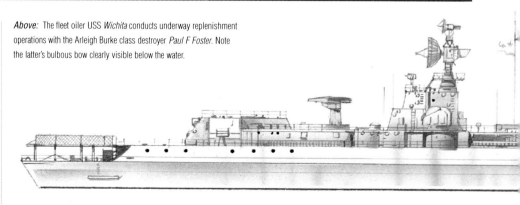

(32,300 ton) Fort Victoria class Fleet Replenishment Ships finally provided the RN with some equivalent of the AOE with a 'one stop' capability for fuel and stores. Plans to fit these ships with combat data systems and Sea Wolf as integrated members of Type 23 groups were abandoned, as were plans for four more, but they can carry five large ASW helicopters and even act as emergency platforms for Sea Harriers. Falklands experience led to the commissioning of RFA *Argus*, a converted Ro-Ro container ship, as a flat-topped aviation training ship that was usable in a wide variety of roles from auxiliary carrier to replenishment vessel.

Starting in 1973, France built the Durance class of multi-product replenishment ship that can also act as a flagship or be used for special forces operations if required. Ships of similar type have been supplied to Australia and Saudi Arabia. Canada also built a flexible Provider class of fleet oiler in the 1960s. The later ships *Protecteur* and *Preserver* were intended to act as a general support vessel with troop space and landing craft to support operations ashore. By the 1990s auxiliaries in medium power navies had crossed the boundary and become combatant warships.

The Rise and Fall of the Soviet Navy

The Soviet Union took a very different approach from Western navies. Aside from considerations of national prestige (not unimportant to Stalin and several of his successors), the USSR's maritime strategy was to deny the seas to various forms of Western naval action and to deploy a sea-going nuclear strike force. The primary importance of their SSBN force and the varying fortunes of the Navy in Moscow's bureaucratic infighting led to a fleet that looked and performed very differently from its intended NATO opponents.

Coastal security was always a major Soviet priority, and throughout the post-war period large numbers of

smaller surface combatants of corvette (500 ton) and fast attack craft size were built for various duties. The advent of the surface-to-surface missile in the Project 183R (Komar) Project 184 (Osa) classes and the later larger Project 1234 (Nanuchka) and 1241.1 (Tarantul) classes gave coastal forces a decisive new capability. The 560-ton Nanuchkas were also large enough for distant deployment. The Soviets also put great emphasis on mine warfare with all their surface combatants rigged for minelaying and a large mine countermeasures force.

During the 1930s Stalin had committed himself to something much more ambitious: a full-scale fleet of both surface ships and submarines to rival those of the other major powers. Several enormous battleship hulls were taking shape when the 1941 German invasion halted construction. In 1945 the Navy proposed to

Above: The highly capable Udaloy class destroyers have been building since the early 1980s. Here *Admiral Luchenko* visits the UK.

resume this grandiose programme, proposing battleships, cruisers, carriers, destroyers large and small and submarines in three sizes. A new 16-in (406-mm) gun battleship was projected and considerable work done on the 36,500-ton Project 82 class large cruiser armed with 12-in (305-mm) guns. The battleship was abandoned in 1952, but three of the latter were actually ordered in 1951 and laid down. Stalin saw them as useful commerce raiders but his successors were less keen and the ships were cancelled on his death in 1953; the lead ship, *Stalingrad*, only months from launch. A parallel design armed also with cruise missiles for strategic strike lasted only a little longer. The lead ship was cancelled and

Below: The Soviet navy commissioned ten Kresta II class cruisers during the 1970s. Their main weapons were anti-submarine torpedoes delivered up to 30 miles away by its SS-N-14 missiles.

Kresta class

data:

Displacement standard	6,000 tons
Displacement full load	7,600 tons
Length	520 feet
Beam	56 feet
Design draught	20 feet
Complement	400

Class: *Kronstadt, Admiral Isakov, Admiral Nakhimov, Admiral Makarov, Marshal Voroshilov, Admiral Oktyabrisky, Admiral Isachenkov, Vasily Chapayev, Admiral Yumashev*

Armament:
8 x SS-N-14 'Silex' missiles
2 x twin SA-N-3 launchers
4 x 57-mm guns
4 x 30-mm CIWS systems
2 x RBU 6000 ASW rocket launchers
2 x RBU 1000 ASW rocket launchers
10 x 21-in torpedo tubes

Machinery:
Steam turbines, 100,000 shp
2 shafts
34 knots

scrapped shortly after launch in 1955 and the programme was replaced by ten 4,400-ton Project 58 (Kynda) class 'missile cruisers' the first one of which was laid down in 1960.

The main big ship programme that did see service was the Project 68B Sverdlov class 13,600-ton light cruiser developed from the pre-war Chipaev class and armed with twelve 6-in (152-mm) guns. Twenty-five were ordered but only 14 completed in 1951–5 before Stalin's successors halted the programme. The Sverdlovs provided very useful ammunition to Western planners who insisted that a powerful anti-surface capability be retained by Western navies in case they were used as raiders.

To support the cruisers in operations closer to home, 250 destroyers were planned, later reduced to 188. The new ships were of two types, Project 30B (Skoriy class) and 41 (Neustrashimiy class) both very conventional designs with guns and torpedoes. Sixty-eight of the former were completed from 1949–53, but only one of

Below: As Soviet naval expenditure escalated through the 1980s, four giant Kirov class missile cruisers were constructed, dwarfing those of other nations. The final unit was slowly completed by the post-Soviet Russian navy but they have spent little time at sea in the last few years.

Left: An Oscar II nuclear-powered submarine of the Russian Northern Fleet seen in 1994. The Oscar class are armed with SS-N-19 anti-ship missiles with a range of some 250 miles.

the latter, as the 3,100-ton design was considered to be too large. A 2,662-ton Project 56 (Kotlin) design was developed instead and put into production in 1953; 27 were built before production was stopped by Khrushchev in 1955. The smaller coastal patrol vessels of 1,900 tons and a reduced 1,160 tons were equally limited in modern capability and the programme was also cut short in 1955.

Stalin was less keen on submarines but the Navy saw them as its primary striking force. The primary role of the Soviet submarine fleet was still seen as coastal defence, although longer-ranged submarine operations would, like those of the surface raiders, contribute to tying down Western strength if it came to war. At Stalin's death, plans stood at 96 Project 611 (NATO code name: 'Zulu') class boats, 288 Project 613 ('Whiskey') class and 36 Project 615 ('Quebec') class. All reflected previous Soviet practice but were affected by knowledge of captured German U-boats. The 611s were 1,900-ton vessels built with large battery capacity to double underwater speed and triple underwater endurance. The

Below: Built in the 1970s, the Kara class were large and fast cruisers primarily designed to attack NATO submarines, but with a useful anti-aircraft capability.

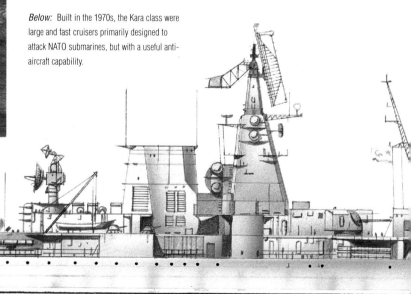

Kirov class

data:

Displacement standard	22,000 tons
Displacement full load	24,300 tons
Length	827 feet
Beam	93 feet
Design draught	29 feet
Complement	692

Class: (as re-named) Admiral Ushakov, Admiral Lazarev, Admiral Nakhimov, Pyotr Velikiy

Armament:
20 x SS-N-19 missiles
12 x SA-N-12 SAM launchers
2 x SA-N-4 SAM launchers
2 x SA-N-9 SAM launchers
2 x SS-N-14 ASW missiles
2 x SS-N-15 ASW missiles
2 x 3.9-in guns (Ushakov)
2 x 5.1-in guns (Others)
6 x 30-mm CIWS
4 x ASW rocket launchers

Machinery:
CONAS (2 nuclear reactors plus oil-fired boilers for steam turbines), 150,000 shp
30 knots

surfaced range was 20,000 miles and they were intended for long-range duties. The 1,050-ton 613s had only half this range and were for operations close to home as an outer coast defence layer. They had characteristic Type XXI features: not only high-capacity batteries but slow-speed creep motors. Both classes were initially built with deck guns and were only partially streamlined; the 613's underwater speed was only 13 knots. Both were later more fully streamlined and were fitted with snorkels, making them more clearly the kind of threat that Western intelligence seems to have interpreted them as being from the start. Twenty-six of the larger boats were built in the early 1950s and an incredible total of 215 Whiskey class boats between 1950 and 1956. The 615 was a tiny 460-ton coastal boat with closed cycle diesel propulsion another factor limiting their range; 31 were built.

These submarine programmes seem to have survived Stalin's death. They may have been curtailed as a result of Khrushchev's policy changes of the mid-1950s but it is possible that the orders for the two larger designs were

Kara class

data:

Displacement standard	8,200 tons
Displacement full load	9,700 tons
Length	568 feet
Beam	61 feet
Design draught	22 feet
Complement	525

Class: Nikolayev, Ochakov, Kerch, Azov, Petropavlosk, Tashkent, Tallinn

Armament:
2 x twin SA-N-3 SAM launchers
2 x twin SA-N-4 SAM launchers
2 x quadruple SA-N-14 ASW missiles
4 x 76-mm guns
4 x 30-mm CIWS
4 x ASW mortars
10 x 21-in torpedo tubes

Machinery:
COGAG gas turbine system, 120,000 shp
2 shafts
34 knots

Above: This Tarantul type missile boat was supplied to East Germany and acquired by the US Navy after German reunification.

changed to improved Project 641 (NATO code name: 'Foxtrot') and 633 ('Romeo') submarines. These were larger: respectively 1,330 tons and 1,957 tons (surface displacement), longer-ranged and deeper-diving. It seems that it was hoped to put both these classes into mass production with plans to build 221 and 336 respectively, but production was curtailed at 21 and 62 units. Reduced construction plans were reluctantly adopted by Khrushchev (who was an enthusiast for nuclear power) beginning in 1957. Shorter-ranged, coastal submarines like the Romeo were considered outmoded and production ceased in 1962. The ocean-going Foxtrots continued to be built until the early 1980s, the production line kept going mainly for exports.

Soviet nuclear submarine development began in about 1950. Its objective was to deliver giant 24-mile-range torpedoes with nuclear warheads as strategic weapons against the USA. The design was altered in the mid-1950s to a more general attack role with eight normal

Above: the Kamov Ka-27 has been the standard helicopter embarked on Russian warships for many years. The 'A' model seen here is the ASW version, equipped with dipping sonar, sonobuoys and able to carry either two homing torpedoes or a nuclear depth bomb.

Left: Baku, seen here off Italy in 1988 was the fourth unit of the Kiev class. Her air group comprised 14 Yak-38 V/STOL aircraft, 14 Kamov Ka-27s and 3 Kamov Ka-25 helicopters. The gigantic cylinders across her foredeck are launchers for SS-N-12 missiles which have a maximum range of about 300 miles.

torpedo tubes and a better sonar fit. The first Soviet SSN *K-3* came into service in 1959. Developed as Project 627, it was the first of 12 boats, one of which (Project 645) had an experimental liquid metal reactor. NATO called them all the 'November' class. The last boat, *K-50*, was laid down as a strategic cruise missile submarine but the missile she was to carry was cancelled and she was completed as a standard 627 type. The reason the strategic torpedo was cancelled was that it was found practical to match a short-range R-11 ballistic missile (NATO code-name: 'Scud') with the standard Zulu class ocean-going submarine. The first firing, by *B-67*, took place in 1955 and five boats were converted to carry two missiles each (Zulu V class). The missile fitted to the new cruisers was also mated in pairs with the Project 613 hull to produce the Project 644 strategic submarine ('Whiskey twin cylinder' to NATO).

Nuclear weapons and guided missiles lay at the heart of the revolution in military affairs that Nikita Khrushchev declared to be the strategic dimension of 'de-Stalinisation' in 1955. Admiral Gorshkov was appointed to re-orientate the Navy in the new direction. Numerous programmes were cancelled and a fleet of reduced size designed around the new weapons. Khrushchev felt that the traditional surface ships being

built in the mid-1950s could not survive against modern aircraft, but he was willing to allow the marrying of the *Shchuka* (NATO code-name: 'SS-N-1') anti-ship and anti-shore cruise missile with three Project 56 hulls, which became the Kildin class. Eight Krupny class 3,500-ton double-ended Project 57B missile ships armed with the same weapon were built during 1958–61. The gun-armed patrol ships were replaced in production by 950-ton ASW vessels equipped with light guns, rocket launchers and torpedoes.

Such vessels needed support even in coastal home defence tasks. The Soviets were becoming less anxious about NATO amphibious landings and more concerned to counter America's increasingly long-range carrier aircraft. In 1956 a new class of large 3,400-ton destroyer, the Project 61 (Kashin class) was authorised to provide cover for ships in the coastal zone against submarines, aircraft and missiles. The ships emerged in the 1960s as 3,400-ton gas-turbine-powered double-ended SAM (Surface-to-Air Missile) ships also carrying light guns, ASW torpedoes and an ASW helicopter. Twenty were built from 1962 to 1973. The *Volna* SAM (NATO code-name: SA-N-1) was tested single-ended in a Project 56 destroyer and eight more ships of the older class were modified to supplement the newer destroyers in the

AAW (Anti Air Warfare) role.

Khrushchev at first supported the Navy in the strategic strike role, and new conventional and nuclear-powered submarines were developed to carry both ballistic and cruise missiles. These were handicapped by relatively short range. The conventionally powered Foxtrot-derived Project 628 (Golf class) carried three ballistic missiles in an extended fin; initially fitted with Scuds, they were later modified to carry the 350-mile-range R-13 missile (SS-N-4). Production began in 1958. The Project 658 (Hotel class) was started in the same year: a similar layout three-missile variant of the Project 627 (November class) nuclear-powered boat. A total of 23 Golf class and 8 Hotel class were built. A further five nuclear-powered hulls were built in 1957–62 as Project 659 (Echo I class) to carry six of the P-5 (SS-N-3) land-attack cruise missiles each.

By the time these boats entered service their mission had been undermined by another sudden lurch of policy. In 1957 the USSR launched the world's first ICBM and two years later, the Strategic Missile Forces formed from the Army were given a monopoly of the strategic strike role. The only compensation was a naval take over of all long-range missile-launching aircraft intended to attack US aircraft carriers. The Soviet Navy's role became more

clearly that of strategic defence against NATO carriers and missile-firing submarines. This rationale supported the building in the 1960s of two 11,200-ton helicopter cruisers, *Moskva* and *Leningrad*, to provide the basis for a long-range SSBN-hunting group. The existing Kynda class missile cruisers could be converted to carry *Progress* (SS-N-3) anti-ship missiles, but they were felt to lack enough anti-aircraft weapons to survive against NATO airpower. The design was recast after four ships as Project 1134 (Kresta I class) with two SAM launchers and only four anti-carrier cruise missiles. *Progress* missiles were also deployed in conventional and nuclear-powered submarines built in the mid 1960s: Project 651 (Juliett class) and Project 675 (Echo II class) respectively. These long-range weapons relied on external targeting from long-range aircraft.

Shorter-range missiles not reliant on external targeting were developed for a new generation of submarines and surface ships. The Project 661 (Papa class) high-speed

titanium-hulled anti-carrier missile boat proved too expensive, and a simpler design, the Project 670 (Charlie class), entered production in 1968. The Charlies were built in two variants with different missiles until 1980. Torpedo-firing attack submarines were also built: the conventional Project 671 (Victor class) and the radical Project 705 (Alfa class). The latter were titanium-hulled high-speed boats capable of diving to astonishing depths, but incredibly noisy at speed.

Shorter-ranged anti-ship missiles were also intended for an improved Project 1134 missile cruiser and a new Project 1135 patrol ship but priorities changed. These were completed as Kresta II and Krivak class large anti-submarine ships equipped with missiles that delivered an anti-submarine homing torpedo. The new designation reflected another policy shift that followed Khrushchev's overthrow. The Navy recovered a part of the strategic nuclear mission, and the Project 667 (Yankee class) submarines were reconfigured from their anti-carrier

Above: A Delta III SSBN seen in 1994 flying the St Andrew's cross ensign of the pre-revolutionary Russian navy.

role. The rest of the fleet was to protect them from Western ASW forces, especially submarines; longer-ranged Western SLBMs also implied a more dispersed anti-submarine screen. The SSNs were modified with ASW missiles, a new ASW version of the Foxtrot, the Project 641 (Tango class) was built, and the cruiser programme emerged as ten Kresta IIs and seven enlarged gas-turbine-powered Project 1134B (Kara class) were built in the 1970s. The Moskvas were replaced in production by the more powerful enlarged project 1143 (Kiev class) operating primitive vertical take-off fighters and a new anti-submarine ship, the 6,200-ton Project 1155 (Udaloy class).

The introduction of longer-ranged missiles into its SSBN force changed the priorities of the Soviet fleet. The new generation of SSBNs would not need assistance breaking out into the Atlantic or Pacific. Since they could practically hit the USA from their home ports, they intended to operate from 'bastions' off the Soviet coast. This required new classes of anti-surface as well as anti-submarine warships to defend them. Soviet exercise experience indicated that such surface forces had to be commanded from flagships rather than from ashore. Bastion defence also required better organic air cover. In addition to this shift to a limited sea-control strategy, Soviet thinking in the 1970s edged towards a more political role for the fleet, seeing it as a national status symbol as much as an instrument of limited naval force. Hence the construction in the 1980s of new and impressive classes of ship for the anti-surface mission, the giant Project 1144 (Kirov class) missile ships of 24,000 tons; the 10,000-ton Slava class missile cruisers, and the 6,200-ton Project 956 Sovremennyy class missile destroyers – the latter follow-ons to the Karas and Krestas respectively.

As the Soviet Union entered its final days, the last Project 1143 ship emerged as a 60,000-ton through-deck carrier to operate the latest jet fighters by the STOBAR (short take-off but arrested recovery) system. In the submarine fleet the Project 671 boats were progressively and significantly modified with improved quietening, and a new hunter killer boat, the Project 945 (Sierra class), was developed alongside the Project 971 (Akula class) cruise-missile-firing boat, and the gigantic Project 949 (Oscar class) anti-carrier submarine. A new conventional boat, the Project 877 (Kilo class), was produced with exports partly in mind. The building programme was impressive indeed, but in the end defeated itself, contributing in no small measure to the economic strains that caused the Soviet Union to implode.

Other Navies

The proliferation of nation states in the post-1945 period has led to the creation of many new navies. The old established Latin American navies tended to hang on to older type ships and retain a predominantly anti-surface emphasis, with traditional cruisers and destroyers supplemented over time by more modern surface combatants obtained either new or second-hand. Other navies tried to capitalise on the apparent fast missile craft revolution until the vulnerability of this type to air attack forced the development of larger, more comprehensively equipped corvette type ships. The need to police expanded 200-mile exclusive economic zones also led states to acquire seagoing capabilities, the most cost-effective answer to this requirement being the lightly armed offshore patrol vessel. Only the richer new states could afford proper major surface combatants, but there were enough of these to make it worthwhile to develop special types of surface combatants in both the frigate and corvette category to augment the always ready supply of obsolescent second-hand warships.

Two major navies are worthy of specific mention. India tried hard from the 1950s onwards to become the major power in the Indian Ocean. Two carriers obtained from the UK gave power projection capability, while surface combatants of Western and Soviet provenance, together with domestic construction combining both traditions, provided the other components of seagoing task forces. India also developed innovative tactics for towing smaller missile attack craft to increase their strategic reach. A submarine fleet was developed, again along both Soviet and Western lines, and a nuclear submarine hired from the Soviet Union. By the 1990s, however, the future of the fleet was coming under serious question. Protracted construction periods for the domestically built destroyers and frigates have driven up costs; there are grave doubts about the promised nuclear-powered submarine programme, and the carrier force seems unsustainable.

After the Communists won the civil war in 1949, Chinese naval policy concentrated on coast defence. Old Soviet technology was adopted and developed to create a surface and sub-surface force that was impressive more in quantity than quality. The general shape of the Chinese surface combatant of the 1970s and 80s was a 1950s style Soviet hull, of either destroyer or patrol vessel (frigate) category with torpedoes replaced by copied Soviet surface-to-surface missiles. Air defence remained very limited indeed as China struggled to produce its own surface-to-air missiles. Only in the early 1990s were modern combatants delivered in the shape of the 5,700-ton (full load) Luhu class, but even this programme was constrained by dependence on foreign technology withheld for political reasons.

The big Chinese success story was the building of a class of five 5,000-ton nuclear-powered attack submarines launched between 1970 and 1990. However, development was very troubled and the operational capability of the boats remains questionable. Significantly, only one SSBN has been built and the SLBM converted for mobile land-based use. Despite ambitious plans to expand into a blue-water navy, the actual performance of the 'Peoples' Liberation Army Navy' remained decidedly limited.

Below: A B-6 (Tupolev Tu-16 copy) of the Chinese naval air force armed with anti-ship missiles.

Chapter 10 – Naval Warfare 1945–97

The main form of naval warfare after World War II has been the projection of maritime power ashore. The first days of the Korean War saw some one-sided action between North Korean fast attack craft and Western surface ships, but after the destruction of the Communist vessels the only serious maritime opposition came from mines.

American and British Commonwealth carriers maintained a constant contribution to the UN air offensive from the start of the Korean war to the end. Battleships, cruisers, destroyers and frigates carried out repeated shore-bombardment missions. The main maritime operation was the landing at Inchon in September 1950, which turned the tide of the first phase of the war. The invasion force comprised some 230 ships and the heavy covering forces comprised four cruisers, HMS *Kenya*, HMS *Jamaica*, USS *Rochester* and USS *Toledo*. There was limited air opposition: aYak-9 fighter and Il-2 'Shturmovik' bomber attacking the cruisers. *Rochester* was hit by a bomb that failed to explode and a sailor was killed when *Jamaica* was strafed. The 'Shturmovik' was shot down.

To a lesser extent warships (including carriers) supported operations ashore against the Communist insurgents in both Indochina and Malaya. A particular feature of the first named conflict was the development by the French of specialised 'Dinassaut' riverine forces with small landing ships converted into command and fire support vessels and landing craft modified into river monitors; armoured landing craft were used as transports. Britain and France together attacked Egypt from the

sea in November 1956, 100 British and 34 French warships taking part, with naval air cover provided by three British and two French aircraft carriers. Shore bombardment was kept to destroyer guns to limit casualties. The British amphibious force was made up of old tank landing ships and craft whose mobilisation and slow speed had delayed the British response, but the French deployed a landing ship dock, and the British pioneered the LPH concept by landing troops by helicopter from *Ocean* and *Theseus*. The Egyptian Navy lost three major warships in 1956. In the Red Sea south of Suez the frigate *Domiat* (ex-HMS *Nith*) was sunk by the British cruiser *Newfoundland*, and her sister *Abikir* (ex-HMS *Usk*) was scuttled as a block ship in the Suez Canal. The Egyptian Hunt class frigate *Ibrahim El Alwal* (ex-HMS *Mendip*) was captured by the Israelis while on a shore-bombardment mission off Haifa. The frigate was engaged by the French *escorteur d'escadre* the *Kersaint* and by the Israeli destroyers *Eilath* and *Yaffa* (ex-HMS *Zodiac* and *Zealous*) after being damaged by rocket-firing Israeli Ouragan fighter-bombers. The Egyptians had tried to scuttle *Ibrahim El Alwal* but the sea cocks were rusted closed. Two newly delivered Soviet-built Project 30B destroyers were damaged at Alexandria by Anglo-French air attack. Although a political fiasco for the British and French, militarily the Suez operation was something of a success and a very useful demonstration of the strengths and weaknesses of available naval capabilities.

The 1960s saw South East Asia become the focus for maritime operations. The main area was Vietnam where the American escalation of the war against the North was facilitated by clashes in August 1964 in the Gulf of Tonkin between American destroyers and North Vietnamese motor torpedo boats. From 1965 to 1973 US carriers played major roles, both on 'Yankee Station' in the strategic bombing of the North itself and on 'Dixie Station' giving support to US, South Vietnamese and other allied forces. In 1972 carrier-based Grumman A-6 Intruders were used to mine North Vietnamese ports.

Surface combatants, including the reactivated battleship *New Jersey*, were used for shore-bombardment missions against targets in North and South Vietnam. Missile equipped ships sometimes engaged North Vietnamese aircraft, the cruiser *Chicago* obtaining a kill at a range of 65 miles with the long-range Talos SAM system. First destroyers, then radar-equipped destroyer

Left: Intermittently active since the 1950s, all four Iowa class battleships were re-commissioned during the 1980s as the US Navy expanded. Here, USS *New Jersey* fires a Tomahawk cruise missile: a feat repeated in anger by her sistership *Missouri* during the Gulf conflict. The end of the Cold War has finally concluded the fifty year career of these veteran warships.

Left The Colossus class light fleet carrier *Theseus* was one of the British carriers supporting UN ground forces during the Korean war. Her airgroup at the time included Supermarine Seafires, Hawker Sea Fury MkIIs and Fairey Fireflies.

escorts (converted as part of the US's strategic defences), minesweepers, coastguard cutters and small patrol vessels were used for 'Market Time' patrols to stop seaborne infiltration of the South by North Vietnamese forces. The Americans also built up a large River Patrol Force for 'Game Warden' operations to deny the Communist forces the use of South Vietnam's rivers, notably the Mekong delta. A new type of river patrol boat (PBR) was rapidly developed and deployed. For operations in the Delta region a Mobile Riverine Force

was created with a fleet of heavily armed and armoured small landing craft converted into assault craft of various kinds. The riverine forces were passed to the South Vietnamese on American withdrawal.

Amphibious forces were used to land the first American troops in South Vietnam at Da Nang in March 1965 and continued to be used in operations against the Viet Cong such as Operation Starlite when under cover of a cruiser and two destroyers the 7th Fleet Amphibious Ready Group landed forces that contributed to the

neutralisation of the First Viet-Cong Regiment.

While the US Navy's involvement in Vietnam escalated, British and Commonwealth maritime forces were involved in the 'Confrontation' between Malaysia and Indonesia. The latter, backed in terms of materiel by the USSR, tried to strangle the new Malaysian Federation at birth. LPHs supported operations ashore in Sarawak and Malaya with their helicopters, and minesweepers were used for coastal and riverine patrol that sometimes led to clashes with Indonesian forces.

Left Cold War confrontation: A Kashin class DDG seen from a US warship during search operations for the Korean Boeing 747 airliner shot down by Soviet fighters in the Sea of Japan.

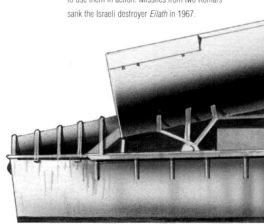

Below: The Soviets built about 100 Komar class missile craft during 1959-61. Used for coastal defence, they were sold to many other navies including the Egyptian forces who were the first to use them in action. Missiles from two Komars sank the Israeli destroyer *Eilath* in 1967.

Above Vast quantities of 16-in shells manufactured during World War II were available for the re-commissioned Iowa class battleships. Here *Iowa* opens fire during NATO exercises off the UK in 1985.

Komar class

data:

Displacement full load		80 tons
Length		27 feet
Beam		21 feet
Design draught		6 feet
Complement		11

Armament:
2 x SS-N-2A 'Styx' SSMs
2 x 25-mm guns

Machinery:
4 diesel engines, 4,800 hp
4 shafts
40 knots

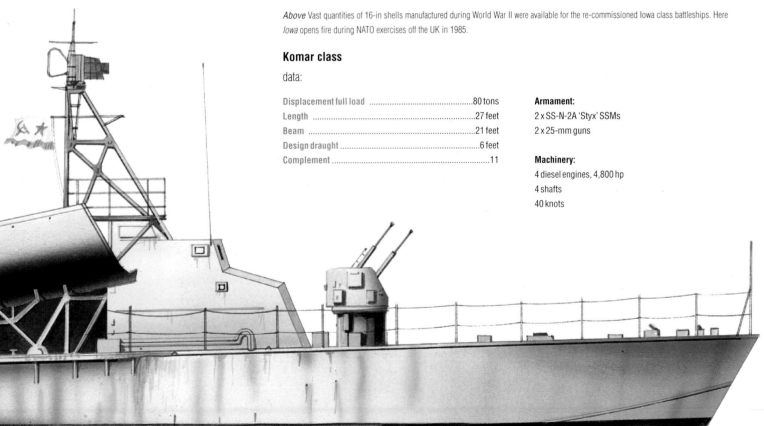

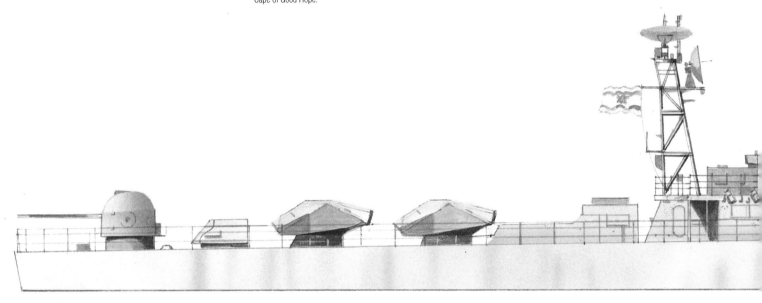

Below: The Israeli navy has enjoyed considerable success with its Sa'ar type missile boats. Several have sailed into the Red Sea via Gibraltar and the Cape of Good Hope.

The frigate *Ajax* foiled an attempted landing north of Koala Lumpur. In 1964 over a third of the entire British surface fleet was operating in Malaysian waters, supporting a campaign that both sustained Malaysia and discredited the Indonesian regime.

The most significant naval event of 1967 was the sinking in October of the Israeli destroyer *Eilath* fourteen miles off Port Said by three Soviet supplied 'Styx' missiles fired from Egyptian fast attack craft moored alongside. The old Israeli ship had been cruising off Egypt in the aftermath of the Six Day War (June 1967).

Below A Nanuchka III class missile corvette of the Russian navy seen in St. Petersburg.

In July she and two Israeli motor torpedo boats had sunk two Egyptian MTBs off Sinai. In the succeeding years, as the so-called 'War of Attrition' was waged between Israel and Egypt, Israeli tank landing craft were used for a deep penetration armoured raid while Israeli aircraft sank the Egyptian destroyer *El Qaher* (formerly HMS *Myngs*) in the Red Sea in May 1970. A Komar class missile boat was also destroyed in the same attack.

Even before the sinking of the *Eilath* the Israelis had begun development of a counter to the Arabs' FACs (Fast Attack Craft): the 220 ton Saar class gunboats. Designed in Germany and built in France from 1965, some escaped in dramatic circumstances at the end of 1969 when France placed an embargo on arms exports to

Israel. A small semi-active radar homing missile, Gabriel was developed for these craft and this weapon proved itself against Arab FACs in the war of 1973. Thirteen Saars were in service as missile boats including two larger (415-ton) Saar 4s. They faced about 37 Komar and Osa class boats operated by the Egyptians and the Syrians, whose Styx missile systems were not really suitable for the engagement of other small craft, and whose homing systems were vulnerable to Israeli countermeasures.

On the first night of the war five Israeli missile boats patrolled off the Syrian coast. A Syrian motor torpedo boat was encountered and sunk by gunfire. Off Latakia Reshef, first of the Saar 4s sank the minesweeper *Hittine* (a Soviet T-43 type) with Gabriel missiles. Three Syrian Osas retaliated with Styx missiles, which were avoided or decoyed, then the Israeli Gabriels accounted for all three Syrian craft. Two days later, off Damietta, six Israeli craft on a shore-bombardment mission avoided Styx missiles fired by four Egyptian Osas, three of which were then sunk by missiles and gunfire. The Israeli fast attack craft, operating with helicopters to assist in missile guidance and ECM (Electronic Counter Measures), dominated the coastal waters off Syria, Sinai and in the Gulf of Suez. Tying down Syrian ground forces for coastal defence and preventing maritime support of the Arab armies in Sinai, the Israelis claimed 38 enemy vessels sunk, including ten missile boats. Later, in 1981–2 the Israelis used their missile gunboats to attack PLO Headquarters in Tripoli and to support the seaward flank of the invasion of Lebanon. The 76-mm (3-inch) guns of the Saars proved very effective in the shore-bombardment role.

The Indian Ocean was the scene of an even larger-scale naval conflict in the 1970s when India and Pakistan went

Sa'ar 4 class

data:

Displacement full load	450 tons
Length	58 feet
Beam	8 feet
Design draught	2.5 feet
Complement	45

Armament:
8 x Harpoon or
4 or 6 x Gabriel SAM missiles
1 or 2 x 76-mm guns
2 x 20-mm guns
1 x 20-mm CIWS

Machinery:
4 diesels
15,000 hp
4 shafts
30 knots

to war over the future of East Bengal. Naval forces had played very little role in the previous Indo-Pakistani conflict in 1965, except for the bombardment of Dwarka by the Pakistani Battle class destroyer *Khaibar* (ex-HMS *Cadiz*). The Indian Navy was determined to take the initiative next time and exploit India's superior naval strength. The result was a plan, Operation Trident, to attack Karachi with newly delivered Osa class missile attack craft towed to their target area by Petya class frigates. This was put into effect on the evening of 4 December 1971 by the Osas *Kiltan*, *Nipat*, *Nirghat* and *Veer*. Six Styx missiles were fired at radar contacts, scoring two hits on the destroyer *Khaibar*, one on the Bluebird class minesweeper *Muhafiz* and at least one on the merchantman *Venus Challenger*; all were sunk. Another missile hit the oil storage tanks ashore.

The rest of the Western Fleet, with two more Osas being towed by Petya class frigates, was meant to deliver a follow up-attack, 'Operation Python', the following day but this was delayed and in the end on 8 December only one Osa, *Vinash*, supported by the Type 12 frigates *Talwar* and *Trishul* pressed home an attack. *Talwar* sank a Pakistani picket with gunfire and *Vinash* fired all four of her missiles. These sank the merchantman *Hermattan*, damaged the *Gulf Star* and the Pakistani Naval auxiliary

Below An Osa-I missile craft of the type widely used by several Arab navies in clashes with the Israelis.

Above An IAI Dagger flies over the LSL *Sir Bedivere* during Argentine air strikes against the British beachhead at San Carlos, 1982.

Dacca, and set fire once more to the oil tank complex.

It was intended to bombard the Makran Coast that same night using the cruiser Mysore, destroyer *Ranjit* and frigate *Betwa*, which between them deployed nine 6-inch (152-mm), four 4.7-inch (119-mm) and four 4.5-inch (114-mm) guns. Operation Grand Slam never took place, however, as the position of the surface action group was compromised when a Pakistani merchantmen was sighted and captured. Another, more serious, reverse for the Indians occurred on 9 December when the frigate *Khukri*, forming with her sister Type 14 *Kirpan* half of an ASW search and attack unit sent to hunt down a Pakistani submarine contact, was itself torpedoed and sunk with heavy loss of life by the Daphne class submarine *Hangor*. This was the first surface ship to be sunk by a submarine since the end of the World War II.

Khukri was revenge for the sinking of the partially modernised US-built Pakistani submarine *Ghazi*, which had been sent to the Bay of Bengal to mine the entrance to the fleet base at Vishakapatnam. Interrupted in her work by the destroyer *Rajput* and seaward defence boat *Akshay*, she sank herself on her own mines when returning to her partially laid minefield. *Vikrant*, escorted by the Type 41 AA frigates *Brahmaputra* and *Beas*, was already at large and struck at airfields and vessels in East Pakistani ports with her airgroup of Hawker Sea Hawks. The Indian carrier group helped prevent a Pakistani seaborne evacuation of their East Bengal garrison. The 115-ton Pakistani patrol craft *Jessore* and *Sylhet* were sunk by the Sea Hawks and a third by IAF Hunters. On 16 December the Indian LSTs *Magar*, *Garial* and *Guldar* supported by the two frigates landed Gurkhas at Cox's Bazaar to pre-empt a cease-fire. After the war a combined Soviet-Indian minesweeping force helped remove mines from the waters of the newly independent Bangladesh.

The most spectacular naval fighting of the entire post-1945 era occurred just over a decade after the Indo-Pakistani engagements. On 2 April 1982 an Argentine amphibious group occupied the Falkland Islands. The British had already decided to make a naval response and two task forces were in process of being formed: Task Force 317, of carrier and amphibious assets, and Task Force 324, of submarines. Both were commanded by Admiral Fieldhouse, the British Fleet Commander in Northwood. The closest available ships, destroyers and frigates exercising close to Gibraltar under the command

Above: Conqueror became the first British submarine to sink an enemy ship since 1945 when she torpedoed the cruiser *General Belgrano* in 1982.

of Rear Admiral John ('Sandy') Woodward were sent south to Ascension Island as a vanguard. The core of his group, however, would be formed by the carriers *Hermes* and *Invincible*, which were sailed from Portsmouth on 5 April with great publicity; they carried respectively twelve and eight BAe Sea Harriers. Two days later the DLG *Antrim* and frigate *Plymouth* were detached together with the auxiliary *Tidespring* to recapture the island of South Georgia that had also been illegally occupied. A week later, as the carriers approached their rendezvous with the surface ships, Woodward despatched three Type 42 destroyers, two frigates and an auxiliary to push ahead to the Falklands area in case there should be a last minute freeze on deployment; he then shifted his flag to *Hermes*. Together with the carriers came the first of the amphibious task group including its flagship, the LPD *Fearless*, together with two more frigates. The Task Force Commander flew down for a conference, and it was agreed that Woodward should take the carrier group, Task Group 317.8., down to the Falklands to enforce a 'Total Exclusion Zone' and perhaps draw the Argentine Navy into battle. The amphibious Task Group, TG 317.0 carrying the landing force (TG 317.1) would then join after necessary reorganisation at Ascension.

On 24 April TG 317.8 concentrated, minus the frigate *Brilliant*, which had been ordered to reinforce the South Georgia Task Group after the loss of some of that group's helicopters. During the operation, ASW helicopters from the DLG and the frigates, plus those of the ice patrol ship *Endurance*, sank the Argentine submarine *Santa Fe* (an old American boat), which had been transporting reinforcements to the island. The re-taking of the island on 25–6 April, after a shore bombardment by *Antrim* and *Plymouth* had triggered the Argentine surrender, was a great boost for the British.

On 1 May operations opened in earnest around the Falklands. Sea Harriers and surface combatants hit Argentine air bases on the islands. The Argentines delivered a major air strike on the Task Group, which the Sea Harriers – equipped with the vastly superior AIM-9L Sidewinder missile – had little difficulty in beating off, with some losses to the attackers. This was a decisive defeat; never again would the Argentines attempt air-to-air combat with the carrier-based fighters. ASW assets also beat off an attack by the German-designed Type 209 submarine *San Luis*, whose torpedo malfunctioned.

The main threat to the British now came from the Argentine surface fleet, a threat of which the Group commander was particularly aware, having succeeded in a successful DLG Exocet missile 'attack' on an American carrier group in the Indian Ocean only shortly before. There were three Argentine groups on the prowl, a carrier force based on the *Veinticinco de Mayo*, an Exocet-equipped frigate group and a surface action group composed of the cruiser *General Belgrano* and two Exocet-equipped destroyers. Primary cover against these forces came from the submarines of TF 324, but only HMS *Conqueror* was in contact – with the *Belgrano* group. Woodward pressurised his Task Force commander into changing the SSNs' rules of engagement and the Belgrano group was duly attacked and the cruiser sunk: a notable first in naval history for the SSN *Conqueror* and her skipper, Commander Chris Wreford-Brown. A planned strike by the other two groups proved abortive, and the Argentine fleet, with no answer to the SSNs, retreated back inside territorial waters.

Land-based aviation remained the Argentines' only

Below: Coventry sinks after being hit by three 1,000 lb bombs from Argentine air force A-4Bs.

chance of averting a British landing. The cutting edge of this offensive was the small force of Exocet-equipped Super Etendards, which succeeded in their second attempt at hitting a British unit, the prototype Type 42 destroyer *Sheffield*. She caught fire and had to be abandoned. This contributed to allowing the Argentines a little respite, but within a few days Sea Harriers and surface ships were again harassing the islands and scouting for minefields. Argentine submarines were frustrated by faulty torpedoes and air attacks by Air Force Skyhawks broken up by Sea Harrier CAPs and the warship's SAM systems. Even if aircraft dropped their bombs, they were at too low an altitude for them to explode.

On 18 May the amphibious Task Groups arrived, along with the transport *Atlantic Conveyor* carrying aircraft reinforcements, both Sea Harriers and RAF Harriers. The landings to recover the islands took place on the night of 20–21 May, and the seven covering escorts fought a heroic battle against Argentine air attacks. HMS *Plymouth* shot down an Israeli-built Dagger fighter-bomber with a Sea Cat missile, but the DLG *Antrim* was hit by a bomb that failed to explode. Her neutralisation as air defence coordinator was completed by strafing attacks, but the Type 22 *Broadsword* shot down one of the Daggers with Sea Wolf and her sister-ship *Brilliant* took over the DLG's role. The Leander class frigate *Argonaut* was hit by Skyhawks but the bombs again failed to go off. Less lucky was *Ardent* whose Sea Cat malfunctioned, allowing a Dagger to attack at sufficient height for the bomb to explode; Skyhawks then followed up, including naval aircraft carrying retarded bombs designed for use at low altitude. Hit by no less than nine bombs, of which seven exploded, the frigate had to be abandoned. During the day, Sea Harriers shot down ten

Above: Practice rounds for the Sea Dart SAM used for long range air defence in the Falklands.

Argentine aircraft.

The air attacks resumed on 23 May. A recently arrived Type 21, *Antelope*, was hit by a bomb which failed to explode, but which eventually detonated during disposal operations, sinking the ship. Two Argentine aircraft were shot down, one by multiple weapons, the other by a Sea

Above: The *General Belgrano* was an American Brooklyn class cruiser (USS *Phoenix*) transferred to Argentina in 1951.

Harrier. On the 24 May four Argentine kills were obtained and the bombs that hit two Landing Ships failed to explode.

The best day for the Argentines was their National Day, 25 May. The British had placed a complementary destroyer/frigate 'combo' comprising HMS *Coventry* and

HMS *Broadsword* north of the islands to act as a missile trap. This it did at first, *Coventry's* Sea Dart claiming two Skyhawks, but more of these aircraft exploited technical and tactical defects on the British side to damage the Type 22 with a bomb that failed to explode

Below: A French Etendard IVM. Equipped with Exocet missiles. The Super Etendards sold to Argentina were handicapped by a lack of missiles in 1982.

Above: The Falklands war vindicated the Sea Harrier which operated in conditions no other carrier aircraft could have. This is an FA2 aboard *Illustrious* in 1995.

and to sink *Coventry* with three 1,000-lb (454-kg) bombs which did. Then Super Etendards struck the main force with two Exocets that were diverted by chaff onto the *Atlantic Conveyor*, setting ablaze both her and her precious cargo of helicopters needed for the attack across the island.

Despite this near disaster most of the forces ashore were able to march on Port Stanley; those that could not were transported by sea, an operation that led to a final serious setback for the British when a badly handled sea lift to Bluff Cove led to the loss to air attack of the landing ship *Sir Galahad* and serious damage to another. Woodward had received welcome support in the shape of

Right: Seven Type 21 frigates including the *Arrow*, seen here, served in the Falklands war.

Above: The Aegis cruiser *Vincennes* which engaged in gun actions with Iranian speed boats in 1988.

more destroyers and frigates when the final Argentine air attack was delivered on the carrier Task Group. The last Argentine Etendard-fired Exocet was decoyed away by the frigate HMS *Avenger*'s chaff and the Type 42 destroyer *Exeter* dealt with one of the supporting Skyhawks; *Avenger*'s gunfire shot down a second. The British destroyers and frigates helped support the final attack on Stanley with gunfire, the DLG *Glamorgan* being damaged by a surface-to-surface Exocet taken off an Argentine surface ship, flown into the islands and fired from an improvised launcher ashore.

The British task forces had been responsible for a remarkable feat of maritime power projection. The surface, air and subsurface components of Argentina's maritime forces had been sufficiently neutralised to allow the insertion and support of ground forces strong enough to restore UK sovereignty. Aircraft from *Hermes* and *Invincible* had accounted for 33 Argentine aircraft both in the air and on the ground, and although 6 Sea Harriers and 4 Harriers had been lost for various reasons, none had been shot down in air-to-air combat.

Even before the Falklands war broke out, Iraq and Iran had gone to war in 1980. At first, naval activity was minimal, the more powerful Iranian Navy containing the Iraqis near its Umm Qasr base and mounting a small amphibious operation on the Fao peninsula. Sporadic attacks were carried out on merchantmen, notably by Iraqi Super Frelon helicopters firing Exocet missiles (indeed such attacks may have been carried out even before the Falklands use of this weapon). In 1983 this campaign became more systematic as Saddam Hussein

declared a naval exclusion zone in the Northern Gulf, including the important oil terminal on Kharg Island. Iran began to convoy shipping, and Saddam extended the exclusion zone. In October Exocet-firing Super Etendards were delivered to Iraq on loan, greatly increasing her maritime striking range, and these were credited with their first success in March 1984 against a Greek merchantman. As attacks were stepped up the Iranians began to retaliate against Arab shipping with Maverick missiles fired by F-4 Phantom IIs and later by helicopters. Many ships were hit but the effectiveness of

the missiles against large merchantmen such as tankers was limited, although some ships were lost.

The 'War of the Tankers' dragged on through 1985 and 1986 with mines adding to the missile threat. Kuwait requested outside help to defend her tankers and in early 1987 Kuwaiti ships were reflagged with the US flag to be protected by US Navy ships in Operation 'Earnest Will'. In May the American frigate *Stark* was accidentally attacked by an Iraqi Exocet-firing Mirage F-1 and almost sunk by two hits. At about the same time Iranian Revolutionary Guard (Pasdaran) armed speedboats began

to attack neutral shipping, and the mining threat from Iran became more serious. In September 1987 an Iranian minelayer was captured by the Americans and the following month there was a clash between Iranian boats and US minehunting helicopters, in which one of the Iranian craft was sunk. Iranian strikes with Chinese-made Styx-type coast defence Silkworm missiles on the anchorage off Kuwait's main oil port led to a punitive attack on an Iranian oil platform by four US destroyers and a frigate.

The British, French and later the Italians also stepped

Left: Attacks on neutral tankers led the US Navy to intervene in the Gulf, escorting vessels like the SS *Gas Queen* seen here in 1987.

up their escort effort, being helped by their greater mine countermeasures capability. In 1988 the Western European Union was used as a political framework to both concert European MCM operations and facilitate the deployment of a Belgian-Dutch MCM force operating in close tactical co-operation with the British and under the protection of the surface combatants of the UK's Armilla Patrol. The Europeans were unwilling to place their forces under American command as they were unsure of US intentions, which became increasingly anti-Iranian.

In April 1988 the frigate USS *Samuel B Roberts* sailed into an Iranian minefield and struck a mine. In retaliation the US Navy began Operation 'Praying Mantis', which turned into its largest surface action since 1945. Two oil platforms were destroyed, each by a three-ship surface action group of a cruiser and two destroyers. An Iranian missile boat, the 249-ton *Joshan*, counterattacked with a Harpoon missile that was decoyed away; four American Harpoons then demolished the *Joshan*. Two Iranian Phantoms were driven off by the cruiser *Wainwright*'s missiles, while Pasdaran speedboats were engaged by US carrier-based aircraft, one being sunk. The 1,250-ton Iranian British-built frigate *Sahand* then came up to support the speedboats, fired a Sea Killer surface-to-surface missile but was then hit by three Harpoons and at least one bomb jointly contributed by the destroyer *Joseph Strauss* and carrier-based A-6s. A second Iranian frigate, *Sabalan* entered the fray. She used both Sea Killer and Sea Cat – ineffectively – against the Americans, but her back was broken by laser-guided

Above: The Los Angeles class attack submarine *Baton Rouge* engaged Iraqi forces ashore with cruise missiles during the Gulf conflict.

bombs and she was only saved by the American decision (ordered from the White House) not to finish her off.

Tension was high in July and the stage was set for tragedy when the Aegis cruiser *Vincennes*, already engaging in a clash with Pasdaran speedboats, fired a missile at what she mistakenly thought was an Iranian F-14 fighter. It was in fact an airliner that was destroyed with the loss of all on board. This apparent further demonstration of US support for Iraq, coupled with the clear ability of the USA to control Iran's vital sea communications, added to the general war weariness in Iran to bring the war to an end.

Iraq suddenly became the enemy in 1990 when she invaded Kuwait, and the USA led an international coalition first to contain further Iraqi expansion and then to eject Iraq from her conquest. US carriers provided invaluable mobile air power in the early days of Operation 'Desert Shield' and a powerful amphibious force was built up to threaten the Iraqi flank. A massive sealift brought in millions of tons of equipment, supplies and fuel for the build-up of US and Coalition forces in Saudi Arabia, while a maritime blockade of Iraq was also mounted. When Operation 'Desert Storm' began in January 1991, aircraft from six carriers were integrated in the air campaign, and sea-launched cruise missiles were used against the heavily defended areas in and around Baghdad; in the first twenty-four hours over 100 Tomahawks were fired by battleships *Missouri* and *Wisconsin*, cruisers and destroyers.

Carrier aircraft attacked the Iraqi Navy and sank three Osa class missile boats in Umm Qasr with Harpoon

Above: The Kilauea class ammunition ship *USS Flint* (AE 2)
during her Gulf War deployment, 1991.

missiles. The Iraqis mainly concentrated on minelaying,
but on 29 January, they sortied with seventeen craft to
support attacks on the town of Khafji. The forces
included three landing ships, two captured Kuwaiti
German-built Exocet-armed missile boats and a
minesweeper. The Iraqis were assailed by Sea Skua
missile-firing Lynx helicopters from British destroyers
and land and carrier based aircraft. Four vessels were
sunk and the rest damaged. Over the next day and a half
the rest of the Iraqi navy then tried to escape to Iran. In
the resulting Battle of Bubiyan twenty-five Sea Skua
missiles were fired by British Lynx sinking or damaging
three former Kuwaiti fast attack craft, four smaller patrol
craft, a landing craft and a minelayer. Vessels damaged
by Sea Skua were finished off by carrier-based A-6s,
which also contributed to sinking about a dozen other
vessels with missiles and bombs. Only one damaged Osa
class vessel got away.

A major minesweeping operation was required to allow

Coalition forces to operate off Kuwait. This was led by
the American LPH *Tripoli* operating MCM helicopters,
but the key assets were probably the British Hunt Class
minehunters. *Tripoli* was mined herself as was the Aegis
cruiser *Princeton*, but a cleared area was created from
which fire support could be provided from the battleships
to the troops ashore. A Silkworm missile attack on the
battleship *Missouri* was defeated by a Sea Dart missile
from her escorting destroyer HMS *Gloucester*. The
18,000-man embarked American amphibious force also
continued to keep the Iraqis preoccupied. as their forces
were defeated ashore.

The Gulf War was a classic example of the 'enabling'
function of maritime forces. Maritime power could not
eject the Iraqis from Kuwait, but without it 'Desert
Storm' could not have been carried out. Naval forces
made vital contributions to the land campaign by their
operations in the 'littoral' environment that is coming to
dominate post-Cold War naval thinking. Moreover, the
war was also remarkable for the international nature of
the naval contribution; states such as Australia, Canada
and even Argentina finding the commitment of warships

to such duties as carrier or auxiliary escort their most
convenient and significant contribution to the
maintenance of the 'New World Order'. After the
conflict was over even Japan contributed an MCM
flotilla to the clearing up operation.

Gunboat diplomacy and maritime policing

Naval forces are relevant in many circumstances short of
war. They are classic diplomatic instruments and they
have major roles in maintaining order and sovereignty in
offshore waters. The latter duties have become much
more extensive with the acceptance of the concept of
200-mile economic zones. The Icelanders can probably
claim most credit for asserting the latter concept with
their successful 'Cod Wars' fought with robust little
offshore patrol vessels against the warships of the Royal
Navy in 1958–61, 1971–3 and 1975–6.

The British have been major exponents of limited
naval force in the post-war era. In 1946 a major incident

occurred in the Corfu Channel when attempts to exert rights of innocent passage through the Corfu Channel led to the mining of the destroyers *Saumarez* and *Volage* and the requirement for a heavily escorted minesweeping operation covered by the carrier *Ocean*. Shortly afterwards British warships had the thankless task of trying to limit Jewish immigration into Palestine, and when the British were forced to withdraw they successfully covered the evacuation. In 1949 the frigate *Amethyst* was engaged by Communist batteries on the Yangtze as she tried to sail upriver to stand by the embassy in Nanking. This led to a major battle between the cruiser *London* and frigate *Black Swan* on the one hand and Chinese shore batteries on the other, in which the British came off rather the worst. Eventually *Amethyst* escaped and rejoined the fleet.

In 1950 the Americans began patrolling the Taiwan strait to protect the Nationalists in Taiwan. In 1954 the US Navy evacuated Nationalist forces from the Techen Islands, successfully deterring Communist intervention, and in 1958 during the crisis over Quemoy and Matsu the US Navy escorted Nationalist convoys to within three miles of the islands. A major carrier force of six units was deployed to the area to provide cover. As late as 1996 the deployment of US carriers was required to counter Chinese military pressure on Taiwan.

The American Sixth Fleet had been used to exert pressure on the Anglo-French invasion force in 1956, but less than two years later it was carrying out its own controversial landing, this time unopposed, in Lebanon to shore up the pro-Western government in the context of civil war in Lebanon and revolution in Iraq. Three amphibious squadrons were used, supported by the carriers *Essex* and *Saratoga*. In 1961 the first full British LPH conversion, HMS *Bulwark*, landed her commando in Kuwait when the newly independent kingdom was threatened. Supported by the carrier *Victorious* and other forces brought in by sea and air, the Commandos successfully deterred Iraqi attack.

The following year perhaps the most significant use of limited naval force of the entire post-war era was the American use of their maritime superiority to 'quarantine' Cuba and pressurise the Soviet Union into withdrawing their strategic nuclear missiles. This contributed to, though it did not begin, the rise of Soviet Naval power, and by 1973 the Soviets were able to use powerful anti-carrier forces to neutralise much of the effect of the presence of the Sixth Fleet in the 1973 Arab-Israeli War. By the 1970s, although less ready to use force than its more experienced Western counterparts, the Soviet Navy was a diplomatic force to be reckoned with on a global scale, contributing, in Gorshkov's words, to supporting the USSR's state interests.

The end of super-power competition has seen no slackening of the use of maritime power, indeed its utility in peace support operations has been clear; both landing troops and evacuating them, carrying out embargo operations in support of UN sanctions resolutions and providing national support platforms for forces deployed ashore in confused and dangerous situations. In the early 1990s as Yugoslavia dissolved in chaos, carrier groups from the USA, France and the UK countries plus NATO-WEU multinational squadrons were deployed in the Adriatic as part of the peace support effort.

The future

This post-Cold War world is seeing major developments in naval forces. At the technical level the development of improved interconnections between platforms, notably the impressive 'Cooperative Engagement Capability' developed in the USA will allow the deployment of truly integrated forces capable of action using pooled sensor data. this may well lead to the deployment of floating magazines, so-called 'arsenal ships' to operate with more conventional platforms in a range of roles. Forces afloat can be integrated with those ashore to provide, for example, air defences that will soon be able to take on ballistic missiles. The increased use of cruise missiles from maritime platforms will also further enhance the already considerable power of maritime forces to affect what goes on ashore, but aircraft carriers will remain important as power projection assets, especially with the further development of STOV/L aircraft.

The trend to more stealthy platforms will continue with special 'stealth' shaped small combatants which may reverse the trend that seemed to be favouring the

Above: An SH-2 refuels aboard *USS Wainwright* (CG 28) during operations in the Gulf, 1988.

helicopter as a fast attack craft killer. Air independent propulsion systems will enhance the capability of stealthy conventional submarines in relatively restricted waters, but the SSN will retain its supremacy as a capital striking asset of unparalleled stealthy mobility.

Novel types of hull design may find more general acceptance, but it seems unlikely that conventional monohull warships will be generally replaced. Indeed the main challenge for the newer navies will be the acquisition of surface warships of similar quality to those of the traditional maritime powers. The highly maritime and increasingly rich Asia-Pacific region will no doubt continue to see a relative build-up of naval capabilities, and these may be used as they have been in the past in support of disputed territorial claims. Nevertheless, Jane's first century ends as it has continued for most of its course with the naval trident firmly held by the North Atlantic powers. Fred Jane would probably be pleased.

Index